DRESSING CONSTITUTIONALLY

The intertwining of our clothes and our Constitution raises fundamental questions of hierarchy, sexuality, and democracy. From our hairstyles to our shoes, constitutional considerations both constrain and confirm our daily choices. In turn, our attire and appearance provide multilayered perspectives on the United States Constitution and its interpretations. Our garments often raise First Amendment issues of expression or religion, but they also prompt questions of equality on the basis of gender, race, and sexuality. At work, in court, in schools, in prisons, and on the streets, our clothes and grooming provoke constitutional controversies. Additionally, the production, trade, and consumption of apparel implicate constitutional concerns including colonial sumptuary laws, slavery, wage and hour laws, and current notions of free trade. The regulation of what we wear – or don't – is ubiquitous. Ruthann Robson, a noted constitutional scholar and commentator, examines the rights to expression and equality, as well as the restraints on government power, as they both limit and allow control of our most personal choices of attire and grooming.

Ruthann Robson is Professor of Law and University Distinguished Professor at the City University of New York School of Law. She is the author of *Sappho Goes to Law School* (1998); *Gay Men, Lesbians, and the Law* (1996); and *Lesbian (Out)Law: Survival under the Rule of Law* (1992); she is the editor of the three-volume set, *International Library of Essays in Sexuality and Law* (2011).

D0732680

Dressing Constitutionally

HIERARCHY, SEXUALITY, AND DEMOCRACY FROM OUR HAIRSTYLES TO OUR SHOES

Ruthann Robson

City University of New York School of Law

CAMBRIDGE UNIVERSITY PRESS
Cambridge, New York, Melbourne, Madrid, Cape Town,
Singapore, São Paulo, Delhi, Mexico City

Cambridge University Press
32 Avenue of the Americas, New York, NY 10013-2473, USA

www.cambridge.org
Information on this title: www.cambridge.org/9780521140041

First published 2013

Printed in the United States of America

A catalog record for this publication is available from the British Library.

Library of Congress Cataloging in Publication data
Robson, Ruthann, 1956–
    Dressing constitutionally: hierarchy, sexuality, and democracy from our hairstyles
to our shoes / Ruthann Robson, City University of New York School of Law.
        pages   cm
    Includes bibliographical references and index.
    ISBN 978-0-521-76165-9 (hardback) – ISBN 978-0-521-14004-1 (paperback)
    1. Clothing and dress – Law and legislation – United States.   2. Beauty, Personal –
Government policy – United States.   3. Constitutional law – United States.   I. Title.
    KF390.5.C56R63   2013
    344.7304′235–dc23   2013002996

ISBN 978-0-521-76165-9 Hardback
ISBN 978-0-521-14004-1 Paperback

Contents

Introduction

From our hairstyles to our shoes, constitutional considerations both constrain and confirm our daily choices. In turn, our attire and appearance provide multilayered perspectives on the United States Constitution and its interpretations. Dress raises a plethora of constitutional concerns. In addition to the First Amendment issues of expressive speech or religion that come most immediately to mind, our apparel prompts problems of equal protection based on classifications of sex/gender and race. Moreover, our habiliments and the profits to be made from their production, trade, and consumption have motivated important constitutional revisions of both doctrine and text. The intertwining of our clothes and our Constitution raise fundamental questions of hierarchy, sexuality, and democracy.

While we most often do not think our wardrobe selections are of constitutional magnitude, the legal regulation of dress is ubiquitous. The most obvious regulations are direct ones: laws criminalizing indecent exposure; laws prescribing and proscribing military uniforms; or regulations detailing the attire of government employees, prisoners, or public school students. Less obvious are the more indirect ways in which the law constrains our apparel. Our daily choices of how to look and what to wear are circumscribed by legal doctrines that fail to protect women from sexual violence, or limit antidiscrimination laws, or allow law enforcement officers and judges wide discretion to consider our appearance. Additionally, our available options of apparel in the marketplace are the product of legal forces. All of these provoke constitutional issues.

The interaction of constitutions with all types of regulation of dress generally falls into the two major categories of constitutional concerns: rights and structures. Under the United States Constitution, the rights that are most often interposed against regulations of dress are the First Amendment guarantees of freedom of speech (expression) and freedom of religion. Regulations of dress may also raise issues of equal protection, introduced into the Constitution by the Fourteenth Amendment passed after the Civil War. The Due Process Clause in the Fourteenth Amendment and

Fifth Amendment both guarantee "liberty" – at least to the extent that the state and federal governments cannot deprive it without due process of law – a concept that would seem to encompass one's choice of what to wear. But these rights have not only been asserted by individuals; they have also been advanced by private parties such as employers seeking to enforce their dress codes or labor policies. There are also important criminal procedure protections in the Constitution – including search and seizure, the right to confront witnesses, and the Eighth Amendment's cruel and unusual punishment that are relevant to restrictions on dress in criminal and prison contexts.

In addition to rights, constitutions are concerned with the structures of government. In the United States Constitution, this is a rather complicated affair, of both separation of powers of the branches of the federal government and federalism as the relationship between the federal government and the fifty states. In the constitutions of individual states, there are also issues of separation of powers among the state branches of government, at times including an administrative branch, as well as issues regarding divisions of power between a state and its subdivisions, such as counties or cities. Additionally, the United States includes territories, both as a historical and present matter, with complex relationships and questions of authority. These issues of horizontal and vertical power distribution raise questions about whether the government entity regulating dress has the constitutional authority to do so. Moreover, in the United States, the doctrine of state action embodies the notion that the Constitution is concerned only with the actions of the government. With the notable exception of the Thirteenth Amendment – important in the production of apparel – actions by individuals, corporations, or other "private" entities that might infringe the constitutional rights of others are not cognizable.

The themes of hierarchy, sexuality, and democracy animate the constitutional concerns surrounding attire and appearance. While hierarchy is not usually acknowledged as central to constitutionalism, the constitution itself is a document that allocates power in hierarchal, or even anti-hierarchal balancing, fashions. Additionally, concepts of rights essentially invoke matters of hierarchy, whether it is the hierarchy between the state and the individual or group, or between individuals or groups with differing claims to rights. The doctrines that develop to elaborate constitutional rights are hierarchal ones: rights of political expression are valued more highly than rights of sexual expression. Moreover, and more controversially, constitutional interpretation often involves a choice between maintaining hierarchy or dismantling hierarchy.

Sexuality itself is a controversial candidate for being central to constitutionalism. Yet constitutional quarrels in recent decades have highlighted issues of sexuality, sexual freedom, bodily autonomy, sex, and gender. In the realm of attire and appearance, sexuality undergirds much of the constitutional reasoning, even when it is not explicit.

Democracy is most readily recognizable as a concept at the heart of our constitution, although it does not appear in the text of the document. Nevertheless, democracy remains problematical whenever there is judicial review of acts passed pursuant to democratic processes. It is also disputable whenever the democratic franchise is partial, as before the Fifteenth Amendment (for black men), the Nineteenth Amendment (for all women), and presently for noncitizens as well as citizen inhabitants of territories.

Other themes emerge from the exploration of constitutionalism from the perspective of dress. First, this examination uncovers the importance of clothing to the constitutional text itself. The Eleventh Amendment and the Reconstruction Amendments are traceable to controversies surrounding cloth. The Commerce Clause contemplated a lively trade in textiles, while the slavery "compromises" in the Constitution failed to contemplate the importance of cotton. The inclusion of the Patent Clause, despite objections to monopolies, would influence the cotton gin and sewing machine. A proposed sumptuary power for the federal government did not survive the Constitutional Convention but would have empowered Congress to legislate a national dress code. Arguments against inclusion of a freedom of assembly provision in the First Amendment were debated, and seemingly defeated, by reference to William Penn's hat. Additionally, textiles were not only important to the Civil War, but also to the Revolutionary War's creation of the nation.

Second, doctrinal incoherence, isolationism, and blurring make understanding and litigating constitutional issues of dress challenging. While these problems are not unique to matters of attire and appearance, doctrinal incoherence seems especially prominent in First Amendment disputes, whether they involve free expression or the religion clauses. The conjoined problems of doctrinal isolationism and doctrinal blurring confuse matters further. For example, courts often note that a challenge to a dress code might be raised as a First Amendment challenge or an Equal Protection Clause challenge but then proceed as if only one is implicated, at least until a stray concept from the excluded doctrine makes its appearance. Similarly, courts determining a criminal defendant's objection to attending trial in jail attire struggle with Sixth Amendment fair trial principles, due process fair trial principles, and even First Amendment concerns. Relatedly, there is often doctrinal asymmetry, again especially pronounced in the First Amendment area. In such instances, the government requires a certain appearance, while courts place a burden on persons resisting that mandate to prove that their deviation has a specific message other than deviation.

Third, the "common sense" of judicial and legislative actors permeates the issues, leading to an interpretative slovenliness. Perhaps because matters of dress and appearance seem so commonplace, judges quickly resort to their own understandings, despite the fact that the litigation itself demonstrates that there is not universal consensus. For example, judges have opined that a cornrow hairstyle is not indicative of African Americans (taking judicial notice of Bo Derek); that moustaches are not cultural symbols for African American men, but that goatees are; and that veils are cultural rather than religious. At times, the slovenliness of the reasoning is palpable, as when a judge opined that the high school graduation cap and gown is a "universally recognized symbol" while the significance of traditional Lakota clothing is less easily understood, even when 90 percent of the graduating class is Lakota. At other times, the slovenliness approaches the cavalier, as when a federal appellate court stated that the difference between female and male breasts, supporting mandated covering of the former but not the latter, was one of those "self-evident truths about the human condition – such as water is wet." Courts do accept evidence regarding social facts, including "expert" testimony about the indicia of gang membership including clothing and tattoos, or the link between dancers wearing pasties and g-strings and the prevention of criminal activity like loan-sharking. Yet this evidence seems to confirm stereotypes and biases rather than providing rigorous proof.

Fourth, the mirrored themes of trivialization and fetishization loom large in many disputes. The condescension and trivialization by many courts when youth are involved is especially pronounced, from the plethora of male student hair-length cases of the 1970s to the increasing number of student gender appropriate attire cases in the courts at present. Even when a judge might ultimately find in favor of a litigant, there can be trivializing language: a judge described an argument that an ordinance criminalizing cross-dressing was unconstitutional as based on the premise that the law prevented the person "from 'doing his own thing' in the vernacular of the 'pepsi generation.'" The concomitant fetishization of dress and grooming is evident in many of the regulations subject to constitutional challenge. Such regulations prohibit display of the "female breast below a point immediately above the top of the areola"; or sideburns from extending below the lowest part of the exterior ear opening; or skirts three inches above the knee (with the measurement to be taken when the woman is "seated with feet flat on the floor and at the highest point of the skirt; e.g., if the skirt has a slit, then the measurement would be taken at the top of the slit," and if "the slit is in the front or side of the skirt, the measurement would be taken while seated; if the slit is in the back of the skirt, the measurement may be taken" while she is standing). Perhaps in an attempt to be objective, such regulations echo the Tudor sumptuary laws proscribing the attire for persons occupying different statuses in the hierarchal social structure, including the famous Knights of the Garter.

Fifth, and last, constitutional issues endemic to sartorial and grooming matters are steeped in history. Separation of powers and nascent rights recognition developing in Tudor constitutionalism are intertwined with the sumptuary laws. Constitutional challenges to contemporary statutes criminalizing the wearing of masks are infused by complicated legislative histories considering carnival, land disputes, and the KKK. The production of clothes is imbued with constitutional conflicts over slavery, laissez-faire, and the treaty power. The historical discourse is often superficial, inaccurate, or opportunistic. Even a matter as simple as an attorney's being mandated to wear a "tie" in court can become fraught: the attorney's bandanna tied above the collar was not a tie according to the judge who held him contempt, despite a reference book on nineteenth-century western wear and a dictionary to support the claim.

These themes infuse the seven chapters of *Dressing Constitutionally*. Briefly, the first chapter, "Dressing Historically," begins with the Magna Carta juxtaposed with the Tudor sumptuary laws, and then considers the structural and rights issues in the English "constitution" raised by the regulation of attire and the economic interests expressed in regulations regarding wool and foreign cloth. It also examines how regulations of habiliments, hairstyles, and plaid contributed to sovereignty and nation building. The colonizers of what would become the United States brought a penchant for the regulation of apparel, including as a mark of a crime, as in *The Scarlet Letter*, as well as other means of badging, scarring, and marking criminals, the morally deviant, poor persons, and slaves. The relationship of the colonies to the wool-exporting and calico-trading mother country was an important aspect of the Revolutionary ethos. The Constitution itself was deeply affected by the trade in textiles, although the proposed sumptuary power for Congress was not included.

"Dressing Barely" begins with Thomas Paine's observation that government, like clothes, is a necessary evil. The chapter pairs two contradictory aspects of government approaches to a lack of clothes and the constitutional ramifications of each. Forced nudity, as in strip searches or other criminal contexts, raises Fourth Amendment and Due Process Clause claims, usually unsuccessfully even if the government action was ill-founded. Chosen nudity or partial nudity, criminalized by indecent exposure statutes, raises First Amendment, as well as Due Process Clause and at times Equal Protection Clause claims. The First Amendment doctrine of obscenity is applied to nudity, even as doctrinal exceptions for regulated media, funding schemes, and secondary effects ultimately extinguish distinctions between obscenity and nudity. The Equal Protection Clause and its limited interpretations provides little protection for nudists and for bare-breasted women.

Chapter 3, "Dressing Sexily," centers the constitutionality of government's major weapon in the control of sexuality: the policing of attire. This policing focuses not only on the lack of clothes, but also on the styles of clothes and other aspects of appearance such as hair, jewelry, cosmetics, shoes, and bodily enhancements or markings. One aspect of this policing is directed at the boundary between the two recognized sexes, female and male. Dressing sexily in this instance means dressing in gender appropriate ways. So-called cross-dressing – wearing clothes of a member of the "opposite" sex – may subject one to criminal sanctions, to discrimination, to interference with familial and educational relationships, and to private violence. The other aspect of this policing seeks to control sexuality, especially but not only female sexuality. Dressing sexily in this sense means dressing in a sexy, erotic, or not sufficiently unsexy manner. So-called dressing provocatively may subject one to discrimination as well as to private violence with government acquiescence, at times in service of a criminal defendant's constitutional rights.

"Dressing Professionally," Chapter 4, begins by examining the federal protections for dress and grooming in the private sphere, protections that are under attack for their lack of constitutional grounding. These statutory protections are uneven and incoherent, especially as they seem to exempt corporate "look policies" that seek to "brand" employees. Government branding of its employees, exemplified by the uniform, is prominent in military and paramilitary contexts. This robe may be another type of uniform, or as some would have it a "cult," but both its use and its absence pose constitutional problems in courtrooms, as well as in academic settings.

Classrooms and protests birthed the First Amendment standard of disruption central to Chapter 5, "Dressing Disruptively." The notion that attire is capable of disruption presupposes not only a normative style of dress but also a normative community that is capable of being disturbed merely by a person's apparel or grooming. In schools, Confederate flag clothing and anti-gay T-shirts have prompted extended litigation about students' First Amendment rights. The disruption standard also has relevance in the courtroom, specifically when litigants including criminal defendants as famous as William Penn refuse to doff their hats. When criminal defendants disrupt the proceedings by appearing in judicial attire, or refuse to be silent and are shackled, gagged, and bound – both of which occurred at the infamous Chicago Eight Conspiracy Trial – questions of courtroom decorum are evaluated in light of the constitutional right to a fair trial. A disruption of the wider social fabric was claimed in the case centering on the most famous outerwear in First Amendment jurisprudence: Cohen's "Fuck the Draft" jacket. The jacket's words made the First Amendment claim more discernible than claims by those wearing saggy pants, or even those wearing masks.

Chapter 6, "Dressing Religiously," examines "religious garb" and implicates one of the most contentious issues of constitutional adjudication. Perhaps because religion has been so historically divisive and continues to be so, the doctrines and theories governing religion are themselves subject to marked divisions, including divides between the Free Exercise Clause and the Establishment Clause, belief and practice, doctrinal and legislative interpretations of the standard of constitutional scrutiny to be applied, and divisions between majority religions and minority religions, as well as between religion and nonbelief. The practice of tattooing and the Church of Body Modification raise constitutional issues and disparate results. The accommodation of religious attire and grooming standards in prisons under both the First Amendment and various statutes has led to anomalous results. Women's religious dress, including Catholic habits and Muslim niqab and hijab, prompts divisiveness and little constitutional resolution.

Last, Chapter 7, "Dressing Economically," focuses on the constitutional issues raised by the labor necessary to produce apparel. The entwinement of slavery and cotton, the laissez-faire *Lochner*-era struggles in sweatshops and textile mills, and the contemporary reign of international free trade have challenged and changed the constitutional contours of our attire. There are intransient constitutional problems not merely with what one wears but with how those items are produced. Just as Tudor sumptuary laws sought to regulate sartorial options to maximize economic profits, so too has United States constitutional doctrine reckoned with cotton, cloth, and clothes as imperative to capitalist success.

Thus, while we may casually assume that the Constitution affords us freedom to dress as we please, the Constitution cabins, channels, and constrains these choices. Moreover, our attire reflects the Constitution, including its text and controversial doctrines.

1

Dressing Historically

The first laws regulating dress in the English realm appeared well after the creation of the foundational documents of democracy. The most famous instrument, the Magna Carta of 1215, still resonates as a quasi-constitution that allocates power and recognizes individual liberties. It also contained a specific provision regulating textiles: "There shall also be a standard width of dyed cloth, russett, and haberject, namely two ells within the selvedges."[1] It did not, however, impede the creation of laws regulating dress.

The sole law passed by the English Parliament in the year 1337 was devoted to matters of wool, cloth, and fur.[2] Although there were certainly ancient Greek, Roman, and Asian laws as well as medieval European and Asian laws governing attire, this law promulgated by Parliament in the eleventh year of the reign of Edward III is the first recorded statute addressing attire in the English realm. The statute forbade the exportation of wool and the importation of foreign cloth; it also governed the "Cloth-workers of strange Lands," who would be welcome in the realm and granted franchises. Taken together, these provisions evince a government concerned with the economy: the statute banned exports and imports but encouraged foreign entrepreneurs to relocate within the realm. The remaining two sections of the statute, however, expressed slightly different concerns. They banned the wearing of imported cloth and the wearing of fur and they included exemptions to these bans.

I. TUDOR REGULATION OF APPEARANCE

Provisions banning the wearing of imported cloth and furs, presumably more costly and rare than domestic items, may be viewed as sumptuary laws. Sumptuary laws target sumptuousness: they are intended to restrain luxury, which was considered a sin in medieval Christianity, as well as to prevent over-consumption, which could be detrimental to society. The 1337 statute can be considered an extension of the earliest known English sumptuary law, passed the year before and aimed at curbing the consumption not of clothing but of food, limiting meals to two courses except on feast days when "three courses at the utmost" were permitted.[3] The 1336 food law recognized the harms caused by "excessive and over-many sorts of costly Meats," even as it stated that these harms affected different classes of persons differently: "the great men, by these excesses, have been sore grieved, and the lesser People, who only endeavor to imitate the great ones in such sort of Meats, are much impoverished." It was not only the hierarchal structure but also its purpose that was made explicit in the law: the impoverishment of the "lesser People" was troubling because they were "not able to aid themselves or their liege Lord in time of need, as they ought." Nevertheless, the law cited a concern with "Souls" and applied to men with a democratic impulse: "no man, of whatever estate or condition soever he be, shall cause himself to be served" more than two courses.

The provisions of the 1337 law of attire were even more hierarchal. The statute of attire was not concerned with articulating different harms but with promulgating different rules for the different estates. The distinctions were articulated by means of exceptions to the general rules of prohibition. The proscription against wearing imported cloth contained an exception for "the King, Queen, and their Children." The banning of wearing fur contained a more extensive exception for "the King, Queen, and their Children, the Prelates, Earls, Barons, Knights, and Ladies" as well as "People of Holy Church" who had benefices worth a hundred pounds per year. There was no mention of souls.

Edward III's Parliament would substantially expand on these laws in A Statute Concerning Diet and Apparel promulgated twenty-six years later.[4] The 1363 statute begins with a confirmation of the Magna Carta. After addressing other matters including the price of poultry and gilting in silver, the statute prescribes the dress of various classes: servants; people of handicraft and yeomen; esquires and gentlemen; merchants, citizens, and burgesses; knights; clerks; clergy; and ploughmen and oxherds. The classes are defined in the statute not only by occupation but also by their net worth. The "Wives, Daughters, and Children" were generally subject to the same conditions as the men, but specific attire for women such as veils, or what might now be called kerchiefs or headscarves, were mentioned. The clothes were defined by their cost as well as their attributes, with attempts at specificity, such as "no higher price for their Vesture or Hosing, than within Forty Shillings the whole Cloth, by way or buying, or otherwise," and "no Manner of Furr, nor of Budge, but only Lamb, Cony, Cat, and Fox."[5] The penalty for violation was forfeiture of the offending clothes, a rather hefty economic penalty in an era when clothes were not only expensive but also scarce. The statute exhorted "Makers of Cloths within the Realm" and the Drapers to maintain the law, although they were to be "constrained by any Manner way that best shall seem to the King and his Council."

English lawmakers spent considerable energy over the next several centuries regulating dress in accordance with social hierarchies. The laws were generally comprehensive statutory schemes, such as those passed during the reign of Edward IV in 1463 and 1482.[6] There were also occasional laws such as during the reign of Henry V, limiting silver for use in knights' spurs or all the apparel for barons or higher estates.[7] The statutory schemes reached their apex during the long reign of Henry VIII. During Henry VIII's first year as king, 1510, Parliament passed "An Act against wearing of costly Apparrell."[8] Repealing earlier statutes of apparel, the 1510 Act portrayed a complexly hierarchal society. The statute prohibited purple "cloth of gold" and silk except for those in the royal family, prohibited sables to those under the degree of earl, prohibited blue or crimson velvet to those under the degree of Knight of the Garter, prohibited foreign furs to those under the degree of Gentleman, and prohibited foreign wool to those under the degree of Lord or Knight of the Garter. As in earlier statutes, the punishment was generally forfeiture, although servants of laborers who wore hose above the price of "x d. the yerde" did so "uppon payne of imprisonament in the Stokkys by thre days." Subsequent acts addressing apparel from Henry VII's Parliament were passed in 1514, 1515, and 1533.[9] Each of these acts reserved certain types of attire to people of a certain status, prohibiting appropriation by persons of lesser rank. In her multifaceted study of clothing during the reign of Henry VIII, scholar Maria Hayward provides an excellent comparison, in table form, of the extensive and shifting details in the four acts of apparel, the first three which are separated by only five years.[10] Despite the minutia, the stated rationale in the statutes was not the maintenance of hierarchy but the prevention of poverty and crime. As the 1510 statute explained, and the next two statutes repeated, "the greate and costly array and apparrell used wythin this Realme contrary to good Statute therof made hathe be the Occasion of grete impovisshing of divers of the Kinge Sugieft and evoked meny of them to robbe and to doo extorcon and other unlawfull Dedes to maynteyne therby ther costeley arrey."

After Henry VIII's death in 1547, royal leadership was in disarray: Henry VIII's only son, Edward VI, a minor, ruled 1547–1553, and Henry VIII's daughter, Mary ("Bloody Mary") ruled 1553–1558. It would be Henry VIII's other daughter, Elizabeth (whose mother was the executed Anne Boleyn), who would reign the longest, from 1558 until 1603. Under all of these monarchs, statutes of apparel continued to be passed.[11]

These statutes – with their hierarchy of social classes and their reservations of purple and ermine – are recognizable as paradigmatic sumptuary statutes. Under the guise of preventing crime and forestalling excess consumption, the laws regulate societal status. Yet the laws portray a society as much in flux as its sovereigns. The laws rely not only on title or "estate," such as Knight of the Garter, but also economic worth, such as possessing lands and annuities to the value of £100 a year.

The inclusion of new occupations such as "merchant" also marks a shift toward recognition of a rising urban class. As preeminent sumptuary scholar Alan Hunt has noted, sumptuary law was directed at images of the social order, including attempts to protect hierarchal conceptions of social relations by resisting change deemed inconsistent with the prevalent vision of the social order.[12]

However, even paradigmatic sumptuary acts of apparel reveal other governmental interests, including economic ones. Indeed, the economic is inextricably intertwined with any sumptuary provision, for definitions of luxury rest upon economic considerations. The economic fitness of the realm, including the balance of trade between imports and exports, is evident in laws prohibiting imports or reserving imported cloth for only certain classes. Additionally, Parliament occasionally sought to mandate the wearing of local products, particularly English wool. For example, a 1666 Act entitled "An Act for Burying in Wool Only" prohibited the burial shirt, shift, or sheet to be made of anything other than wool, and it similarly prohibited the coffin from being lined with anything other than wool.[13] While this may be called a sumptuary law, the stated rationale was not excess in apparel or over-consumption but to encourage the woolen manufacturers of the kingdom and to prevent money being spent on the importation of linen. Importantly, it applied uniformly across classes; the only exception was for a person who had died of the plague.

An earlier and better known law was the Elizabethan Cap Act. A serious decline in employment for "cappers" and other wool workers was the stated motivation for the Act for the making of Cappes, passed by Parliament in 1571 during the reign of Elizabeth I.[14] The act's remedy for the decline in the wool trades was to require "every person" above the age of six years to wear a cap upon Sabbath and Holy Days. However, although the act recited that the wearing of the caps was decent and comely for all estates and degrees, it specifically exempted "Maydens Ladyes and Gentlewomen," as well as those who were noble personages, Lords, Knights, and Gentlemen of possession of twenty marks land by the year, as well as their heirs." Thus, the act essentially mandated the cap as a marker for lower class status.

A similar marking of the lower classes occurred by the practice of "badging" the poor, prompted by economic interests of a different sort. Beggars had been required to wear badges indicating their eligibility for alms in some English parishes and towns since the reign of Henry VIII, and the famous Elizabethan poor law of 1563 required licenses for those receiving poor relief in some cases.[15] However, the badging requirement imposed by a parliamentary statute of the realm in 1697 provided that every person receiving relief, including the wife and children of such person, shall

> upon the Shoulder of the right Sleeve of the uppermost Garment of every such Person in an open and visible manner weare such Badge or Mark as is herein after

mentioned and expressed that is to say a large Roman P, together with the first
Letter of the Name of the Parish or Place whereof such poor Person is an Inhabitant
cutt either in red or blew Cloth as by the Churchwardens and Overseers of the Poor
it shall be directed.[16]

The impoverished were subject not only to badging but also to branding. During
the brief reign of Edward VI, Parliament in 1547 passed An Act for the Punishment
of Vagabonds and for the Relief of the Poor, providing that the punishment for both
male and female loiterers who did not apply themselves to honest labor was to be
marked with a hot iron in the breast with the letter V and to serve as a "slave" for
two years to the person who captured him or her. If the vagabond attempted to run
away, he or she would be branded again, this time with the letter S on the forehead
or ball of the cheek and would then be a slave forever. A second attempted escape
would result in the death penalty.[17] Indeed, branding was not an especially harsh
punishment, especially in comparison with an earlier statute under Henry VIII that
provided the punishment of being tied to the end of a cart naked and beaten with
whips throughout the town until the "Body be blody" or standing on the pillory and
having an ear cut off.[18] Slavery, however, was extreme and soon repealed, although
vagabond children over the age of five were allowed to be "taken into service."[19]
A series of vagabond statutes throughout the Tudor era criminalized the impoverished, migratory laborers and those who "refused" to work in an era that witnessed
the end of feudalism, the plague, and the beginnings of manufacturing.[20]

In addition to economic hierarchies, statutes of attire addressed gender hierarchies, although often less explicitly. Most notably, the English acts of apparel were
directed primarily at males, with the 1510 statute specifically exempting women (as
well as, among others, minstrel players).[21] Perhaps this was because males were more
preoccupied by clothes than women, or perhaps it was because males in the targeted
classes were more visible than women, or perhaps men were deemed to be citizens
worthy of regulation while women were subsumed into their male-headed households. However, the statutes of apparel implicitly and at times explicitly presume a
gendered division of attire, even if their regulatory focus was otherwise.

The acts of apparel occasionally address sexuality. For example, in 1463 the
Parliament of Edward IV criminalized men's sexually revealing attire. It prohibited
the wearing of any gown, jacket, or coat "unless it be of such Length that the same
may cover his privy Members and Buttocks." The act applied to knights who were
less than lords, esquires, and gentlemen, as well as other persons, and extended the
prohibition to tailors who made garments of this short length.[22] Women's sexuality
was also subject to attire regulations, although not in the major acts of apparel. The
Parliament of Scotland passed a law in 1458 that regulated silk and furs in a familiar
hierarchal manner and provided that "no labourers or husbands wear any colour
except grey or white on work days; and on holy days only light blue, green or red,"

but also contained a specific prohibition for women: "no woman come to church nor market with her face hidden or muffled so that she may not be known, under pain of escheat of the cap."[23] More than a century later, the sumptuary laws were augmented with a moralistic imperative for women expressed in an exceedingly terse statute: "it be lawful for no women to wear above their estate except whores."[24] By providing an exemption from the sumptuary hierarchy to "whores," this brief statute regulates other women, who, as Alan Hunt notes, must conform to the social class regulations of attire in order to "protect and confirm their own respectability."[25] The City of London took a different tactic; in a Proclamation by Edward III in 1351, it prohibited "common lewd women" from furs and silk linings, while also mandating the women wear striped and unlined hoods.[26]

II. CONSTITUTIONAL CONCERNS AND TUDOR REGULATION

The regulation of clothing played a pivotal role in developing quasi-democratic principles regarding constitutional separation of powers between the legislature and the royal "executive." As Edward III's proclamation demonstrates, the matter of dress was not only a subject of parliamentary concern, but also of royal edicts. Indeed, many monarchs were quite attentive to matters of apparel and cloth; the definitive collection of Tudor proclamations evinces such attention amid the 851 royal documents that address various other matters such as food, guns, traitors, religion, wages, wars, coinage, and the plague. There are four proclamations from Henry VIII "enforcing" statutes of apparel, including two in the same year of 1534, as well as several relating to wool. The brief reign of Henry VIII's son, Edward VI, and then the equally brief reign of Henry VII's daughter, Mary, witnessed only a few proclamations concerning the wool trade and none regarding statutes of apparel. However, the available royal decrees from Henry VIII's other daughter, Elizabeth I, include nine separate proclamations entitled "Enforcing Statutes of Apparel," as well as several other proclamations on apparel, two specifically enforcing the "Act for the making of Cappes," and a few mitigating or enforcing statutes regarding wool manufacturing, and one focused on patents for luxury cloth. Not only are Elizabeth I's proclamations the most numerous on the subject of dress, but they also illuminate the quasi-constitutional tension between Parliament as legislature and the Queen as "executive."

This tension did not begin with Elizabeth I. The rise of democracy occurred in juxtaposition to the absolute rule of the monarch, with the Magna Carta being a notable document shifting the balance. However, the balance was always a tenuous one. The Statute of Proclamations in 1539 under Henry VIII's reign resulted from intense negotiations between Parliament and the Crown, and ultimately gave enhanced powers to the Crown to legislate through proclamation. While there is an argument that the statute marked a turn toward despotism, the Crown's precise powers and their constitutional significance remain subject to debate centuries later.[27] In any event, the repeal of the Statute of Proclamations under Henry VIII's successor, the child Edward VI, did not prevent subsequent monarchs – especially Elizabeth I – from issuing proclamations that might be viewed as usurping Parliament's arguably more democratic role.

Elizabeth I's proclamations enforcing the statutes of apparel illustrate the trajectory of her royal power. In her second year as Queen, Elizabeth I sought to enforce the extant statutes of apparel – 24 Henry VIII and 1&2 Philip & Mary – by directing the Privy Council, the mayors, sheriffs and justices of the peace, and noblemen to enforce the laws, that are then encapsulated.[28] Two years thereafter, a 1562 proclamation declared there was a "monstrous abuse of apparel almost in all estates, but principally in the meaner sort."[29] The stated target of the poorer classes may have been disingenuous given the proclamation's focus on attire of the higher classes. This proclamation was accompanied by three additional proclamations designated as action from the Queen's Privy Council.[30] Arguably, the imprimatur of the Privy Council lent a less imperious tenor to the proclamations, although the council was a body of the queen's advisors who served at her pleasure and political judgment. Taken together, these proclamations from Elizabeth I's fourth year as queen attempt to streamline the array of specific attire regulations in previous statutes as well as address new outrages, including men wearing double ruffs or billowing hose.[31]

Eighteen years later, Elizabeth I's 1580 proclamation quite obviously exceeded its title "Enforcing Statutes of Apparel." While it first recited the usual state of "mischief" "specially in the inferior sort" causing the need for enforcement, and then provided a basic outline of the regulations, its third section announced "necessary additions." This section reads like a parliamentary statute. For example, numbered paragraph 9 provides:

> Item, that all apprentices at the law and utter barristers of the Inns-of-Court, and all merchants of any society, and all that keep household in city or town, and such as may dispend £20 by the year, may wear a welt of velvet in their gowns, jackets, or coats.[32]

Seventeen years later, Elizabeth I again issued an enforcement proclamation, but most interestingly this edict in 1597 does not limit itself to enforcing statutes but is entitled "Enforcing Statutes *and Proclamations* of Apparel." The text refers to "special parts and branches of the law now standing in force" and "her majesty's said proclamations," and then lists the specific regulations first for men's apparel, then for women's, that "her majesty straightly charge and command."[33] In a separate proclamation, entitled "Dispensing Certain Persons from Statutes of Apparel," Elizabeth

I provides particular exemptions and rules for various classes of persons, including again "students of the Inns-of-Court or Chancery."[34]

Thus, the relative quasi-constitutional powers of Parliament and the Crown are deeply implicated in the regulation of dress in the British realm. Indeed, Alan Hunt and N. B. Harte argue that the demise of formal sumptuary regulation during the first year of the reign of James I, after the death of Queen Elizabeth, is attributable to the constitutional struggle between the Parliament, notably the Commons, and the Crown who would prefer to rule by proclamation rather than legislative actions.[35] This constitutional struggle occurred without a unitary written "constitution" and without a coequal judicial body to act as referee, since judges were generally under the power of the monarch. The contest was therefore political rather than adjudicatory. Parliament won, passing an extensive statute that repealed previous sumptuary laws, as well as a raft of other types of laws, while reaffirming a few laws and not recognizing the Crown's right to issue proclamations.[36] Parliament did entertain several types of sumptuary bills, but there was no agreement about the allocation of powers between itself and the Crown. As both Hunt and Harte observe, this essentially ended paradigmatic sumptuary statutes in England much earlier than they might have otherwise, and much earlier than they ceased in Continental Europe, although other regulations of attire persisted.[37]

In addition to constitutional structures, the English government's regulation of dress implicates questions of nascent constitutional rights. The Magna Carta specified several particular rights and liberties. None of these rights explicitly concern personal attire, although there are several mentions of property disposition that would include clothes as items of valuable property in this era, and there are also mentions of rights of marriage (and nonmarriage) that could be viewed as rights of personal autonomy, even as they are intertwined with rights of property. However, notions of rights and liberties may have played a part in the overall efficacy of laws of attire. For example, a satirical critique of badging laws, as recounted by scholar Steve Hindle, advocated that the poor should disregard wearing badges because they were "established by act of parliament, and the common people knew that all such injunctions were 'great infringements of their liberties.'"[38] Of course, the satirist's argument was exactly the opposite, but the invocation of infringement of liberties is telling. Perhaps this sentiment contributed to the lack of compliance with the badging of the poor.[39] And perhaps it contributed to lack of compliance with more paradigmatic laws of attire, for, as the numerous acts and proclamations indicate, enforcing regulations of dress was not easily accomplished. While the proclamatory bemoaning of the sad state of affairs caused by failure of the population to abide by previous regulations of apparel may be high rhetoric, it is nevertheless noteworthy. There seem to be very few records of actual enforcement proceedings; there is also no known interpellation of a "right" to be free to wear what one pleased.

At the risk of anachronism it is worth speculating how statutes of attire would fare under contemporary American standards of constitutional scrutiny. The statutory exemptions obviously create classes of persons that would support equality challenges, and gender classifications would be subject to a more rigorous scrutiny than those based on economic status. There would possibly be due process challenges regarding liberty, and a constellation of free expression challenges as well. But importantly, whatever the challenges, there would be an assessment of the government's goals and the measures enacted to achieve those goals, a means-ends analysis. For example, the stated government goals repeated in several statutes of preventing the impoverishment of people and also preventing people from robbing and extorting to maintain their costly attire would be evaluated as to whether they were worthwhile government interests. Phrased as contemporary U.S. constitutional doctrine, it might be asked whether these goals are legitimate or important, or less likely, compelling, government interests. The answer will depend, at least in part, on political perspective. For example, a strict libertarian would presumably not agree that the government has any interest in preventing individuals from becoming impoverished.

Assuming there is a sufficient government interest, the means chosen of accomplishing that interest must also be analyzed. Preventing the impoverishment of people by forbidding them to spend their money on certain expensive objects seems to lack rationality under current thought. Likewise, preventing robbery and extortion by criminalizing clothes purchased with the proceeds of crimes (or perhaps stolen clothes) seems much more tenuous than criminalizing the crimes of robbery and extortion themselves. Yet one could also imagine the arguments that a government could make that there is a sufficiently close fit between the desired ends and the strictures on attire. Again, the ultimate conclusions will be based at least in part on political perspective as well as views of human nature.

The discussion of rights, whether anachronistic or not, implicitly assumes an oppositional relationship between the government and the individuals asserting rights. The statutes of attire in medieval England would seem to be products of an oppressive government controlling the dress of its citizens to enforce social hierarchies. However, there is persuasive evidence that the statutes were much more democratic than that, at least with respect to the higher classes. As medieval scholar Kim M. Phillips compellingly argues, the calls for regulation of attire originated in Parliament's Commons (the lower house, composed of knights, esquires, gentlemen, burgesses, and citizens of the towns), although it was certainly developed with collaboration from the Lords and Council.[40] Focusing on knights, Phillips speculates regarding their petitions to limit their own attire, even as they, more understandably, sought to limit the attire of those beneath them in the social hierarchy. Phillips contends that there must have been economic and pragmatic considerations: "Given the extraordinary expense of high-status fabric, furs, and jewels it is likely that the petitioners were seeking a means by which they could prevent excessive demands on their incomes without losing face."[41] More provocatively, Phillips posits that the knights were pleading for a "distinctiveness in dress" as a method to "assert a distinctive model of manliness" in the "homosocial networks and complex structures of masculine hierarchy." While Phillips does not use the word "democracy," she contends that there was much for the knights to gain in their "collusion" with the broader governmental arrangements in exchange for losing the right to wear "cloth of gold, sables, pearls, and sexually revealing outfits."[42]

Likewise, there was something to gain for the poor who lost the right to wear clothes without also wearing the parish badge indicating poverty. As in the case of knights, there were practical and economic effects: a badge entitled an impoverished person to survival benefits and alms. But as Steve Hindle argues, the badge could be semiotically read not only as a sign of stigma but also as a sign of belonging. Hindle analogizes it to livery – the badges, clothes, or colors that a landed noble bestowed on servants or tenants – symbolizing both subordination and patronage.[43] However, unlike the knights, there is little evidence that those who were impoverished participated in democratic institutions that resulted in regulating their choice of attire. Moreover, regulations of the poor could not only badge and brand their bodies but also serve to expel them from the body politic. It would be a vagabond statute that would introduce the punishment of transportation: dangerous rogues to be conveyed "unto such part beyond the Seas" as shall be determined for that purpose by the Privy Counsel, with a return to England being a felony punishable by death.[44] The same statute, under Queen Elizabeth, criminalized bringing vagabonds, rogues, and beggars from Ireland, Scotland, or the Isle of Man into the Realm of England or Wales.[45]

III. NATIONAL DRESS

Questions of the place of the poor in the kingdom were accompanied by questions regarding the country's boundaries. What might be named "nation building" was at the heart of many of the laws of attire with their specific proscriptions regarding foreign cloths and furs for specific classes of persons. Yet even as the classes were subject to flux, so too were definitions of "foreign." For example, the first act of apparel, passed in 1337, defined foreign as outside the "Lands of England, Ireland, Wales, or Scotland, within the King's Power."[46] Almost two centuries later, Parliament under Henry VIII, prohibited cloth made "oute of this Realme" to the lower classes in 1514, with a more specific definition of the realm as England, Ireland, Wales, Calice, and Berwik.[47] Notably absent is Scotland, although Berwick abutting Scotland is included. Notably present is Calice (Calais), across the English Channel, which was subsequently recaptured by France. In the next act of apparel under Henry VIII, passed only a year later, a provision prohibited the lower classes from wearing furs whereof there is no like kind growing within this realm of England, Wales, or in any other land under the king's obeisance.[48] Thus, the precarious predicament of sovereignty is evident in the acts of apparel.

Regulations of dress as nation building are also evident in English attempts at defining hierarchies between the English and the Irish. Ireland, when known as the English Pale (borderlands), was subject to English rule, including proscriptions on dress. Initially, the law was directed at differentiating between the Irish and the English living in the Pale, because, according to a 1297 statute, "the killing of Englishmen and Irishmen requires different modes of punishment."[49] In this same statute, the Parliament held in Ireland declared that Englishmen had become "degenerate in modern times, attire themselves in Irish garments," and were wearing an Irish hairstyle, the culan, with the head half-shaven, but long hair in the back of the head. The parliamentary solution was a prohibition of the culan and "that all Englishmen in this land wear, at least in that part of the head which presents itself most to view, the mode and tonsure of Englishmen," to be enforced by seizure of lands and chattels, and arrest of body and imprisonment. Fifty years later, there were still anxieties about distinguishing the Irish and the English. The "Statute of Kilkenny," passed by a Parliament held in Ireland in 1367, addressed the worry that the "conquest" of Ireland was being threatened by English settlers who were "forsaking the English language, manners, mode of riding" and were living "according to the manners, fashion, and language of the Irish enemies." The third chapter of the statute – after a provision recognizing the church and a provision prohibiting the English from sexual or family relations with the Irish, or selling the Irish horses or armor – mandates that the English use the English language and English name and "that every Englishman use the English custom, fashion, mode of riding apparel according to his estate."[50]

English law later became less concerned with preserving distinctions than imposing Irish assimilation. As scholar Margaret Rose Jaster has noted, English regulations regarding Irish apparel reveal the essential contradiction of colonization: an insistence on the inherent difference of the Irish while mandating conformity through clothing to eliminate that difference.[51] Conformity in the legal arena received special attention in an act in 1495: The lords, both spiritual and temporal, in the Parliament held in Ireland were admonished to appear in their Parliament robes, "in like manner and form as the lords of the foresaid realm of England doth appear to the Parliament," upon penalty of a fine.[52] More famously, in 1537 the Parliament held in Ireland under Henry VIII, forbade very specific Irish styles to all of the populace, again regulating hair, in the style known as "glibbes" but previously called "culan," as well as attire:

no person … shall be shorne, or shaven above the eares, or use the wearing of haire upon their heads, like unto long locks, called glibbes, or have or use any hair growing on their upper lippes, called or named a crommeal, or use or wear any shirt, smock, kerchor, bendel [band or ribbon], neckerchour, mocket [bib], or linnen cappe, coloured, or dyed with saffron, nor yet use, or wear in any their shirts or smockes above seven yards of cloth, to be measured according to the King's standard and that also no women use or wear any kyrtell, or cote tucked up, or embroidered or garnished with silk, or courched nor layd with usker [jewels], after the Irish fashion; and that no person or persons of what estate, condition, or degree they be, shall use or wear any mantles, cote or hood made after the Irish fashion.[53]

The statute's stated purpose is not subjugation but unity, an abolition of the diversity that is betwixt the peoples of Ireland in "tongue, language, order, and habit" and which "by the eye deceiveth the multitude" that the people are of separate countries instead of "wholly together" as one nation.[54] Within a few years, Parliament would pass the Crown of Ireland Act, declaring that the King of England was now the King, rather than the Lord, of Ireland, arguably uniting Ireland and England.[55]

The relationship between England and Scotland was also mediated through laws passed by the English to regulate appearance. Rather than moustaches, hairstyles, and mantles, however, the target of the Scottish attire regulations was plaid. While Scotland and England had at times been united, after the 1688 deposing of the controversial and Catholic King James (known as James II as King of England and Ireland, and as James VII as King of Scotland), there were continuing battles and royal contestations. In 1746, after another Jacobite "uprising" in the north, Parliament under King George II passed an "An Act for the more effectually disarming the Highlands in Scotland; and for the more effectually securing the Peace of the said Highlands; and for restraining the Use of the Highland Dress; and for further indemnifying such Persons as have acted in Defence of His Majesty's Person and Government, during the unnatural Rebellion."[56] While much of the act concerns firearms, including permissible search and seizure processes, section 17 prohibits Scottish dress:

no man or boy, within that part of Great Briton called Scotland, other than shall be employed as officers and soldiers in his Majesty's forces, shall on any pretence whatsoever, wear or put on the clothes commonly called Highland Clothes (that is to say) the plaid, philibeg, or little kilt, trowse, shoulder belts, or any part whatsoever of what peculiarly belongs to the highland garb; and that no tartan, or partly-coloured plaid or stuff shall be used for great coats, or for upper coats.[57]

By its terms, the provision only applies to males, but it is otherwise quite different from the "acts of apparel" of two centuries before. The punishment to be imposed reflects the severity of the infraction as a crime of "unnatural Rebellion" as well as

the status of "Great Briton" as an empire: a first offense is imprisonment without
bail for six months; a second offense would render a person "liable to be transported
to any of his Majesty's plantations beyond the seas, there to remain for a space of
seven years."[58]

IV. COLONIAL HIERARCHIES

Given this history, it is not surprising that many colonists to what would become the
United States – whether they were transported to America for their crimes of plaid
or came to the continent's shores under different circumstances – would include
regulations of dress in their legal schemes. To be sure, many colonists did not have
exclusive power to govern themselves. Most were essentially members of chartered
companies, "one body corporate and politique in fact and name" as the Charter of
the Colony of Massachusetts Bay phrased it.[59] Moreover, when colonists exercised
lawmaking power, their laws had to be consistent with the laws of England, including their laws regarding attire.[60]

In regulating dress, the colonists displayed their concerns regarding hierarchy,
sexuality, and democracy. A classic of American literature, *The Scarlet Letter* by
Nathaniel Hawthorne, illuminates some of these themes.[61] Although published
in 1850, the novel is set more than two centuries earlier in the Massachusetts
Bay Colony. The novel's heroine, Hester Prynne, makes her first appearance
walking out of the prison door with her three-month-old baby and an elaborately
embroidered red "A" on her dress. She proceeds to the "scaffold of the pillory,"
although she is not subject to "that gripe about the neck and confinement of
the head." She returns to prison, and upon her release must wear a red A on her
clothes for the rest of her life.

Hawthorne, who reputedly studied the records of the Massachusetts Bay Colony,[62]
described the Puritan founders as "a people amongst whom religion and law were
almost identical, and in whose character both were so thoroughly interfused." Early
in the novel, Hawthorne communicates this intertwinement through the dialogue
among some townspeople objecting to Hester Prynne's punishment as too lenient.
"At the very least, they should have put the brand of a hot iron on Hester Prynne's
forehead," one person says, while another person voices the desire for an even
harsher penalty – she "ought to die" – under the law "both in the Scripture and
statute-book."[63] Hawthorne's twinning of the statute-book and scripture is substanti-
ated by the colony's statute-book itself, which included an instruction in 1647 that
the copying of the laws should be with two large margins, with one margin for the
"heads of the law" and the other for any references, scriptures, or the like.[64]

The crime of the character Hester Prynne – seemingly adultery although the
character's marital status is unclear and the word is not contained in Hawthorne's

novel – is punished by imprisonment, the pillory, and through a life sentence of badging with the appropriate letter. The Records of the Governor and Company of Massachusetts Bay include other such badging punishments. In 1634, one Robert Coles was disenfranchised and ordered to wear about his neck and hang outside his garment at all times a "D, made of red cloathe and sett upon white" and in 1636, one William Perkins to wear "a white sheete of pap on his brest, having a greate D made upon it." Their crimes were stated as drunkenness. For gross offenses in attempting lewdness with various women, in 1639 John Davies was censured to be severely whipped and to wear the "letter V vpon his breast vpon his vppermost garment."[65] Presumably the "V" represents the first letter of uncleanness.

Hawthorne's novel explores the various meanings of his heroine's wearing of the red letter A as her punishment. Interestingly, Hawthorne describes Hester Prynne's badge as violative of another aspect of the Colony's regulation of dress:

> On the breast of her gown, in fine red cloth, surrounded with an elaborate embroi-
> dery and fantastic flourishes of gold thread, appeared the letter A. It was so artisti-
> cally done, and with so much fertility and gorgeous luxuriance of fancy, that it had
> all the effect of a last and fitting decoration to the apparel which she wore; and
> which was of a splendor in accordance with the taste of the age, but greatly beyond
> what was allowed by the sumptuary regulations of the colony.[66]

Hester Prynne not only breaches the sumptuary laws by her embroidered A, but she also makes her living in their shadow. Hawthorne's only other mention of the colony's sumptuary laws in *The Scarlet Letter* is in the context of Hester Prynne's exercise of her livelihood of "needle-work," which, was "then as now, almost the only one within a woman's grasp." Prynne had elevated needlework to an art; one she advertised with her letter A and in the clothing of her child. Her work was in demand, because despite the Puritan's renowned "sable simplicity":

> Public ceremonies, such as ordinations, the installation of magistrates, and all that
> could give majesty to the forms in which a new government manifested itself to
> the people, were, as a matter of policy, marked by a stately and well-conducted
> ceremonial, and a sombre, but yet a studied magnificence. Deep ruffs, painfully
> wrought bands, and gorgeously embroidered gloves, were all deemed necessary to
> the official state of men assuming the reins of power; and were readily allowed to
> individuals dignified by rank or wealth, even while sumptuary laws forbade these
> and similar extravagances to the plebeian order.[67]

Again, although Hawthorne's work is a novel and written two centuries after the incidents it describes, it seems consistent with the historical evidence. The Records of the Governor and Company of the Massachusetts Bay Colony reveal several sumptuary regulations from the era in which the novel is set.[68] A 1634 order from the General Court, a body having both legislative and adjudicatory powers, discussed

meals, beer, and tobacco, and then turned to the great, superfluous, and unnecessary expenses occasioned by new and immodest fashions, as well as the wearing
of silver, gold, silk, and lace.[69] The order prohibited such apparel, upon penalty
of forfeiture. The order addressed some specific problems: overly "slashed" clothes
(though one slash in each sleeve and another in the back is specifically permitted); "cuttworks, imbroderied or needle worke capps, bands & rayles" (the last being
most probably a type of neckerchief or scarf)[70] and gold or silver girdles (cords worn
around the hips or waist), hatbands, belts, ruffs, and beaver hats. All of these were
prohibited. An order in 1636 prohibited the making or selling of "bone lace, or other
lace" to be worn on garments or linens, upon penalty of a fine, with an exception for
"binding or small edging laces."[71] In 1644, without explanation, the Records state:
"It is ordered, that all those former orders made about apparel & lace are hereby
repealed."[72]

This was not the end of laws of attire in the Massachusetts Bay Colony. Indeed, it
is a law in 1651 that most closely mirrors the sumptuary legislation of Tudor England
with a concern for enforcing hierarchies through apparel.[73] The General Court first
conveyed its frustration that the previous declarations and orders "against excess
in apparel" for both men and women had not been effective, but that "intolerable
excess" had "crept in upon us." The worst offenders were, not surprisingly, "people
of mean condition." The General Court declared that it was detestable and intolerable that "men and women of mean condition should take upon them the garb
of gentlemen by wearing gold or silver lace, or buttons, or points at their knees, or
to walk in great boots; or women of the same rank to wear silk or tiffany hoods, or
scarves which, though allowable to persons of greater estates or more liberal education." Therefore, the Court ordered that

> no person within the jurisdiction, nor any of their relations depending upon them,
> whose visible estates, real and personal, shall not exceed the true and indifferent
> value of £200, shall wear any gold or silver lace, or gold and silver buttons, or any
> bone lace above 2s. per yard, or silk hoods, or scarves, upon the penalty of 10s. for
> every such offense.

However, unlike Tudor Parliaments, the General Court bemoaned the difficulty of
setting down "exact rules" to govern all sorts of persons. It avoided the multileveled
hierarchies of many of the Tudor statutes in favor of vagueness and delegation. The
order gave wide discretion to the selectmen in every town: whosoever the selectmen "shall judge to exceed their ranks and abilities in the costliness or fashion
of their apparel in any respect, especially in the wearing of ribbons or great boots
(leather being so scarce a commodity in this country) lace, points, etc., silk hoods,
or scarves," would be subject to fines assessed by those same selectmen. The law

further provided that it "shall not extend to the restraint of any magistrate or public officer of this jurisdiction, their wives and children, who are left to their discretion in wearing of apparel, or any settled militia officer or soldier in the time of military service, or any other whose education and employment have been above the ordinary degree, or whose estate have been considerable, though now decayed."[74] Nevertheless, the Massachusetts scheme sought to recognize and enforce class hierarchy as clearly as any Tudor sumptuary regulation that contained specific items of attire of the Knights of the Garter.

As in Tudor England, the existence of recognized liberties did not deter the promulgation of laws of attire. The precise legal status of the Massachusetts Body of Liberties of 1641 at that time remains subject to scholarly debate. However, the Body of Liberties is now considered the Massachusetts Magna Carta and a precursor to not only the Massachusetts Constitution but also the U.S. Constitution's Bill of Rights. The Massachusetts Body of Liberties contains some very progressive articulations of rights, especially with regard to due process and criminal procedure. For example, it includes a right against double jeopardy; a right included in the Fifth Amendment to the U.S. Constitution. However, almost three hundred years after the Massachusetts Body of Liberties, the United States Supreme Court would hold the double jeopardy right not sufficiently fundamental so as to be applicable to the states,[75] only reversing this conclusion in 1969.[76] Additionally, the Body of Liberties recognizes rights, albeit limited, for women, children, and animals. However, the Body of Liberties was not limited to an articulation of rights, but set out a framework for religious society, including as it did a "Declaration of the Liberties the Lord Jesus hath Given to the Churches." There was also a catalogue of "capital laws," supported by marginal biblical citations, enumerating twelve offenses that warranted the death penalty. These included worshipping "any other god but the lord god" after conviction, being a witch, blasphemy, murder, bestiality (in which the animal would also be slain and buried), male homosexuality, and adultery.[77] Thus, taken as a whole the Body of Liberties provides little that would support a right of liberty or equality, and even less to support a right of conscience or speech, that would be sufficient to challenge a branding, badging, sumptuary, or dress regulation.

Reports of enforcements of the dress regulations are scattered among the records of the colony. In 1652 a session of the Salem Quarterly Court considered accusations against Jonas Fairbanks for "wearing great boots," Henrye Bulllocke for "excess in his apparel in boots, ribbons, gold and silver lace," and Marke Hoscalle for "wearing broad lace."[78] The statements in the records are generally quite succinct, with women and silk seeming to be the most common offenders. For example, records for a session of court held at Ipswich in 1653 include several women summoned for

wearing silk hoods. The women are unnamed except as "wife" of their named husbands, and the judgments of their cases depends upon their husbands' worth:

> Wife of John Hutchings, presented for wearing a silk hood, was discharged upon
> testimony of her being brought up above the ordinary rank. Wife of Rich. Knight,
> presented for wearing a silk hood, discharged, her husband being worth above two
> hundred pounds. Joseph Swett's wife fined ten shillings for wearing a silk hood.
> Wife of William Chandlour fined ten shillings for wearing a silk hood. Wife of
> John Whipple, presented for wearing a silk hood, discharged, her husband being
> worth two hundred pounds.[79]

Although brief, it is sometimes obvious from the records that the court heard the
testimony of witnesses or received letters. The court also evaluated the evidence:
"Rich. Brabrooke's wife presented for wearing a silk scarf. Not proved."[80] Moreover,
while the statutory element was the husband's worth, this was not necessarily determinative: "Thomas Harris, Thomas Wayte and Edward Browne, upon proof of their
wives' education and bringing up, discharged of their presentments." This entry has
a footnote, seemingly of testimony of one of the husbands, which not only discusses
the wife's education and previous status, but also includes a legal argument. He
noted that the purpose of the law was to eliminate the sins of pride and excess in
apparel and argued that there was no pride in this case because she wore her scarf
only during the seasons when it was cold or wet.[81] While not an invocation of rights,
this argument reflects a notion of entitlement to fairness. Moreover, the argument
was successful and included in the record.

Massachusetts may have been the most vigorous in its regulations of dress, but it
was not alone. The first general assembly in Virginia, consisting of the colonial governor, the council members appointed by the governor, and elected burgesses from
the colonists, was convened in 1619. It quickly reached the matter of enacting regulations against idleness, gaming, drunkenness, and excess of apparel. The enactment
contains no definition of excess of apparel but seems to delegate its definition and
enforcement to religious authorities: every man was to be assessed "in the Churche
for all publique contributions" if he is unmarried for his own apparel and if married,
for his own and his wife's apparel.[82]

In South Carolina, there was concern for the clothing of slaves. The first "Act for
the Bettering Ordering of Slaves," promulgated in 1690 by the colonial proprietors
for Carolina, included a general directive that slaves be provided clothes.[83] In the
Acts of 1735 and 1740, those legislating for the colony of South Carolina enacted a
dress code for slaves.[84] The 1735 and 1740 acts, though separated by a notable slave
uprising in 1739, differ very little from each other with respect to their attention to
attire. One notable exception was that the post-Stono Rebellion act in 1740 included
a provision that those having responsibility for slaves should allow them sufficient

clothing, although the act did not include any right of recourse for the slaves them-selves.[85] It is possible, however, that criminal sanctions were not unthinkable. In at least one case – albeit from Tennessee and more than a century later – the court affirmed a conviction for lewdness of a slave owner based on his failure to pro-vide "decent" clothing for a female slave beyond tattered and dirty rags that did not adequately cover her. The criminal fine was $25.[86]

Otherwise, both acts seek to remedy the same situation: "many of the slaves of this Province wear clothes above the condition of slaves." Both laws essentially set an upper limit on the types of fabric permitted for slaves: nothing "finer, other, or greater value than Negro cloth, duffels, kerseys, osnabrigs, blue linen, check linen or coarse garlix, or calicoes, checked cottons, or Scotch plaids." The only exception the laws provided was for "livery men or boys."

The South Carolina slave codes provided punishments of marking the body with letters rather than wearing letters upon one's clothes. The letter R would be branded on the cheek or the forehead for a slave's crime of "running away."[87] Branding could be a consequence of other crimes, inflicted on slaves and nonslaves alike. Additionally, branding on the thumb could be a substitute "punishment" when a person asserted "benefit of clergy." While benefit of clergy developed in England to immunize religious officials from civil punishment, it was extended to persons who were literate, or could imitate literacy, by "reading" from a particular passage of the Bible; Psalm 51 came to be known as the "neck verse" because it could save one's neck from the noose. However, this benefit could be asserted only once. Hence, the person's thumb or thumb joint was branded with an appropriate letter for the crime, M for manslaughter/murder; T for theft.[88]

The branding of thumbs plays an important part in the constitutional history of South Carolina and the colonial United States. In 1712, the Lords and Proprietors of the Province of South Carolina selectively adopted a series of statutes of the English Parliament.[89] While South Carolina did not include any of the acts of apparel, it did adopt the Great Charter. It also incorporated various acts regarding benefit of clergy. For example, South Carolina made "of force" the 1623 Act of Parliament that extended the benefit of clergy to women committing "small felonies" (worth less than ten shillings). The punishment for the first offense was to be "branded and marked in the hand, upon the brawn of the left thumb, with a hot burning iron, hav-ing the Roman T upon said iron." The branding was to occur in open court before the judge and performed by the jailer. Further punishment such as whipping and imprisonment was also within the discretion of the judge.[90]

Importantly, however, the law regarding benefit of clergy with its mark of branding for specific crimes was not identical in England and the colony of South Carolina. This led to what may be termed a constitutional conflict in the famous 1736 case of *Rex v. Mellichamp*.[91] Mellichamp was convicted of counterfeiting, but his attorney essentially argued that the South Carolina law that proscribed his punishment without benefit of clergy was unconstitutional, as it exceeded the powers of the colonial government and conflicted with British law. The chief judge invoked the Magna Carta and waxed eloquent on the British constitution: "founded on Reason and the Law of Nature, and extracted, refined and collected from the Laws of Nations, calculated as well for the Honour, Strength and Support of the Crown, as for the Freedom, Safety and Wellfare of the People." The judge referred to the English constitution as a singular entity: "This Constitution thus framed and settled by the Wisdom of our Ancestors, we have long experienced to be salutary and good, and may be esteemed the best in the World, being thereby secured in the peaceable Enjoyment of our Lives, Liberties, Estates, and Properties, free from Oppression and arbitrary Violence, and subject to no Laws but those of our own making, that is by King, Lords and Commons in Parliament assembled."

The judge posited himself as a protector of individual rights, bound to "demand and protect all his Majesty's Subjects in the safe and free Enjoyment of their Lives, Liberties, Estates and Properties, so far as by Law I may, and as I would by no means suffer the Prerogative of the Crown to be lessened, so I would be careful not to extend it to the prejudice of the People, nor to encroach on the Liberties of the Subject." This autonomous judicial role might be contrasted with the criticism in the Declaration of Independence forty years later, that King George III had "made Judges dependent on his Will alone, for the tenure of their offices, and the amount and payment of their salaries." Yet whether Thomas Mellichamp was accorded benefit of clergy and escaped the death penalty with only a branding is uncertain. The chief judge was alone in his conclusion, an assistant justice disagreed, and the court adjourned "in expectation of a fuller Bench to decide the case by a Majority."[92]

It is difficult to imagine an analogous case involving a slave. South Carolina never allowed slaves to assert benefit of clergy, even assuming they could be deemed literate.[93] The slave code statutes of 1722 and 1735 provided that slaves guilty of crimes such as theft where "a white man is allowed benefit of clergy and ought to be punished by burning in the hand," a slave "shall be burned with the letter R in the forehead."[94] Indeed, theft by slaves might be considered "running away": an assertion of rights and a form of escape from servitude.[95] As such, an indelible brand rather than a removable badge or rough textiles would serve as a marker of status, not only of being enslaved but also of being rebellious.

The same issue of the *South Carolina Gazette* in May of 1736 containing *Rex v. Mellichamp* also included this entry:

BROUGHT TO THE GAOL IN CHARLESTOWN

April 10. A Negro Fellow with white Negro Cloth Jacket and breeches, taken up by a Negro Fellow belonging to *Wm. Bull* Esq;

13. *Jemmy* a Negro Boy, has on a white Cloth Jacket and Trowsers, taken up by *Peter Mason* Tanner.

23. A Negro Girl, has on a Negro Blanket taken up by *Jeremiah Taylor.*

May 3. *Primus* a Negro Fellow belonging to Doctor *Lewin* taken up by Mr. *Starling.*

6. *Tom* A Negro Fellow has on a Negro Cloth Jacket & breeches, taken up by one of Mr. *Harvey's* Negros.[96]

Instead of *Rex v. Mellichamp* in which the judge invoked the Magna Carta and liberties, the docket of persons brought to the jail – presumably in accordance with the slave codes that mandated temporary jailing for running away – contained no reference to rights or adjudication. People are merely described by their race, as well as by their gender; they are less likely to be accorded even a partial name than to be described by their attire.

V. THE ENDS OF EMPIRE

Managing hierarchy in the colonies was a complex process, accomplished in part through regulation of attire and infliction of bodily marks. Similarly, managing the complications of morality and sexuality employed regulations of apparel and other appearances. However, in addition to the interests of maintaining hierarchy and morality, the colonists of British America had substantial economic interests regarding cloth. The plans to produce silk in the southern colonies, including South Carolina and Virginia, were unsuccessful. In the Massachusetts Bay Colony, several laws promoted wool and other local textiles. Unlike the Elizabethan cap act mandating the wearing of wool caps, the Massachusetts approach championed production. For example, in 1645 an act referenced the brutal civil war in England, noting there was a scarcity of wool by reason of the wars in Europe killing both the sheep and the workers of wool. The solution was a preservation of clothes, as well as allowing sheep to be kept on the commons.[97] An act a few years later mandated death by hanging for any dog that attacked a sheep.[98]

In 1656, with Charles I beheaded and England under the Protectorate of Oliver Cromwell, wool was apparently still in short supply in the colony, so the Massachusetts Court required an assessment of households for spinning capacity, a setting of a quota, and a possible penalty for failure to meet the quota. The same act encouraged local officials to encourage the sowing of hemp and flax and the clearing of commons where sheep could be kept and bred.[99]

In the decades that followed, developments such as the Glorious Revolution in 1688, the establishment of a constitutional monarchy, and the Act of Settlement of 1701, stabilized England. So too did the possession of colonies. In its empire – what historian T. H. Breen has labeled an "empire of goods"[100] – England employed its legal powers in the service of capitalism, especially with regard to wool. At home,

Parliament's Woolen Manufacture Act of 1725[101] began the process of what scholar Christopher Tomlins names the "criminalization of employment contract breach." Tomlins describes how Parliament transformed the employment relation into that of master-servant, with criminal consequences for uncooperative servants,[102] solidifying a source of labor. For its possessions, England employed its legal powers to create colonies of customers. Insufficient wool in British America was not simply attributable to a lack of success in keeping the sheep safe from attacking dogs. For example, the Royal Privy Council used power to void colonial laws to veto two acts from the Virginia Assembly: An Act Prohibiting the Exportation of Any Iron, Wool, Woolfells, Skins, hides, or Leather; and An Act for Encouragement of the Manufactures of Linen and Wollen Cloth.[103] More comprehensively, Parliament passed various "Navigation Acts" that sequestered the commercial activities of the colonies within the empire. First passed during the Protectorate of Oliver Cromwell, the navigation acts essentially provided that the American colonies could trade only with Great Britain.[104] Not surprisingly, by 1773, American colonists purchased almost 26 percent of all the goods being domestically produced in Great Britain[105]; about half of these goods were various kinds of finished cloth, with a predominance of woolens.[106] In the American colonies, England had finally found – or created – a reliable buyer for its manufactured wool. Additionally, America was a profitable stop in Great Britain's global trade, a large portion of which featured textiles and articles of clothing.

Breen notes that this arrangement was widely admired: the "empire of goods" that "gained strength from equipoise" was analogized to the "crown, lords, and commoners" of England's "famed balanced constitution" that was a "source of liberty and prosperity."[107] Breen quotes George Mason writing to George Washington in 1769: "Our supplying our Mother-Country with gross Materials, & taking her Manufactures in Return is the true Chain of Connection between us; these are the Bands, which, if not broken by Oppressions, must long hold us together, by maintain[in]g a constant Reciprocation of Interest."[108]

The "oppressions" that broke the "reciprocation of interest" were largely the result of the economic hierarchies between the "mother country" and the dependent American colonies. While tea may be the most famous of commodities fomenting the revolution of the British colonies of America, apparel played an important part. The British Parliament did single out textiles or clothes on a few occasions when it legislated for the colonies. In 1732, Parliament passed a law with the lengthy title of "An Act to prevent the exportation of hats out of any of His Majesty's colonies or plantations in America and to restrain the number of apprentices taken by hat-makers in said colonies or plantations, and for the better encouragement of the making of hats in Great Britain."[109] Not mentioned in the otherwise descriptive title of the act was a provision that prohibited any person "residing in any of his Majesty's plantations in America" from making or causing to be made "any felt or hat of or with any wool or stuff whatsoever," unless he had served as an apprentice for seven years.[110]

More than forty years later, Thomas Jefferson referred to the Hat Act in his *A Summary View of The Rights of British America*, written in 1774 as a draft for the Virginia convention selecting representatives to the Continental Congress and considered a precursor to the Declaration of Independence. In *A Summary View*, Jefferson described the Hat Act as forbidding "an American subject" from making "a hat for himself of the fur which he has taken perhaps on his own soil." He labeled this "an instance of despotism to which no parallel can be produced in the most arbitrary ages of British history."[111]

But the Hat Act is not the pinnacle of Jefferson's rhetoric. Of more immediate concern to Jefferson than the Hat Act passed under George II were the acts passed by Parliament under the reign of King George III. Jefferson argued that the acts under George III were part of "a deliberate and systematical plan of reducing us to slavery." Among the laws under George III, Jefferson listed "An act for granting certain duties in the British colonies and plantations in America, &c."[112] While Jefferson did not expand on the law, contemporary readers would have been well aware of the law more commonly known as the Sugar Act passed in 1764. It placed duties not only on sugar:

> For every pound weight avoirdupois of wrought silks, bengals, and stuffs, mixed silk or herbs, of the manufacture of Persia, China, or East India, imported from Great Britain, two shillings.
>
> For every piece of callico painted, dyed, printed, or stained, in Persia, China, or East India, imported from Great Britain, two shillings and six pence.
>
> For every piece of foreign linen cloth, called Cambrick, imported from Great Britain, three shillings.
>
> For every piece of French lawn imported from Great Britain, three shillings.[113]

The imposition of duties on items such as wrought silk and French lawn (a type of fine cloth) might be interpreted as a kind of hierarchal sumptuary legislation. The Sugar Act targeted luxury items and created status hierarchies between those who are able to afford to pay the extra tax in opposition to those who were not. Unlike more direct sumptuary regulations, however, the imposition of duties preserved a zone of consumer autonomy. A segment of the population could choose whether or not to purchase Cambrick and pay the extra three shillings or buy a less lavish textile that was untaxed. However, democratic impulses would successfully contravene the consumer choice construction of the import duty.

The role of apparel in revolutionary rhetoric was disproportionate to its direct regulation. For example, appearing before Parliament's House of Commons in 1766 to speak about the hated Stamp Act that required purchase of a stamp for legal documents and other parchments, Benjamin Franklin talked about clothes. Answering a query, Franklin stated that if the Stamp Act was not repealed, there would be a "total loss of the respect and affection the people of America bear to

this country, and of all the commerce that depends on that respect and affection."
Regarding the effect on commerce, Franklin stated that the Americans would take
"very little of your manufactures in a short time" and indeed had the ability to do
without them: "The goods they take from Britain are either necessaries, mere con-
veniences, or superfluities. The first, as cloth, etc., with a little industry they can
make at home; the second they can do without till they are able to provide them
among themselves; and the last, which are mere articles of fashion, purchased and
consumed because the fashion in a respected country; but will now be detested and
rejected. The people have already struck off, by general agreement, the use of all
goods fashionable in mourning." Franklin added that the Americans would replace
their pride in English fashions with wearing "their old cloathes over again, till they
can make new ones."[114]

While Parliament did repeal the Stamp Act, the colonists pursued their "general
agreement" to forgo British fashions and imports. As T. H. Breen has persuasively
demonstrated, the nonimportation and nonconsumption compacts among colonists
forged an American identity in resistance to "unconstitutional" taxes on consumer
goods. Wearing "homespun" apparel became a mark of American patriotism. While
the compacts were unenforceable – they were, after all, extra-legal documents under
colonial law – strategies such as local associations and committees, signatory and
subscription lists, newspaper letters, social shaming, and other pressures within and
across the colonies were effective in equating "liberty" with eschewing a silk ribbon.
This politicization had a distinctively democratic tone, often highlighting the role
of women as decision makers for households, although generally neglecting those
unable to make consumer choices, such as slaves and nonadults.

The anti-importation rhetoric also possessed a pronounced sumptuary inflection.
The Articles of Association of the First Continental Congress in 1774, essentially an
agreement to boycott British goods, included a provision that

> We will, in our several stations, encourage frugality, economy, and industry, and
> promote agriculture, arts and the manufactures of this country, especially that of
> wool; and will discountenance and discourage every species of extravagance and
> dissipation, especially all horse-racing, and all kinds of games, cock fighting, exhi-
> bitions of shews, plays, and other expensive diversions and entertainments; and on
> the death of any relation or friend, none of us, or any of our families will go into any
> further mourning-dress, than a black crepe or ribbon on the arm or hat, for gentle-
> men, and a black ribbon and necklace for ladies, and we will discontinue the giving
> of gloves and scarves at funerals.[115]

This echoed earlier discourse arguing that it was the "folly and extravagance of
the people in imitating the customs and dress of foreigners" and the "extravagant
dress and luxury" that had the "fatal effect" of inducing the British to believe that

Americans were more prosperous than they were and therefore capable of paying more taxes.[116] Similarly, it was argued that the colonists had grown "more Luxurious every Year" causing them to "run deeper and deeper in Debt to our Mother Country," so that it was time to revive the virtues of "industry and Frugality."[117] According to T. H. Breen, this virtue was a new sort of consumer virtue – a "bourgeois virtue" – distinct from the other religious or political types of virtue. Nevertheless, the emphasis on virtue was certainly linked to the Puritan and Christian virtue that had animated the sumptuary laws of the Massachusetts Bay Colony. And it was also linked to the notion of virtue in civic republicanism that prized independence from the corrupting influence of commerce.[118]

Perhaps it was this notion of civic republicanism that best explains the effort to include sumptuary laws as among the enumerated powers of the federal government in the U.S. Constitution drafted in 1787. The Constitutional Convention occurred because the Articles of Confederation, a document entered into during the Revolutionary War and consolidating a league of sovereign states, came to be perceived as unsatisfactory, at least by those who supported a more unified government. But even those who supported more unification did not necessarily support the Constitution as drafted, including George Mason, a delegate from Virginia who ultimately did not sign the document. The same Mason who had written George Washington a decade earlier concerning the commercial reciprocation of interest between the colonies and Great Britain was advocating a federal power to make sumptuary regulations. According to the Records of the Federal Convention, Mason argued for a Sumptuary Clause to enable Congress to enact sumptuary laws: "The love of distinction it is true is natural; but the object of sumptuary laws is not to extinguish this principle but to give it proper direction."[119] The motion failed by a vote of 8–3, with only the delegates from Delaware, Maryland, and Georgia voting in the affirmative. A few weeks later, Mason "had not yet lost sight of his object," according to the Records, and he was "descanting on the extravagance of our manners, the excessive consumption of foreign superfluities, and the necessary of restricting it."[120] Mason this time moved for a committee to be appointed, which did occur, although the committee apparently never made a report.[121] The Constitution as drafted and ratified did not include among the enumerated powers of Congress a mention of sumptuary laws, or any references to the power to direct individuals' "love of distinction."

Yet popular rhetoric continued to include judgments about individuals' "love of distinction." As scholar Linzy Brekke has noted, post–Revolutionary War America was beset by an economic malaise and imported textiles were an easy scapegoat.[122] Brekke argues that George Washington was a "particularly contradictory figure" during this period, seen as both a person with "homespun" clothes and politics, as well as someone less genuine. One report criticized him as someone who was not nearly as patriotic as his rhetoric: he "dressed in manufactures of foreign nations" and thus almost "every article he wears is repugnant to his words."[123]

In addition to declamatory judgments, there were genuine issues regarding the advisability of government legislating on aspects of dress in a constitutional democracy. John Adams, who would become the nation's second president, wrote in his pamphlet "Thoughts on Government" that

> The very mention of sumptuary laws will excite a smile. Whether our countrymen have wisdom and virtue enough to submit to them, I know not; but the happiness of the people might be greatly promoted by them, and a revenue saved sufficient to carry on this war forever. Frugality is a great revenue, besides curing us of vanities, levities, and fopperies, which are real antidotes to all great, manly, and warlike virtues.[124]

Adams thus links support for sumptuary laws with the Revolutionary War effort. He also valorizes frugality as a masculine virtue, decidedly superior to the effeminacy of "fopperies." The invocation of rights is implicit and negative: the countrymen may not be sufficiently "wise" to submit. Yet there is also a latent claim of equality (or at least male equality), especially because Adams's passage on sumptuary laws follows one on universal education: "Laws for liberal education of youth, especially of the lower class of people, are so extremely wise and useful, that, to a humane and generous mind, no expense for this purpose would be thought extravagant."

Similarly, Mason's support for sumptuary laws may be linked to republican virtue. Jeff Broadwater, a Mason biographer, argues that Mason's concept of republican virtue was not necessarily in conflict with liberal rights, but a "delicate balance" in which individual freedoms rested upon the "virtue of the citizenry." Moreover, Broadwater notes that the conflicts of Mason's time were not between "the public good and individual rights but those between majority rights and an undemocratic government."[125]

From a federalism perspective, Mason's advocacy of federal power to enact sumptuary laws is less explicable. While John Adams remains in reputation a staunch federalist, George Mason continues to be celebrated as a champion of states' rights. If adopted, Mason's proposal would have arrogated to the federal government the power to adopt mandatory dress codes for everyone in the United States.

But the lack of an explicit "sumptuary power" does not mean that the federal government cannot constitutionally concern itself with clothes. Congress now legislates attire primarily through the commerce clauses, both interstate and foreign.[126] Additionally, Congress has among its powers taxing, imposing duties, and regulating the armed forces, and it may provide for the "general welfare," so that its funding may have conditions attached. The government as an employer, or as a custodian as in the case of prisons, routinely regulates aspects of bodily appearance. Moreover, the judicial powers allocated by the Constitution, including to the United States Supreme Court and inferior federal courts, allow courts to adjudicate controversies about the contours of the Constitution; this includes constitutional limitations regarding regulations of dress and other matters of appearance. These controversies often involve laws or policies promulgated by nonfederal levels of government – states, localities, tribal sovereigns, and territorial governments – that supervise specific aspects of bodily presentation.

The most basic of the laws governing appearance, and perhaps the most constitutionally controversial, are laws that govern whether or not people must cover or uncover specific parts of their bodies.

2

Dressing Barely

Government – like dress – is a "badge of lost innocence."[1] Thomas Paine, who made this observation on the first pages of his famous American revolutionary pamphlet, "Common Sense," was primarily concerned with government rather than dress. However, his further characterizations of government as a "necessary evil," prompted by human "wickedness" and intended to restrain human vices and create distinctions, might also be extended to clothes. Presumably, in Thomas Paine's paradise, there would be no need for government or for bodily coverings.

Paine's imagined paradise is far from reality. Both government and clothes seem necessities. Moreover, government requires its subjects to be clothed, or, more precisely, that certain parts of certain bodies be covered under certain circumstances. However, the government may also require a lack of clothes. Strip searches and forced nudity, indecent exposure, nude dancing, and gender disparities in mandated coverings prompt complex constitutional issues implicating hierarchy, democracy, and sexuality.

I. STRIPPED OF RIGHTS

A majority of the provisions of the U.S. Constitution's Bill of Rights pertain to criminal procedure. The Fourth Amendment guarantees the "right of the people" "against unreasonable searches and seizures." The Fifth Amendment includes a version of the Magna Carta's due process clause, repeated in the Fourteenth Amendment: that no person shall be deprived of life, liberty, or property without due process of law. The Eighth Amendment prohibits "cruel and unusual punishments" from being inflicted. When the government enforces nudity or partial nudity in the criminal or quasi-criminal context, these constitutional proscriptions may limit government power.

One of the most prominent issues is that of the "strip search" as evaluated under the Fourth Amendment standard of reasonableness. Such a search might range from a partial disrobing (a shirt lifted, for example) to full nudity, as well as extending to a search of body cavities. It might also occur in a variety of contexts, including during the initial investigation and arrest or as a person is being jailed. The reasonableness of such searches under constitutional law often reach the courts through civil actions by those who have been searched against those who executed the search. As such, the question of the immunity of the defendants is often also an issue, especially when monetary damages are sought.

The courts granting relief to the plaintiffs who have been searched – and even some courts that do not grant relief – acknowledge that forced nudity is humiliating and an affront to personal dignity. Yet this acknowledgment generally extends beyond the person's lack of clothes. Perhaps because of the egregious facts necessary to surmount immunity, the reported cases generally involve other factors contributing to the kind of humiliation inimical to democracy, enforcing hierarchy and insinuating sexuality. For example, in *Evans v. Stephens*, decided by the Eleventh Circuit in 2005, the court held that a police officer's strip search must be supported by "at least" reasonable suspicion that there might be evidence of a crime hidden on the person's body; a standard that was not satisfied.[2] More important, the court also looked to "the manner" in which the officer conducted the search. The court stated it did not require the search to be "delicately conducted in the least intrusive manner," but it did require the search be "conducted in a reasonable manner" and not "in an abusive fashion."

The "abusive fashion" of the search of the plaintiffs in *Evans* is evident from the court's opinion. Not only were the plaintiffs "forced to disrobe" but there were subsequent events in the "broom closet" where the officer "inserted the same baton or club – without intervening sanitation – in each Plaintiffs' anus and used the same baton or club to lift each man's testicles." There was also physical violence against the plaintiffs. The police officer punctuated all of this with racial slurs and threats. In sum, the court found "the totality of the circumstances – for example, the physical force, anal penetration, unsanitariness of the process, terrifying language, and lack of privacy – collectively establish a constitutional violation, especially when the search was being made in the absence of exigent circumstances requiring the kind of immediate action that might make otherwise questionable police conduct, at least arguably, reasonable." In this context, the police officer's orders to one of the plaintiffs to remove shoes and shirt, then the rest of the clothes, and insist upon the removal of the underwear, or even to pull down the underwear of one of the plaintiffs to the ankles, is only part of a sexualized, hierarchal, and humiliating scenario.[3]

The court in *Evans* distinguished that search from searches that occur when jailers, for security and safety purposes, conduct strip searches of inmates – or persons about to become inmates – in the general jail population. The United States Supreme Court in 1979 upheld a similar type of search, even in the absence of probable cause, and even when the persons were pretrial detainees who had not been convicted of any crime.[4] Extending this principle, the Court's 2012 opinion in *Florence v. Board of Chosen Freeholders*, upheld the constitutionality of a strip search of a person arrested for a minor crime when that person is being committed to the jail's general population.[5] In a 5–4 decision, the majority relied on the deference that should be given to jail officials. However, although Justice Alito concurred, he stressed that the Court did not hold that it was "*always* reasonable to conduct a full strip search of an arrestee whose detention has not been reviewed by a judicial officer and who could be held in available facilities apart from the general population."[6] This would seem to leave undisturbed cases such as *Mary Beth G. v. City of Chicago*, in which the Seventh Circuit invalidated a policy that required strip searches of all women – but not men – who were detained in city jails.[7] Yet it may leave males in a more vulnerable position. In an interview before the case reached the United States Supreme Court, Albert Florence stressed the anti-democratic, hierarchal, and sexualized aspects of his experience of standing naked before several guards and being told to "spread your cheeks": "I consider myself a man's man," said Mr. Florence, a finance executive for a car dealership. "Six-three. Big guy. It was humiliating. It made me feel less than a man. It made me feel not better than an animal."[8]

A different situation, but presenting similar Fourth Amendment issues, arises when the search occurs at a person's home in which she or he is naked or only partially clothed. Again, the constitutional issue of the reasonableness of such searches often reaches the courts through civil actions filed by those who have been searched, and again, the facts need to be especially egregious to surmount the immunity that protects law enforcement. Indeed, two Supreme Court cases might serve as object lessons in the perils of sleeping in the nude.

In *Monroe v. Pape*, the Court considered the Monroes, a married heterosexual black couple, who had been asleep and naked in their Chicago bed in the autumn of 1958, when, according to their complaint, "13 Chicago police officers broke into petitioners' home in the early morning, routed them from bed, made them stand naked in the living room, and ransacked every room, emptying drawers and ripping mattress covers."[9] Discussing these allegations, Justice Frankfurter, dissenting in part, noted "the calculated degradation of insult and forced nakedness" as among the "manifold aggravating circumstances" of the intrusion. Frankfurter opined that the "essence of the liberty protected by the common law and by the American constitutions" was the right to resist unauthorized entry of a dwelling by government officials.

As legal scholar Myriam Gilles has shown, *Monroe v. Pape* was imbued with the hierarchal racial relationships between a white police force and the African American community during a decade of rapid change in Chicago.[10] The precise issue before the Court was not whether the Fourth Amendment had been violated, but whether the Monroes could bring a civil suit for damages. The lower federal courts found that the Monroes could not litigate their claims of constitutional deprivation. Reversing, a majority of the Supreme Court found that the Monroes could proceed against the defendant law enforcement officer Frank Pape and other detectives, although the Monroes' claims against the defendant City of Chicago could not be maintained because the city was not a "person" capable of being sued for a violation of constitutional rights. The Monroes did win a jury verdict for damages against the defendant detectives. And the Court eventually reversed its conclusion regarding municipalities as appropriate defendants.[11]

Forty years or so later, the Court in *Los Angeles County v. Rettele* again considered whether a sleeping in the nude heterosexual couple had a claim for relief against the law enforcement officers who had entered their bedroom.[12] However in *Rettele*, the officers had a search warrant and the couple's race was white. These were both important factors because the couple, Rettele and Sandler, argued that the search warrant being executed was based on probable cause to believe certain African American men lived at the address, and because Rettele and Sandler were Caucasian, the officers should have immediately stopped executing the warrant. The Court's per curium opinion dispatches this "unsound proposition" quickly: "it is not uncommon in our society for people of different races to live together."

That the officers should have allowed the couple to cover their naked bodies after arousing them from bed gets only slightly more attention. After relating the facts, including that the couple was held at gunpoint for one to two minutes and not allowed to move to get clothes or use the sheet as a covering, the Court observed that blankets and bedding can conceal a weapon, which was especially relevant because one of the actual suspects was known to own a firearm: "The Constitution does not require an officer to ignore the possibility that an armed suspect may sleep with a weapon within reach." Additionally, the Court noted there was no allegation that the deputies prevented Sadler and Rettele from getting dressed any longer than necessary, and that once the deputies realized there was no threat – and that they had made a mistake – they urged the couple to put on some clothes as quickly as possible.

However, even an expeditious strip search may be humiliating. Especially of a young person by school officials. And perhaps especially if that young person is female. And perhaps especially if the infraction being investigated is a relatively minor one, for example, the possession of prescription strength ibuprofen and over-the-counter naproxen, both pain relievers, both perfectly legal, but both banned under school rules without advance permission.

Such was the situation in *Safford Unified School District No. 1 v. Redding*, decided by the Court in 2009.[13] Suspecting thirteen-year-old Savana Redding of possessing prescription pain relievers, the assistant principal directed an administrative assistant and the school nurse, both women, to take Savana to the nurse's office and search her. According to the Court, the women "asked Savana to remove her jacket, socks, and shoes, leaving her in stretch pants and a T-shirt (both without pockets)," then asked Savana to remove the pants and T-shirt, and then told Savana to "pull her bra out and to the side and shake it, and to pull out the elastic on her underpants, thus exposing her breasts and pelvic area to some degree."

The Court credited Savana's subjective expectation of privacy as evident in her account of the search as "embarrassing, frightening, and humiliating." The Fourth Amendment requires not only that there be a subjective expectation of privacy, but that the expectation be reasonable. The Court considered "the consistent experiences of other young people similarly searched, whose adolescent vulnerability intensifies the patent intrusiveness of the exposure."[14] Yet it is not only youth that is important in the Court's analysis. Relying on previous school search precedent, albeit involving the search of a purse rather than a strip search, the Court reiterated that the scope of a search must be evaluated in light of "the age and sex of the student and the nature of the infraction."[15]

While Savana's age and minor infraction are explicitly addressed, the role of Savana's sex merely flickers throughout the Court's opinion, without being directly confronted. Justice Thomas, however, provides a contrary view. In a footnote in his dissent, he states that Savana's "age and sex, if anything, *increased* the need for a search," given the finding that among 12- to 17-year-olds, females are "more likely than boys to have abused prescription drugs."[16] Perhaps prudently, Thomas does not add an argument that females are presumably more likely to store these prescription drugs in their under garments.

Sex, gender, and sexuality hierarchies are implicit in the Fourth Amendment "reasonableness" of searches that require removing clothes. As in Savana's school situation, the usual practice or policy has become to prefer the searcher and the "searchee" to share the same sex/gender. Arguably, this diminishes unacceptable hierarchies and ameliorates the potential for sexual violence as well as humiliation, although Albert Florence and the young men in *Evans* might have a different view. For searches of transgender and gender nonconforming persons, police and prisons are slowly developing protective policies, yet transgender persons are additionally vulnerable to humiliating strip searches seeking to find their "sex."

The degree of humiliation constitutionally recognizable from having one's clothes forcibly removed should not necessarily vary by the character of the searchee. As in the context of sexual violence, the operative principle is consent. A 2011 case in Florida federal court highlights this issue.[17] The plaintiffs were employees subject to strip searches during the execution of a warrant seeking unlawful prescription drugs. The place of employment, notably, was a "gentleman's club" and two of the plaintiff employees were exotic dancers. Clad in their work attire at the time the warrant was executed, they were searched by a female officer, although in an area open to view by others. The search included pulling out a bikini top as well as the bottoms, front and back, and exposing genitalia. Under Florida law, adopted in the local law enforcement policy, a strip search was defined "as the removal or re-arrangement of some or all of the clothing so as to permit visual or manual inspection of the genitals, buttocks, anus, or breasts, in the case of a female, or undergarments of such person."[18] Denying a motion for summary judgment by the city and its law enforcement officers, the federal judge noted that he was "not impressed" by the defendants' arguments that because "nothing more could have been exposed during the searches than is normally revealed during the plaintiffs' dances," this "mitigates the illegality of the strip search." The case was later settled with damages paid to the employees who had been searched.[19]

Outside the context of a search for evidence of a crime or weapons, law enforcement would seem to have little rationale for imposing forced nudity. However, there are three other justifications for the removal of clothes in the criminal context: interrogation, discipline, and suicide prevention.

First, and most pervasively, the humiliation of nudity is a technique of interrogation. In *Malinski v. New York*, which reached the United States Supreme Court in 1945, the Court quoted the prosecutor's summation to the jury that sought to support the veracity of Malinski's confession:

> Why this talk about being undressed? Of course they had a right to undress him to look for bullet scars, and keep the clothes off him. That was quite proper police procedure. That is some more psychology – let him sit around with a blanket on him, humiliate him there for a while; let him sit in the corner, let him think he is going to get a shellacking.[20]

The Court noted that if "the confession had been the product of persistent questioning while Malinski stood stripped and naked," it would be "a clear case" that the confession had been coerced and was therefore unconstitutionally procured. But even where the nakedness lasted only two hours, the suspect later had "shoes, socks, and underwear back on and a blanket in which to wrap himself," and the interrogation occurred only after he was again clothed, the Court concluded that the lack of clothing contributed to the coerciveness of the confession. The Court's constitutional concern was the Due Process Clause of the Fourteenth Amendment, which, in addition to the Equal Protection Clause, according to the Court, summarized "the history of freedom of English-speaking peoples running back to Magna Carta."[21]

For citizens of the United States, protections against unconstitutional interrogation are grounded not only in the due process clauses of the Fifth or Fourteenth Amendments, for federal and state actions respectively, but also in the criminal procedure protections such as the privilege against self-incrimination and the right to counsel of the Fifth and Sixth Amendments. For noncitizens detained in the United States, these constitutional criminal procedure provisions are also applicable. However, for noncitizens detained by the United States overseas, there are few if any constitutional constraints on interrogation techniques or treatment. The operable hierarchies are not only between citizens and noncitizens, but between different sources of law, including constitutional criminal procedure protections, international treaties, or, as the government once argued in the context of the "War on Terror," little law at all.

Forced nudity as an interrogation technique has been prominently used against detainees in Iraq, Afghanistan, Guantanamo Bay, and elsewhere, pursuant to the War on Terror. As various U.S. government reports themselves acknowledge, detainees have been subjected to removal – or to reward – of clothing as an interrogation technique, not only during interrogation but also as a generalized "ego down" strategy to render detainees more cooperative.[22] The line between "ego down" and "humiliation" was not one that was sharply defined, as the government reports attest. The distinction between humiliation and dehumanization was also blurred. Detainee nudity, as one of the reports on the Iraq War's Abu Ghraib Prison states, was "employed routinely and with the belief that it was not abuse," although the investigating officer finds the use of clothing as an incentive was "significant in that it likely contributed to an escalating 'de-humanization' of the detainees and set the stage for additional and more severe abuses to occur."[23] If nudity conveys innocence, as Thomas Paine opined,[24] it also conveys something other than the usual circumstance of "civilized" humans. In 2004, the Special Rapporteur of the Commission on Human Rights on torture and other cruel, inhuman, or degrading treatment or punishment, specifically referenced "certain methods that have been condoned and used to secure information from suspected terrorists," including "depriving them of clothing" and "stripping detainees naked and threatening them with dogs." According to the Special Rapporteur: "The jurisprudence of both international and regional human rights mechanisms is unanimous in stating that such methods violate the prohibition of torture and ill-treatment."[25]

Moreover, there was a marked inflection of gender and sexual hierarchies. The notorious Abu Ghraib incidents illustrated by photographs of multiple naked detainees in a pyramid, or with a solitary naked hooded detainee standing on a box, or with a naked detainee on a leash, are undoubtedly intended to be sexually humiliating. Moreover, nudity was at times combined with apparel meant to be demeaning, as when male detainees were naked except for wearing women's underwear on their heads.[26] While the detainees were more likely than not to be male, the government reports contain a few references to women detainees, including this one in the Fay/Jones Report by the Department of Defense investigating incidents at Abu Ghraib:

Incident 38:. Eleven photographs of two female detainees arrested for suspected prostitution were obtained.... In some of these photos, a criminal detainee housed in the Hard Site was shown lifting her shirt with both her breasts exposed. *There is no evidence to confirm if these acts were consensual or coerced*; however in either case sexual exploitation of a person in U.S. custody constitutes abuse. There does not appear to be any direct MI [Military Intelligence] involvement in either of the two incidents above.[27]

In no other instance did the Fay/Jones Report speculate on whether there was "evidence" to "confirm" a finding that a detainee's removal of clothing was coerced. Indeed, it is difficult to imagine the issue of consent being raised for a male detainee being photographed partially naked.

In addition to its use as a technique of interrogation, the second rationale for full or partial nudity is discipline. In overseas facilities operated as part of the War on Terror, nudity was acknowledged in the report regarding FBI involvement as a "disciplinary measure in response to detainee misconduct."[28] Within U.S. prisons, the rationale of discipline has also surfaced; however, prisoners within the United States are protected by the Eighth Amendment's prohibition of "cruel and unusual punishment." When applied to prison conditions, the Eighth Amendment as interpreted by the courts requires both a serious deprivation of the prisoner's needs and "deliberate indifference" by the jailers.[29] Generally, prisoners' allegations of forced nudity are made in combination with other factors, such as cold temperatures.[30] Additionally, forced nudity as accompanied by clothing as a reward has been alleged with regard to behavior modification programs for inmates with disciplinary issues.[31]

The third rationale for forced nudity of a prisoner is as a response to a suicide threat. This rationale has surfaced in the overseas detainee context[32] and in the domestic United States.[33] The high profile detention of Bradley Manning, a private first class in the U.S. Army, accused of leaking classified military documents to WikiLeaks, included allegations of forced nudity. When Manning was first detained in the military prison in Quantico, Virginia, known as the "Brig," the authorities limited his nightclothes to underwear for the first eight months. Manning was under Prevention of Injury (POI) watch, despite the fact that the Brig's own psychiatrists declared that Manning was not a suicide risk. In March 2011, Manning was denied even his underwear at night and the mandatory standing at attention each morning was done while he was naked.[34] Manning's forced nudity might also be considered in the context of his sexual orientation and gender identity; as a nonheterosexual man who possibly identifies as female, Manning occupies a subordinate status even apart from being a prisoner forced to be nude.[35] Interestingly, the United Nations Special Rapporteur on Torture attempted to investigate Manning's treatment, but the U.S. government blocked access to Manning at the Brig. Manning was transferred to Leavenworth Prison in April 2011, where his treatment was believed to be much better, including being provided clothes. However, the Special Rapporteur was still denied an opportunity to speak with Manning privately.[36] According to his attorney, Manning was thereafter able to receive correspondence, although photographs including nudity or partial nudity were specifically disallowed.[37]

II. INDECENT EXPOSURES

If Bradley Manning removed his own clothes at the Brig rather than being forced to do so, he might be guilty of a crime: indecent exposure. The common law crime of indecent exposure is generally defined as the intentional exposure of the "private parts" of one's body in a public place observable by others. A claim by Manning that the prison was not a "public place" might not be a successful one. It was not a successful contention in a 2010 case involving Daniel Genies, an inmate temporarily housed in a medical unit because, as the court noted, the exposure occurred "in a room with a large glass window that oversaw the bed which was located right next to that window" that was observable by staff.[38] It was also not a successful claim in a 1998 case involving Jerome Minor, given that the Georgia public indecency statute specifically provides that "public place" shall "include jails and penal and correctional institutions."[39]

The extension of the "public" is not limited to prisons. In an English sixteenth-century case, Mr. Sidley was punished for being naked on his balcony.[40] In an American case from 1981, a Georgia court upheld the conviction of man who was "sunbathing in the nude on his back porch wearing only white socks and black shoes."[41] And an Indiana appellate court in 2008 rejected a constitutional vagueness challenge and upheld a conviction for "appearing" nude in a "public place": the defendant was naked by the fence separating his yard from his neighbor's yard, when "his neighbor drove his truck on to the sidewalk and pointed his headlights" at the figure he had seen in the dark.[42] These imprecisions in the definition of "public" are captured by this instruction to a jury, approved by the New Jersey Supreme Court in 1884:

> The true principle is, and I so instruct you, that as a general proposition the place where the exposure is made should be public; but that it is sufficient if the place is not ordinarily public, but only so in consequence of persons being temporarily assembled there; and further that there is no need that the exposure should be actually seen by any one, provided that it was made to be seen, and those who were there could have seen it if they had looked; and if so made, the place being public, it is immaterial whether the exposure was made to one person or to many.

Based on such a definition, it is not surprising that the court affirmed the defendant's conviction for indecent exposure because he urinated in his own front yard.[43]

Not only may the construction of "public" be more expansive than anticipated, but other aspects of the crime raise constitutional issues such as vagueness and overbreadth. The statutes criminalizing indecent exposure vary, with some requiring lewdness or a sexual element. Additionally, related crimes such as nuisance, breach of the peace, disorderly conduct, or obscenity may be used to prosecute public nudity. At times, courts consider the particular language of the indecent exposure statute to decide whether or not the charged acts are within the prohibition and avoid the constitutional challenge. For example, in *Duvallon v. District of Columbia*, Ms. Duvallon argued that the D.C. Code provision prohibiting any "indecent exposure of his or her person" was unconstitutionally vague.[44] The District of Columbia Court of Appeals held instead that the provision did not apply to her actions of protesting outside the U.S. Supreme Court building wearing only a cardboard sign that covered "the front of her body from the neck to below the knees," but exposing her buttocks. Citing English and American cases, the court held that the word "person" was "a euphemism for the penis." Since the code provision criminalized the exposure of "his or her person," the provision applied to "comparable portions of the male and female anatomy," that is, "human genitalia." The court reversed her conviction, based on the definitional disparity between buttocks and genitalia. To do otherwise, the court noted, would risk unconstitutional vagueness.[45]

The Nevada Supreme Court, writing in 2010, upheld the constitutionality of a similarly worded statute.[46] In *State v. Castaneda*, the court considered whether the prohibition against the "open and indecent or obscene exposure of his or her person" was so vague as to violate due process. As the court correctly articulated, the general test for unconstitutional vagueness is that the law either fails "to provide a person of ordinary intelligence fair notice of what is prohibited" or is "so standardless that it authorizes or encourages seriously discriminatory enforcement."[47] Relying on history and the common law, the court found that it is well understood that "person" means "private parts" or more specifically "penis." Thus, people have fair notice, presumably because they understand history and the common law, and the standard is sufficiently precise. For the court, Castaneda's actions in front of the police station encompassed exposure of his "private parts," although the court declined to read the statute as expansively including buttocks, as the prosecution had argued.[48]

A law that does not rely upon common law and historical understandings of indecency is vulnerable to a constitutional challenge for vagueness. For example, although an Iowa statute contained the word "indecent," the Iowa Supreme Court held that it was unconstitutionally vague.[49] The Iowa court later upheld the revised, and more precise, state statute that included genital exposure and also a sexual intent.[50]

Similarly, terms other than "indecency" that do not rely upon common law and historical understandings may make them vulnerable to a constitutional vagueness challenge. "Customary street attire" is such a term. The rather unique ordinance challenged in *People v. O'Gorman* provided: "No person over the age of sixteen (16) years shall be permitted to appear in bathing costume or in any other than customary street attire upon any public street or thoroughfare in the City of Yonkers."[51] The defendants did not have on bathing costumes, but were dressed for the summer solstice thusly: "The girl had on 'white sandals, no stockings, yellow short pants and a colored halter, with a yellow jacket over it and no hat'; the boy or young man 'had on white sneakers, white anklets, short socks, yellow trunks, short pants, a blue polo shirt, brown and white belt, no hat.'" New York's highest court in 1937 had little difficulty declaring the law invalid, stating that when "it comes to the kind and sufficiency of clothes one must wear to appear decently in public we of the law have generally left such matters to the good sense and force of public opinion." The court found the ordinance was not "definite nor limited; in fact, it is so vague and meaningless as to reach many harmless and insipid foibles." At times the court seemed to be musing, stating that customary street attire "has rather a drab appearance; if some desire to color it up a bit, where is the harm?" While the court was clear that nudity could be prohibited, the "Constitution still leaves some opportunity for people to be foolish if they so desire."[52]

The New York court's view that the Constitution leaves room for people to wear foolish clothing, including yellow short pants or yellow trunks, is belied by a much more recent Florida case. Jeffrey Ross went shopping at a Wal-Mart in Broward County wearing what the court described as "extremely short shorts"; the court did not mention their color. At his bench trial, the complainant, a fellow shopper, testified that Ross was "exposed," while Ross not only testified on his own behalf but also "donned the shorts to demonstrate to the trial judge that he would not be exposed." The trial judge noted, for the record, that Ross "did not have underpants on." The trial judge found Ross guilty and the appellate court upheld Ross's conviction in *Ross v. State* for "exposure of sexual organs" criminalized by the Florida statute. Ross, proceeding pro se, did not make a constitutional argument.[53]

Luckily for Ross, his conviction for "exposure of sexual organs" did not mean he became a "sexual predator" subject to registration, community notification, and other requirements. In Florida, the sexual predator status requires a felony conviction, which would include the felony of indecent exposure to a person younger than sixteen years of age. However, if the complaining witness in Mr. Ross's case had been accompanied by a child, Mr. Ross might now be classified as a sexual predator. Similarly, if Mr. Ross had visited a Wal-Mart in the neighboring state of Alabama wearing his short-shorts, he would most likely be deemed a "sex offender." In Alabama – as in approximately half the states – a conviction of the misdemeanor of indecent exposure results in the classification of a person as a "sex offender," required to meet reporting and registration requirements, and barred from certain types of employment. Moreover, while Mr. Ross may not be classified as a sexual predator in 2010, there is no guarantee that the Florida legislature will not change its statute to include misdemeanor indecent exposure and make that change retroactive. This may seem as if it would be unconstitutional as an ex post facto law; however, the U.S. Supreme Court has upheld the practice, reasoning that the sex offender regulations are civil, rather than criminal, and thus excluded from the ex post facto prohibition.[54] The Court has also rejected a constitutional procedural due process challenge to such a law,[55] as well as rejecting constitutional challenges to indefinite civil commitment statutes for sex offenders.[56]

The sex offender, including a person who becomes one through a failure of attire, has arguably replaced the "homosexual" in the hierarchical relations of law.[57] The first sexual offender registration law, in California in 1947, was aimed in part at gay men and included among its registrable offenses "lewd vagrancy" and indecent exposure,[58] both common charges against gay men entrapped by police officers. More dramatically, the sex offender may be viewed as "monstrous other within," as legal theorist John Douard has phrased it.[59] While monster may seem hyperbolic, the dehumanization of the sex offender is similar to the dehumanization that occurs in the forced nudity of detainees. In both situations, clothes are an indication of hierarchal superiority; they represent not only civilization but also humanity. As Albert Florence phrased it, he was made to feel "not better than an animal."[60] This linking of the nudity and inhumanity is evident in a 1858 Supreme Court of Indiana opinion that noted "public indecency" includes both "public displays of the naked person" and the "exhibition of a monster."[61]

III. THE FIRST AMENDMENT, OBSCENITY, AND SECONDARY EFFECTS

"He was a monster, black dressed in leather," Jim Morrison of The Doors sang, presumably about himself, in a song released in 1970.[62] That same year, a Florida jury would consider events at an earlier Doors concert and convict Morrison of indecent exposure. While Morrison's actions occurred before a packed audience in a relatively small venue, there is little agreement about what those actions were. On one generally accepted account, an inebriated Morrison asked the audience if they would like to see his sexual organs, and then "Morrison waved his shirt in front of his crotch in bullfighter tradition" and taking his shirt away "for an instant," taunted the audience: "Did you see it?"[63] Although Morrison was charged with the felony of lewd and lascivious behavior, and six misdemeanors, he was convicted only of profanity and indecent exposure. Morrison, represented by attorneys, was in the process of appealing his conviction when he died in Paris in 1971, at the age of twenty-seven. Forty years after Morrison's conviction, Florida governor Charlie Crist pardoned Morrison posthumously. Governor Crist's stated rationales included

Morrison's denial of the indecent exposure, the denial's corroboration by witnesses, the fact that Morrison was not arrested until days later, the trial judge's refusal to allow additional evidence of the "community standards" of other rock performances of the era that would have "offered cultural context," and the fact that he died while his case was on appeal.[64] Crist, soon ending his term, was also reportedly a Doors fan and Jim Morrison was among Florida's most famous natives.

Jim Morrison, waving his shirt in "bullfighter tradition" in front of his crotch, and Jeffrey Ross, pulling up his extremely short-shorts, were convicted, thirty years apart, of violating the same Florida indecent exposure statute. But a stage occupies a more privileged place in the hierarchy of First Amendment venues than a Wal-Mart. While alive, Morrison was interviewed about the conviction and claimed "artistic freedom." His discussion not only included his own supposed indecent exposure but also presumably related to the fact that the musical *Hair* was being shown quite near his Miami concert venue.[65]

Hair, a play that debuted in late 1967, had a brief scene with all the characters naked at the end of the first act. It was also controversial for its themes of sexual freedom, youth culture, racial equality, and pacifism. But it was nudity, along with profanity, that was the articulated basis for its notoriety. When the play reached the U.S. Supreme Court, it was because the directors of the Chattanooga Memorial Auditorium, a municipal theater in Tennessee, had "understood from outside reports that the musical, as produced elsewhere, involved nudity and obscenity on stage." The directors therefore rejected the application of Southeastern Productions to stage the play, explaining only that the production would not be in the "best interests of the community." In *Southeastern Promotions, Ltd. v. Conrad*, the Court reversed lower courts that upheld the Chattanooga directors' action.[66] Interestingly, as the Court noted, the lower courts relied in part on the Chattanooga ordinance that criminalized any person appearing "in a public place in a state of nudity" or "in public in an indecent or lewd dress." The Court did not reach the issue of the ordinance's applicability or constitutionality but instead based its holding on the more narrow ground that the Chattanooga directors' rejection of the application to use this public forum "accomplished a prior restraint under a system lacking in constitutionally required minimal procedural safeguards."

Within a few months, the Court would declare unconstitutional a local ordinance regulating performances including nudity. In *Erznoznik v. City of Jacksonville*, decided in June 1975, the Court considered a Florida city's law regulating "drive-in theaters."[67] The ordinance made it unlawful and a nuisance for any "ticket seller, ticket taker, usher, motion picture projection machine operator, manager, owner, or any other person connected with or employed by any drive-in theater" to show "any motion picture, slide, or other exhibit in which the human male or female bare buttocks, human female bare breasts, or human bare pubic areas are shown" if it is "visible from any public street or public place." The Court repudiated the city's argument that the ordinance was merely protecting unwilling viewers from offensive material, retorting that the city had singled out films with nudity, "presumably because the lawmakers considered them especially offensive to passersby." This type of content discrimination, the Court held, was unconstitutional.

The city in *Erznoznik* had conceded that the ordinance was broader than one aimed at obscenity. First Amendment doctrine in the United States has been clear that governments may constitutionally criminalize obscenity, although whether this is because obscenity is absolutely and categorically excluded from constitutional protection is somewhat less clear. First Amendment doctrine, at least since *Miller v. California* in 1973, has enshrined a three part test to evaluate regulations of obscenity, and thus to define "obscenity."[68] Obscenity can be criminalized if the work depicts or describes sexual conduct, as defined by state law, in a "patently offensive way"; and taken as a whole, according to community standards, appeals to the prurient interest in sex; and last, again taken as a whole, does not have serious literary, artistic, political, or scientific value. This definition departs from the English common law rule from *Regina v. Hicklin*, once popular in the United States, that considered the "tendency of the matter charged as obscenity" as to whether it would "deprave and corrupt those whose minds are open to such immoral influences and into whose hands a publication of this sort may fall."[69] On this view, the most sensitive members of society – those who could be corrupted – became the mainstays of morality. Given the *Miller* test's emphasis on community standards, it might be argued that it reinvigorates the *Hicklin* view.

However, the *Miller* test does uncouple nudity from obscenity, as the Court in *Erznoznik* made clear. Generally, there must be some sexual element for expressive nudity to become capable of being regulated as obscene. Terms such as "lewd" or "lascivious" are often employed in order to sexualize nudity. While such terms are vague, they are not considered by courts to be unconstitutionally vague.

The regulation of nudity when it has an expressive context must therefore come within the ambit of constitutionally defined obscenity, subject to three important exceptions. These exceptions allow the government to proscribe nudity or partial nudity, often in the guise of "decency," even in the face of a First Amendment challenge. Thus, government efforts have been constitutionally upheld when the regulation occurs in an otherwise regulated medium, such as television; when the regulation occurs in a government funding scheme; and when the government regulation is targeted not at the nudity itself but at its "secondary effects."

Regulated Media

The regulated medium of television in the United States is subject to a federal statute prohibiting the broadcast of "indecent" material.[70] It is also subject to the promulgated regulations of a federal agency, the Federal Communications Commission

(FCC), that prohibit the broadcast of any material "which is indecent" between 6 A.M. and 10 P.M.[71] This prohibition includes partial nudity and profanity even if it is "fleeting" and has been preoccupying the federal courts for several years. One incident is the so-called wardrobe malfunction of Janet Jackson during the evening Super Bowl XXXVIII Halftime Show in 2004, also known as "nipplegate," which occurred during a live broadcast dance and song between Janet Jackson and Justin Timberlake. As described by the Third Circuit Court of Appeals, Timberlake was singing "gonna have you naked by the end of this song," and simultaneously "tearing away part of Jackson's bustier," resulting in Jackson's bare right breast being "exposed on camera for nine-sixteenths of one second."[72] In another instance, an episode of the television series *NYPD Blue* showed the "nude buttocks of an adult female character for approximately seven seconds and for a moment the side of her breast. During the scene, in which the character was preparing to take a shower, a child portraying her boyfriend's son entered the bathroom. A moment of awkwardness followed."[73]

These incidents, as well as expletives by various celebrities during award shows broadcast live, have been litigated on the basis of administrative law principles, as well as constitutional law challenges based on the First Amendment and the Due Process Clause.[74] In its 2012 opinion, focusing on the *NYPD Blue* nudity, the Court held invalid the fines because the FCC policy was void for vagueness and thus violated the Fifth Amendment's Due Process Clause. The Court sidestepped the First Amendment challenge, although free speech concerns certainly animated its analysis. The line between permissible nudity and impermissible nudity was highlighted during oral argument: an advocate for the television station pointed out that the friezes in the courtroom itself include nude buttocks; Justice Ginsburg asked about a television broadcast of *Hair* or the opera *The Makropulos Case* that includes a nude woman entering a bathtub.[75] The Court also sidestepped the recurring issue of whether the rules for broadcast media and other media (including cable television) continues to be a constitutionally sustainable one in light of technological changes.[76]

The exception of regulated media, which allows the regulation of mere indecency that does not necessarily meet the constitutional definition of obscenity, does not extend to unregulated media. Thus, the Internet is not within this exception. Congress has attempted on several occasions to regulate indecency on the Internet, focusing on content available to minors, who are presumably more corruptible than adults. The earliest provisions, contained in the Communications Decency Act of 1996, criminalized the dissemination of "indecent material" to minors, relying on the model of prohibiting indecency in broadcast media. The Court soundly rejected the analogy in *Reno v. American Civil Liberties Union*.[77] "Cyberspace," as the Court stated, was clearly distinguishable, and the Communications Decency Act was a unique attempt by the government to supervise and regulate "the vast democratic forums of the Internet."

The Court noted that the problem with prohibiting "indecency" was that it threatened to reduce the Internet to only that material acceptable for children. This was unconstitutionally overbroad under the First Amendment. Congress quickly reacted. It sought to again protect children from accessing "adult" material by passing the Child Online Protection Act (COPA). COPA replaced "decency" with "harmful to minors," defined in a manner that tracked the obscenity definitions of *Miller v. California*.[78] The litigation surrounding COPA was complex, with two returns to the U.S. Supreme Court, a full trial, and the Court declining certiorari in 2009, thus letting stand the Third Circuit's conclusion that COPA was unconstitutional.[79] Meanwhile, however, Congress pursued another avenue to promote decency on the Internet, relying on a different exception to the general rule that obscenity is the constitutional requirement for regulating nudity and partial nudity.

Government Funding Schemes

Funding is the second exception that allows a government to survive a First Amendment challenge to its regulation of expressive nudity or partial nudity even though the constitutional criteria of obscenity are not met. It might be reasoned that in a government-funding scheme, the government is not "regulating" at all. Instead, the government is merely attaching strings to its money. The recipient is perfectly free to accept the money and the string, and equally free to reject both. Or so the argument goes. The doctrine of unconstitutional conditions – which some believe is not a viable doctrine – would place constitutional limits on the conditions that the government can attach to funding.

The Children's Internet Protection Act (CIPA), passed by Congress in 2000, attached a condition to the receipt of government discounts or grants to libraries and schools supporting computer use.[80] The condition was the installation of software on all computers to prevent minors from accessing harmful material. Such filters would mean, for example, that a library patron could not freely access information regarding Janet Jackson's wardrobe malfunction. This would be true because a search for "Super Bowl XXXVIII" would be blocked: XXX would be a filtered term. Similarly, a search for "breast," even if accompanied with "cancer" or "chicken," would be blocked. Arguably, an adult library patron could consult with a librarian and have the software disabled. The American Library Association challenged CIPA based on the forfeiture of First Amendment rights as an unconstitutional condition. In its decision in 2003, a majority of the Court upheld CIPA, with only Justices

Stevens, Ginsburg, and Souter dissenting.[81] Justice Rehnquist, writing for the plurality in *United States v. American Library Association*, phrased it succinctly:

> CIPA does not "penalize" libraries that choose not to install such software, or deny
> them the right to provide their patrons with unfiltered Internet access. Rather,
> CIPA simply reflects Congress' decision not to subsidize their doing so. To the
> extent that libraries wish to offer unfiltered access, they are free to do so without
> federal assistance.[82]

Whether or not a library could continue to exist or to finance computer access for its
patrons without these federal subsidies was not a relevant inquiry.

The Court in *American Library Association* relied upon its 1998 decision in
National Endowment for Arts v. Finley.[83] Karen Finley, one of the six plaintiffs, was
an artist whose performance piece of her nude but chocolate-covered body became
notorious. Finley had been recommended for a National Endowment for the Arts
(NEA) grant, but was vetoed at the highest levels. Congress had recently mandated
the NEA to ensure not only that artistic excellence and merit were criteria, but
also to take into consideration "general standards of decency and respect for the
diverse beliefs and values of the American public."[84] This change was motivated by
congressional disapproval of the previous use of NEA money by a museum funding
a retrospective of the photography of Robert Mapplethorpe, which included nudity
and homoeroticism, and by a different arts organization that had funded the work
of Andres Serrano, maker of the controversial *Piss Christ*. In considering Finley's
First Amendment challenge that the decency provision was unconstitutional viewpoint discrimination, the Court stressed that Congress did not compel any particular
action by the NEA but only required the NEA to "take into consideration" general
standards of decency in making its funding decisions. Moreover, decency could
mean different things to different people; the Court contrasted "a septegenarian
in Tuscaloosa and a teenager in Las Vegas." The vagueness of "decency" worked
in favor of it not being a preclusion of a particular viewpoint, even as the Court
rejected the argument that "decency" was unconstitutionally vague. The status of
the government as funder was pivotal: "when the Government is acting as patron
rather than as sovereign, the consequences of imprecision are not constitutionally
severe."[85]

Thus, if there are strings attached to government funding, those strings may be
opaque or oblique. A person is always free, according the Court, to reject both the
subsidy and the strings. The concept – or the conceit – is that the government is
not primarily regulating expressive nudity, but is only declining to subsidize it. The
notion of primary and nonprimary regulation is also operative in the third and final
exception to the general rule that obscenity is the constitutional requirement for
regulating expressive nudity.

Secondary Effects

When a municipality or state enacts an ordinance that prohibits nude dancing entirely, or only in certain circumstances such as where alcohol is sold or within proximity to other establishments, there may be a First Amendment challenge. The argument is that nude dancing is expressive speech, similar to other recognized expressions such as in ballet, theatre, cinema, painting, sculpture, or literature. The Supreme Court would agree with such a formulation, more or less. A plurality of the U.S. Supreme Court has stated that "nude dancing" is indeed "expressive conduct, although" it "falls only within the outer ambit of the First Amendment's protection."[86] Another, earlier, plurality similarly opined that nude dancing "is expressive conduct within the outer perimeters of the First Amendment" although "only marginally so."[87] The placement of nude dancing at this marginal, outer perimeter site is attributable to notions that the core of First Amendment protection is reserved for speech necessary for democracy. As Justice Stevens famously stated, "every schoolchild" understands our duty to defend the right to speak whether or not we agree with the content of "political oratory" or "philosophical discussion." However, Stevens continued, "few of us would march our sons and daughters off to war to preserve the citizen's right to see 'Specified Sexual Activities' exhibited in the theaters of our choice."[88] On the hierarchy of constitutional values, sexual speech occupies a low position. Given this inferior position, the government would presumably need to meet a minimal standard to survive constitutional scrutiny.

Yet prohibitions on nude dancing are not analyzed in such a straightforward manner. Instead, such prohibitions are analyzed as if the government's true target is not nude dancing but the "secondary effects" that accompany nude dancing. The litany of these effects include generalized references to "crime" or "serious criminal activity," as well as specific crimes such as prostitution, rape, incest, assault, and public intoxication, and more general concerns such as property values, public health safety and welfare, the debasement of both women and men, and the promotion of violence.[89]

As the true targets of the government action, these "effects" – which are not themselves speech – mean that the government action is analyzed as one that has an incidental burden on speech. The government regulation is deemed content-neutral and viewpoint-neutral. Thus, the level of constitutional scrutiny employed by the judiciary is less than strict; the regulation is therefore most likely to be upheld as constitutional.

The term "secondary effects" originated in a footnote authored by Justice Stevens. Writing for the Court in the 1976 case of *Young v. American Mini Theatres* – the same case in which he had referred to marching "our sons and daughters off to war" – Stevens referred to the government's determination that a concentration of "adult" movie theaters causes the area to deteriorate and become a focus of crime, effects that are not attributable to theaters showing other types of films. He continued, it "is this secondary effect which these zoning ordinances attempt to avoid, not the dissemination of 'offensive' speech."[90] He specifically contrasted this type of regulation to the drive-in movie ordinance involved in *Erznoznik v. City of Jacksonville*.[91]

Justice Stevens would seemingly come to regret his footnote, or at least the manner in which a plurality of the Court came to construe it. By 2000, Justice Stevens was dissenting in a "secondary effects" case, *Erie v. Pap's A. M.*, in which the Court upheld an ordinance that prohibited nudity and simulations of nudity. Stevens argued that the secondary effects doctrine was limited to zoning and did not properly extend to "the total suppression of protected speech."[92] A "total ban" of nude dancing was, for Stevens, "the most exacting of restrictions." He was not swayed by the fact that almost-nude dancing – attire consisting of "pasties" and a "G-string" – would be permissible. And he was troubled by the fact that the city of Erie seemed to be targeting not merely nudity but also the nude dancing at Kandyland, the particular club at issue, while permitting more traditional theatrical productions such as *Hair*.[93]

Justice Souter, who dissented in part in *Erie v. Pap's A. M.*, was even more explicitly regretful. Although, unlike Stevens, he had no part in inventing the phrase, he had concurred in an earlier opinion upholding Indiana's prohibition of nude dancing on the basis of the secondary effects doctrine. In 2000, Souter argued that there needed to be an evidentiary showing of secondary effects; his previous lapse was a "mistake," attributable to "ignorance." The government, he wrote, "must toe the mark more carefully than I first insisted."[94]

The "mark," however, is not necessarily clear. The last three decisions of the Court on secondary effects have been fractured. Justice Kennedy, concurring in a 2002 case, used the term "fiction" to describe the Court's approach in secondary effects cases. Scholars have criticized the doctrine: it is incoherent, intellectually dishonest, confused and confusing.[95]

This doctrinal incoherence is compounded by interpretative slovenliness regarding the "effects," even when there are social facts in evidence. There are important gaps in the quantum of evidence necessary to prove an effect, judicial willingness to defer to local lawmakers, and the use of studies from one city as evidence to support effects in another city that may be of a different size and in a different state. But more fundamentally, the question of causation is unresolved and perhaps unresolvable. Although the name of the doctrine is secondary effects it might just as easily be named "secondary correlations" or "secondary accompaniments." Indeed, the courts themselves often speak in terms of correlation rather than causation.

Moreover, the "remedy" of pasties and G-strings undermines the efficacy of the secondary effects doctrine, with sloppy reasoning approaching dishonesty. It seems that no one on the Court actually believed that there was a link between nudity and secondary effects that would be broken by skimpy attire. Justice O'Connor, writing for the plurality in *Erie*, was "sure," that "requiring dancers to wear pasties and G-strings may not greatly reduce these secondary effects."[96] Justice Scalia, concurring, wrote: "I am highly skeptical that the addition of pasties and G-strings will at all reduce the tendency of establishments such as Kandyland to attract crime and prostitution, and hence to foster sexually transmitted disease."[97] Justice Souter, concurring and dissenting, observed, "It is not apparent to me as a matter of common sense that establishments featuring dancers with pasties and G-strings will differ markedly in their effects on neighborhoods from those whose dancers are nude."[98] And Justice Stevens, dissenting, expressed incredulity: "To believe that the mandatory addition of pasties and a G-string will have any kind of noticeable impact on secondary effects requires nothing short of a titanic surrender to the implausible."[99]

For Justice Stevens, the City of Erie's ordinance should be subject to the highest scrutiny as a content regulation. First Amendment arguments regarding content regulations are similar to equality arguments: the perceived problem is that the government is discriminating among types of speech. An implicit hierarchy inherent in the Supreme Court's nude dancing cases is between "high art" and "low art," with unarticulated but concomitant distinctions between their consumers. As one appellate judge noted, "while the entertainment afforded by a nude ballet at Lincoln Center to those who can pay the price may differ vastly in content (as viewed by judges) or in quality (as viewed by critics), it may not differ in substance from the dance viewed by the person who, having worked overtime for the necessary wherewithal, wants some 'entertainment' with his beer or shot of rye."[100] The cases reverberate with concerns that the regulations could reach the "nude ballet at Lincoln Center" – or even *Hair* – yet this implies that there is a fundamental, or at least important, distinction between their substance and their secondary effects.

Class hierarchy also permeates the other two exceptions to the general obscenity requirement that allow for the regulation of nudity or scant clothing. The government funding exception enforces a class hierarchy. If one is sufficiently wealthy, one does not need a federal grant to subsidize one's artistic pursuits of chocolate-covered nakedness or to use the computer at the public library to access Internet images of Karen Finley's strategically chocolate-smeared naked body. The regulated media exception, likewise, has a class hierarchy element. The distinction between television and the "vast democratic forums of the Internet" is one that may also replicate the digital divide between economic and social classes.

In addition to class hierarchies, two other types of hierarchies permeate the legal regulation of nudity under discussion. Classifications based on nudity itself (those who are wearing clothes and those who are not) and classifications based on gender/sex both implicate constitutional doctrines of equal protection.

IV. EQUALITY: OF NUDISTS AND WOMEN

Nudists, also known as naturalists, are subject to indecent exposure laws with only minimal protection for their expression under the First Amendment. The Fourteenth Amendment might provide some recourse to nudists as a social group who are prosecuted and discriminated against, assuming they can be considered to constitute a class deserving of judicial attention.

The 1938 case of *United States v. Carolene Products* provides the inaugural inquiry.[101] In *Carolene*, the Court distinguished the challenge before it – a challenge to a federal statute regulating the shipment of "filled milk" (skimmed milk to which nonmilk fat is added so that it may seem more like whole milk or even cream) – from other types of constitutional challenges that might deserve a *"more exacting judicial scrutiny"* under the Fourteenth Amendment. In its famous footnote four, the Court specified the types of statutes requiring a higher level of judicial scrutiny as those "directed at particular religious, or national, or racial minorities, whether prejudice against discrete and insular minorities may be a special condition, which tends seriously to curtail the operation of those political processes ordinarily to be relied upon to protect minorities." Although *Carolene Products* did not involve the Equal Protection Clause, footnote four became the standard for evaluating the level of scrutiny afforded specific classifications. Thus, courts will consider whether the group is a minority, whether the minority is discrete and insular, whether there is (historical and legal) prejudice against the minority, and whether the minority is exiled from the normal political processes.

Interestingly, although immutability has become central in discussions of equal protection, the original *Carolene Products* formulation did not contain the term. The Supreme Court introduced immutability into equal protection doctrine as it struggled with sex/gender classifications. In its 1973 plurality opinion in *Frontiero v. Richardson*, the Court reasoned, "sex, like race and national origin, is an immutable characteristic determined solely by the accident of birth" without reference to "individual responsibility."[102] The immutability consideration assumes centrality in any argument regarding equal protection for nudists or naturalists: nudity can be altered simply by wearing clothes.

Yet immutability is not always essential. Equality arguments based on sexuality have often encountered the choice/"born this way" dichotomy, with the evolving view minimizing the necessity of "accident of birth." Moreover, the original *Carolene Products* formulation included as one of its examples "religious" minorities, an identity that is not immutable or an "accident of birth" as religions themselves stress in concepts such as conversion, faith, and sin.

If immutability is no longer the sine qua non of illegitimate disadvantage in equality theory, as British legal theorist Davina Cooper has noted, then nudists may have viable equality claims.[103] Or, at the very least, as Cooper argues, a consideration of nudism can illuminate equality discourse, especially as it relates to more radical notions of structural inequality. Cooper contends that as a "constituency, nudists experience considerable discrimination and marginality," while ordinarily clothed people – known as "textiles" – experience considerably less regulation of their lives. Indeed, the classification of the majority of people as "textiles" as well as phrases such as "textile supremacy" and "clothing's contemporary hegemony" make clear the hierarchal relationship between being clothed and being naked, in much the same way as the forced nudity of Bradley Manning does. Yet as Cooper rightly observes, although equality may be extended to "subjugated and despised groupings," it tends to remain a "murmur" until "constituencies, identities or lifestyles cross a threshold of socially recognized (or constituted) value." She posits that nudists can, or even have in some locales, crossed such a threshold. However, as a matter of constitutional doctrine, nudism cases in the United States eschew the Fourteenth Amendment's equal protection clause in favor of First Amendment notions of expression. This is true even if a person's identity as a "nudist" rather than particular nude expressions is at issue. For example, a federal district court found in favor of "a practicing nudist" who had been denied employment with a police force solely on the basis of his nudism and his "private non-political association with those who espouse nudism" under the First Amendment.[104] Interestingly, the court rejected an analogy to homosexuality, which would have been a clearly constitutional basis to deny him employment at the time of the case in 1970. He was not secretive (and thus not susceptible to blackmail) and there was nothing to "indicate that he had any emotional hang-up concerning his association." Moreover, he was stable: "while there is much argument, and some validity apparently, to the question of instability in reference to homosexuals, there has been absolutely nothing to indicate any psychological defect insofar as the practice of nudism is concerned."[105]

The relationship between nudism and other hierarchies, including ones based on sexuality, is complex. On one view, "textile dominance" solidifies inequalities, especially those based on class and gender. Cooper refers to a utopian novel by the author Dickberry in which the sudden and inexplicable disappearance of all clothing in Edwardian London does more "for human equality than all the philanthropists' efforts, or the anarchists' steel blade." The novel is *The Storm of London*, subtitled "A Social Rhapsody," originally published in 1904; and Dickberry is the pseudonym of Blaze DeBury, a woman writer.[106] Feminist utopian scholar Darby Lewes situates Dickberry/DeBury in a tradition of women writers borderlined "between centuries of patriarchal past and tantalizing glimpses of an egalitarian future."[107] Lewes writes that these women, who often published pseudonymously, reflected their own confused status in the disorientation of their novels, such *The Storm of London*'s sudden disappearance of all clothing, textiles, carpets, and draperies, as well as all

books. Dickberry/DeBury links the end of clothing with the impending cessation of
hierarchies: "Democracy was at hand"; "Scotland Yard is to be turned into a public
gymnasium"; "militarism will inevitably die out with the disappearance of military
distinctions"; and the inevitable "reform of the relations between the sexes, between
employers and employees, and goodness only knows what next."[108] Yet, as literary
scholar Darby Lewes asserts, there is a "ladylike" quality to such novels that forestalls
radical envisioning. Gender and class hierarchies remain in place throughout the
novel, despite assurances of metamorphosis. At the end of *The Storm of London*, the
possibility of social change retreats when the disappearance of clothing is revealed as
a semi-conscious reverie of the character Lord Somerville. The lord is not, however,
unchanged. He says he will leave London Society and depart for the Continent; his
fiancé/nurse says she will follow him. Presumably they will wear clothes.

Even if the absence of clothing may not abolish – or even ameliorate – gender
hierarchy, certainly the absence of clothing has asymmetrical consequences across
the bodies of the genders. This disparity can be captured in a word: breasts. If Janet
Jackson had torn at Justin Timberlake's shirt during a Super Bowl Halftime show
causing a "wardrobe malfunction," there would be no "nipplegate," no FCC fine,
and no prolonged litigation.

The constitutionality of differential *legal treatment* of women's breasts as compared to men's breasts is said to rest upon the differential *nature* of female and male
breasts. Courts have generally rejected any expert testimony that there is no variance
in the composition of the flesh of male and female breasts; that the breasts do not
form a primary sex characteristic but a secondary one; that the degree of development of the breasts does not determine sex; or that some men have breasts as large
as those of some small-breasted women.[109] For a panel of the Fifth Circuit Court of
Appeals writing in 1995, the difference between male and female breasts was one
of those "self-evident truths about the human condition – such as water is wet."[110]
Although the court disparaged the need for a trial on such a self-evident matter, it
approvingly quoted expert testimony that "distinguishing between male and female
breasts in defining nudity is 'certainly consistent with what we know medically about
human sexual response.'" In this court's view, "human sexual response" was a universal, and impliedly heterosexual male, condition. An earlier state court, however,
also considering an ordinance from a Texas city, had rejected the notion that female
breasts evoke sexual arousal as a "viewpoint" subject to "reasonable dispute, depending on the sex and sexual orientation of the viewer."[111]

Once a court concludes that there are real differences in male and female breasts,
the constitutional equality analysis is truncated. For the Fifth Circuit court, further
reasoning was unnecessary because the challenged law was not making a classification "simply on the basis of gender." Apparently the law's classification was not
"simply" on gender, but on the gender of the breasts. Only slightly more analysis

appeared in a Fourth Circuit opinion several years earlier, upholding the conviction of a woman who removed her bathing suit top while walking on the beach on the Chincoteague National Wildlife Refuge.[112] The court rejected her equal protection challenge, concluding that the gender "distinction here is one that is substantially related to an important governmental interest." The important governmental interest, according to the court, was "the widely recognized one of protecting the moral sensibilities of that substantial segment of society that still does not want to be exposed willy-nilly to public displays of various portions of their fellow citizens' anatomies that traditionally in this society have been regarded as erogenous zones." The court added that such zones "still include (whether justifiably or not in the eyes of all) the female, but not the male, breast." Thus, the woman's male companion, whose attire the court does not mention but who might have also been "topless," would not have offended the moral sensibilities of the lone witness, the federal Fish and Wildlife Service officer who made the arrest.[113]

Feminists have attacked the gender disparity in nudity regulations through protests and litigation. Activist Nikki Craft and other women challenged the Cape Cod National Seashore regulation that defined prohibited nudity fetishistically to include the "female breast below a point immediately above the top of the areola."[114] In addition to a First Amendment claim, the women argued that the regulation violated equal protection because, as the judge expressed it, the regulation permitted "males to walk and play and swim 'shirtfree' upon the Seashore whereas it denies women the same 'rights.'" After articulating the constitutional standard for gender classifications, the judge foundered in an attempt to apply it. The judge did find that the government's interest was to protect the moral and aesthetic sensitivities of the public but never concluded that this was a sufficiently important interest to satisfy the standard. Instead, the judge discussed the "natural" differences in male and female bodies, even as he relied upon the principle that "nudity is a social concept" to defer to legislative choice. Candidly, he wrote that he would not part company from the other courts that had rejected equal protection challenges to laws banning public display of female, but not male, breasts.

Yet at least some judges have been sympathetic to an equality challenge. Earlier litigation involving Nikki Craft and other women reached a more receptive audience at New York's highest court the 1992 case of *People v. Santorelli*.[115] The case originated when the women staged an action in a Rochester park; they were arrested for public nudity based upon exposure of their breasts. A trial judge rejected their equal protection challenge, while dismissing the charges against them based upon a First Amendment analysis of their publicized protest in the park, but an appellate court reversed.[116] When the case reached New York's highest court, the court's succinct memorandum opinion evaded the constitutional issues by holding that the statute was not intended to apply to the type of situation before it, but only "topless waitresses." However, concurring Judge Vito Titone essentially accused his colleagues of historical inaccuracy, arguing that the "topless waitress" statute was a precursor statute and that the new provision under which Craft and others were convicted "was aimed at filling a gap" to clearly proscribe "nude sunbathing by ordinary citizens" and "either men or women appearing bottomless in public places." Joined by one other judge, Titone's opinion argued that the court should have taken the equal protection issue more seriously and suggested that any recognition of a governmental interest of protecting public sensibilities that are based on a gendered distinction is itself a constitutional problem. For Titone, the "underlying legislative assumption that the sight of a female's uncovered breast in a public place is offensive to the average person in a way that the sight of a male's uncovered breast is not" is an assumption that replicated gender bias rather than confronting and eradicating sex inequality. Titone's concurring opinion stands as one of the most supportive judicial statements of the unconstitutionality of legally imposed gender differentials in required clothing.[117]

The discordant treatment of unclothed breasts is exemplified by two "topless jogger" cases from Florida. Belinda McGuire was arrested for jogging without a bathing suit top on a beach that had been considered clothing optional until it became state property. The Florida Supreme Court upheld her conviction for violation of a regulation that provided: "In every bathing area all persons shall be clothed as to prevent any indecent exposure of the person. All bathing costumes shall conform to commonly accepted standards at all times."[118] The court rejected Ms. McGuire's vagueness and overbreadth challenges and held the regulation constitutional. Around the same time, Allen DeWeese was also charged with jogging without a top. He violated a Palm Beach ordinance that made it unlawful "for any person to walk, run, jog, ride or otherwise be conveyed over or upon any street, alley, sidewalk, roadway, thoroughfare or other public place in the Town of Palm Beach with the upper part of his or her body uncovered." The Eleventh Circuit Court of Appeals, applying the lowest possible standard of judicial scrutiny, nevertheless found that the ordinance was not rationally related to any legitimate governmental interest.[119] The court found that the town did not have a legitimate interest in regulating "the dress of its citizens at large," as encompassed by its stated purposes of maintaining the quality of life and unique character of Palm Beach. Further, "prohibiting male joggers from appearing in public without a shirt" was irrational, and any justification was beyond the court's "imagination."[120]

Judicial imagination, for the most part, seems securely bounded by gendered understandings of people's upper bodies. As Canadian feminist legal scholar Janine Benedet has noted, the crucial question may be whether women can ever expose their breasts in a manner that is not "sexual."[121] One possible answer is breast-feeding. Perhaps paradoxically, this response accepts the only universally agreed upon difference between male and female breasts – the ability to lactate – and the only situation in which exposure to a minor – the feeding baby – is guaranteed. Nevertheless, some states and localities have amended their public exposure laws to exempt breast-feeding. So, for example, in 1993 Florida amended its statute – the same law under which Jim Morrison on stage in Miami and Jeffrey Ross in a Wal-Mart were convicted – to exempt breast-feeding.[122]

Arguably, breast-feeding exceptions do little to dismantle sexualized hierarchy given their applicability only to women in their role as mothers. Yet arguments that would require men to cover more of their bodies also seem unsatisfactory. However, while claims that the display of male breasts should be considered offensive or sexually provocative have generally had little success in the equality context, male breasts have been deemed sexually relevant in other determinations. For example, rejecting the argument that sexual contact could not include touching the chest of an adolescent male, a federal court denied relief to an adult male based on evidence that he rubbed a fifteen-year-old male's "stomach and breasts" under his shirt.[123] Similarly, in an Oregon court, it was the sexual nature of the male perpetrator's breasts that was the issue. The victim's allegation was that the defendant "forced her to suck on the nipples of his breasts," and the court held that evidence that the male defendant "cross-dressed" was relevant to this allegation. The court stated that male breasts are "not sexual or intimate parts of the body *unless* the person whose breasts are at issue considers them to be so." Because the state was required to prove that the defendant considered his breasts sexual, the evidence that he "dresses as a woman" was probative.[124]

Nudity regulations, including but not limited to differentiation of breasts, sustain sexual and gender hierarchies. At times, nudity and "cross-dressing" are entwined. The Oregon case considering the admissibility of defendant's cross-dressing practices is one such example. However, many of the topless cases, including most notably the arguments by Nikki Craft, might also be viewed as advocating a type of cross-dressing, or at least the seeking of male privilege through equality in (un)dress. Further, a law itself might make the link, as an Akron, Ohio, ordinance did when it provided that "No person shall appear upon any public street or other public place in a state of nudity or in a dress not belonging to his or her sex, or in an indecent or lewd dress."[125] So-called cross-dressing regulations, both direct and indirect, articulate and maintain separate and unequal sexual and gender hierarchies, as do direct and indirect requirements focusing on women's attire.

3

Dressing Sexily

A major weapon of the governmental maintenance of sexual hierarchies is the policing of attire. This policing focuses not only on the lack of clothes but also on the styles of clothes and other aspects of appearance such as hair, jewelry, cosmetics, shoes, and bodily enhancements or markings.

One aspect of this policing is directed at the boundary between the two recognized sexes, female and male. Dressing sexily in this instance means dressing in gender-appropriate ways. So-called cross-dressing – wearing clothes of a member of the "opposite" sex – may subject one to criminal sanctions, to discrimination, and to private violence with government acquiescence.

The other aspect of this policing seeks to control sexuality, especially but not only female sexuality. Dressing sexily in this sense means dressing in a sexy, erotic, or not sufficiently unsexy manner. While women, but not men, who bare their breasts may be subject to criminal sanctions, so-called dressing provocatively may subject one to discrimination as well as to private violence without government protection.

The U.S. Constitution has not proven to be an effective safeguard of dressing sexily, either in the sense of dressing gender appropriately or provocatively. One drawback has been the cramped interpretations of sex/gender equality typical of constitutional equal protection doctrine under the Fourteenth Amendment. The other, and more systemic, problem is the Constitution's failure to encompass private actions, other than in the realm of slavery and involuntary servitude as prohibited by the Thirteenth Amendment. Both of these constitutional concerns contribute to the lack of democracy and the maintenance of hierarchy especially with regard to sexuality and gender.

I. CROSS-DRESSING

The Columbus, Ohio, ordinance providing that "No person shall appear upon any public street or other public place in a state of nudity or in a dress not belonging to his or her sex, or in an indecent or lewd dress,"[1] was not a solitary effort by government to mandate sex-distinct attire. Ordinances in other cities such as Cincinnati, Houston, Chicago, and New York had similar goals. Constitutional challenges to the laws met with mixed success.

The initial judicial reaction to the Columbus, Ohio, ordinance in *City of Columbus v. Zanders* was to reject the constitutional challenge to the ordinance, but protect the particular defendant from its criminal sanction. The constitutional challenge to that ordinance was that it constituted a deprivation of a right of expression guaranteed by the First Amendment, a deprivation of the right of privacy guaranteed by the Fourth Amendment, a deprivation of due process guaranteed by the Fifth Amendment, and it was cruel and unusual punishment contrary to the Eighth Amendment as applied to the due process clause of the Fourteenth Amendment. The judge trivialized these constitutional claims by denominating them as a request "to declare the ordinance unconstitutional inasmuch as it prevents him from 'doing his own thing' in the vernacular of the 'pepsi generation.'" Given such language, it is not surprising that the judge concluded the ordinance was constitutional. However, the judge took more seriously the argument that the ordinance should not be applied to Zanders given his status as a "true transsexual." The judge approvingly discussed various medical authorities to support the conclusion that a "true transsexual suffers from a mental defect over which he has little practical control." Thus, Zanders's "course of conduct in dressing and posing as a female is more the result of an irresistible impulse or a loss of will power than a deliberate act or violation" of the ordinance. In short, the court circumvented the serious constitutional challenges by fetishizing and pathologizing Zanders.[2]

Other courts likewise engaged in pathologizing and fetishization to exempt transsexuals from the cross-dressing proscriptions but did so through a constitutional analysis. The Illinois Supreme Court in *City of Chicago v. Wilson* focused on the medical status of the challengers to an ordinance that provided "Any person who shall appear in a public place ... in a dress not belonging to his or her sex, with intent to conceal his or her sex, ... shall be fined not less than twenty dollars nor more than five hundred dollars for each offense."[3] The court described the defendants' arrest "minutes after they emerged from a restaurant where they had had breakfast," with reference to their attire: "Defendant Wilson was wearing a black knee-length dress, a fur coat, nylon stockings and a black wig. Defendant Kimberley had a bouffant hair style and was wearing a pants suit, high-heeled shoes and cosmetic makeup." Taken to the police station, they "were required to pose for pictures in various stages of undress. Both defendants were wearing brassieres and garter belts; both had male genitals." The defendants challenged the ordinance on the basis of unconstitutional vagueness, overbreadth, and denial of equal protection. The court focused on the defendants' status as transsexuals and found that the city's asserted reasons for banning public cross-dressing, including preventing "crimes in washrooms" and "inherently antisocial conduct which is contrary to the accepted norms of our society," did not apply to cross-dressing "when done as part of a pre-operative therapy program." The court's language was expansive, essentially concluding that gender conformity in clothes was a mere "aesthetic preference" and that governmental regulation of appearance interfered with constitutional "values of privacy, self-identity, autonomy, and personal integrity." Yet the court held that the ordinance was only unconstitutional as applied to individuals pursuing sex reassignment surgery. The ordinance could be constitutionally applied to others.[4]

A federal district court in Texas, in *Doe v. McConn*, reached a similar conclusion in 1980 regarding Houston's cross-dressing ordinance that made it unlawful "for any person to appear on any public street, sidewalk, alley, or other public thoroughfare dressed with the designed intent to disguise his or her true sex as that of the opposite sex."[5] The challenge, by several plaintiffs "in various stages of sexual transition," joined by a treating psychiatrist, attacked the constitutionality of the ordinance on various grounds. Relying on the Illinois Supreme Court's conclusion regarding the Chicago ordinance, the court found Houston's governmental interests likewise did not survive even minimal scrutiny and could not overcome the liberty interests of "true transsexuals" who were undergoing therapy in preparation for sex-reassignment surgery. Interestingly, the court did not refer to *Mayes v. Texas*, a denial of certiorari by the United States Supreme Court six years earlier involving a constitutional challenge to the same Houston ordinance.[6]

The Columbus ordinance involved in *Zanders* also experienced more than one challenge, with the subsequent one being more successful. Less than five years after *Zanders*, the Ohio Supreme Court found the ordinance unconstitutionally vague, without limiting the finding to "true transsexuals." Writing in 1975, the unanimous court in *City of Columbus v. Rogers* applied its own common sense understandings of the ambiguity of gender-specific attire:

> Modes of dress for both men and women are historically subject to changes in fashion. At the present time, clothing is sold for both sexes which is so similar in appearance that "a person of ordinary intelligence" might not be able to identify it as male or female dress. In addition, it is not uncommon today for individuals to purposely, but innocently, wear apparel which is intended for wear by those of the opposite sex. Once it is recognized that present-day dress may not be capable of being characterized as being intended for male or female wear by a "person of ordinary intelligence," the constitutional defect in the ordinance becomes apparent. The defect is that the terms of the ordinance, "dress not belonging to his or her sex," when considered in the light of contemporary dress habits, make it "so vague that men of common intelligence must necessarily guess at its meaning and differ as to its application."[7]

The court therefore held that the Columbus ordinance violated the Due Process Clause of the Fourteenth Amendment to the Constitution.

Of course, the very notion of cross-dressing relies upon gender-segregated clothing, a notion the Ohio Supreme Court found to be unintelligible given "contemporary dress habits." Yet the court's casual use of "innocently" to characterize those who might "purposely, but innocently" wear "apparel which is intended for wear by those of the opposite sex," not only preserves a strict sex/gender differentiation of persons but also implies that some purposeful wearing of "opposite-sex" apparel is not "innocent."[8] Some laws prohibiting cross-dressing linked a lack of innocence not to lewdness, as in the Columbus, Ohio, ordinance, but to vagrancy.

The connection between vagrancy and cross-dressing is the fear of disguise. A New York statute passed in 1845 prohibited vagrancy as defined as a person "who, having his face painted, discolored, covered or concealed, or being otherwise disguised, in a manner calculated to prevent his being identified, appears in a road or public highway, or in a field, lot, wood or inclosure."[9] This version of the law was specifically prompted by economic insurrections, the so-called anti-rent riots, and not by people such as Saviro Luechini of Buffalo, a "young man" with "his face all painted up" who was wearing women's clothes, a wig, and slippers in the lobby of a theater in 1912.[10] The appellate judge reasoned that there must be some other indicia of vagrancy, such as inability to support oneself by lawful means, lest "the disguised circus 'barker,' the midway 'ballyhoo,' or even the masquerader at the ball" be convicted under the statute. The trial judge deemed irrelevant the testimony of a detective that Luechini's feminine garb was meant to represent the "White Slave": "There is no "white slavery" crime involved here, nor am I called upon to pass, even incidentally, upon the character of the entertainments furnished by any of our moving picture show houses." The appellate judge, separating morality from vagrancy, reversed Luechini's conviction.[11]

Another young man, convicted more than fifty years later for violating the same statute was not so fortunate.[12] Mauricio Archibald was arrested on a New York City subway platform "wearing a white evening dress, high heel shoes, blonde wig, female undergarments, and facial makeup," in the early morning hours, returning from a masquerade party. A majority of the three-judge appellate court rejected arguments that the vagrancy law was unconstitutionally vague. The dissenting judge, however, cast doubt on the very concept of vagrancy, noting that New York's highest court had recently held the first subsection of the statute, criminalizing idleness, unconstitutional.[13] Yet while acknowledging the roots of the vagrancy provision in the anti-rent riots, the dissenting judge contended that a contemporary and seemingly proper purpose of the cross-dressing subsection was to discourage "overt homosexuality in public places which is offensive to public morality." But again, gender segregation in attire was deemed a questionable reality. "Today," the dissenting judge proclaimed, hair lengths, hair dyes, facial makeup, and clothing styles of men and women "are becoming increasingly similar." Moreover, he concluded that the statute would logically criminalize "strangely attired 'hippies', flowing-haired 'yippies' and every person who would indulge in the Halloween tradition of 'Trick or Treat.'" For the dissenting judge, there was no rational relationship between the state's interests in the promotion of the health, safety, comfort, and welfare of the community and the criminalization of cross-dressing.[14]

Creative New York prosecutors seeking to bring charges against those who were cross-dressing could also avail themselves of the impersonation statute. In a case in Brooklyn against Gene Simmons – seemingly not the pseudonymous Gene Simmons of the rock band KISS famous for its use of heavy facial makeup and costuming – the prosecutor had not only charged larceny and prostitution but also criminal impersonation, all arising from an incident on Coney Island.[15] The court construed the meaning of the criminal prohibition of "impersonating another," and while not specifically considering constitutional arguments, implicitly found that the statute could not be constitutionally applied to the defendant because he was not impersonating "another" specific person by wearing "a woman's wig, dress, makeup and shoes."

The question of impersonation also arises in cases in which a biological woman dressed as a man and had sexual relations with women. In her work analyzing a high-profile case in Israel involving this situation, scholar Aeyal Gross also discusses two such prosecutions in the United States, *People v. Clark* in Colorado in 1996 and *State v. Wheatley* in Washington in 1997.[16] Importantly, the prosecuting witnesses in both *Clark* and *Wheatley* were underage, so the charges of rape were actually charges of statutory rape and not predicated on deception facilitated by gender nonconforming clothes. Clothes in these cases are not the direct object of the government regulation and there is no constitutional challenge, but such prosecutions evince the connection between criminalization and clothes in the service of maintaining gender hierarchies.

Despite the United States Supreme Court's failure to review the constitutionality of a cross-dressing law when presented the opportunity in *Mayes v. Texas* in 1974,[17] the direct criminal sanctions for gender inappropriate dress have faded and prosecutions for "impersonation" are rare. As some courts observed, social change in dress made the notion of gender-appropriate dress incoherent, rendering cross-dressing laws unconstitutionally vague. Yet the direct imposition of gender-appropriate dress remains a vital strategy for controlling certain segments of the population, especially the young.

II. BOYS AND GIRLS

The U.S. Supreme Court has long recognized the constitutional right of parents in the care, custody, and control of their children, naming it "perhaps the oldest of the fundamental liberty interests" the Court has adjudicated.[18] The twin pillars of this right are a pair of cases decided shortly after World War I. In *Meyer v. Nebraska*, the Court held that the "liberty" protected by the Due Process Clause includes the right of parents to "establish a home and bring up children" and "to control the education of their own."[19] A few years later in *Pierce v. Society of Sisters*, the Court proclaimed that the "liberty of parents and guardians" includes the right "to direct the upbringing and education of children under their control."[20] Even more expansively, the Court opined that the "fundamental theory of liberty" in the United States "excludes any power of the State to standardize its children": a "child is not the mere creature of the State; those who nurture him and direct his destiny have the right, coupled with the high duty, to recognize and prepare him for additional obligations." Yet in two recent cases in Ohio, the state power to standardize the dress of children according to gender was vindicated at the expense of the parents' constitutional liberty to "cross-dress" their children.

Smith v. Smith was a custody dispute between two biological parents.[21] In the original divorce proceeding, the parties had entered into a settlement agreement awarding the mother residential custody of the couple's two children, both boys. The father, as the court phrased it, "had very little contact with the children" for the next several years. However, when the father learned that the mother was allowing the older boy to wear "girl's clothes" as he wanted, the father petitioned for an emergency change in custody, which the trial judge granted. After a lengthy trial, the trial judge changed the custody of both children to the father and specifically ordered that the elder child was "not to be encouraged or permitted to wear girl's clothes." The appellate court affirmed, relying upon the trial judge's own slovenly conclusions: in his interview with the child in chambers, the trial judge "did not sense anything particularly feminine" about the child and opined that "the boy had little interest in being a girl other than in his desire to wear girl's clothing."[22]

The constitutional right of care, custody, and control of one's children was a problematical constitutional claim in *Smith v. Smith* because the custody dispute was between two legal parents, both of whom have the same rights, despite the father's lack of attention to the children before the matter of dress came to his attention. On appeal, the mother did raise an objection to what the court characterized as "judicial meddling," a claim that the court did, however, acknowledge was based on the fundamental constitutional right that parents have "in the care, custody and management of their children." For the court, however, this claim evaporated because of the divorce – not because the father is also a parent with equal rights, but because "the court is called upon to exert the authority of parens patriae, which literally means 'parent of his or her country,' and refers to the role of the state as sovereign and guardian of children and others under legal disability." The court, acting as an organ of the sovereign state, must guard its children from cross-dressing.

The court may also exercise its parens patriae role to overcome the constitutional rights of both parents to prevent children from cross-dressing. For example, in the unreported case of "Aurora," the child was the subject of abuse and neglect proceedings, with social workers removing the child from the parents.[23] The "gag" order on the parents and the unreported nature of child protective proceedings make information about the case difficult to obtain. However, given the nature of abuse and neglect proceedings, it is doubtful that the parents would risk raising a constitutional claim lest they be deemed uncooperative and not dedicated to their child's best interests.

In both "Aurora" and *Smith v. Smith*, cross-dressing was linked to gender identity disorder. This is unsurprising because the medical definition of gender identity disorder of children (GIDC), introduced in 1980 into the *Diagnostic and Statistical Manual of Mental Disorders* (DSM-III), includes choices in attire as an important factor in diagnosing the disorder in children. In both the original iteration, and subsequent modifications, the text seems to struggle to situate the "disorder" into a society with gendered norms regarding gender-segregated clothing. The DSM-III explained that boys may have a "preference for dressing in girls' or women's clothes, or may improvise such items from available material when genuine articles are unavailable," and that "three-fourths of the boys who cross-dress begin to do so before their fourth birthday." The DSM-III explained that girls, however, generally "begin to acquiesce to social pressure during late childhood or adolescence and give up an exaggerated insistence on male activities and attire." Similarly, in the DSM-IV, promulgated in 1994 and revised in 2000, the attention to cross-dressing as a symptom of GIDC is gendered: "in boys, preference for cross-dressing or simulating female attire; in girls, insistence on wearing only stereotypical masculine clothing."[24] The problem, of course, is that in most contemporary practices, both boys and girls wear pants, which have at times been considered exclusively masculine, but presently dresses, skirts, and makeup are generally considered within the exclusive province of females. Thus, it is far easier for boys to violate gender norms than for girls. The proposed DSM-V continues to attempt to cope with this recognition, revising the cross-dressing symptom to provide "in boys, a strong preference for cross-dressing or simulating female attire; in girls, a strong preference for wearing only typical masculine clothing and a strong resistance to the wearing of typical feminine clothing."[25] The proposal would also change the name of the diagnosis itself to "Gender Dysphoria," in order to remove the stigmatizing label of "disorder."

Yet the existence of GIDC as a "disorder," or at least a medical diagnosis, has assisted children resisting sex-segregated dress. In *Doe v. Bell*, a seventeen-year-old living in a state-operated and gender-segregated foster care facility filed a complaint in New York state court seeking an injunction to allow her to wear feminine attire.[26] Doe had been the subject of a memo from the facility's director, stating that Doe was not permitted to wear "female attire" in the facility, except if "he is walking directly out of the facility" and except that Doe would be allowed "to wear scarves, 'nails,' brassieres, and enhancers." The court found that Doe had a recognized disability and was entitled to reasonable accommodation under state law. Rejecting the government's argument that accommodation would expose others to adverse and harmful effects, the court relied in part on the exceptions the facility had allowed. The government "cannot explain," the court stated, why Doe may wear "fake breasts, make-up, women's blouses, scarves, nails, hair weaves," but "may not wear skirts or dresses without endangering the safety of the facility and its residents."[27]

It is difficult to argue with the court's conclusion that there is "simply no rational basis for treating dresses and skirts differently than the other feminine accouterments" that Doe was allowed to wear. Yet this rationale is not necessarily helpful for deciding cases in which the government did not make any concessions to gender-segregated dress. Moreover, although Doe did include a constitutional argument based upon freedom of expression, the court did not reach this ground given the resolution on the state law disability claim.

The standardization of youth into boys and girls by enforcement of gender-segregated dress occurs not only in foster care, custody, and abuse and neglect situations, but with even more vigor in educational settings. In the public school cases, the constitutional challenges are generally more explicit. However, courts struggle with whether wearing non-gender-conforming clothes is best conceptualized as being protected by equal protection or being protected by the constitutional right of free speech (expression). The opinions are fraught with doctrinal blurring and incoherence.

Clearly, prohibitions on gender nonconforming sartorial choices implicate both equality and expressive constitutional concerns. A school policy itself may make a gender classification – boys may not wear earrings; boys may not have long hair; girls must wear a dress to the prom; girls must wear a "drape" for a high school yearbook portrait – inviting a constitutional inquiry regarding sex equality. Additionally, students, like others, dress as a matter of self-expression and in order to make a statement.

In many of the cases from the 1970s, the sex equality claim was nascent at best. For example, sex is barely mentioned in *Karr v. Schmidt* when the Fifth Circuit en banc considered a constitutional challenge to an El Paso, Texas, school board regulation that provided "FOR BOYS: 1. Hair may be blocked, but is not to hang over the ears or the top of the collar of a standard dress shirt and must not obstruct vision. No artificial means to conceal the length of the hair is to be permitted; i.e., ponytails, buns, wigs, combs, or straps."[28] The district judge at trial did find an equal protection violation, but on the basis of a classification between those [males] being denied free public education based upon the length of their hair and those [males] not being so denied. In reversing the trial judge's finding on equal protection, the majority of the Fifth Circuit en banc court did note that another circuit court had held there was a violation of the equal protection clause on the basis of sex, but this was irrelevant given the trial court's rationale.[29]

The several dissenting judges in *Karr v. Schmidt* likewise did not find sex equality worth more than a cursory mention. Vigorously objecting to the court's statement of doctrine and analysis, Judge Wisdom, writing for himself and four other judges, explained the correct standard as being that a "classification 'must be reasonable, not arbitrary, and must rest upon some ground of relation to the object of the legislation,'" citing *Reed v. Reed*, decided by the Supreme Court the previous year.[30] Yet *Reed v. Reed* was not especially significant for its articulation of the rational basis standard of equal protection, but for its extension of equal protection under the Fourteenth Amendment to a classification based on sex; in *Reed*, the Court held unconstitutional a probate rule that gave preference to males over females in appointing the administrators of decedents' estates. Earlier in Wisdom's dissenting opinion, there is also a reference to sex equality. In refutation of the majority's trivialization of constitutional challenges to public school hair length regulations, Wisdom's opinion stated that the crowding of federal dockets was no reason to "blink a violation of liberty which obviously means a great deal to many young people." Indeed: "Almost every day, the federal courts spawn new classes of litigation – most recently, perhaps, litigation over the constitutional rights of women."[31]

The judicial inability – as well as the inability of the lawyers – to analyze, and perhaps even to perceive, the sex classification inherent in a regulation that provides one rule for boys and another for girls demonstrates the tenacity of heterosexuality and gender hierarchy in constitutional understandings. Certainly, sex equality was in the air as the Fifth Circuit judges were deciding *Karr v. Schmidt* in 1972. Not only had the Supreme Court decided *Reed v. Reed* the year before as the Fifth Circuit noted, but the Equal Rights Amendment (ERA) had passed both Houses of Congress by March and Congress passed Title IX to the Civil Rights Act providing for sex equality in education programs in June. In January, Shirley Chisholm announced she was a presidential candidate; *Ms. Magazine* published its first free-standing magazine. By 1972, the National Organization for Women was celebrating its sixth year and Title VII, including the prohibition of sex discrimination in employment, was eight years old. Yet issues of sex equality remained difficult to articulate.

The First Amendment free expression claim, at times conjoined with a liberty clause claim under the Fourteenth Amendment's Due Process Clause, was more robust in the 1970s, even if not usually successful. The Supreme Court's pronouncement in *Tinker v. Des Moines Independent Community School District* that students did not "shed their constitutional rights to freedom of speech or expression at the schoolhouse gate" required schools to demonstrate that the expression was a substantial disruption or material interference with appropriate school discipline.[32] The expression at issue in *Tinker* was the wearing of a black armband in protest of the Vietnam War, and the Court found it important to explicitly distinguish this from "regulation of the length of skirts or the type of clothing, to hair style, or deportment" in the schools. This distinction illustrates the doctrinal – and political – asymmetry in the school hair and dress cases. The schools imposed dress codes that began to include hair length for boys because the schools determined that long hair symbolized something, yet the students' constitutional claim often faltered on their failure to prove precisely what their long hair symbolized.

The Court refused to grant certiorari in at least nine male hair length cases involving students, often over a dissent by the cantankerous and controversial Justice Douglas if the Circuit Court had found the school policy constitutional.[33] Douglas's opinions provide a window into the controversies. Writing the year before *Tinker*, in his brief dissent from the denial of certiorari of a case from the Fifth Circuit involving a group of male students with a musical group and the Beatles-style haircuts to match, Justice Douglas situated the right as grounded within liberty: "I suppose that a nation bent on turning out robots might insist that every male have a crew cut and every female wear pigtails. But the ideas of 'life, liberty, and the pursuit of happiness,' expressed in the Declaration of Independence, later found specific definition in the Constitution itself, including of course freedom of expression and a wide zone of privacy."[34] Interestingly, Douglas's formulation assumed that the denial of liberty would occur on a gendered axis: crew cuts for boys and pigtails for girls.

Writing several years after *Tinker*, in his longer dissent from certiorari in a case from the Ninth Circuit, Douglas noted the doctrinal incoherence in the male student hair length cases; they produced a conflict in the circuits that is deep, irreconcilable, and recurrent, with the federal court "decisions in disarray."[35] Again, Douglas stressed the liberty aspects, including this time the liberty of parental rights to direct the upbringing of their children. Douglas also discussed equal protection, but it is again the equality between those who are accorded benefits (such as public education) and those who are not: the state cannot "set hair styles for patrons of its schools, any more than it could establish a welfare system only for men with crew cuts and women with bobbed hair."[36] The problem of different rules for hairstyles depending upon the sex of the body that they topped had little constitutional valence, even for Justice Douglas.

Even if the Supreme Court had entered the fray and adjudicated the constitutionality of school regulations prohibiting long hair on male students, entrenched notions would most likely have obscured recognition of the different hairstyles for male and female students as raising a gender classification worthy of constitutional consideration. Perhaps this was because the hair regulations were aimed at males and at first blush did not impact females, thus not squarely presenting a case of women's disadvantage. Yet part of the government rationale prohibiting boys from having "long hair" was the maintenance of sexualized hierarchy. In one case, the principal testified "if boys were allowed to wear long hair so as to look like girls, it would create problems with the continuing operation of the school because of confusion over appropriate dressing room and restroom facilities."[37] Concurring in the same case, a judge found it worthwhile to dispute the link between male hair length and "effeteness."[38]

A Supreme Court intervention in the early 1970s would have also suffered from the lack of development in constitutional sex equality doctrine. In *Craig v. Boren* decided in 1976, the Court carefully articulated the standard for review for sex classifications under the Equal Protection Clause, holding that "classifications by gender must serve important governmental objectives and must be substantially related to achievement of those objectives."[39] However, in order to apply the standard, courts must recognize a sex classification. More than a decade after *Craig v. Boren*, the federal judge in *Harper v. Edgewood Board of Education* flatly proclaimed that there was no sex equality implication when school officials refused admission, and then called police officers to forcibly eject, a cross-dressed couple seeking to attend the Junior-Senior Prom.[40] The couple, a sister and brother, dressed inappropriately according to the court: he wore "earrings, stockings, high heels, a dress, and a fur cape"; she "wore a black tuxedo and men's shoes." But the federal judge perceived no viable equal protection issue. The dress code did not "differentiate based on sex" but merely required "all students to dress in conformity with the accepted standards of the community."[41]

More recently, two other prom cases, both of which settled, deemphasized the sex equality aspects in litigation. Constance McMillen wanted to wear a tuxedo to her high school prom in Fulton, Mississippi, as well as bring her girlfriend as a date. After she was denied permission, she contacted the ACLU, which contacted the school board, which withdrew its support for the prom, in effect cancelling it. The complaint, filed in federal court in 2010, sought a preliminary injunction based solely on the First Amendment claim. The district judge found that McMillen intended to communicate a message about her sexual orientation by wearing a tuxedo and that "this expression and communication of her viewpoint falls squarely within the purview of the First Amendment."[42] The judge nevertheless denied the motion for preliminary injunction, based in part on representations that the private parent-sponsored prom that was being finalized would be open to all students, and presumably McMillen would be able to wear a tuxedo. However, as events transpired according to the amended complaint, there seemed to be two proms, and the one that McMillen attended had only a few students, while the majority of students attended a parent-organized prom at another location. The accepted offer of settlement included monetary damages, reasonable attorney fees, and the adoption of a policy that addressed equality concerns including sexual orientation.

Similar in some respects is the situation of Kevin Logan, who the court described as a "young homosexual transgendered man" and who was excluded from the prom for wearing a "prom dress of the type normally worn by high school girls."[43] Logan had been wearing "feminine attire" during the school year, was supported by at least some students when the principal excluded Logan from the prom, and according to the complaint, a woman was allowed to attend the prom wearing a tuxedo. The dress code provision relied upon by the school board after the incident prohibited "Clothing/accessories that advertise sexual orientation, sex, drugs, alcohol . . ." Given the reliance on this policy, not surprisingly the district judge characterized Logan's First Amendment claim as "pivotal" and did not address the equal protection claim, when denying the motion to dismiss. Again, the case eventually settled for monetary damages and changes in policy.[44]

In one of the most discussed cases involving student cross-dressing, *Doe v. Yunits*, the Massachusetts state court judge issued a preliminary injunction requiring the school officials to allow Doe to attend school "wearing clothes and fashion accouterments that are consistent with her gender identity."[45] Judge Linda Giles's analysis centered on the free speech claim, under the Massachusetts state constitutional provision as "guided by federal free speech analysis." The judge first found that Doe's dress was symbolic speech, noting that Doe's message was well understood by school officials as evinced by the "vehement response." Yet the judge found that the vehement response by school officials as well as some students was not sufficient to satisfy the material disruption requirement laid out by the Supreme Court in *Tinker*[46] when curtailing school speech, lest "contentious students" be granted a "heckler's veto." However, what is most noteworthy about Judge Giles's opinion is the simultaneous recognition of the state constitutional sex discrimination claim and the conceptual interdependence between the free expression claim and the sex equality claim. The judge rejected the school officials' argument in the free expression context that "any student" who dressed in "distracting clothing" would be subject to discipline, by stating that "if a female student came to school in a frilly dress or blouse, make-up, or a padded bra, she would go, and presumably has gone, unnoticed by school officials." For the judge, the expression is linked to its gender disparity. Thus, the school would not be allowed to ban "gender-identified dress but should be permitted to ban clothing that would be inappropriate if worn by any student, such as a theatrical costume." Yet when considering the sex equality claim, the judge highlighted Doe's gender identity and biological sex:

> Since plaintiff identifies with the female gender, the right question is whether a female student would be disciplined for wearing items of clothes plaintiff chooses

to wear. If the answer to that question is no, plaintiff is being discriminated against on the basis of her sex, which is biologically male.[47]

Judge Giles specifically distinguished *Harper*, the case involving the brother-and-sister cross-dressed couple who sought to attend the prom: Doe is "expressing her personal identity," and "not merely engaging in rebellious acts to demonstrate a willingness to violate community norms." It would seem that to be protected under constitutional provisions regarding free speech or sex equality, cross-dressing must be a matter of sincerity and deeply felt identity.

However, even if a student simply does not "feel comfortable" with mandated gender-segregated attire, there may still be a valid sex equality constitutional claim. Indeed, a person's subjective response to inequality should not determine whether or not there is a denial of equal protection. In litigation commenced in 2010 concerning the mandatory attire for high school yearbook portraits, Ceara Sturgis argued that she should not be forced to wear the "scoop-necked 'drape,' a curtain-like garment that causes the female students to look as if they are wearing a dress or blouse," because although she "identifies as a female, she feels deeply uncomfortable in clothing such as dresses, blouses, and skirts that are traditionally associated with the female gender."[48] The complaint alleged that this was sex-stereotyping in violation of the Equal Protection Clause, as well as federal statutes prohibiting sex discrimination in educational institutions. A federal district judge denied a motion to dismiss, agreeing that although there is "no fundamental right to appear in a yearbook," Sturgis relied on sex equality arguments, contending that the "women-must-wear-drapes" requirement amounts to sexual stereotyping that is facially discriminatory.[49] The judge noted that the defendant school district "countered that the policy is sex neutral because both sexes were required to wear specific clothing – boys were not allowed to wear drapes." While this type of formal equality argument can be common, it has been enervated at least since 1967 when the Supreme Court decided *Loving v. Virginia*.[50] In *Loving*, Virginia had argued that because its miscegenation statutes prohibiting interracial marriage "punish equally both the white and the Negro participants in an interracial marriage, these statutes, despite their reliance on racial classifications, do not constitute an invidious discrimination based upon race." The Court soundly rejected what it called the "equal application" theory, stating that there was no question that the miscegenation statutes rested solely upon distinctions drawn according to race and proscribed "generally accepted conduct if engaged in by members of different races." However, without reference to *Loving*, the district judge in *Sturgis* found that the school district's argument had "some appeal," as did Sturgis's argument, and thus the decision should be made on a more complete record. The judge also ordered the parties to mediate, perhaps hoping for a settlement as occurred in a similar "drape" lawsuit several years earlier, although that settlement did not occur until the federal judge issued a final order and an appellate brief had been filed.[51]

What the "drape" cases manifest, however, is not simply the gender segregation of the clothing policies, but their sexuality. As thousands of current yearbook portraits attest, the so-called drape is most commonly arranged off both shoulders. If not sexually revealing, it is certainly sexually suggestive. Its sexuality is further heightened by a comparison with the mandated male attire: male shoulders are ensconced in a shirt and a jacket, with the neck barely visible under its shirt and bow tie.

This is not to contend that sex-segregated dress codes for students generally promote expressions of female sexuality. Indeed, it is often quite the opposite. Although never as prominent as male hair length in the litigation, issues of skirt length, clothing tightness, and visible bra straps permeate the school dress code cases that primarily address male hair. Within the overall dress code, the school's purpose for regulating female dress is generally articulated as mandating "modest dressing," and thus to prevent disruption because the presumptively heterosexual male students would be distracted. Courts easily accepted such justifications, with little or no discussion, implicitly finding the government control of girls' sexuality through dress permissible and unremarkable.[52]

Importantly, however, whether the regulation of girls' dress is intended to prevent girls from appearing too sexual or insufficiently sexual, it attempts to place girls in sexualized and gendered hierarchies. Mandated sex-segregated attire operates to similar ends. When the government standardizes children into two (and only two) classifications – girls and boys – "cross-dressing" among young people threatens the government's project. Further, when the government standardizes the category of "girl" with regard to acceptable sexuality, girls who are either too sexual or insufficiently sexual jeopardize the goal. While apparel regulations are certainly not the sole method of enforcing gendered and sexualized standardizations of children, they are a crucial one. For adults, including adult women, the government involvement may be less direct but is no less influential in maintaining a sexualized hierarchy.

III. PROVOCATIVE CLOTHING, SEXUAL VIOLENCE, AND STATE PROTECTION

Women's dress provokes (heterosexual) men to sexual violence. This "common sense" hypothesis underlies the mandate, whether directly or indirectly enforced, that female dress should not be "provocative." A rarely discussed but important instance of direct governmental control of women's attire occurs in the context of prison visitation. The Federal Bureau of Prisons has promulgated a "visiting room dress code," which mandates that visitors wear clothing "that is appropriate for a large gathering of men, women, and young children. Wearing inappropriate clothing (such as provocative or revealing clothes) may result in your being denied visitation."[53] The information for visitors then provides specifics that will bar admission to the prison: revealing shorts; sundresses; halter tops; bathing suits; see-through garments of any type; crop tops; low-cut blouses or dresses; leotards; spandex; miniskirts; backless tops; hats or caps; sleeveless garments; skirts two inches or more above the knee; dresses or skirts with a high-cut split in the back, front, or side; or any clothing that looks like inmate clothing (such as khaki or green military-type clothing).[54]

The bulk of the Federal Bureau of Prisons' examples of prohibited clothing concern arguably "provocative" female dress. Certainly there are legitimate security concerns that should govern regulations of apparel of visitors to penal institutions. The most obvious exclusions would be loose or baggy clothing, in which weapons or other contraband could be hidden, although this is not mentioned on the Federal Bureau of Prisons list, or clothes that resemble inmate or correctional officer uniforms. Yet the focus in the Federal Bureau of Prisons, as well as most state departments of correction, is preventing provocative clothing.

The fetishized attention to attire rivals Henry VIII's attention to the Knights of the Garter. For example, short skirts are generally prohibited, but it is important to define "short." The Michigan Department of Corrections allows skirts to be an inch higher than the federal system but has delineated guidelines regarding calculating the three inches:

> Measurements are to be taken when the visitor is seated with feet flat on the floor and at the highest point of the skirt; e.g., if the skirt has a slit, then the measurement would be taken at the top of the slit. (If the slit is in the front or side of the skirt, the measurement would be taken while seated; if the slit is in the back of the skirt, the measurement may be taken while the visitor is standing).[55]

In addition to short skirts, bras have received special attention. The Michigan guidelines specifically mandate that "adult females must wear a brassiere." Yet there is also a problem with visitors who wear a bra. While the New York guidelines prohibit "provocative attire" including short skirts, low tops, plunging necklines, backless blouses or dresses, and see-through clothing, they also demonstrate the problem with mandating bras: "Please be advised, if your bra makes the metal detector go off, you will have to take it off and/or be searched by an officer."[56]

One of the few cases involving a constitutional challenge to visitor dress involves a bra. Scharlette Holdman, then director of the Hawai'i ACLU, sought entry to a prison and was searched by a matron who discovered Holdman was not wearing a bra.[57] The matron denied Holdman entry, relying upon a directive that required visitors to be "properly dressed," "fully clothed including undergarments," and stated "provocative attire is discouraged." Holdman's challenge stressed equal protection, under both the United States and Hawai'i state constitutions, arguing that the requirement that women wear bras while men need not constituted sex discrimination. Writing in 1978, the Hawai'i Supreme Court expressed some consternation about the slight record, but relying in part on deference to prison officials, the court found that dress standards are "intimately related to sexual attitudes" and "the omission of a brassiere as a conventional article of women's clothing" has been "regarded as sexually provocative by some members of society." The court questioned whether such "attitudes were reflected in the prison population" but concluded that the prison officials could assume that prisoners held such attitudes. Thus, the policy satisfied the standard for equal protection, even if the state constitutional standard was the higher strict scrutiny. The fact that Scharlette Holdman's lack of a bra became evident only upon a tactile search was irrelevant: the prison could still find it would be sexually provocative to the male inmates.

In most situations in which the lack of a bra or a plunging neckline or a short skirt garners judicial attention for provoking male sexual interest, there is no direct governmental regulation. Instead, the more common scenario involves legal proceedings involving male violence or harassment, either criminal or civil. In these cases, any constitutional protection for the woman's choice of arguably provocative dress is not at issue. Yet it is important to consider why the woman's constitutional rights are not implicated.

The U.S. Constitution protects persons from governmental action and not private action, with the exception of the Thirteenth Amendment prohibiting involuntary servitude and slavery. The doctrine of state action and the concomitant theorization of positive versus negative rights are at the heart of this constitutional issue. The Fourteenth Amendment introduced equality into the Constitution by providing that "No State shall" deny persons equal protection. The First Amendment begins with the words "Congress shall make no law." Undoubtedly, the framers, both of the original Constitution and of the Reconstruction Amendments, were focused on protecting individual liberties from the overreaching of federal and state governmental powers, respectively. Thus, the exercise of private power, whether individual or corporate, is not deemed a violation of "rights," constitutional or otherwise, and the government, whether federal or state, is not deemed to have a duty to protect persons from the exercise of that power. This American view may be increasingly diverging from international norms.

The case of Jessica Gonzalez, now Jessica Lenahan, is illustrative. She had a restraining order against her husband based on his violent acts. When she discovered that he took their three children without permission, she contacted the police department several times and was essentially told to call back later each time. Mr. Gonzalez murdered all three children. In 2005, the United States Supreme Court decided *Castle Rock v. Gonzales* holding that she did not have a constitutional right under the due process clause to have a restraining order enforced by law enforcement.[58] Six years later, the Inter-American Commission on Human Rights of the Organization of American States issued a lengthy report and concluded that the failure to protect Lenahan and her daughters constituted a form of sex discrimination in violation of the 1948 American Declaration of the Rights and Duties of Man, since they took place in a context where there has been a historical problem with the enforcement of protection orders; a problem that has disproportionately affected women since they constitute the majority of the restraining order holders.[59] Thereafter the UN Special Rapporteur on violence against women "urged the United States Government to reexamine its current policies on dealing with violence against women."[60]

A landmark case in 2001, *Carmichele v. Minister of Safety and Security*, from the highly respected South African Constitutional Court, also concluded that the government has a duty to protect women from private violence.[61] This may not necessarily be a stretch for the court because the South African constitutional text explicitly guarantees a right "to be free from all forms of violence from either public or private sources," although the case was actually litigated under the Interim Constitution which did not contain such a clause.[62] As South African legal scholar Marius Pieterse has explicated, the constitutional provision means that both the state and its citizens are at the very least under a constitutional obligation to refrain from violence, the government has the further duty to actively endeavor to prevent private violence that would violate the right to be free from violence, and perhaps even private actors have a duty to protect others from private violence.[63] Carmichele involved the government action of not detaining a man accused of rape, although there were specific facts that the man might pose a danger to others, including specific facts about Carmichele. Indeed, Carmichele was subject to a brutal attack, for which the man was convicted of housebreaking and attempted murder. Considering Camichele's suit against public authorities, the South African Constitutional Court acknowledged the U.S. constitutional distinction between what it labeled "action" and "inaction," but declared that the provisions of the South African (interim) Constitution "point in a different direction," as do the provisions of the European Convention on Human Rights.[64] Moreover, the Court held that the South African Constitution embodies "an objective normative value system" that includes the dignity, freedom, and security of the person, which for women means "freedom from the threat of sexual violence," a vital component of eliminating gender-based discrimination.[65]

The exercise of governmental responsibility to protect women from sexual assault, whether constitutionally mandated or not, does take many forms, including law enforcement liaisons to communities. However, such events can produce their own controversies. In 2011, a police officer was on a "routine visit" to Osgoode Hall Law School in Toronto to advise students on their personal safety. Before an audience of ten students, the police officer reportedly said, "I've been told I'm not supposed to say this – however, women should avoid dressing like sluts in order not to be victimised."[66] The reasons the officer was told not to voice such opinions soon became clear as students organized a "SlutWalk" to protest the officer's remarks. Moreover, the phenomenon of SlutWalks soon gained global enthusiasm, with organized protests of women, some dressed provocatively and some not, throughout the United States, Europe, South America, and Asia.

While the SlutWalk participants did not articulate their concerns in terms of constitutional specifics, they certainly used the rhetoric of rights. The basic message was that women should have the right to wear whatever they want and that deprivation of this right is a matter of sex inequality. Some signs proclaimed that the government should be telling men not to commit sexual assault rather than telling women how to dress. Other signs confronted "victim blaming": "No one is responsible for violence perpetrated against them, no matter what they wear."

The use of women's provocative clothing to mitigate responsibility for sexual assault is rooted in "common sense" attitudes, confirmed as a social fact by some sociological studies, that link a woman's consent to sexual advances, even violent ones, to her mode of dress.[67] The use of a sexual assault victim's clothing can create a sense that the victim was "asking for it" and that the perpetrator acted in a normal – noncriminal – manner. In this sense, women's provocative clothing is understood as provoking men to sexual acts for which they should not be held criminally responsible.

In reaction to this situation, Congress enacted a rape shield law in 1978, now codified as Federal Rule of Evidence 412.[68] Generally, rape shield laws "shield" the victim of sexual assault from interrogations about her sexual behavior, a process some women's advocates described as a "second rape." The federal rule focuses on the victim's sexual history rather than attire, although the Advisory Committee Notes to the rule explicitly include the "alleged victim's mode of dress, speech or lifestyle." States have generally followed the federal rule in adopting their own rape shield provisions, but a few states including Georgia and Alabama have incorporated the advisory notes regarding dress into the text of the rule itself.[69] Yet whether state or federal, the rape shield laws do not operate as an absolute bar to such testimony. Rape shield laws are subordinate to the defendant's constitutional right to present a defense and the right to a fair trial, grounded in the Due Process Clauses of the Fourteenth and Fifth Amendments, as well as the Sixth Amendment's Confrontation Clause and Compulsory Process Clause.[70]

The defendants' constitutional rights necessarily trump. In part this is because the victims' rights are not articulated as constitutional ones. Instead, the rape shield statutes barring evidence of matters including "mode of dress" are rules of evidence based upon relevancy. As the federal judge considering Florida's rape shield statute in *Johnson v. Moore* opined, the "evidentiary proscription" was "soundly grounded in both reason and experience," in order to "protect the complainant's reasonable expectation of privacy, to avoid invasive and demeaning inquiry into a complainant's intimate conduct, to encourage the reporting and pursuit of complaints of sexual battery, and to avoid the prejudice that results from the introduction of a distracting, confusing, and inflammatory irrelevancy."[71] Only the "reasonable expectation of privacy" rationale approaches the status of a current constitutional right, although taken together these interests could support an articulation of a constitutional guarantee of sex equality.

The excluded evidence being considered by the federal judge interpreting the constitutional ramifications of Florida's rape shield law in *Johnson v. Moore* included testimony that the victim – a thirteen-year-old – was seen "provocatively dressed," waving vehicles over to her, getting in those vehicles, and exiting a short time later. The defendant proffered testimony that the victim often exchanged sex for drugs. The attire evidence did thus not explicitly raise the issue of the specific provision in Florida's rape shield statute that excludes evidence of dress as provocation: "evidence presented for the purpose of showing that manner of dress of the victim at the time of the offense *incited* the sexual battery shall not be admitted into evidence in a prosecution."[72] Instead, the defendant in *Johnson* argued that the apparel evidence was relevant to consent, a position with which the judge ultimately agreed given the victim's testimony and the prosecutor's arguments that "opened the door" to issues of the victim's sexual experience.

The relationship between a victim's specific apparel and the level of consent necessary to negate an element of the offense of rape or sexual assault, in light of a defendant's constitutional rights, has proved particularly vexatious to the New Hampshire Supreme Court. The New Hampshire statute specifically provides that the "victim's manner of dress at the time of the sexual assault shall not be admitted as evidence in any prosecution under this chapter to infer consent."[73] The New Hampshire state senate had doubts about the constitutionality of the original bill, and therefore sought an advisory opinion from the New Hampshire Supreme Court, a proceeding allowable under the state constitution but that would not be permitted in the federal system. The justices concluded that the exclusion of manner-of-dress evidence as to the issue of consent did not infringe on a defendant's constitutional rights, although the advisory opinion specifically noted it was "necessarily qualified" because it could not "anticipate every possible fact pattern that may arise and test the limits of the bill."[74] Several years later, the New Hampshire justices had the opportunity to consider whether a fact pattern had arisen in which the victim's dress – a T-shirt and a quilt – was so probative of consent as to constitute a denial of the defendant's constitutional rights if the dress evidence was excluded.[75] The court considered the "contemporaneous conduct" of the victim and held exclusion did not violate the defendant's constitutional rights, although whether or not such attire evidence could ever be introduced to support consent was not resolved.

The characterization of attire as "provocative" or as communicating sexual consent is deeply problematical. Law professor Duncan Kennedy, writing as an avowedly heterosexual white male in his 1992 essay *Sexy Dressing*, provided his own definition: "costumes conventionally regarded as sexy in the sense of provocative generally choose exposure over covering, tightness over looseness, brightness (or black) over soft color, transparency over opaqueness, and symbolic shaping of breasts, waist, buttocks, and feet over 'natural' lines."[76] However, writing around the same time, several other authors noted that any communication is fraught because the person perceiving the clothes may not "have the same experience or knowledge, share the same culture, or view clothing within the same context" as the person wearing the clothes.[77] In essence, critics rightly accuse Duncan Kennedy of the same sort of interpretative slovenliness that mars so many opinions in which judges apply their own "common sense" understandings, seemingly not cognizant of their limits.

An important point that Duncan Kennedy does contribute, however, is the insistence on the relevance of the setting (both time and place) in which apparel is worn: "Sexy dress is sexy *in terms of* the dress codes that regulate virtually all social space." Kennedy attempts to map this variety, with nighttime being a time of "more sexy" dress for women and daytime being "less sexy." However, Kennedy's charting of workplace apparel could again be faulted for its interpretative slovenliness. His category of "More sexy" women's dress contains these (and only these) examples: "Sales work; Street prostitutes; Actresses & models enacting sexuality." His category of "Less sexy" women's dress contains these (and only these) examples: "Professional work; High priced call girls; Women script writers."[78] However, whether or not one agrees with Kennedy's categorizations of appropriate dress for women "script writers," certainly the arena of the "workplace" is a contested setting for women's dressing sexily. Yet women are not alone in this. And even apart from dressing sexily or sexed, dressing professionally poses problems of constitutional magnitude.

4

Dressing Professionally

Attire can communicate professional status. At times, apparel is the metonym for the profession – for example, "robes" is understood to mean "judges" in the American legal context. At other times, there are rigidly established conventions of dress, such as military uniforms, that convey hierarchies. And at most times, customs of dress and grooming are subject to fluctuating policies that may or may not be explicit, specific, or even understood, even as such policies are usually sexualized, hierarchal, and undemocratic. In all of these situations, however, there are constitutional concerns.

In private employment, dress and grooming policies are subject to federal statutory protections against discrimination. However, the reach of these protections is incomplete, often incoherent, and subject to constitutional constraints and challenges. In public employment, the military uniform serves as a paradigmatic dress code. Even as military uniforms have shaped constitutional development in recondite ways, they have also been subject to constitutional challenges, both by authorized and unauthorized wearers. Government interests in uniformity have extended to paramilitary uniforms, such as those worn by police officers and even bus drivers, and judges have accorded deference to government justifications over individual constitutional rights of free expression. Professional dress in academic and legal contexts is rooted in the history of the clerical gown, yet contemporary practices raise constitutional questions of rights, as well as constitutional structures and symbolism.

It is worth noting that if all professional dress codes were subject to a strict judicial scrutiny requiring a compelling employer interest and a narrow tailoring – or even to a rigorous rational basis judicial scrutiny requiring a truly legitimate employer interest to which the dress code was rationally related – few would survive constitutional review. Only occasionally is there a close fit, or even a truly rational one, between the regulations of professional dress and the actual practice of the profession. For example, for those whose profession is to communicate as translators or interpreters, including in legal forums, the major concern should be how they "dress" their language. But their bodily presentation also receives attention. One state regulation provides that an "interpreter shall display professional demeanor and conduct" by wearing "appropriate professional clothing, which includes: 1. A skirt or dress; 2. A business suit; 3. Slacks and a jacket; or 4. Similar attire."[1] In a regulation from another state, an interpreter's dress will be as "unobtrusive" as possible, including avoiding patterned clothing.[2] Both of these policies govern sign language interpreters. Only the latter, however, is clearly rational, concerned as it is with clothes that would "tire the eyes of deaf consumers" or otherwise interfere with the efficacy of the sign language interpreter's professional work.

I. AT WORK IN THE PRIVATE SPHERE

The authority of private employers to condition employment on specific types of attire and other appearance requirements is expansive, but not absolute. The status of employers as private insulates them from constitutional norms, but equality concerns do appear in federal, state, and local laws that prohibit various types of "discrimination" in employment. The best known of these laws is Title VII of the 1964 Civil Rights Act that makes it an unlawful employment practice "to fail or refuse to hire or to discharge any individual, or otherwise to discriminate against any individual with respect to his compensation, terms, conditions, or privileges of employment, because of such individual's race, color, religion, sex, or national origin."[3] Under Title VII, as well as similar laws, employees have a civil action against employers for adverse employment actions based on discrimination in the covered categories. Yet Title VII, by text and judicial interpretation, is problematical as a sufficient bulwark against employer control of employee attire and appearance. The problems include the reach of Title VII, the strict and often incoherent application of Title VII, and the constitutional attacks on Title VII.

Statutory Inclusions and Exclusions

First, Title VII has a limited reach. Some of these limitations are manifestations of the constitutional grounding of Title VII, at least in part, in congressional power under the Commerce Clause, Article I, §8 c. 3: covered employers are defined as those "engaged in an industry affecting commerce who has fifteen or more employees for each working day in each of twenty or more calendar weeks in the current or preceding calendar year." This excludes employees of small businesses and domestic workers. Other limitations are the product of political choices. Indeed, Congress originally chose to exempt governments from the definition of employer. Congress altered this to include most federal, state, and local government employees in 1972,[4] while continuing the exemption of Congress itself as a covered employer until 1995.[5] Foreign employers (within the United States) and foreign employment (even if both employer and employee are Americans) pose special problems. Employers that are religious organizations are not automatically exempt, but an often broadly construed "ministerial exemption" allows religious organizations wide latitude under the theory of First Amendment free exercise of religion. Moreover, not all employment relations are embraced within Title VII and similar laws; uncovered categories include students, volunteers, independent contractors, and prisoners.

The political choice to establish an administrative agency, the Equal Employment Opportunity Commission (EEOC), and to require the exhaustion of administrative remedies as a prerequisite to seeking judicial redress can serve as a limit to Title VII. This political choice is further subject to political shifts, such as the presidential control over the commissioners. Perhaps the most famous chair of the EEOC is Clarence Thomas, appointed by Ronald Reagan, accused of sexual harassment at the EEOC by Anita Hill and others, and now a member of the United States Supreme Court.

Political choices are also inherent in the classifications to be protected. Sex was not an obvious inclusion in the 1964 Civil Rights Act and may have been the product of an effort to defeat the bill. The classifications of Title VII have been supplemented with other acts addressing age and disability, but as of 2012 sexual orientation and gender identity remain uncovered grounds of discrimination in federal law.

Political choices also inhere in the causation requirement. A finding of discrimination requires the adverse employment action be "because of" the classification, raising problems when there are various classifications operating (e.g., an Asian woman) or when the employer may have mixed motives or when the discrimination does not fit neatly into a classification (e.g., pregnancy or language use). Discrimination excludes other nonequality-based objections to one's treatment: an employer policy that treats all employees terribly is not an issue of discrimination.

Look Policies

In addition to the incomplete reach of Title VII, judicial treatment, while inconsistent, has generally afforded wide latitude to employers to govern employee dress and appearance. As Title VII scholar Merrick Rossein has explained:

> Employers are permitted to protect the company's business image or brand by requiring all of their employees to be clean shaven with short hair; their female employees to wear skirts or dresses, and sometimes even high heel shoes and makeup; and their male employees to wear suits and ties. Employers can lawfully prohibit visible tattoos, body piercings and unconventional hairstyles such

as dreadlocks, cornrows and braids, and can impose weight limits. Women can be sanctioned for wearing too much make-up where male employees are also required to dress conservatively. Courts have permitted a prohibition of jewelry for men and not women. Many employers require "professional" dress and disallow "revealing" or "provocative" clothing, particularly worn by women because of their concern that sexualized clothing might result in unwanted attention leading to problems with sexually hostile work places.[6]

Two well-known cases involving women at work and what they should wear demonstrate the inability of Title VII to adequately address the gendered aspects of women's professional dress. In *Price Waterhouse v. Hopkins*, the U.S. Supreme Court found that the accounting firm discriminated against Ann Hopkins by denying her a promotion to partner based upon her sex, or more precisely, sex-stereotyping.[7] The Court's plurality labeled the coup de grace the evidence that Hopkin's chief supporter advised her that in order to improve her chances at a partnership at the next opportunity, she should "walk more femininely, talk more femininely, dress more femininely, wear make-up, have her hair styled, and wear jewelry." However, this has not been interpreted to foreclose an employer's ability to mandate that women (but not men) wear makeup or have styled hair. In *Jespersen v. Harrah's Operating Company, Inc.*, the en banc Ninth Circuit found that the adoption of a policy by Harrah's Casino of a gender-defined grooming code did not violate Title VII.[8] The policy required that women's hair "must be teased, curled, or styled" and "worn down," and that for women, "Make up (face powder, blush and mascara) must be worn and applied neatly in complimentary colors. Lip color must be worn at all times." On the contrary, the policy provided that for men, "Eye and facial makeup is not permitted," as well as mandating that hair must not extend below the top of the shirt collar. The Ninth Circuit agreed with the weight of authority that gender-differential dress and grooming codes by employers do not constitute sex discrimination under Title VII and further held that the employer was not engaging in unlawful sex-stereotyping. The court distinguished *Price Waterhouse v. Hopkins* by noting that "Harrah's grooming standards do not require Jespersen to conform to a stereotypical image that would objectively impede her ability to perform her job requirements as a bartender,"[9] rejecting Jespersen's argument that wearing makeup did impede her authority over rowdy patrons. The court's unsatisfying distinction may be attributable to the class hierarchies involved, or to the difference between explicit and implicit grooming codes, or to the judicial propensity to recognize individual discrimination and not systemic inequality, or to some combination. Whatever the underlying rationale, courts have generally interpreted Title VII to give wide latitude to employers to enforce gendered dress by employees.

Courts have also allowed employers to dictate racialized grooming standards for employees without contravening Title VII. For Black women, the issue of hair has been especially fraught, a matter explored by legal scholars such as Paulette Caldwell, Angela Onwuachi-Willig, and D. Wendy Greene.[10] The notorious case of *Rogers v. American Airlines* decided by a federal district judge in 1981 roundly rejected a challenge to the employer's rule prohibiting all-braided hairstyles, known as cornrows, by all employees.[11] The judge found the policy did not implicate a sex or a race classification. He found it noteworthy that men had hair as long as women and that white women could also wear cornrows, specifically referencing "the white actress [Bo Derek] in the film '10.'" The judge distinguished the hypothetical prohibition of an "Afro/bush" style "because banning a natural hairstyle would implicate the policies underlying the prohibition of discrimination on the basis of immutable characteristics," and "an all-braided hairstyle is a different matter. It is not the product of natural hair growth but of artifice" and was not immutable, but rather easily changeable.

Yet while all employees may be prohibited from wearing the braided style of Bo Derek in the 1980 movie, some – but seemingly not all – employees may be prohibited from replicating her hair color. Legal scholar D. Wendy Greene has analyzed a trio of cases involving an employer's disapproval of a black woman's blonde hair.[12] In *Santee v. Windsor Court Hotel*, Ms. Santee had applied for a position as a housekeeper but was told that the employer had a policy prohibiting employees from "having extremes in hair color."[13] Santee was asked whether she would change her hair color, she stated she would not, and she was not offered employment. In *Bryant v. BEGIN Manage Program*, Ms. Bryant was terminated from her employment for insubordination and she alleged discrimination based upon her supervisor's comments that she was a "wannabe" because she dyed her hair blonde (and wore a suit rather than "Afrocentric" clothing).[14] And in *Burchette v. Abercrombie & Fitch Stores*, Ms. Burchette was ordered by her supervisor at the Fifth Avenue store to remove the blonde highlights from her hair and ordered her to have the hair color she was "born with" or he would terminate her.[15]

The federal judges reached varying conclusions. In *Santee*, the judge found that Santee's claim was based on hair color, a changeable feature, rather than race, an immutable characteristic, and was therefore not protected by Title VII. The judge accepted the employer's argument that "all employees" were subject to the "extremes in hair color" policy. Surprisingly, the judge stated that even if "further discovery revealed employees who have the same color hair as the Plaintiff, such evidence is not probative of whether the Defendant failed to hire Santee on the basis of her race." Not surprisingly, the judge granted summary judgment in favor of the employer. In both *Bryant* and *Burchette*, the facts are more complicated as is typical when there has been a course of employment rather than a simple failure to hire based on a single interaction. In *Bryant*, the judge found the general grooming cases inapposite, stating that Bryant's claim was that "as a black woman, she was obligated to dress in a particular manner, despite the fact that the dress code was flexible as applied to others." The judge denied the motion for summary judgment and the case eventually settled. On the contrary, in *Burchette*, the judge granted the motion for summary judgment in favor of Abercrombie & Fitch because Burchette could not produce satisfactory evidence that other nonblack employees were being treated differently for failure to comply with the "natural" hair policy and that Ms. Burchette simply needed to change her hair color to continue her employment.

The different outcomes may be explicable by their underlying facts and by the presentation of those facts by the plaintiffs and their attorneys. Or it may be that the judge in *Bryant* was especially sympathetic, or was made more sympathetic by Bryant's status (relatively higher than that of a hotel maid or a sales clerk) or by the fact that her supervisor was also black and sought to enforce "Afrocentric" dress and hairstyles.

Despite the doctrinal incoherence and occasional recognition of discrimination, these cases exemplify the hierarchal relationship between employer and employee. Indeed, the employer may be most able to regulate the attire and appearance of its employees when it explicitly seeks to "brand" them.[16] There is judicial deference to both the Abercrombie & Fitch "Look Policy" ("a professional image that is consistent with our reputation as the best in the fashion industry") and the Harrah's "Personal Best" policies (intended to create a "brand standard of excellence" by regulating the appearance of service employees throughout Harrah's twenty casinos). Such judicial deference makes it difficult to recognize the hierarchal relations of race, class, gender, or sexuality, and impossible to ameliorate the hierarchal relations of employer-employee in the private employment sphere.

Constitutional Attacks on Statutory Protections

Although limited, the existence of statutory protections for private realm employees is an improvement over the absence of legislative safeguards. The power to enact and enforce such legislation, however, is itself subject to constitutional constraints. There are three constitutional concerns raised by the 1964 Civil Rights Act, including Title VII and its amendments: the power of Congress to enact such legislation; the constitutional rights of employers; and statutory protections that may conflict with changing equal protection doctrine.

The power of Congress to enact the 1964 Civil Rights Act is grounded in the Commerce Clause or the Fourteenth Amendment's enforcement section. Although it may be "unthinkable" that the act could be declared unconstitutional given "the shared norms of the current governing consensus,"[17] shared constitutional norms shift. As legal scholar Paul Boudreaux has written, although "it may seem unthinkable that the Court could revisit the constitutionality of the discrimination statutes," such as the 1964 Civil Rights Act, it is "instructive to consider how an emboldened federalist Court might scrutinize such laws today." Boudreaux cautioned that although the opinions upholding the Civil Rights Act under the Commerce Clause "now hold forty years of precedential value," that is "only half as long as the period in which the Supreme Court adhered to the precedent of 1883's *Civil Rights Cases* that Congress could not regulate discrimination at privately-owned accommodations."[18]

The *Civil Rights Cases* centered the Reconstruction Amendments as a basis for congressional power to enact the 1875 Civil Rights Act.[19] The Court rejected the ability of Congress to reach private rather than state action pursuant to the Fourteenth Amendment's enforcement power. The Court likewise rejected the Thirteenth Amendment as a basis of congressional power to prohibit racial discrimination. Although the Thirteenth Amendment is unique in that it does reach private action, the Court held that the abolition of slavery was far narrower than racial discrimination. Importantly, the *Civil Rights Cases* have never been overruled. When the Court upheld provisions of the 1964 Civil Rights Act in the companion cases of *Heart of Atlanta Motel Inc. v. United States* and *Katzenbach v. McClung (Ollie's Barbecue)*, it did so under the Commerce Clause, despite congressional reliance on the Fourteenth Amendment and despite Justice Douglas's concurring opinion that the "decision should be based on the Fourteenth Amendment, thereby putting an end to all obstructionist strategies and allowing every person – whatever his race, creed, or color – to patronize all places of public accommodation without discrimination whether he travels interstate or intrastate."[20]

The "obstructionist strategies" to which Justice Douglas referred presumably included conservative arguments surrounding the 1964 Civil Rights Act. The cases involving *Heart of Atlanta Motel* and *Ollie's Barbecue* were argued a month before – and decided a little more than a month after – the 1964 presidential election between Lyndon Johnson and Barry Goldwater. Goldwater's conservative stance included an opposition to the 1964 Civil Rights Act, buoyed by scholarly opinions from William Rehnquist, then in private practice in Arizona, and Robert Bork, then a law professor.[21] Bork had also advanced his arguments against the Civil Rights Act in an infamous essay in the *New Republic*, arguing that congressional power under either the Commerce Clause or the Fourteenth Amendment was insufficient to overcome individual liberty and impose "moral or aesthetic" judgments about the wrongfulness of racial discrimination.[22]

As Bork's libertarian arguments demonstrate, the constitutional objections to the 1964 Civil Rights Act including Title VII are not confined to the absence of congressional power but extend to the presence of countervailing individual constitutional rights possessed by the employer. At times, the employer's right is merely implicit.

For example, while Bork was a judge on the D.C. Circuit Court of Appeals he wrote (and was joined by then-judges Antonin Scalia and Kenneth Starr) that evidence that the "plaintiff wore provocative clothing" was relevant to the sexual harassment claim and that the employer company should not be held vicariously liable "in the unique context presented by sexual harassment claims," given the traditional rule excluding employer liability for "employee's intentional torts involving sexual escapades."[23] On certiorari, in an opinion written by Justice Rehnquist, the U.S. Supreme Court held that the plaintiff Mechelle Vinson had a claim for hostile environment sexual harassment, that the employer bank might be held liable for the actions of its manager under agency principles, and that evidence of the plaintiff's "provocative dress" could be admitted at trial on the issue of whether the sexual advances were unwelcome.[24]

The arguments that employers possess a countervailing constitutional right to overcome discrimination laws, often expressed as a First Amendment right, can be more explicit in some conservative legal scholarship. For example, one scholar has contended that workplace harassment law is a "nationwide speech code" and has urged employers' attorneys to raise First Amendment defenses in order to prompt judges to consider the evidence more carefully and "give the defendant another shot."[25] While the U.S. Supreme Court rejected a free association and free speech defense to a Title VII sex discrimination claim,[26] some argue that sexual harassment and hostile environment claims have content-regulation at their center in the same way that regulation of hate-speech and obscenity do.[27] Yet the Court has upheld consideration of hate-speech as an enhancement to a crime (certainly more severe than a civil penalty to an employer) and has routinely upheld regulations of obscenity.[28]

In addition to First Amendment and liberty arguments relating to employer freedoms as a general counterargument to anti-discrimination laws, there are arguments against the constitutionality of the specific provision of disparate impact. Under Title VII, the disparate impact on a protected class by an employer's action can give rise to a claim. For example, an employer prohibition of the cornrow hairstyle could be race or sex discrimination if it could be shown that the prohibition had a disparate impact on African Americans or women. This is distinct from the Court's doctrine under the Fourteenth Amendment's Equal Protection Clause declaring that disparate impact alone is insufficient; a discriminatory intent is also required.[29] Thus, a government employer would have greater latitude under the Equal Protection Clause than under Title VII: the prohibition of the cornrow hairstyle would not be race or sex discrimination even if it could be shown that the prohibition had a disparate impact on African Americans or women unless it could also be demonstrated that the employer intended to discriminate against African Americans or women.

In the 2009 "white firefighters" case from New Haven, Connecticut, *Ricci v. DeStefano*, Justice Scalia concurred specially to observe that there had merely been a postponement of "the evil day on which the Court will have to confront the question: Whether, or to what extent, are the disparate-impact provisions of Title VII of the Civil Rights Act of 1964 consistent with the Constitution's guarantee of equal protection?"[30] For Scalia, "the war between disparate impact and equal protection will be waged sooner or later." While this does not necessarily mean that the disparate-impact provision of Title VII will be vanquished, it will most certainly be altered.[31]

Thus, the constitutional uncertainties surrounding the disparate-impact provision of Title VII, the countervailing rights of employers, and the very foundations of congressional power threaten to erode the statutory protections for employees in the private realm. These threats further weaken civil rights statutes that courts interpret to provide wide latitude to employers to control employee attire and appearance. Political and constitutional choices in civil rights statutes exclude many employees from even this limited protection. In short, although Title VII and similar statutes have ameliorated the hierarchy between employer and employee by prohibiting discrimination on the basis of certain classifications, a private employer retains almost absolute power over an employee's "professional" dress, including her hairstyle and color.

II. UNIFORMITY

The military uniform is the quintessential attempt of a sovereign to brand and professionalize a class of its employees. The first important constitutional case decided by the U.S. Supreme Court, *Chisholm v. Georgia*, involved both clothes and sovereignty.[32] The soldiers who fought on behalf of the American revolutionists were by all accounts a ragtag lot; they were poorly clad whether they were part of the Continental forces raised by the new Congress or the militia organized by individual colonies.[33] Georgia's Continental regiments wore locally made uniforms that included kilts, but as one of the poorest and sparsely populated states, the uniforms were far from uniformly available.[34] Georgia seemingly tried to remedy the situation of ill-clothed troops in 1777 when the Executive Council of Georgia authorized Thomas Stone and Edward Davies to contract for the sale of material by Robert Farquar, a South Carolina merchant. While the Court in *Chisholm* did not specifically describe the items for purchase, and commentators variously describe the goods as "military goods" or "cloth and uniforms," the Georgia scholar Doyle Mathis avers that the merchandise under contract included "cloth, thread, silk, handkerchiefs, blankets, coats, and jackets."[35] Although the goods were delivered, Farquar was never paid. After Farquar's death his executor, Alexander Chisholm, pursued the debt of $169,613.33[36] (about 3.6 million in contemporary dollars).

By the time of the lawsuit in 1792, the American Revolution had been successful, Georgia was a state within the United States, and the Articles of Confederation
had been abandoned in favor of the recently ratified Constitution to be interpreted
by a U.S. Supreme Court. The Constitution included Article III §2, providing
that the "judicial power shall extend" to "controversies between a state and citizens of another state." Yet when Chisholm sued Georgia, Georgia relied upon an
extra-constitutional notion of sovereignty, essentially arguing its superiority to both
the federal courts and to the individual claimant based upon theories that a sovereign state, like a king, could "do no wrong." Four of the five sitting justices of the
Court, all of whom could be called "framers" of the Constitution,[37] held Georgia's
claim of sovereignty untenable under the new Constitution. Deeply controversial,
Chisholm v. Georgia was unpopular from an anti-federalist and states' rights perspective, but also because Georgia was not the only state to be heavily indebted due to
the Revolutionary War. Congress quickly proposed the Eleventh Amendment "overruling" the Court's decision in *Chisholm* and the requisite number of states ratified
it within two years. Today, the Eleventh Amendment continues to be especially
contentious because the Court extended it beyond its plain text to include citizens
of a state suing their own state in federal court. Thus, a lawsuit about Revolutionary
War uniforms is the genesis of doctrines that can immunize a state against a lawsuit
by one of its employees for discrimination, including discrimination based upon
professional dress.[38]

The highly stylized contemporary military uniform – as well as the specter of
haphazard Revolutionary War combat attire – made a more explicit appearance in
constitutional law when the U.S. Supreme Court considered religious discrimination under the First Amendment in its 1986 opinion in *Goldman v. Weinberger*.[39]
S. Simcha Goldman was an Air Force officer and psychologist who had worn a
yarmulke on his head even while indoors without incident for many years, despite a
regulation prohibiting "headgear" to be worn while indoors, except by armed security police. The 190-page document of uniform regulations also allowed an exception for headgear worn indoors during religious ceremonies, and a Department
of Defense Directive gave military commanders discretion to permit "visible religious headgear" in designated living areas and "nonvisible items generally." The
particularity of the military regulations supported the Court's opinion, authored by
Rehnquist, that the Court should defer to the military's judgment that a yarmulke
"would detract from the uniformity sought by the dress regulations." The military's
professional judgment was that "the traditional outfitting of personnel in standardized uniforms encourages the subordination of personal preferences and identities
in favor of the overall group mission," and uniforms "encourage a sense of hierarchical unity by tending to eliminate outward individual distinctions."

Justice Stevens, concurring, agreed that the military's "plausible interest" was entitled to deference, although he expressed two doubts concerning the propriety of the military's interest. The first doubt was simply expressed as "personal experience." Although Stevens did not elaborate in the opinion, his personal experience included service at the Navy's Pearl Harbor communications intelligence unit, code-named Station Hypo, where military decorum including compliance with uniform requirements was notoriously informal.[40] Stevens's second doubt was expressed as "admiration for the performance of the 'rag-tag band of soldiers' that won us our freedom in the Revolutionary War." Although he joined the majority, he wrote that these two doubts "might persuade us that the Government has exaggerated the importance of that interest."[41]

Goldman was controversial, and like *Chisholm v. Georgia* two centuries earlier, Congress quickly reacted to "overturn" the opinion.[42] This is not to say that all members of Congress agreed with the proposal to require the military to relax its dress regulations. For example, Senator Barry Goldwater, apparently unaware of the preferred uniform of Georgia's Continental regiments during the Revolutionary War, argued that the congressional proposal to negate *Goldman* could be "stretched" so far that one "might see someday a man in kilts" in the military.[43] Nevertheless, Congress passed the "accommodation of religious apparel in the military" provision as part of the defense appropriations act in 1987; President Reagan signed it into law. The statute now provides that a member of the armed forces may wear an item of "religious apparel" while wearing the uniform of the member's armed force, except that the secretary of defense may prohibit items that he determines would interfere with the performance of military duties or if the "item of apparel is not neat and conservative."[44]

If a man in a kilt would undermine the "sense of hierarchical unity," then a woman in a skirt might do the same. Indeed, a woman, whether or not she wears a skirt, has the capacity to undermine the military's masculine identity. In *Virginia v. United States* (VMI), the U.S. Supreme Court found that the exclusion of women from the Virginia Military Institute violated the Equal Protection Clause of the Fourteenth Amendment, notwithstanding the fact that Virginia provided a sister school for women.[45] The sister school interestingly had not mandated uniforms for women, so when VMI had to enroll female students, the school confronted issues of women's appearance.[46] The essential dispute was a classic one posed in equality doctrine. On the one hand, simply issuing entering female students the "standard" uniform meant that women had to conform to a male standard. On the other hand, changing the standard for women meant treating them differently, and thus unequally. Originally, female cadets were to wear the same uniforms as male cadets, although "tailored to fit women's bodies." Soon, skirts (knee-length) were allowed for "social occasions," although some women later opted to wear them in the classroom. With skirts came the problem of "pantyhose," which then produced a policy worthy of the Knights of the Garter:

> Panty hose will be worn with the gray skirt and the white shirt. They will match, or be no more than one skin tone darker than the color of the skin and will not have visible runs. There should be enough elasticity to avoid bagging around the ankles and knees; panty hose will be neatly worn at all times. Female cadets may use their own preference in regard to sheen and style of garment top. Panty hose with seams up the back of the leg and other designs are not permitted.[47]

In addition to uniforms, there were other matters of dress: the shaved head for entering students, nudity in swimming classes, jewelry, and makeup. The developed guidelines allowed some accommodation but stressed the "conservative"; for example, female cadets were allowed to wear "conservative cosmetics" including "noneccentric lipstick."[48] The notion of conservative deviation, whether based on gender or religion, relaxes the judgment that uniforms "encourage a sense of hierarchical unity by tending to eliminate outward individual distinctions," as accepted by the Court in *Goldman*. Presumably, an outward distinction that is not conservative would undermine that unity.

Yet the sense of unity is explicitly a "hierarchal unity." Indeed, Rehnquist completed his statement in *Goldman* that uniforms eliminate distinctions with an important qualification: "except for those of rank." Thus, it is not actually uniformity that is at stake; it is the hierarchy of distinctions within the military that may be obscured by other differences.

The military uniform also promotes another type of hierarchy: the distinction between those who wear the uniform and those who do not. A general federal criminal statute prohibits wearing the uniform of the armed forces "without authority" and allows imprisonment of six months for doing so.[49] A different statute specifically governing the military outlines when a person not on active duty may wear a specific uniform, such as permitting a retired *officer* of the Army, Navy, Air Force, or Marine Corps to wear the uniform of his retired grade.[50] Another permitted circumstance within that statute is for an actor "portraying a member of the Army, Navy, Air Force, or Marine Corps," in a "theatrical or motion-picture production" with the caveat that "the portrayal does not tend to discredit that armed force." Although this provision remains in the United States Code, the U.S. Supreme Court declared a portion of it unconstitutional in *Schacht v. United States*.[51]

Schacht arose from a skit performed outside an Armed Forces Induction Center during the Vietnam war. As part of that skit, Schacht, dressed in an army uniform, used a water pistol filled with red liquid to shoot a person costumed in Viet Cong apparel. When the victim fell down, Schacht would exclaim that the victim was a pregnant woman.

The Supreme Court unanimously reversed the Fifth Circuit's affirmance of Schacht's conviction for violating the general criminal law of wearing a uniform without authority. However, the Supreme Court had no question that the criminal law was constitutional. Without analysis, the Court simply cited its precedent for expressive conduct, *United States v. O'Brien*.[52] *O'Brien*, decided two years earlier and also involving a Vietnam War protest – the burning of a draft card – had set out a standard for expressive conduct that certainly could support a conclusion that the criminalization of wearing military uniforms was unconstitutional.

However, the Court accepted Schacht's argument that he was sheltered by the "theatrical provision" exception in the statute regulating persons not on active duty. One issue was that of statutory interpretation: whether the anti-war skit on a public street was within the definition of a "theatrical production." The Court rejected arguments that such productions must be staged and professional, melding artistic and political speech in its reasoning.[53] The other issue was one of constitutionality: whether the limitation that "the portrayal does not tend to discredit that armed force" survives a First Amendment analysis. The Court's opinion does not label the caveat "viewpoint discrimination," but the caveat is a classic illustration of a law criminalizing speech based on viewpoint and thus deserving the strictest of scrutiny. What the Court does say is that a provision that "leaves Americans free to praise the war in Vietnam but can send persons like Schacht to prison for opposing it, cannot survive in a country which has the First Amendment."[54]

In 2012 in *United States v. Alvarez*, the Court found that the so-called Stolen Valor Act, criminalizing false claims about receiving military medals, could not survive First Amendment scrutiny.[55] The opinion did not reach the companion statutory provision criminalizing the wearing of military medals without authorization. The important distinction between the two provisions, however, was not between "stating" and "wearing," but between the absence of an element of fraud in the Stolen Valor Act and the important requirement of "anything of value" in the wearing prohibition.[56] As the Court stated in *Alvarez*, the "American people do not need the assistance of a government prosecution" to express high regard for military awards; the truth "needs neither handcuffs nor a badge for its vindication."[57]

It may be that the unauthorized wearing of a uniform or medal always expresses a viewpoint, for example, the idea that there should be no distinctions by uniform in a democracy or that medals for military performance are anti-democratic. In the paramilitary context of law enforcement, the wearing of police uniforms by unauthorized persons raises the specter of criminal disguise. However, even when there is not a risk of treachery, the unauthorized use of police uniforms may be sanctioned without a First Amendment violation. Appearing before the Court as the anonymous John Roe, a San Diego police officer challenged the termination of his employment for violating department policies including conduct unbecoming an officer, outside employment, and immoral conduct.[58] Roe sold sexually explicit videos of himself, partially masked and dressed in a police uniform, although not identifiable as the San Diego police uniform. The videos were apparently geared toward a gay male audience; in one video custom-made upon request by an undercover officer, Roe appeared in "police uniform, issuing a traffic citation but then revoking it after undoing the uniform and masturbating." In its per curiam opinion in *City of San Diego v. Roe*, the U.S. Supreme Court announced it had "no difficulty" concluding that Roe's expression, "designed to exploit his employer's image," was not a matter of public concern and thus not susceptible to First Amendment protection.[59]

A concern over the sexuality of a person wearing a paramilitary uniform also preoccupied the Court in *Boy Scouts of America v. Dale*, decided in 2000.[60] The Court relied on the First Amendment right of the private organization to exclude an assistant scoutmaster because of his sexual orientation, notwithstanding a state non-discrimination law. Relying on the right of an organization to control its message, Justice Rehnquist writing for the majority focused on the sexual identity of James Dale: the "presence of an avowed homosexual and gay rights activist in an assistant scoutmaster's uniform sends a distinctly different message from the presence of a heterosexual assistant scoutmaster who is on record as disagreeing with Boy Scouts policy." For Justice Stevens, dissenting, this transformed Dale's sexuality into a "symbol of inferiority." Stevens disapprovingly quoted from the Boy Scout's counsel at oral argument who stated that when Dale revealed his sexuality, he "put a banner around his neck" and he "can't take that banner off."[61]

The paramilitary uniform, whether private or public, seems to be a message that subordinates the wearer to that which is worn, notwithstanding anti-discrimination or constitutional concerns. The U.S. Supreme Court has declared that a police department, like the military, is entitled to great deference in its grooming policies given its interests of discipline, uniformity, and esprit-de-corps. In *Kelley v. Johnson*, decided in 1976, the Court rejected a challenge to the hair policies of the Suffolk County, New York, police department. The policies prohibited hair from touching the ears or the collar, sideburns from extending below the lowest part of the exterior ear opening, moustaches from extending over the top of the upper lip or beyond the corners of the mouth, and all beards and goatees, except for medical reasons. The policy also prohibited wigs with an exception for cosmetic reasons to cover baldness or disfigurement. The county patrolmen's benevolent association challenged the policies on the basis of the liberty component of the Due Process Clause. Justice Rehnquist, writing for the Court, applied the most deferential version of scrutiny, placing a burden on the challengers to demonstrate the absence of rational connection between the regulation and government interests. Justice Brennan, dissenting, joined by Marshall, reasoned that the liberty interest encompasses the right to dress to one's own taste, as consonant with the "values of privacy, self-identity, autonomy, and personal integrity" the Constitution was designed to protect. The Court assumed that such a right might exist, but found it inapposite in the context of government employment, citing several First Amendment cases and concluding "there is surely even more room for restrictive regulations of state employees where the claim implicates only the more general contours of the substantive liberty interest protected by the Fourteenth Amendment."[62]

Governmental interests in uniformity extend beyond the military or paramilitary, and the Second Circuit in *Zalewska v. County of Sullivan* upheld such interests in a constitutional challenge to a dress code covering county employees driving "Meals on Wheels" vans.[63] Grazyna Zalewska, employed as such a driver for several years, objected when the county instituted a uniform policy mandating pants. Ms. Zalewska sought to wear a skirt because it was her lifelong practice as a matter of familial and cultural custom. Writing in 2003, the court found her skirt preference did not rise to the level of expressive conduct under the First Amendment's asymmetrical burdens. Although the employer had an interest in the message pants conveyed, a skirt did not convey any particularized message, contrasted, according to the court, to the "nun's habit and the judge's robes."

The court also found that assuming a liberty interest in dress existed, it survived rational basis scrutiny under a due process analysis, and that the gender-neutral pants-only policy survived rational basis scrutiny under an equal protection analysis. The county's articulated interests – promoting esprit-de-corps among van drivers, encouraging respect by clients, professionalism, a positive image for the county, and safety – were not so irrationally related to the dress code as to be unconstitutional. The court was most approving of the safety rationale, focusing on the job duties in relation to wearing a skirt, although not referencing Zalewska's previous skirted performance. The court was much less approving of professionalism and respect: "Were it our decision to make, we would perhaps not embrace the notion that skirts are inherently unprofessional or that wearing them does not encourage customer respect or enhance the service's public image." But the county's sartorial decisions were entitled to great deference.

Judicial deference to government means that government employers, like other employers, are free to mandate that employees dress uniformly, in the interests of esprit-de-corps, branding, and professionalism, as well as safety. Not all government employees wear uniforms, of course, yet these notions, as well as hierarchy, pervade government employment. They extend to the paradigmatic government venues of classrooms and courtrooms.

III. THE CULT OF THE ROBE?

Professional dress in classrooms and courtrooms shares the common ancestry of academic and legal robes, both of which are related to the dress of religious clerics. By the Tudor era, various regulations attended to the specific requirements of various ceremonial robes, while more generally graduate students and barristers were essentially equated with gentlemen and allowed to dress accordingly.[64] Fashions changed: black replaced more colorful garments during the mourning for monarchs; wigs substituted for hoods as head coverings.[65] Yet the main purposes are hierarchical: a person's individuality is subsumed by a costume that symbolized respect for the profession and the dignity of it.

Academic Dress

While teachers no longer wear robes except for special occasions such as graduation ceremonies, the necktie might be considered a modern vestige of the robe, or at least the ruff that often encircled the neck of a robe. In considering whether or not a dress code that mandates a tie can constitutionally be applied to public school teachers, courts have often acknowledged the government's interests in promoting respect, professionalism, a semblance of uniformity, and even dignity. Courts have differed, however, regarding the constitutionality of the means of achieving these interests. Such differences appear whether the challenge is based upon free expression or liberty or other constitutional arguments. They implicate not only individual constitutional rights but also local control of school boards and the judicial role. Ruling on a teacher's challenge to a dismissal based upon attire and facial hair, the future Justice Stevens, then a Seventh Circuit judge, wrote, "just as the individual has an interest in a choice among different styles of appearance and behavior, and a democratic society has an interest in fostering diverse choices, so also does society have a legitimate interest in placing limits on the exercise of that choice," and the federal courts should be hesitant to substitute their own judgment for that of the school board "on a question of manners."[66]

Extensive litigation beginning in the mid-1970s that challenged the mandatory (for male teachers) necktie policy of the Board of Education of East Hartford, Connecticut, is illustrative.[67] The teacher objected to the necktie policy not only on the basis of his personal autonomy, but he also argued that the absence of a necktie actually enhanced his ability to teach by allowing him a "closer rapport" with his students. The district judge dismissed the constitutional challenge to the policy, noting that a teacher's positive example in dress and grooming "enlarges the importance of the task of teaching, presents an image of dignity and encourages respect for authority." The district judge proclaimed that such school policies are necessary to forestall the possibility of teachers "wearing 'Bermuda shorts' or similarly inappropriate forms of flamboyant dress." A panel of the Second Circuit reversed the district judge, finding that the school board's asserted interests of establishing a professional image for teachers and maintaining respect within the classroom were not served by the tie requirement. The panel opinion waxed on the expressive

nature of attire – the robe of "priest and judge alike" has been a mark of authority –
and favored the (American) liberty interest in dress over the unfortunate (Chinese
and Russian) history of "oppression accomplished by body-tegument conformity."
In another reversal, the en banc Second Circuit credited the board's interest in
"promoting respect for authority and traditional values, as well as discipline in the
classroom, by requiring teachers to dress in a professional manner," and further
applauded the school board's good faith in distinguishing between a "traditional
English class" during which the teacher was required to wear a tie, and the "'alternative' class in filmmaking," when he was not. During an era when school busing
cases dominated other circuits, the Second Circuit en banc stated that "it is not the
federal courts, but local democratic processes, that are primarily responsible for the
many routine decisions that are made in public school systems." Judicial restraint
was especially appropriate because the teacher's "interest in his neckwear" did not
"weigh very heavily on the constitutional scales"; he could "remove his tie as soon
as the school day ends."[68]

Compared to mandatory tie requirements, regulations of teachers' hairstyles have
the potential to be more burdensome: the moment it takes to remove a necktie after
work is obviously not sufficient to re-grow a beard. Additionally, courts have discussed the relationship between beards (and other hair) and race, although just as in
the Title VII cases involving black women's hair, the constitutional cases involving
black male teachers and hair display a marked doctrinal incoherency. For example, one court rejected any possibility that "the wearing of a mustache had been so
appropriated as cultural symbol by members of the Negro race as to make its suppression either an automatic badge of racial prejudice or a necessary abridgement
of First Amendment rights."[69] On the other hand, a different court found that the
teacher's goatee was "worn as 'an appropriate expression of his heritage, culture and
racial pride as a black man.'"[70]

Yet the most important distinction in the cases regarding teachers' attire and hair
is the level of the school at issue. Considering its hair regulation jurisprudence in
1982, the Fifth Circuit stated that there is a "bright line" between public colleges
and public secondary or elementary schools. The asserted needs for professionalism,
respect, and discipline are simply not sufficient at the college level. Interestingly,
however, the court rejected an argument that the line should be between adults
and adolescents: requiring all school employees, even bus drivers, to adhere to the
dress code for students served the interests of the school in discipline and authority,
as well as uniformity.[71] While many of the challenges to schools occurred during
the "counter culture" era, provoking judicial hostility or sympathy, it is nevertheless
remarkable that judges cite cases involving students and teachers interchangeably.
While the rhetoric is that of respect, hierarchy, and professionalism, it is as if the

teachers' status as adult employees and the students' status as minors legally compelled to attend school are commensurate.

For students, their entry into adulthood might be said to be at high school graduation, a ceremony during which they traditionally wear robe-like attire. As one federal judge described it, the cap and gown is the "universal symbol of achievement and honor in the academic world." The judge used this universality to defeat the First Amendment claim of a high school senior who wanted to wear his traditional Lakota clothing at graduation in *Bear v. Fleming*, decided in 2010. The judge found that the student's expressive activity must yield to the school board's interests, including an interest in "demonstrating the unity of the class and celebrating academic achievement." The judge noted that "not all of the audience members will be Lakota or will understand the significance of Mr. Dreaming Bear's traditional Lakota clothing," repeating that in contrast, the cap and gown "is a universally recognized symbol." But as the court's opinion also noted, the graduating class consisted of ten seniors, nine of whom were Lakota. Tellingly, the judge reasoned that the "graduation proceedings celebrate not only the students' achievements, but also the school's achievement as an institution of learning and the teachers' and administrators' achievements as educators."[72]

Traditional Court Dress

When the judge presided over the hearing on Dreaming Bear's request for preliminary relief, presumably he was attired in the usual manner for modern federal judges, wearing a black judicial robe over his clothes but not a judicial wig or head covering. While there is no specific dress mandate for federal judges, some states have rules of court that require a judge in open court to wear a judicial robe, or more specifically a "suitable black judicial robe," or even more specifically a black robe that "must extend in front and back from the collar and shoulders to below the knees" with "sleeves to the wrists."[73]

The early American controversies regarding how similar the dress of Article III judges would be to their British counterparts implicated style and nation building, but also the symbolism of democracy and constitutionalism. The eventual compromise abandoned the British fashion for various types of court wigs, but adopted British gowns that gradually eschewed scarlet and silk evolving to the stereotypical robe of black polyester.[74]

Even as customs settled, however, disagreements over judicial attire remained. Writing in 1945 while he was a respected Second Circuit judge, the legal realist Jerome Frank argued to jettison the robe entirely.[75] Frank's essay, "The Cult of the Robe," contended that the "pretense that judicial reactions are uniform manifests itself in the demand that judges wear uniforms." Moreover, Frank argued that the "judge's vestments are historically connected with the desire to thwart democracy by means of the courts." He criticized the "atavistic robe" as analogous to an "esoteric judicial vocabulary" that conflicted with the "fundamental democratic principle" disfavoring secrecy. In calling for abandonment of robe-ism, Frank invoked the ordinary citizen who would be unused to courthouse ways and disquieted by the "strange garb of the judge."[76]

Frank's view has not prevailed, perhaps in part because the robe has become the metonym for the judge in contemporary popular culture as many a political cartoon illustrates. An argument in favor of this metonymic relationship is that robes not only obscure individualism, but that they foster the judicial independence so important to democratic constitutionalism. In this way, the judicial uniform in the United States – one that does not generally communicate rank – conveys an institutional message that each judge "belongs to the judiciary."[77]

This metonymic relationship, however, can raise constitutional issues. For many state court judges who are elected, the question of whether wearing a robe can be a feature of their campaign literature is a vexed one, implicating their First Amendment rights. In general, the concern articulated in ethics opinions from various state committees is the misleading potential of a judicially garbed candidate, but the effect is to maintain a hierarchy of judges. For example, in Nevada, the committee on judicial ethics and campaign practices has opined that a person who has served as an "alternate municipal judge" or as an "unpaid part-time judge" or as a "full-time judicial master" may not wear a judicial robe in campaign literature; however, a person who is a "continuing part-time judge" may wear a judicial robe in campaign literature.[78] Prohibitions on being portrayed wearing robes in judicial elections may be susceptible to the same sort of First Amendment challenge as a prohibition of announcing views on disputed legal issues in judicial elections, a prohibition declared unconstitutional by the U.S. Supreme Court in *Republican Party of Minnesota v. White*.[79]

While the election context raises the most obvious clash between the ethical and constitutional considerations of judges donning robes, even a sitting judge may encounter such a conflict. In *Jenevein v. Willing*, the Fifth Circuit partially expunged the censure of a Texas judge by the state's commission on judicial ethics "to the extent that it reached beyond" the judge's "use of the courtroom and his robe to send his message."[80] As part of contentious litigation in 2003 that spawned allegations of bribes, favors, and sexual misconduct, Judge Jenevein held a press conference in the courtroom – and importantly, wore his judicial robe – to announce his withdrawal from the case and his institution of grievance proceedings against the attorney who had made the allegations. The attorney, however, filed a grievance against Judge Jenevein for holding the press conference, and the state commission issued a censure against the judge, without addressing the First Amendment defenses the judge had raised. Judge Jenevein thereafter brought an action in federal court challenging the constitutionality of the censure. The Fifth Circuit held that while the judge was indeed an employee, the First Amendment doctrine governing government employee speech emphasizing the divide between matters of public and private concern was inapposite.[81] Instead, the court applied strict scrutiny. Considering whether judicial impartiality was a compelling governmental interest, the court held that it could not be gainsaid that the "state's interest in achieving a courtroom that at least on entry of its robed judge becomes a neutral and disinterested temple" was compelling. The state's compelling interest extended to the "judicial use of the robe, which symbolically sets aside the judge's individuality and passions." On the issue of whether the censure was narrowly tailored, the court had more difficulty separating the content of the judicial statements from their environment. The court found the judge's use of the "trappings of his judicial office to boost his message," particularly "stepping out from behind the bench, while wearing his judicial robe, to address the cameras," could constitutionally support a censure. In a limited victory for the state judge, however, the court ruled that the content of the statements could not be constitutionally censured. The Fifth Circuit emphasized that the judge was publicly addressing abuse of process, that the communication was between the judge and "his constituents," and it was on a matter of "judicial administration" rather than the merits of a case.[82]

Judges have become more administrative and less judicial, at least according to Justice Rehnquist in his own "The Cult of the Robe" essay published in 1976.[83] While Rehnquist did not even allude to matters of habiliment, he stressed the less attractive aspects of uniformity. Perhaps not coincidentally, after Rehnquist assumed the status of Chief Justice of the United States, he adorned his robe with gold stripes, reportedly inspired by "a production of Gilbert and Sullivan's *Iolanthe*, in which the lord chancellor wore a similar robe."[84] Justice Ginsburg described the stripes as resembling those "of a master sergeant more than those of a British Lord," explaining that even though he was "a man not given to sartorial splendor," he said he "did not wish to be upstaged by the women." Ginsburg added that Justice O'Connor, the first woman Supreme Court Justice, "has several attractive neck pieces, collars from British gowns, and a frilly French foulard," while Ginsburg herself wears "British and French lace foulards too, and sometimes one of French Canadian design."[85]

For female attorneys in the United States, the choices of courtroom attire are more complicated than lace collars. The early American adoption, albeit partial, of British judicial attire did not extend to British customs regarding advocates. Until recently, the "court dress" in Great Britain featuring wigs and robes applied to both jurists and barristers, but not to solicitors, even when solicitor-advocates appeared in court. In late 2011 the UK Supreme Court, established only a few years earlier, noted that its justices did not "wear legal dress themselves and have decided not to impose this obligation on advocates appearing before them." The Court directed that "provided that all the advocates in any particular case agree, they may communicate to the Registrar their wish to dispense with part or all of court dress," the Court would "normally agree" to the advocates' preference with regard to legal dress.[86] Advocates' preferences, however, might well be to don the traditional garb that has long symbolized status, as well as its gradations. It is not mere coincidence that barristers who have been appointed to the rank of Queen's Counsel are called "silks" or that solicitors have argued that they be entitled to wear wigs.[87] Moreover, it might not be mere coincidence that at the very time the British legal profession is being diversified, the symbols of its status are being abandoned.

While rationales for maintaining formal court dress include hierarchy, as well as tradition, status quo, and "branding," another benefit is perceived gender equality.[88] A somewhat curmudgeonly call for the adoption of robed (if not wigged) attorneys in the United States, pointed to problems with women's apparel:

> Courtroom decorum is adversely affected as more and more women appear at bar in a tremendous variety of color and design – pants, dresses, suits, blouses (with and without neckties). The necessary respect of the courtroom is absent when lawyers are higgledy-piggledy in attire. This is not to say that the woman who appears in gaucho pants is intentionally flouting the court's decorum, but rather that no discernible tradition or norm has developed in woman's dress in the court room. But were they robed, all lawyers would be dressed equally and have a great and conscious feeling of what they were about. Lawyers would immediately be inconspicuous and their causes would be foremost – which is as it should be.[89]

In the absence of standardized court dress, the professional attire of women attorneys in the United States has been subject to gendered and slovenly interpretations. Just as the wig and robe were once construed as exclusively male apparel, pants can be construed as exclusively male and thus inappropriate for women attorneys as courtroom attire.

As late as 1991, the New York City bar ethics committee was asked whether or not female lawyers could "wear appropriately tailored pant suits or other pant-based outfits in a court appearance." The committee stated that it had been told "judges in this state have remarked negatively in open court on the attire of women lawyers appearing before them," and noted individual judges have "some degree of latitude to regulate the conduct of lawyers in their courtrooms." Nevertheless, the committee stated that while the rules of dress are generally a matter of custom, pants could certainly qualify as respectful and dignified.[90] And as late as 1994, federal district courts in Oklahoma specifically provided by local rule that female attorneys must wear dresses or suits (with skirts).[91] The subject of dress codes, whether explicit or implicit, for women attorneys was included in the many "gender bias in the courts" reports that began in the state courts in the 1980s. By the time of the final report of the federal Ninth Circuit's task force published in 1994, the survey of 232 federal judges revealed only a small percentage of both male and female judges stating that they imposed a "no pantsuit" rule, although a similarly small percentage of judges (all male) stated they preferred not to have female counsel appearing when visibly pregnant.[92] Yet while the gender bias task forces were instituted as a strategy to address gender inequality in the courts among advocates, litigants, and society, they also demonstrate the inadequacy of legal remedies. As the New York City ethics committee noted in its pantsuit opinion, "equality of attire in the courtroom" had a constitutional dimension, but as such it was beyond the committee's "jurisdiction."[93]

The constitutional issues regarding attorney dress can be difficult to litigate. For the most part, attorneys' "dress for success" means elevating their clients' interests above their own, especially in a courtroom context in which pleasing the judge (and jury) is important. In the absence of standardized dress codes, the general advice to women is to err on the side of conservatism, including skirts.[94] Yet there have been a few cases in which the attorney-judge relationship seemed to have devolved into a contempt proceeding, although even then the constitutional issues can be obscured. For example, when Patricia DeCarlo, a legal services attorney in Camden, New Jersey, wore slacks (gray wool), a sweater (gray), and a shirt (green) during a court appearance in January 1975, she was eventually held in contempt by the trial judge. She appealed the contempt order, arguing in part that it constituted "unconstitutional discrimination against female attorneys." The appellate court did not reach the constitutional issue, essentially holding that as a matter of law DeCarlo's dress was suitable. The opinion noted that she was attired at oral argument in the appellate court in the same clothes she wore when the trial judge held her in contempt – a strategy that essentially invoked the judges' common sense and was more successful for Patricia DeCarlo's slacks than for Jeffrey Ross's shorts.[95] Moreover, the trial judge's objection to DeCarlo's apparel eventually focused not on her pants, but on her sweater, or perhaps on her "open-collared blouse." For the appellate court, the lack of "standards or traditions for female attorneys" worked in DeCarlo's favor, especially as contrasted to the established tradition of neckties for men.[96]

Rejecting a gender discrimination challenge to the requirement of a necktie (and jacket) for male attorneys, the Supreme Court of Alaska reasoned that court orders requiring "appropriate conservative business dress" applied equally to men and women: "Though women need not be required to wear a coat and tie, they are required to wear conservative business attire. Such a dress code would not discriminate since the general standard is the same." The court likewise rejected the argument of attorney Martin Friedman that the tie requirement impaired his ability to represent his client zealously, by interfering with his ability to connect with jurors.[97] All ties, however, are not equal. An appellate court in New Mexico upheld a trial judge's interpretation of a local rule requiring male attorneys to wear "ties" as excluding a bandanna tied above the collar. The attorney, Tom Cherryhomes, had "referred to a book on nineteenth century western wear and a dictionary" to argue that his neckwear satisfied the tie requirement. The judge rejected the relevance of history, ordered Cherryhomes to wear a conventional tie, and then held him in contempt when he did not. On appeal, the court circumvented the attorney's First Amendment argument, reasoning that the constitutional challenge was subsumed into the finding of contempt. Cherryhomes should have complied with the order and then challenged its constitutionality. Yet the appellate court implied that such a challenge would not have been successful: it declared that the trial judge's interpretation of the local rule was "reasonable."[98]

Cherryhomes, Friedman, DeCarlo, and other attorneys who have attempted to raise constitutional challenges to orders of attire issued by judges have faced the "cult of the robe" that accords authority to the judiciary, even if it may be mistaken. While the constitutional arguments of Cherryhomes, Friedman, and DeCarlo – at least as contained in the appellate opinions – lack constitutional sophistication, each by implication argued for a standard that would require disruption of the courtroom proceedings.[99] This standard would require something more egregious than simply a lack of dignity, respect, and professionalism. For persons who are not dressing professionally, the ban on dressing disruptively, whether in courtrooms, schoolrooms, or in public is often at issue.

5

Dressing Disruptively

The notion that attire is capable of disruption presupposes not only a normative style of dress but also a normative community that is capable of being disturbed merely by a person's apparel or grooming. As a general matter, perhaps it is difficult to believe that what a person is wearing, other than a weapon, could have that much power. More specifically, it might be difficult to believe that armbands, hats, purses, T-shirts, jackets, saggy pants, or even shackles and masks could be so potent. However, as these examples illustrate, it is less the article of clothing itself than what it symbolizes: a threat to a presumptively democratic status quo.

While the focus is usually on the disruptive agent, the threatened normative order merits closer examination. The commonly accepted candidates, often echoed as the government's interests in litigation regarding the constitutionality of regulating dress or grooming, include school discipline, courtroom decorum and fairness, or even the social fabric. But these formulations are both too narrow and too general. Site-specific constitutional doctrine can obscure the broader issues of hierarchy, democracy, or sexuality that are always at stake. General abstractions seeking to preserve order in schools, courtrooms, or society easily slip into deference to governmental officials and risk a type of fascistic order antithetical to democracy and democratic constitutionalism. The doctrine of disruption, most closely associated with schools, exemplifies these problems.

I. SCHOOL DISCIPLINE AND THE RIGHTS OF OTHERS

The watershed case of *Tinker v. Des Moines Independent Community School District* involved the wearing of black armbands by school students in protest of the Vietnam War.[1] Decided by the United States Supreme Court in 1969, *Tinker* established the substantial and material disruption standard for evaluating school speech. While the Court actually uses the word "interfere" more often than "disrupt," and uses the terms synonymously, what has become known as the *Tinker* disruption standard requires that in order to curtail student speech, school authorities must show that the student speech would materially and substantially interfere with appropriate school discipline. The majority opinion, authored by Justice Fortas, opined that "state-operated schools may not be enclaves of totalitarianism," and favored free speech, the marketplace of ideas, and implicitly, democracy. Justice Black peppered his biting dissent with statements such as "students all over the land are already running loose" and "some of the country's greatest problems are crimes committed by the youth, too many of school age," ultimately objecting to a "new revolutionary era of permissiveness in this country fostered by the judiciary."

While it may seem as if the substantial disruption standard was "created out of whole cloth," *Tinker* itself cited earlier student protest attire cases decided by the Fifth Circuit, as legal scholar Kristi Bowman has noted.[2] These cases involved the suspension of African American students for wearing voting rights buttons with the acronym SNCC (Student Nonviolent Coordinating Committee) at Mississippi schools during a period of intense civil rights unrest and violence.[3] As Bowman argued, the Fifth Circuit probably borrowed its substantial disruption test from non-school civil rights cases that stressed the nonviolent nature of the protests, and then other courts borrowed the standard in school speech cases before the Court decided *Tinker*. Bowman also demonstrated how the various drafts by Justice Fortas returned again and again to the Fifth Circuit cases in developing the *Tinker* standard, thus showing that anti-racism activism is the "legal and social foundation upon which *Tinker* is built."[4]

Perhaps ironically, one of the most contentious types of student attire in post-*Tinker* cases involves clothes featuring the Confederate flag, usually a T-shirt, but including belt buckles and purses. The Confederate flag cases invoke the substantial disruption standard but also encompass two other matters briefly raised in the *Tinker* opinion. First, the Court in *Tinker* noted that the black armbands did not implicate the "rights of other students to be secure and to be let alone," thus suggesting this should be a factor. Second, the Court in *Tinker* found it "relevant" that the school did not prohibit the wearing of all symbols of political or controversial significance, and had allowed the wearing of "buttons relating to national political campaigns," and even "the Iron Cross, traditionally a symbol of Nazism," thus raising the specter of viewpoint discrimination.

In three recent cases decided by three different circuit courts of appeals applying the by-then forty-year-old *Tinker* standard, the courts upheld bans on student Confederate flag clothing.[5] In each case, the appellate court gave great weight to incidents of racial divisiveness in the school district to support the constitutionality of the exclusion of Confederate flag symbols. In each case, the appellate court rejected the argument that the school officials must demonstrate a close link between past incidents and the Confederate flag. Instead, each appellate court found that *Tinker* allowed schools to reasonably forecast the possibility of a disruption and take steps to prevent it, including banning the Confederate flag. Each court also rejected, at least implicitly, any arguments that the Confederate flag ban constituted viewpoint discrimination or that the Confederate flag did not necessarily symbolize racial discrimination. For example, in *A.M. v. Cash*, decided by the Fifth Circuit in 2009, the high school students who had carried purses "bearing large images of the Confederate battle flag," argued that they had seen other objectionable dress at the school: Mexican flag T-shirts, rainbow belts, Malcolm X T-shirts, and a "male student who wears female makeup and clothing."[6] The court in *Cash* rejected this argument under a rational basis equal protection analysis, but the Sixth Circuit in *DeFoe v. Spiva* later confronted a similar argument more squarely within the First Amendment.[7] The court in *DeFoe* rejected a viewpoint discrimination argument, deciding that Malcolm X T-shirts were indeed banned under the school district's dress code that prohibited clothing and accessories from displaying "racial or ethnic slurs/symbols." The court found it less clear whether the Tennessee school district would prohibit the Mexican flag, but added that there was not any indication that it had ever been linked to disruption.

As for the contested symbolism of the Confederate flag, the students usually argued that they did not wear the symbol because of its racial meanings but because – as one of the purse-toting students explained – it is a "venerated symbol of my ancestry, a symbol of my Christian religious faith, and a symbol of the South, a symbol of American history and a political symbol, to me, of limited government and resistance to unconstitutional authority."[8] But while courts have recognized that the Confederate flag may have some meanings unconnected to racism, they have noted that the flag also has racist meanings, and indeed, the very contest over those meanings can be disruptive.[9]

Yet there is some disagreement regarding whether the *Tinker* disruptive standard should be applicable. Concurring in *DeFoe*, Judge Rogers argued that expressions of racial hostility can be controlled by schools even if "students in the attacked racial group happen to be mature, good-natured, and slow to react."[10] Judge Rogers relied upon *Morse v. Frederick*, in which the U.S. Supreme Court upheld the discipline of a student for displaying a banner that read "BongHits4Jesus" because it could be read to condone drug use.[11] Rogers argued that the interest in reducing racial tension was just as important as deterring drug use. Interestingly, another judge of the three-judge panel joined Judge Rogers's concurrence, although the panel's "official" opinion remained the one that hewed much more closely to the established *Tinker* disruption standard, perhaps guaranteeing that the U.S. Supreme Court would decline review.

Courts have also considered anti-gay clothing in schools under the *Tinker* disruption standard, with the constitutional challenge to the dress code more generally successful. Protracted litigation arising in the Indian Prairie School District is illustrative.[12] In 2006, the district's Neuqua Valley High School participated as one of thousands of schools across the United States in a "Day of Silence," a nationwide program organized by Gay, Lesbian and Straight Education Network (GLSEN) to call attention to violence against sexual minority youth. As part of the event, supporters wore T-shirts with the slogan "Be Who You Are." As a counterevent to Day of Silence, the Alliance Defense Fund had organized "Day of Truth," which also included T-shirts with slogans, including "The Truth Cannot Be Silenced." One high school student made her own T-shirt, with the slogans "My Day of Silence, Straight Alliance" on the front and "Be Happy, Not Gay" on the back. After a student complaint, school officials deemed the "Be Happy, Not Gay" message a violation of the student appearance code prohibiting wearing "garments or jewelry with messages, graphics or symbols ... which are derogatory, inflammatory, sexual, or discriminatory." The more general misconduct code disapproved of images and derogatory comments that referred to "race, ethnicity, religion, gender, sexual orientation, or disability." After discussion, the words "Not Gay" were inked-out on the student's shirt. However, as the 2007 Day of Silence and Day of Truth events approached, two students sought a preliminary injunction to allow the phrase "Be Happy, Not Gay," to be worn on T-shirts or otherwise. School officials conceded that students could wear Day of Silence messages: official Alliance Defense Fund clothing with its emphasis on truth, the "My Day of Silence, Straight Alliance" message on the previous year's T-shirt, as well as "Be Happy, Be Straight." However, school officials declared that negative references to being gay would not be permitted.

In denying the injunction, the district judge found that the students had only a slight chance of prevailing on their First Amendment claim, discussing the "uncontested fact that derogatory statements about being gay have a tendency to harm gay youth," the *Tinker* "rights of others" standard, and the school officials' allowance of student protest with a variety of other messages on their clothes. In *Indian Prairie I*, a year later, the Seventh Circuit reversed, in an opinion by the controversial Judge Richard Posner. The Seventh Circuit ruled that a preliminary injunction against the school should issue before the imminent Day of Silence/Day of Truth events, limited to allowing students to wear the phrase "Be Happy, Not Gay." In a nutshell, Posner concluded that "Be Happy, Not Gay" was only "tepidly negative; 'derogatory' and 'demeaning' seems too strong a characterization." In this sense, Posner seemed to be concluding that he would not have made the same judgment that the school officials did, but this is far from constitutional analysis. Instead, Posner's opinion is full of his idiosyncratic "common sense" or what some might call slovenly interpretations, much like his book, *Sex and Reason*, in which among other things, he purports to explain why lesbians are bad dressers and gay men are fashionable dressers.[13] In this opinion, he analogized sexuality to colas: "If you say 'drink Pepsi' you may be showing your preference for Pepsi over Coke, but you are not necessarily deriding Coke. It would be odd to call 'Be Happy, Drink Pepsi' a derogatory comment about Coke." But then he quickly dismisses his own analogy: "Given kids' sensitivity about their sexual orientation and their insensitivity about their preferences in soft drinks, the Pepsi–Coke analogy misses the mark. The plaintiff, like the students who participate in the 'Day of Truth,' is expressing disapproval of homosexuality, as everyone knows. No one bothers to talk up heterosexuality who isn't interested in denigrating homosexuality."

Concurring in the judgment, Judge Rovner stated that she "scarcely know[s] where to begin with the Pepsi/Coke analogy," noting that it not only misses the mark as Posner's opinion admits, but it does so "by a rather wide margin." Rovner criticized Posner's opinion as convoluted, arguing that this is a "simple case" that calls for a straightforward application of *Tinker*. However, for Judge Rovner, *Tinker* seemed to include no "rights of others" analysis. Although she stated that the T-shirt slogan was undoubtedly disparaging, she concluded it did not satisfy *Tinker*'s substantial disruption standard.

Yet the analysis in both opinions regarding the substantial disruption standard is disappointing, especially when compared to the Confederate flag cases. Posner's opinion cites some of the Confederate flag attire cases as illustrating the "rare case" in which schools can prove that substantial disruption will ensue rather than providing the basis for a reasonable forecast. Further, Posner accepted a certain level of disruption as tolerable: "As one would expect in a school the size of Neuqua Valley High School, there have been incidents of harassment of homosexual students." Moreover, the substantial disruption standard seems to require shocking violence. Concurring, Judge Rovner distinguished the environment at Neuqua Valley High from the situation in *Nabozny v. Podlesny*, a peer sexual orientation harassment case decided by the Seventh Circuit ten years earlier, that had featured a mock-rape and repeated beatings of a sexual minority student.[14] Disagreeing with Posner's inartful invocation of *Nabozny*, she nevertheless again stressed causation: this level of violence would not likely occur "as a result" of the T-shirt. Finally, nowhere in the opinions is there any speculation of the number of sexual minority students at the high school. This is different from cases upholding the banning of Confederate flag apparel, in which circuit courts found it relevant to note that the number of African American students enrolled in the school was quite small: less than sixty out of 2,300 students in one case and fifteen to twenty students out of 1,100 in another case.[15] Certainly the number of sexual minority students may not have been placed in evidence by the school, and indeed the school may not have known it – the very point of GLSEN's "Day of Silence."[16] Yet given Posner's wide-ranging speculations on a host of other matters, it might have been more relevant, or at least as relevant, as soft drink brands.

The case returned to the Seventh Circuit three years later, after the district judge granted summary judgment for the students and awarded them nominal damages of $25. Perhaps not surprisingly, Posner's opinion in *Indian Prairie II* is, like its predecessor, less than a model of clarity, although he seemed to blame the doctrine, stating that *Tinker*'s substantial disruption test had not proved "a model of clarity in its application." And again, a "rights of others" analysis under *Tinker* is completely lacking, and indeed subverted. Writing for the unanimous panel, Posner rejected the school's argument that "banning 'Be Happy, Not Gay' was just a matter of protecting the 'rights' of the students against whom derogatory comments are directed." Tellingly, Posner placed quotation marks around "rights" in this passage, as he did throughout the opinion. He countered that "people in our society do not have a legal right to prevent criticism of their beliefs or even their way of life," characterizing sexual orientation in high school as a lifestyle. In support of his proposition, he cited cases that did involve larger society but did not occur in schools. He then continued, completely eliding the fact that there were sexual minority students at the school and making the issue the political debate on same-sex marriage: "Although tolerance of homosexuality has grown, gay marriage remains highly controversial. Today's high school students may soon find themselves, as voters, asked to vote on whether to approve gay marriage, or to vote for candidates who approve of it, or ones who disapprove."[17]

Despite its doctrinal and logical incoherency, Posner's view has become the precedential one, in part because of his expansive interpretation of Article III judicial power. In *Indian Prairie II*, Posner rejected the school's claim of mootness because the students had graduated: "it is not unlikely that one or more" of the high school's students "may someday want to display the slogan." However, in the *Harper v. Poway Unified School District* litigation, Article III power was restrained.[18] The Ninth Circuit had upheld the school's ability to prohibit a T-shirt with an anti-gay message; based upon *Tinker*'s "rights of others" rationale, the U.S. Supreme Court granted a writ of certiorari, vacated the Ninth Circuit opinion, and directed it to dismiss the case as moot. The originally named student had graduated from high school, although other students had joined the litigation as plaintiffs, and the district judge had entered a judgment in favor of the school.[19]

The rejection of the "rights of others" analysis in favor of the substantial disruption standard requires the courts to engage in assessments regarding political norms, which in turn determine the outcome. In the Seventh Circuit's anti-gay T-shirt cases, the political norm is debate of sexuality: the T-shirt slogan furthers debate rather than disrupts it. In the Confederate flag clothing cases, the political norm is racial civility: the symbol of the Confederacy threatens to disrupt it. Thus, it is not only the "common sense" determinations of threats of disruption that are vexing but also the implicit values regarding hierarchy, democracy, and the importance of sexuality.

Additionally, some student clothing raises issues of sexuality in the context of vulgarity, usually conceptualized as being governed not by the disruption standard, but by the post-*Tinker* case of *Bethel School District v. Fraser*, a case arising from a school election speech infused with double entendres.[20] Courts applying *Fraser*'s vulgarity standard, however, often invoke *Tinker*'s disruption standard, either intertwined or as a parallel analysis. For example, in *H. v. Easton Area School District*, a federal judge in 2011 found unconstitutional a school's ban on wristbands with the slogan "I ♥ Boobies."[21] The bracelets, distributed by Keep a Breast Foundation, an organization devoted to breast cancer education and awareness, prompted concerns regarding their vulgarity as well as their potential to disrupt. The judge found the school officials' justifications both incorrect and inconsistent, disagreeing that the word "booby" was vulgar, noting it is also the name of a bird, and that school officials used the word themselves in their announcements. The judge also found that while there may have been some remarks from male students, "isolated incidents are well within a school's authority" to address and did not rise to a substantial disruption. While one principal expressed concerns that allowing "boobies" on these breast cancer bracelets would diminish her authority to prevent other students from wearing clothing with other inappropriate statements, the judge did not credit this rationale.

Given the uncertainties of refereeing student expression on bracelets, T-shirts, and purses, a school might logically wish to prohibit all such expression. In *Palmer v. Waxahachie Independent School District*, the Fifth Circuit upheld a school district's broad authority regarding T-shirts.[22] Retreating from a policy that prohibited clothes that posed a threat of substantial disruption in part because it was labor intensive to enforce, the school district banned all T-shirts with printed messages, unless they were approved school-related slogans or bore logos smaller than two inches by two inches. Paul Palmer, a high school student, unsuccessfully sought approval of non-school related T-shirts, including one with the text of the First Amendment. In rejecting a First Amendment challenge to the banning of a First Amendment T-shirt, the Fifth Circuit reasoned that the school policy was content and viewpoint neutral, and merely a time, place, and manner restriction meriting only intermediate scrutiny. Interestingly, Palmer contended that the school district's allowance of messages on buttons, pins, and wristbands rendered the policy unconstitutional, an argument that the court labeled "perverse." Instead, the court credited the school's button/pin/wristband leniency and the possibility that students could wear their T-shirts during their nonschool hours, as meeting the requirement of ample alternative opportunity for students to express their views. Moreover, banning messaged T-shirts but not messaged buttons was permissible under the school's rationale of preparing students for dress in the "working world."

The Fifth Circuit in *Palmer* relied upon its previous ruling in *Canady v. Bossier Parish School Board*, upholding the constitutionality of mandated school uniforms, requiring navy or khaki pants and specified shirts.[23] The court assumed that student clothing possessed First Amendment protection, but held that the neutrality of the school policy in terms of both content and viewpoint required the school to satisfy only the intermediate standard of scrutiny. The court concluded that the school's stated interest of "improving the educational process" was important, and that students had other avenues of communication open to them during school, as well as being able to wear clothing of their choice outside of school. The school linked mandated school uniforms to improved school discipline and test scores. Interestingly, several years earlier President Bill Clinton's State of the Union address had mentioned a similar, if more specific link. Clinton issued a "challenge" to provide Americans with better educational opportunities and stated that "if it means that teenagers will stop killing each other over designer jackets, then our public schools should be able to require their students to wear school uniforms."[24]

Yet the threshold requirement of expressive speech, assumed arguendo by the Fifth Circuit, is not necessarily satisfied by a designer jacket or by jeans. Attire bearing words or symbols is much more likely to meet the expressive threshold necessary to invoke First Amendment protections. However, even unadorned apparel can speak volumes, as has been the case with the hat.

II. OF HATS AND SHACKLES

When the members of the First Congress debated amending the Constitution to include what is now the First Amendment, Representative John Page argued that whether a man has a right to wear his hat or not was far from trivial.[25] The clause being discussed did not refer to hats or other attire but to the freedom of assembly. Page was responding to the previous remarks of Representative Theodore Sedgwick of Massachusetts, who had argued that the assembly clause was unnecessary: it was encompassed by the speech clause; it was self-evident; it would never be called into question; and it was derogatory to the dignity of the House of Representatives to descend into such minutiae. In support of all his arguments, Sedgwick contended the amendment might just as well declare "a man should have a right to wear his hat if he pleased." It proved not to be the best analogy, provoking a trenchant response by Representative John Page: just as "a man has been obliged to pull off his hat when he appeared before the face of authority," so too have people "been prevented from assembling together on their lawful occasions."[26]

As historian Irving Brant observed, Page's reference had tremendous resonance for the members of the First Congress who would have understood it as alluding to William Penn's famous trial.[27] A decade before Penn received the large land grant in America that would become the state of Pennsylvania, Penn and his co-defendant William Mead were prosecuted in England for "tumultuous assembly" and disturbing the peace. They had preached outside a Quaker meeting house that had recently been closed by Restoration regulations limiting religious dissent from the recently reestablished Church of England. Originally a pamphlet and purported trial transcript, *The Peoples Ancient and Just Liberties Asserted, In the Tryal of William Penn and William Mead at the Old Bailey, 22 Charles II 1670, written by themselves*, became an essential American document. It portrayed Penn and Mead as heroes seeking their rights as Englishmen under the Magna Carta but stymied by arbitrary officials in the king's court.[28]

Their hats were central to this portrait. As Quakers, Penn and Mead denied so-called hat honor, the male practice of doffing one's cap to a superior including removing one's hat in court. The refusal of hat honor, intended to challenge hierarchy, had become a well-known characteristic of the Quakers; a fair number of Quakers had been beaten, jailed, whipped, or fined because of their practice by the time of the Penn and Mead trial.[29] Thus, this colloquy was not surprising:

RECORDER. Do you know where you are?
PENN. Yes.
RECORDER. Do you know it is the King's Court?
PENN. I know it to be a Court, and I suppose it to be the King's Court.
RECORDER. Do you not know there is respect due to the Court?
PENN. Yes.
RECORDER. Why do you not pay it then?
PENN. I do so.
RECORDER. Why do you not put off your hat then?
PENN. Because I do not believe that to be any respect.
RECORDER. Well, the Court sets forty marks a piece upon your heads as a fine for your contempt of the Court.[30]

However, shortly before this interchange, Penn and Mead had been waiting, hatless, for their case to be called. When an official noticed their hats were off, he ordered an officer to "put on their hats again." Seemingly, this command was merely for the purpose of immediately issuing the order to Penn to remove his hat, an order the court would have known as problematic for the Quaker William Penn. Immediately after the Recorder's fine, Penn and Mead both spoke:

PENN. I desire it might be observed, that we came into the Court with our hats off (that is, taken off) and if they have been put on since, it was by order from the Bench, and therefore not we but the Bench should be fined.
MEAD. I have a question to ask the Recorder. Am I fined also?
RECORDER. Yes.
MEAD. I desire the jury and all people to take notice of this injustice of the recorder, who spake not to me to pull off my hat, and yet hath he put a fine upon my head.[31]

The court's actions regarding the hats – provocative, arbitrary, and lacking the essentials of fairness – set the scene for the remaining injustices of the trial, the eventual jury acquittal, the prosecution of the jurors for that acquittal, and the imprisonment of Penn and Mead for contempt for failure to remove their hats.[32]

Thus, Representative Sedgwick's comparison of the right to wear or not wear a hat and the right to assembly as equally trivial rights was not likely to be accepted by those familiar with the Penn and Mead trial. Sedgwick's motion to strike "assembly" from the text of the First Amendment failed by a large margin. But perhaps Sedgwick was correct. Recent constitutional doctrine tends to support the argument that assembly is mere surplusage and the right is encompassed by freedom of speech.[33]

Nevertheless, Penn's hat continues to have some constitutional plangency. Its most famous appearance is in *West Virginia State Board of Education v. Barnette*, albeit in a footnote.[34] The Court evoked William Penn's hat and the Quaker refusal to exhibit deference as an example of compelled speech. Consistent with Penn's spirit, and reversing recent precedent, the Court held that "compelling the flag salute and pledge transcends constitutional limitations on their power and invades the sphere of intellect and spirit which it is the purpose of the First Amendment to our Constitution to reserve from all official control."[35]

Yet wearing a hat in court persists as constitutionally prohibitable. Remarkably relying on an interpretation of the courtroom as a nonpublic forum, a federal district judge in 2009 concluded that requiring a litigant to remove his hat – a baseball cap – did not violate the litigant's asserted First and Fourteenth Amendment rights. There was no issue of viewpoint discrimination, such as prohibiting only Yankees baseball caps. Instead, the generally accepted etiquette of removing hats in a courtroom "out of respect" for the judicial process was reasonable: the litigant had no constitutional right to make a "fashion statement" by wearing clothes he "might have worn to a baseball game" rather than attire "suitable to the dignity of a courtroom."[36]

If a hat can disrupt courtroom dignity, then the prospect of criminal defendants donning judicial robes must certainly be disruptive. If those robes are adorned with symbols of oppression – for example, the yellow star used by the Nazis to badge Jews – the disruption is even more probable. And if the defendants removed the robes to reveal that one of them was wearing the shirt of a police uniform, and if both defendants walked on the judicial robes they had removed, then there should be little doubt of disruption. All of this occurred near the end of the Chicago Conspiracy Trial.[37]

The Chicago Conspiracy Trial, sometimes known as the Chicago Eight or Chicago Seven Trial, shared many features with the equally notorious Penn and Mead trial three centuries earlier. The Chicago Conspiracy Trial also arose from actions involving a tumultuous assembly; the original Chicago Eight defendants were charged under the then-recent federal Anti-Riot Act for their conduct at the

1968 Democratic National Convention in Chicago.[38] Like the Penn and Mead trial, there were possibilities of jury nullification, although the Chicago Conspiracy Trial jurors did return some guilty verdicts and were not imprisoned. Both trials featured confrontations between judicial power and individual rights, including findings of criminal contempt based on the defendants' attire.

The trial transcript of the robe incident does not capture the appearance of the robes or the defendants' actions, but does depict the character of the proceedings, including the relationship between the judge and defense counsel, William Kunstler:

THE COURT: May the record show defendants Hoffman and Rubin came in at 1:28, with their—

MR. RUBIN: The marshal just came and asked us to come in. We came as soon as we were asked.

THE COURT: And also attired in what might be called collegiate robes.

MR. RUBIN: Judge's robes, sir.

A DEFENDANT: Death robes.

THE COURT: Some might even consider them judicial robes.

MR. RUBIN: Judicial robes.

THE COURT: Your idea, Mr. Kunstler? Another one of your brilliant ideas?

MR. KUNSTLER: Your Honor, I can't take credit for this one.

THE COURT: That amazes me.[39]

Federal judge Julius Hoffman issued criminal contempt citations for a multitude of infractions by the defendants as well as their attorneys. The wearing of the judicial robes by defendants Abbie Hoffman and Jerry Rubin were only two of the specifications of contempt among more than 150 for the seven defendants and their two attorneys in the five-month trial the judge described as "marred by continual disruptive outbursts in direct defiance of judicial authority by defendants and defense counsel."

After the Seventh Circuit remanded the cases to be tried before a judge other than the judge who had issued the criminal contempt citations,[40] Judge Edward Gignoux of Maine, sitting by special designation, found that some of the contempt citations lacked merit, but did find Hoffman and Rubin guilty of contempt based upon the robe incident. In his opinion, after describing the episode, he noted that the defendants had testified that their "conduct was 'guerrilla theater' and 'symbolic communication' of their contempt for the judge and the judicial process, as well as their view that judicial robes were simply a cloak for police brutality." This inchoate free expression claim remained implicit. Although Judge Gignoux conceded that "the record does not disclose that the conduct charged to these defendants in these specifications caused any substantial disruption of the proceedings," he found the defendants' actions "so flagrant, so outrageous, and so subversive of both respect for the court and the integrity of the judicial process as to rise to the level of an actual and material obstruction of the administration of justice."[41] Essentially, the judge concluded that the actions of Hoffman and Rubin achieved exactly what they intended: a subversion of the hierarchical order demanded by the judicial process.

Important to this hierarchal order is the notion of professionalization, including not only the attire of attorneys but also the notion that attorneys represent, and generally speak for, the litigants. Bobby Seale, the eighth member of the Chicago Eight, sought to subvert this hierarchy by representing himself when his attorney of choice was hospitalized and Judge Hoffman refused to postpone the trial. Seale vigorously asserted his right, including his right to represent himself,[42] on numerous occasions, including statements addressing the judge thus:

> After you done walked over people's constitutional rights, after you done walked over people's constitutional rights, the Sixth Amendment, the Fifth Amendment, and the phoniness and the corruptness of this very trial, for people to have a right to speak out, freedom of speech, freedom of assembly, and et cetera. You have did everything you could with those jive lying witnesses up there presented by these pig agents of the Government to lie and say and condone some rotten racists, fascist crap by racist cops and pigs that beat people's heads-and I demand my constitutional rights-demand-demand.[43]

For these and other statements, Judge Hoffman adjudged Bobby Seale in contempt of court and declared a mistrial solely for him, thus transforming the Chicago Eight Trial into the Chicago Seven Trial. But first, Judge Hoffman ordered Bobby Seale shackled, bound to a chair, and gagged, a display that continued for several days.[44] The image of Bobby Seale – the only African American defendant – arrayed in muslin face coverings, chained, and tied was one many found shocking. The defendant was dressed in a disruptive manner, albeit not by his own choosing.

In reviewing Seale's appeal from the contempt citations, the Seventh Circuit cursorily approved the restraining attire, citing *Illinois v. Allen*, decided by the United States Supreme Court several months after Bobby Seale had been shackled, gagged, and tied at trial.[45] *Illinois v. Allen* involved the expulsion of a mentally ill defendant during his trial, but the Bobby Seale spectacle was obviously on the minds of the Justices. Justice Black, who in his dissent in *Tinker* the year before had complained of young people and a "new revolutionary era of permissiveness in this country fostered by the judiciary,"[46] wrote for the Court that although it "is not pleasant to hold" that a defendant could be banished from the court for parts of his own trial, disruptive defendants must not be allowed to treat the courts, "palladiums of liberty as they are," with disrespect. The opinion offered "three constitutionally permissible ways for a trial judge to handle an obstreperous defendant": bind and gag him, cite him for contempt, or remove him from the courtroom. Yet the Court made clear that the first of these was the least acceptable. Shackling and gagging was a "last resort" that could significantly affect a jury and constituted "something of an affront to the very dignity and decorum of the judicial proceedings."

Writing separately and neither dissenting nor concurring, Justice Douglas made explicit the connection to "political trials" and extensively quoted from the Penn and Mead Trial.[47] Although not mentioning William Mead, or Penn's hat, Justice Douglas focused on Penn as a member of an "unpopular minority" who was asserting his rights to the consternation of the "sincere, law-and-order" panel of judges who wished something to be done to Penn "to stop his mouth." For Douglas, political trials, presumably including the Chicago Conspiracy Trial, implicated the heart of constitutional democracy in which both majorities and minorities have an important stake.[48]

It is not only in overtly political trials that the constitutional rights of criminal defendants become enmeshed in matters of habiliment. The quintet of cases from the United States Supreme Court – *Illinois v. Allen* (1973), *Estelle v. Williams* (1976), *Holbrook v. Flynn* (1986), *Deck v. Missouri* (2005), and *Carey v. Musladin* (2006)[49] – considered matters of attire in the context of criminal trials and did not involve the manifest challenges to democracy and hierarchy obvious in the Chicago Conspiracy Trial or the Penn and Mead Trial. Nevertheless, the Court's discussions of the relevance of clothes and appearance implicate issues of democracy, hierarchy, and constitutionalism.

Of central concern is whether the attire at issue brands the defendant with the mark of guilt. The Bill of Rights devotes the majority of its provisions to rights in the criminal context, although the presumption of innocence and the right to a fair trial are not specifically enumerated. Instead, the right to a fair trial inheres in the due process clauses of the Fifth and Fourteenth Amendments, although it could be said to flow from the Sixth Amendment as a whole or the provisions relating to a "public trial" or an "impartial jury."[50] Additionally, the Sixth Amendment right to assistance of counsel can be pertinent, not only because the defendant wishes to represent himself as in *Allen*, but because the defendant's attire might inhibit his ability to consult with counsel. As the Court in *Allen* noted, one reason to disfavor restraining a defendant is that the ability to communicate with counsel is "greatly reduced when the defendant is in a condition of total physical restraint."[51]

More important, however, the rights to a fair trial and to an impartial jury are compromised when a defendant wears shackles. Extending *Allen*, a divided Court in *Deck v. Missouri* found this was true even during the sentencing phase, when a jury was deciding whether or not to impose the death penalty on a defendant wearing leg irons, handcuffs, and a belly chain.[52] Although this convicted defendant no longer possessed the presumption of innocence, the right to effective counsel could be implicated given that shackles could "confuse and embarrass" a defendant.

Moreover, the wearing of shackles constituted an affront to the dignity of the court-room that included "the respectful treatment of defendants." While a trial judge could certainly take account of individualized security concerns, including the dangerousness of the defendant, the Court advised that the "symbolic yet concrete objectives" of courtroom decorum should generally not be disrupted by a defendant wearing shackles.[53]

Considerations of dangerousness also inform the Court's unanimous decision in *Holbrook v. Flynn* to uphold the appearance of several uniformed state troopers sitting behind the six defendants.[54] While this deviated from the general practice of extra security details wearing civilian clothes, a combination of factors made this impracticable. The Court rejected the analogy to wearing shackles, noting that the uniformed guards did not necessarily communicate the defendants' dangerousness and could just as easily be interpreted by jurors as guarding against more general disruptions. The Court noted that while it might be the better practice to have officers doff their uniforms when providing security, the Court's role in reviewing a constitutional challenge to a state-court practice was more limited.[55]

The limited role of the judicial review, especially given federalism concerns, governed the outcome in the two other cases of the quintet. In *Estelle v. Williams*, the Court unequivocally held that compelling a defendant to wear "prison garb" during the state court trial was a violation of the right to a fair trial inherent in the Fourteenth Amendment's Due Process Clause.[56] Unlike wearing shackles, there was no state interest possibly served by wearing "jail attire." Further, there were equality concerns because the practice affected those who were unable to afford to post bail prior to trial. However, the Court's majority did not extend relief to Harry Lee Williams, because although he had requested an officer at the jail to return his civilian clothes for court, his attorney did not object to Williams's prison attire. While a state cannot compel a defendant to appear at trial in jail clothes, there must be an objection to preserve this right. The objection requirement not only serves federalism concerns but also preserves the possibility of a defense trial strategy of dressing the defendant in jail attire as a sympathy ploy.[57]

Williams's emphasis on state compulsion foreshadows the problem of government control over a public trial. In *Carey v. Musladin*, the Court considered a constitutional challenge by a convicted defendant who argued that spectators wearing buttons with photos of the victim denied him a fair trial.[58] The Court's opinion was decisively procedural. Because the United States Supreme Court had never ruled on the potentially prejudicial effect of spectators, Musladin's claim was foreclosed by a federal statute limiting habeas corpus relief to constitutional violations that were contrary to clearly established Supreme Court precedent.[59] While the opinion was unanimous, Justice Souter's concurring opinion contended that trial judges had affirmative obligations to ensure a fair trial, including regulating the attire of spectators.[60]

One example of a trial judge taking such an obligation seriously occurred in a homicide trial in New York in which the judge banned the wearing of "obtrusive corsages of red and black ribbons of approximately five to six inches in length."[61] Applying the local courtroom decorum rules prohibiting disruptive conduct, the trial judge used his discretionary power to prohibit all expressive or symbolic clothing and accessories, including armbands, buttons, and flowers, as "disruptive of a courtroom environment, which environment must be scrupulously dedicated to the appearance as well as the reality of fairness and equal." The judge criticized his own past practice in a nonjury trial permitting thirty-five spectators wearing bright yellow T-shirts bearing the blue legend "Justice for Jimmy," the victim. While the vast majority of spectator attire seems to favor the victim and thus possibly prejudice the defendant's right to a fair trial, the judge also referenced the high profile "Central Park Jogger" criminal prosecution, in which the trial judge "barred a spectator-brother of one of defendants from wearing a black sweatshirt with the letters emblemized in white, 'My Brother Antron McCray Is Innocent.'"[62]

Any First Amendment rights of the spectators, even ones that would not prejudice a defendant, are blurred. Concurring in *Musladin*, Souter raised the possibility of the spectators' First Amendment right to wear buttons, although he stated he did not find such an interest "intuitively strong."[63] In the New York corsages case, the trial judge was dismissive: although free expression was at the "very core of our organized democratic society," it had no place in the courtroom, a "holy shrine of impartiality" that was clearly committed to special and defined purposes and not the "airing of general grievances."[64]

The importance of impartiality, and its appearance, supports the ban on expressive dress at the U.S. Supreme Court building and its environs. While the Court's guide for visitors to oral argument prohibits "display buttons and inappropriate clothing,"[65] federal statutes prohibit the display of any flag, banner, or "device" designed or adapted to "bring into public notice a party, organization, or movement" in the Supreme Court building or grounds.[66] In 1983 in *United States v. Grace*, the Court held that the prohibition could not constitutionally extend to the sidewalk, a traditional public forum.[67] Justice Thurgood Marshall contended that the entire statute should be unconstitutional, noting that it "would be ironic indeed if an exception to the Constitution were to be recognized for the very institution that has the chief responsibility for protecting constitutional rights."[68]

Yet Marshall's irony is the current state of the law. Interpretations of "devices that bring into public notice a party, organization, or movement" make clear that they extend to clothes. For example, a D.C. appellate court held that "costumes – the

orange jumpsuit and the black hood – constituted 'devices,'" and another D.C. appellate likewise found the wearing of orange jumpsuits, with or without black hoods,
and the wearing of orange T-shirts with the phrase "Shut Down Guantanamo" to be
covered by the prohibition.[69] Such rulings have revealed two other ironies. First, the
prohibitions invert the usual hierarchy of protected speech classifications so that the
most highly valued category of political speech becomes the least protected. Second,
the prohibitions banish the central issue of disruption. Courts have reasoned that
the statutory prohibition on "devices" was not directed at preventing disruption, but
rather on preserving the "appearance of the Court as a body not swayed by external
influence." Thus, it does not matter that the clothes themselves caused no actual
disruption because they apparently disrupt the notion that the Court is not subject
to democratic influences.

It is therefore not surprising that a person wearing a jacket bearing a political
message that caused no disruption was arrested in the Supreme Court building in
early 2012. The jacket was stenciled with the words "Occupy Everything" and the
wearer had been admitted by the guards and was not part of any protest or action. A
widely distributed video captured a few minutes of guards asking the jacket-wearer
to remove the jacket or exit the building, and then placing the man under arrest.[70]
There is no question that the man could not have been arrested outside the court
building, largely because of a decision involving another man in a jacket rendered
by the U.S. Supreme Court four decades before.

III. RIPS IN THE SOCIAL FABRIC

The most famous jacket in constitutional law bore the words "Fuck the Draft." It
also had the words "Stop War" and two "peace symbols." The year was 1968 and the
place was Division 20 of the Los Angeles Municipal Court in the neighborhood of
110 North Grand, Los Angeles. The person who wore the jacket was Paul Robert
Cohen, age nineteen, who was in the courthouse to testify in a case. He was charged
with the crime of tumultuous and offensive conduct causing a breach of the peace.
He waived a jury trial, was found guilty by a judge, denied probation, and sentenced
to thirty days in the county jail.[71]

As the U.S. Supreme Court noted in *Cohen v. California*, the fact that Cohen
was in the courthouse was irrelevant.[72] He was charged with a generally applicable
California penal statute, negating any government argument that its purpose was
to preserve an "appropriately decorous atmosphere in the courthouse." Instead, the
state court, upholding his conviction, observed that "women and children" were present in that corridor. The U.S. Supreme Court rejected the argument that persons
in the corridor were members of a captive audience that the state needed to protect:
they could simply avert their eyes. Importantly, no "tumult" or actual disturbance

of the peace occurred, but only a vague fear of disruption. As distilled, the issue became whether "one particular scurrilous epithet" can be excised from public discourse under the First Amendment. Writing for the majority, Justice Harlan gave little import to the obscenity of the words on the jacket. He implicitly credited the jacket as political speech, contending that verbal tumult and disruption were necessary side effects of open debate and democracy.

At times, Harlan seemed to be addressing the cultural – and generational – disruption so evident in other cases of the era such as *Tinker*, which the Court cited, and the Chicago Conspiracy Trial. The opinion acknowledges the potential for trivialization – beginning with the apologetic "this case may seem at first blush too inconsequential to find its way into our books" – and invokes relativism – the pithy and much-quoted "one man's vulgarity is another's lyric." Ultimately, however, the decision vindicated Cohen's jacket: "it is largely because governmental officials cannot make principled distinctions in this area that the Constitution leaves matters of taste and style so largely to the individual."[73]

Matters of taste and style are constitutionally fraught in part because it can be difficult to recognize any First Amendment issue. In *Cohen v. California*, the expressive element of Cohen's jacket may seem clear and its political content even more obvious. After all, the jacket had words on it and those words asserted opposition to a controversial government activity. However, three justices dissenting declared that "Cohen's absurd and immature antic" was "mainly conduct and little speech." Moreover, even if there were speech, it was of the type that is categorically excluded from the protection of the First Amendment. The dissent thus chastised the majority's "agonizing over First Amendment values" as both "misplaced and unnecessary."[74]

Similar constitutional uncertainty swirls around the more recent "matter of taste and style" that is known as saggy pants: pants that are worn substantially below the waist with underwear or flesh visible. The fashion implicates the hierarchal relations between established authorities and youth culture, not unlike Cohen's jacket bearing anti-war symbols and words. Additionally, the saggy pants style implicates African American and urban sexuality and masculinity. Perhaps relatedly, there is a somewhat unusual preoccupation with the pedigree of the saggy pants fashion. The general, if suspect, sourcing of the style is to prison dress, focused on an absence of belts and over-large clothes, which have also been argued as rooted in slave attire. There is also lore that highlights sexuality, often as a means to discredit the style, arguing that low pants signal availability for homosexual engagement in prison. Whatever its origin, the attire has become fashionable, as have efforts to eradicate it. Government entities and actors wishing to criminalize the wearing of saggy pants have relied upon three strategies: prosecuting under extant disorderly conduct laws; prosecuting under extant indecent exposure laws; and promulgating specific statutes or ordinances that criminalize saggy pants. Each of these strategies has been subject to constitutional challenge.[75]

Decades after California prosecuted Paul Robert Cohen for tumultuous and offensive conduct causing a breach of the peace, New York charged Julio Martinez with disorderly conduct for wearing "his pants down below his buttocks exposing underwear potentially showing private parts."[76] Unlike Cohen's judge, who not only convicted him but imposed an especially harsh sentence, the Bronx County Criminal Court Judge dismissed the case. The Bronx judge summarily discussed a few of the constitutional cases regarding dress (although not *Cohen v. California*), but rested his decision on the lack of allegations that Martinez's attire "disturbed the public tranquility or violated the public order." While noting that "most of us may consider it distasteful, and indeed foolish, to wear one's pants so low as to expose the underwear," the judge eclipsed this sentiment with a quotation from New York's highest court considering a prosecution for indecency of young people in their yellow shorts in Yonkers in 1937: "the Constitution still leaves some opportunity for people to be foolish if they so desire."[77]

Foolish or not, at least one city's chief of police has argued that this type of dress supports criminal sanctions based on disorderly conduct and indecent exposure laws. The Flint, Michigan, memo instructing law enforcement officers to make arrests of "youths and adults" who were "sagging" prompted a response from the American Civil Liberties Union (ACLU).[78] The ACLU acknowledged that while prosecuting exposure of the naked buttocks might be appropriate, the chief of police had publicized his practice of targeting young men with the tops of their boxer shorts showing, or even with the tops of their boxer shorts covered by shirts that he lifted to expose the sagging pants. The ACLU memo threatened a constitutional challenge.[79]

The ACLU has been active in challenging proposed laws that would criminalize sagging pants, seemingly stopping many of them. However, several municipalities have enacted such laws. For example, the town of Dublin, Georgia, amended its public indecency ordinance in 2010 to include a prohibition against "wearing pants or skirts more than three (3) inches below the top of the hips (crest of the ilium) exposing the skin or undergarments." The ordinance also provides that "it is a defense" if "it is determined, after a hearing or trial, that the person was exercising rights protected by the federal or state Constitution."[80] An earlier Riviera Beach, Florida, ordinance, passed by voter referendum, criminalized "wearing pants below the waist which expose the skin or undergarments," although trial judges soon found the ordinance unconstitutional as violating the wearer's liberty interests.[81]

When the explicit prohibition of saggy pants has been on the agenda of state legislatures, it has not only implicated constitutional rights but also state constitutional structures. Alabama's proposed law criminalizing saggy pants would only be effective in the city of Montgomery.[82] The Alabama constitution favors state over local power even on local issues, a rather unusual constellation of powers. Commentators attribute this increasingly awkward constitutional arrangement to the fear of majoritarian African American local communities that animated the still-in-force 1901 state constitution.[83] The hierarchy between state and local governments is also evident in recent legislative strategies in other states that focus on school dress codes. These statutes shift the responsibility – and the disruption inquiry – to schools by mandating that local school districts adopt dress codes prohibiting saggy pants. For example, a Florida law adopted in 2011 provides that each "district school board shall adopt a dress code policy that prohibits a student, while on the grounds of a public school during the regular school day, from wearing clothing that exposes underwear or body parts in an indecent or vulgar manner or that disrupts the orderly learning environment."[84]

Whether in school or elsewhere, First Amendment challenges to laws prohibiting saggy pants must meet the threshold requirement that the wearing of saggy pants is symbolic speech. The doctrinal asymmetry requires the challenger to demonstrate that he (or his pants) is making a specific statement, while the authorities are free to single out the style for its generalized meanings. This challenger's hurdle becomes more difficult as the fashion is popularized, just as a cornrow hairstyle was less expressive after being worn by Bo Derek in a film.[85] Rejecting a claim by a ninth-grade student subject to a long-term suspension for repeatedly wearing saggy pants, a federal judge in 1995 accepted that while the student may have intended to convey a message of black identity and culture with his saggy pants, the message was not necessarily apparent to those who viewed the "fashion trend followed by many adolescents all over the United States."[86]

Importantly, however, given that the fashion trend is identified with racialized youth, the saggy pants proscriptions can serve as a gateway for other constitutional problems, including those involving search and seizure. Indeed, the ACLU memo directed to the Flint (Michigan) police chief specifically discussed stop and frisk, search, and arrest practices that could arise from a targeting of saggy pants, and argued that these practices would be unconstitutional.[87] In short, the constitutional concern is that saggy pants can operate as a proxy for race, as well as youth, and allow for "racial profiling" without the explicit use of race.

Yet even without criminalizing the wearing of saggy pants, the garment might raise constitutional concerns. For example, it might be proffered as part of the articulable suspicion of criminal activity to support a valid Fourth Amendment stop-and-frisk.[88] Or it may be constitutionally considered in sentencing, as it was when a trial judge referred to the two seventeen-year-old defendants "sagging their pants" before imposing life without possibility of parole. Rejecting a claim of cruel and unusual punishment, a California appellate court found no bias in the trial judge's reference to attire, declaring that this was an allowable consideration of the defendants' demeanor and attitude relevant to sentencing.[89] Or it may constitute allowable discrimination in jury selection, sufficient to defeat a criminal defendant's claim of unconstitutional exclusion of jurors on the basis of race. As one court phrased it, "although the prosecutor may have a bias 'against people who sag,'" that did not mean the exclusion of the juror was "based on race."[90]

At times explicit, but always implicit, in the discussions of saggy pants is the notion that they are "gang attire." Usual definitions of gang attire focus on identification with specific youth gangs. These indicia include specific words or letters or numbers on clothing – for example, Posole; M; 13 – or even prosaic colors of clothes such as blue. The indicia can also include tattoos, again of specific words or numbers, but also of more generic terms such as "nicknames." As a consequence, a young person can be deemed a member of a gang simply because, as one judge phrased it, he "on two occasions wore baggy pants, blue clothes, or 'Los Angeles Raiders' garments."[91]

While the defining characteristics of "gang membership" usually involve some sort of attire or appearance, these indicia, as well as the definition of "gang" itself, vary widely. There is no consensus in the statutes, no consensus among law enforcement, and no consensus among academics.[92] There is, however, widespread agreement about the existence of constitutional problems in identifying and regulating gangs. First Amendment claims of a right to wear gang attire generally fail to meet the threshold requirement of a particularized message. For example, a federal judge rejected an argument that the distinctive vests of members of a motorcycle "club" conveyed a particularized message of fraternity, freedom, and equality that would be understood by others. Seemingly, the judge found no contradiction that the basis of club members' exclusion from the Gilroy Garlic Festival was that their clothing was expressive: law enforcement decided the vests constituted "gang colors or insignia" prohibited by the festival's dress code policy. On appeal, the Ninth Circuit did not plumb this incongruity but engaged with the other threshold peculiarity in the case, state action. A divided en banc court found that although the Gilroy Garlic Festival was held on City of Gilroy property and staffed by City of Gilroy law enforcement officers who were "on duty," the Gilroy Garlic Festival Association, and not the city, was the responsible entity and thus there was no state action sufficient to invoke constitutional protections.[93]

Most constitutional problems with gang attire, however, involve the criminal justice system and thus there is clear state action. Often the governmental attempts at definition and indicia begin with law enforcement field interviews of persons "suspected to be gang members based on their race, ethnicity, gender, age, and clothing," and may include a demand that the person partially disrobe to reveal tattoos.[94] While there are obvious Fourth Amendment concerns with the stop and the search, there are also due process problems with such a self-reinforcing methodology that might, for example, result in law enforcement noticing individual tattoos and classifying them, which then becomes reified as an indicia of gang membership. There are also procedural due process concerns when a person is then identified as a gang member and placed on a local law enforcement list, or in a statewide or national gang database, with no "notice and opportunity to be heard" and little chance to be removed from the list.[95] These concerns are heightened when a law enforcement officer provides "expert testimony" during a court proceeding that certain attire or tattoos are indicia of gang membership, compromising a Sixth Amendment Confrontation Clause right.[96]

The effects of being deemed a gang member because of a nickname tattoo or a proclivity to wear blue can be dramatic. They also raise several constitutional issues. Essentially criminalizing gang membership through loitering ordinances has been one law enforcement strategy. However, in 1999 the U.S. Supreme Court limited this tactic when it declared unconstitutional Chicago's Gang Congregation Ordinance, under which 42,000 people were arrested in three years. Focusing on the shortcomings of "loiter" rather than of "gang member," the Court found the ordinance unconstitutionally vague as a matter of due process.[97] Another strategy has been to use public nuisance laws to seek injunctions prohibiting persons identified as gang members from wearing specific clothing as well as other activities including loitering. The California Supreme Court has upheld this mechanism against constitutional challenge.[98] Moreover, in 2001, a California appellate court upheld the constitutionality of an injunction that prohibited wearing clothing that bore the numbers "'13'; '20'; '13 20'; '16'; '16 20'; '22'; '22 16'; '22 16 12'; '22 16 12'; '22 16 12 19.'" In so doing, the court read an intent requirement into the injunction, stating that it meant to enjoin only "the conscious expression of gang affiliation, support and allegiance." The challenger's overbreadth argument failed, but he could presumably take comfort in the court's assurance that he would not violate the injunction if he wore "a high school football jersey *in a football game* bearing one of the numbers forbidden by the injunction."[99]

Other constitutional issues arise in the criminal context under two of the Eighth Amendment's clauses. First, the Eighth Amendment prohibits "excessive bail." Yet as scholar Babe Howell has demonstrated, a mere allegation of gang membership is usually sufficient to raise the amount of bail, especially in cases in which the charges are not serious or there is weak evidence.[100] Second, the Eighth Amendment prohibits cruel and unusual punishment, which has been interpreted to include a requirement that the punishment be proportionate – or at least not greatly disproportionate – to the crime. However, without more, a gang enhancement will not meet the strict standard regarding Eighth Amendment proportionality or a similar state constitutional provision, resulting in even more minors sentenced to extensive imprisonments.[101]

The specific constitutional concerns of government action intended to combat gang disruption of the social fabric may be less important than the overall constitutional implications. Indeed, the government methods themselves may be disrupting the social fabric in ways that impose hierarchy and thwart democracy. As many scholars have noted, gangs are predominantly conceptualized as a problem of young, male, and racialized persons. In Los Angeles, almost half of African American men between the ages of twenty-one and twenty-four were listed on the gang database; since most did not have criminal records, presumably these men favored "L.A. Raiders" garments.[102] In Minnesota, with a population that is approximately 5 percent African American, a 2009 report notes that African Americans represented approximately half of the persons listed in the gang databases.[103] The report also expressed community concern that the criteria for inclusion in the database highlighted "factors" – including attire and tattoos – "that are synonymous with the urban youth culture," as well as related concerns of racial profiling, bias, and stereotyping.[104] The reality of racial – as well as age and gender – disparities in governmental action against gangs raises clear equality concerns under the constitution.

Nevertheless, these concerns are not cognizable under current equal protection doctrine with its requirement of intent. While this precondition has been compellingly critiqued precisely because it does not address bias and stereotyping,[105] the U.S. Supreme Court in *Washington v. Davis* held in 1976 that mere disparate effect, without intent, is insufficient to support an equality claim.[106] Integral to the majority's rationale was the importance of preventing constitutional protection in situations akin to using racial dress as a criterion for criminalization. As the Court stated, equal protection doctrine that did not require intent would "be far reaching and would raise serious questions about, and perhaps invalidate, a whole range of tax, welfare, public service, regulatory, and licensing statutes that may be more burdensome to the poor and to the average black than to the more affluent white."[107]

The intertwining of race, violence, and dress restrictions occurs in another context that has threatened the social fabric: the specter of the Ku Klux Klan (KKK). While the KKK has had several iterations and is loosely organized, the founding of the white supremacist group is generally attributed to several former Confederate soldiers at the close of the Civil War. During Reconstruction, Congress passed several Force Acts meant to address the power of the KKK, including a provision that made it a felony for two or more persons to "go in disguise upon the public highway" with the intent to intimidate or violate the rights of any person.[108] This provision, like similar congressional acts, raised constitutional issues regarding federal power to address private action, an issue that the Supreme Court skirted by construing this provision so narrowly that it would have little applicability to the KKK.[109]

A spate of anti-KKK state and local provisions especially popular after World War II included criminalizing appearing masked in public. Many of these anti-masking provisions did not require intent to commit another act, such as intent to intimidate or violate other rights. For example, the Georgia statute, passed in 1951 and still in force, makes it a misdemeanor for any person to wear "a mask, hood, or device by which any portion of the face is so hidden, concealed, or covered as to conceal the identity of the wearer" and is either on public property or private property without permission. In 1990, the Georgia Supreme Court upheld the statute against a First Amendment challenge by Shade Miller, who was arrested for appearing in KKK regalia alone near the courthouse in Gwinnett County, purportedly to protest the anti-mask statute.[110] In addressing Miller's argument that the statute was overbroad, the court interpreted the statute narrowly, but not so narrowly as to exclude the KKK. Instead, the court required the mask-wearer to have intent to conceal his identity and further that the statute would "apply only to mask-wearing conduct when the mask-wearer knows or reasonably should know that the conduct provokes a reasonable apprehension of intimidation, threats or violence."[111] The Second Circuit similarly upheld a challenge to an anti-masking statute from New York in *Church of American Knights of the Ku Klux Klan v. Kerik.*[112] The KKK group had sought an injunction against the statute to allow a demonstration while wearing masks. Rejecting the First Amendment claim, the court agreed that the KKK regalia – the robe, hood, and mask – met the threshold requirement for expressive speech, but nevertheless separated the mask in its analysis. In the court's view, the mask was "redundant" and did "not convey a message independently of the robe and hood." Moreover, the court opined that mask-wearing was not integral to the expression but optional even among KKK members. Like saggy pants and motorcycle club vests, doctrinal asymmetry is evident: the mask is prohibited because of what it conveys, but it does not possess sufficient expression to support a First Amendment claim.

The New York statute at issue was not originally an anti-KKK statute, but had a long and circuitous history, exemplifying the multiple rationales supporting anti-masking laws. Like England's notorious Waltham Black Act of 1723, the New York law can be traced to criminalizing actions against the landed gentry. The English Act was directed at a Robin Hood–like gang (the Waltham Blacks) whose extensive poaching was arguably attributable to "social resentment" and "class hatred," and made it a capital offense without benefit of clergy to be armed with one's face blackened or otherwise disguised in places such as forests and highways.[113] The New York law, promulgated in 1845, was directed at a widespread resistance to farming rents assessed by large estate owners, known as the anti-rent riots. This resistance included actions by farmers dressed as "Indians," resulting in escalating encounters until one resulted in the death of two law enforcement officers.[114] The New York statute, like the English one, prohibited being disguised and armed. While the English statute was originally intended to be of short duration, it was reenacted several times and survived for a century, long after the Waltham Blacks were a threat, perhaps becoming seen as essential to maintaining the social fabric.[115]

The 1845 New York statute also included a provision criminalizing three or more persons disguised and assembled in public houses or other places. Read in the context of the entire statute and its history, this would seem to be directed at gatherings of anti-rent supporters, yet this statute supplemented a previous law, An Act for the Prevention of Masquerades, passed in 1829.[116] Thereafter, an attempted revision of the penal law in 1850 moved the anti-mask provisions to vagrancy, but the criminal code was never adopted by the legislature.[117] After the Civil War and a renewed popularity of masquerade balls, some "socially inclined persons" from New York City reportedly came to the state capital to lobby on behalf of amendment, because although the statutes were only occasionally enforced, they could "give excuse, however, for some very troublesome and vexatious proceedings on the part of the police."[118] The lobbyists prevailed, at least in part, and the legislature amended the 1845 act's provision on assemblages to include an exception for "any masquerade or fancy dress ball or entertainment, or any assemblage therefor of persons masked" and "the wearing of masks, fancy dresses, or any other disguise by persons on their way to, or returning from, such ball or other entertainment."[119] The exception also had a proviso: if the event was in a city, permission had to be first obtained from the police authorities. The "socially inclined" persons may have had to pay dearly for their permits: the legislature set the permit fee for New York City as between $5 and $100 in 1888, with the amount collected "for the benefit of the police pension fund."[120] When the laws were recodified in 1909, the prohibition of disguised and masked persons, including the exception, was placed in the consolidated laws sandwiched by "Crime against Nature" and "Disorderly Conduct."[121] When the penal laws were again recodified in 1965, the anti-mask provision was part of a "thoroughgoing revision" and placed under the title "Offenses against Public Order," within the crime of loitering. According to the revisers, such offenses required no intent to cause either public or individual harm, but are "generally unsalutary or unwholesome from a social viewpoint."[122]

Against such a background, courts have struggled with the legislative history in determining the law's purpose as relevant to constitutional challenges, with historical inaccuracies and the appearance of historical opportunism. In addition to KKK and "cross-dressing" cases,[123] courts have addressed disguises in the context of political protests. For example, in 1967, a federal district judge rejected a First Amendment challenge by members of the Bread and Puppet Theater who had been threatened with the law during an anti-war protest.[124] In a brief opinion, the judge found that police threats to prosecute did not rise to the level necessary to support their challenge because the law "by its very terms" could protect their activity as performance, assuming that they had applied for a permit. Implicitly recognizing the inversion of the hierarchy of categories of speech in the First Amendment, the judge stated that it "does not demean the seriousness of the Bread and Puppet Theater's efforts to make the obvious observation that these masquerade protests are entertainment, and none the less so because of any social or political themes or overtones." More recently, a state judge had no trouble rejecting a claim by protesters charged under the present iteration of the New York statute, loitering while masked, which continues to include the duly permitted "masquerade party" exception.[125] Arrested for wearing bandannas on their faces, the demonstrators argued that the permitting scheme was unconstitutionally vague and that the statute was overbroad. The judge relied upon the "anti-rent riots" portion of the legislative history to conclude that "the anti-mask law was enacted originally in order to prevent identification during lawless activity." This supported the judge's construction of the statute as prohibiting wearing masks for no "legitimate purpose." On this construction, the usual First Amendment hierarchies are again inverted: anonymity as an act of political association is not legitimate, while entertainment would be. These interpretations would support the arrests in 2011 of Occupy Wall Street demonstrators for wearing Guy Fawkes masks.[126]

Most other anti-masking statutes, including proposed model anti-masking statutes aimed at curbing the KKK, contain similar, if expanded, masquerade exceptions.[127] Specific mention of Halloween and Mardi Gras, as well as masquerade balls and theater, are common. These exemptions for what might be termed "carnival" reveal the content and viewpoint discrimination inherent in the statutes. Moreover, these exemptions betray the boundaries of permissible hierarchy inversions even in carnival. For example, the Louisiana anti-masking statute's holiday exemption itself has an exemption, not for a permit, but for sex offenders. The statute prohibits anyone convicted of a sex offense "from using or wearing a hood, mask or disguise of any kind with the intent to hide, conceal or disguise his identity on or concerning Halloween, Mardi Gras, Easter, Christmas, or any other recognized holiday for which hoods, masks, or disguises are generally used."[128]

Yet in all cases, the anti-masking statute exemptions make clear that the carnival exceptions are temporary. Although rooted in religious traditions, carnival and other holidays are disruptions in the social fabric, during which the rules, including the rules of attire, may be suspended. For more constant religious observances that include dress, tattoos, hairstyles, or other appearances, the constitutional issues implicate democracy, hierarchy, and sexuality with even more complexity.

6

Dressing Religiously

Religious dress – often called "religious garb" – implicates one of the most contentious issues of constitutional adjudication. Perhaps because religion has been so historically divisive and continues to be so, the doctrines and theories governing religion are themselves subject to marked divisions. Inherent in the well-known language of the First Amendment that "Congress shall make no law respecting an establishment of religion, or prohibiting the free exercise thereof" is the division between the Establishment Clause and the Free Exercise Clause. While religious garb and grooming most often involve matters of free exercise, they may also embrace Establishment Clause concerns. Within the Free Exercise Clause, divisions regarding belief and practice can be paramount. Doctrinal developments within Free Exercise Clause doctrine have produced divisions regarding the level of scrutiny to be applied and legislative interventions have compounded the segmentation. Important to the bisection of the First Amendment provisions regarding religion into the Establishment Clause and Free Exercise Clause is the distinction between the majority religion(s) and minority religions. Additionally, and perhaps the most controversially, there is the division between religions and nonreligion.

All of these concerns animate issues of tattoos and the Church of Body Modification, accommodation of religious attire and grooming standards in prisons, and women's religious dress including Catholic habits and Muslim niqab and hijab.

I. THE CHURCH OF BODY MODIFICATION

Danielle Bar-Navon and Ariana Iacono were both teenagers who wore facial jewelry to their respective schools. Both violated the school's dress code, both were disciplined, and both brought actions under the First Amendment. Danielle Bar-Navon argued that her non-otic jewelry was expressive speech, conveying a message of nonconformity, a claim the Eleventh Circuit rejected.[1] The court stated that even if Danielle's jewelry satisfied the necessary threshold to qualify as expressive speech, the school restriction would merely be subject to intermediate scrutiny, a standard the prohibition easily survived. The court noted that the dress code allowed Danielle adequate alternative methods of communication: she could communicate by talking, by engaging in "active debate," or by wearing "symbolic jewelry through ear piercings." Moreover, the school policy did not prohibit piercings; it only prohibited "wearing jewelry through piercings," and it only applied while she was at school. Thus, Danielle Bar-Navon had no First Amendment right to wear her facial jewelry to high school. Ariana Iacono, however, was much more successful. Ariana was a member of the Church of Body Modification.

Ruling for Ariana Iacono, the federal judge described the Church of Body Modification as having approximately 3,500 members in the United States who "practice ancient and modern body modification rituals – including piercing, scarring, tattooing, and suspensions – through which they strengthen the connection between their bodies, minds, and souls."[2] The judge noted that Ariana had joined the church the month that school had started, had her nose pierced, and now believed, "according to the Church's teachings, she must wear the nose stud at all times." With no analysis, the judge found that Ariana Iacono was likely to prevail on the free exercise of religion claim, and therefore restrained the school authorities from enforcing the dress code against Ariana as it pertained to her nose stud.[3]

The constitutional recognition afforded to Ariana Iacono's piercing because of its religious character is implicit in cases in which courts found no First Amendment protection. In Danielle Bar-Navon's case, the Eleventh Circuit noted that she "stated expressly that her non-compliant piercings were intended to make no religious or political statement."[4] In a case involving a cross tattoo for which the student was disciplined under a gang symbols prohibition, the Eighth Circuit rejected her assertion that the tattoo was political speech and found it significant that she did not "identify her tattoo as representing any form of religious expression."[5] In another case involving students wearing rosaries disciplined under a gang attire prohibition, a federal district judge found that rosaries were essentially religious and therefore protected.[6]

Yet the dissonance over protections for piercings in the cases of Ariana and Danielle depending upon their religious motivations might raise serious concerns in a constitutional democracy. The simple, if unsatisfying, explanation is an argument that "religion" has favored status in the constitutional hierarchy. Textually, this is not supportable, especially given that both freedoms of religion and speech are made explicit, as are freedoms of assembly and press, but only religion is also explicitly constrained. Moreover any favoritism is far from a constitutional consensus and may conflict with the other religion clause: the prohibitionary Establishment Clause. As Justice Stewart phrased it, there is a "double-barreled dilemma" when the government prefers an individual's religious explanation over a secular one and thus violates the Establishment Clause mandate "that the government must blind itself to the differing religious beliefs and traditions of the people."[7] More concisely, Justice Stevens wrote that a "governmental preference for religion, as opposed to irreligion, is forbidden by the First Amendment."[8] On the other hand, Justice Brennan argued that the underlying explanation for one's dress was constitutionally significant. Dissenting in *Goldman v. Weinberger* regarding the right to wear a yarmulke with a military uniform, Brennan wrote that if Goldman "wanted to wear a hat to keep his head warm or to cover a bald spot," there would be no constitutional violation because "[m]ere personal preferences in dress are not constitutionally protected."[9] However, Brennan stated that for Goldman, an Orthodox Jew, the military's ban on the yarmulke "sets up an almost absolute bar to the fulfillment of a religious duty" and required Goldman to "violate the tenets of his faith virtually every minute of every work-day."[10]

Although the Court's majority rejected Goldman's constitutional right to wear religious headgear while in military uniform, the 1986 case of *Goldman v. Weinberger* was situated within the period of maximum doctrinal protection for religious expression, including attire and appearance. The circuitous history of free exercise doctrine begins with *Reynolds v. United States* in 1878, a Mormon challenge to the constitutionality of anti-polygamy proscriptions.[11] Reasoning that polygamy was antithetical to democracy and a feature of Asiatic and African societies presumably lower in the hierarchy of civilization, the United States Supreme Court held that the practice of polygamy may be criminalized although the government could not "interfere with mere religious belief and opinions."[12] This practice-belief divide persisted for almost a century, until the Court decided *Sherbert v. Verner* in 1963, holding that even a neutral law of general applicability that incidentally burdened the free exercise of religion should be subject to strict scrutiny. It was *Sherbert* that prompted Stewart's "double-barreled dilemma" criticism and it was the failure to rigorously apply *Sherbert* that prompted Brennan's dissenting opinion regarding Goldman's yarmulke. In 1990, the Court changed course in *Employment Div., Dept. of Human Resources of Oregon v. Smith*.[13] Without overruling *Sherbert* but distinguishing it into irrelevance, Justice Scalia writing for the Court ruled that a "neutral law of general applicability" was constitutional even if there was a burden on a person's free exercise of religion. This standard was necessary, the Court reasoned, given "society's diversity of religious beliefs" and the unconstitutionality of judging "different religious practices."

These concerns had been apparent in *Goldman*. The worry was that if the yarmulke could not be constitutionally prohibited, then presumably neither should the turban or dreadlock, although any test that considered the sincerity of the religious belief and the effect of the religious practice would risk discrimination among religions.[14] The sincerity of religious beliefs – rather than the truth or falsity of those beliefs – is the usual test of religion, but distinguishing between "religion" and constellations of beliefs is not a simple matter. The Court has been most explicit about this subject in two cases construing a conscientious objector statute during the Vietnam War era. In *United States v. Welsh*, the Court performed what Justice Harlan called "a remarkable feat of judicial surgery" in order to preserve the constitutionality of the statute and affirm its earlier opinion in *United States v. Seeger*, in which the Court defined religion as a "sincere and meaningful belief which occupies in the life of its possessor a place parallel to that filled by God" in the lives of those persons who qualify for the statutory definition of religion that stressed the theistic.[15] Consistent with such rationales, a federal district judge found the "Native American Indian movement" qualified as a religion, and found that even if the wearing of long hair was not a "fundamental tenet" of the religion, it was sufficient if the persons asserting the claim were sincere in their belief that the practice was religious.[16] Thus, the acceptance of Ariana's belief in the Church of Body Modification as a religion is consistent with First Amendment doctrine.

The Church of Body Modification has also been recognized as a religion under Title VII, but there was not the level of protection for wearing pierced jewelry that was accorded Danielle Bar-Navon. Kimberly Cloutier, a member of the Church of Body Modification, worked at the retailer Costco and was terminated because of her noncompliance with a dress code that prohibited her eyebrow jewelry. Cloutier had filed an EEOC complaint under Title VII, prohibiting discrimination based upon religion as well as race and sex. The First Circuit rested its rejection of Cloutier's religious discrimination claim on the fact that accommodating Cloutier's religious preference would pose an undue hardship on the company. The court stressed that Costco was not unique in having a dress code designed to promote its professional public image. Facial jewelry on an employee would compromise the image the corporation desired to convey to its customers, in much the same way as blonde hair on African American employees would impede the desired image of other employers.[17]

However, although the First Circuit panel and the district judge both asserted that they would assume Cloutier satisfied the threshold issue of a sincere religious belief, the opinions make clear that the judges had grave doubts. Costco had argued that the Church of Body Modification was not a religion, and even if it were, its religious doctrine did not require displaying facial jewelry at all times. The EEOC disagreed. When the issue came before the federal courts, they trod carefully. The district judge noted that the term "religious" was elusive, but added that this presented a difficulty for an employer, as well as for courts.[18] As to Cloutier's sincerity, the district judge's recitation of the facts highlighted the timing of Cloutier's joining the church; she had engaged in body modification before joining and seemingly joined after Costco was enforcing its new dress code, and she did not mention her religion when first advised by a Costco supervisor to remove her facial jewelry. The district judge also delved into church doctrine, stating that the church did not demand the constant *display* of body modifications, and that Cloutier's own practice was inconsistent in this regard: "It is perhaps significant that plaintiff does not insist that *all* her body modifications, for example her tattoos, be visible at all times."[19] Essentially repeating these facts, the First Circuit, like the trial judge, nevertheless stated it assumed that Cloutier met the threshold of sincere religious belief. Yet judicial disquiet regarding both the church and Cloutier's sincerity color the conclusion that Costco's accommodation of a warehouse cashier's facial jewelry would be an undue hardship. The undue hardship finding does not rely upon Cloutier's motivation. In *Cloutier*, unlike the comparison between the students Bar-Navon and Iacono, there is equality between the religious and the secular.

While Title VII may seem more balanced than the First Amendment, Title VII privileges religion by absolving it from the overall goal of anti-discrimination. Title VII of the 1964 Civil Rights Act exempts any "religious corporation, association, educational institution, or society with respect to the employment of individuals of a particular religion to perform work connected with the carrying on by such corporation, association, educational institution, or society of its activities."[20] The initial exemption was narrower, but Congress broadened it in 1972 to omit the word "religious" before activities and thus include the secular activities of any religious organization. In this form, it was upheld against an Establishment Clause challenge in the United States Supreme Court's 1987 decision, *Corp. of Presiding Bishop of Church of Jesus Christ of Latter-day Saints v. Amos.*[21] The case began as a lawsuit by several employees against several employers connected with the Church of Latter-Day Saints, also known as the Mormon Church. The plaintiffs had been terminated from their jobs solely because each of them was unable or refused to satisfy the Mormon Church's worthiness requirements for a temple recommend,[22] a certificate "issued only to individuals who observe the Church's standards in such matters as regular church attendance, tithing, and abstinence from coffee, tea, alcohol, and tobacco."[23] Most of the plaintiffs were employees of Beehive Clothing Mills, which manufactured "temple clothing, garments and temple veils."[24] By the time the case reached the U.S. Supreme Court, it did not involve temple attire, and concerned only one plaintiff and one employer. The employer was an indisputably secular enterprise, the Deseret Gymnasium, open to the public. The employee terminated for lack of his temple recommend performed indisputably secular work as a building engineer, essentially maintaining the building and gym equipment for the past sixteen years. In a unanimous opinion, the Supreme Court approved the termination under the religious employers exemption to Title VII. The Court held that the Title VII exemption was a constitutional means of accommodating the religious practices of the employer – including running a gym open to the public – and did not violate the Establishment Clause.[25]

This exemption for religious employers extends to an employee who raises a religious discrimination claim based on dress. Lori Kennedy, a member of the Church of the Brethren, as a matter of religious principle, wore "modest garb that includes long dresses/skirts and a cover for her hair." At some point during her thirteen years as a geriatric nursing assistant, her supervisor informed her that her attire was inappropriate and made residents and their family members uncomfortable. If Kennedy had been employed by a secular nursing-care facility, there would be no question that she would have a claim. However, as the Fourth Circuit explained, Kennedy's employer was the Villa St. Catherine, a nursing-care facility with statues of the Virgin Mary, Jesus, and St. Catherine Laboure adorning the facility's landscape and a crucifix on the wall of every resident's room.[26] As a religious employer, Villa St. Catherine's termination of Kennedy because of her Church of Brethen dress was insulated from Title VII review.

Perhaps more surprisingly, courts have extended this religious exemption to insulate an employer who "terminates an employee whose conduct or religious beliefs are inconsistent with those of its employer."[27] This means that a religious employer has carte blanche with regard to employment decisions, including employee's attire and grooming. Thus, if Ms. Kennedy had worn her skirt too short, had not worn a cross, or had painted her nails, she could still be terminated if Villa St. Catherine contended these acts were inconsistent with its mission. Additionally, the so-called ministerial exception, constitutionalized by a unanimous Court in 2011, provides support for religious employers to have absolute authority over anyone they deem as having a ministerial function, including a teacher in a private school.[28] Thus, in this hierarchical structure, religion trumps. However, perhaps it is more accurate to conclude that employers trump.

The criminal context yields different results, as two Texas death penalty cases illustrate. Upholding the death sentence of Irving Alvin Davis, a Texas court affirmed the requirement that Davis "lift his shirt and stand before the jury" to display the "inverted pentagram on his chest."[29] The pentagram, which the court describes as having been etched, burned, or carved on Davis's body, and then labeled a "tattoo," was introduced as evidence of Davis's Satanism. Davis objected to the viewing of the "tattoo" as well as expert testimony on Satanism, but the appellate court in *Davis v. State* relied on precedent that the Constitution "does not erect a *per se* barrier" to the admission of evidence protected by the First Amendment, and implicitly concluded this included religious beliefs.[30] Likewise, in *Robles v. Quarterman*, a federal court upheld admissibility of a defendant's tattoo described as "depicting a demon eating Christ's brain."[31] Applying the more deferential standard of post-conviction review, the judge rejected the argument that the tattoo's admission into evidence violated a right to free exercise of religion. Importantly, in both *Davis* and *Robles*, the opinions stressed that the tattoos were introduced in the penalty phases as relevant to the issue of future dangerousness. Essentially, having Satanic markings on one's body supports that body's state-sanctioned demise.

II. ACCOMMODATION IN THE PENITENTIARY

In addition to the inverted pentagram on Davis's flesh to prove his Satanism, the state also offered a grievance form filed by Davis while he was a prisoner. In this form, Davis stated that he had been a Satanist for several years and "that he was also a 'blood sorcerer' who had taken up vampirism, and that he was without the materials that he needed to practice his religion."[32] While the prison authorities presumably did not supply Davis with blood, Davis's grievance illustrates recognition by prisoners that they are entitled to religious accommodation while incarcerated. Among the most common religious grievances in state and federal prisons are those related to hair and "headgear."[33]

While prisoners generally have less robust constitutional rights than others, they arguably have more religious freedom than employees or students, at least as a matter of positive law. This anomaly is the result of a complex constitutional interaction between the United States Supreme Court and Congress. In 1990 the Court decided *Employment Div., Dept. of Human Resources of Oregon v. Smith* – a case involving the religious use of peyote – and held that a neutral law of general applicability did not merit judicial application of strict scrutiny.[34] This change of the standard for First Amendment Free Exercise claims did not go unnoticed by Congress. In response to *Smith*, Congress enacted the Religious Freedom Restoration Act (RFRA) in 1993.[35] Congress invoked the Framers and specifically stated its purpose was "to restore the compelling interest test as set forth in *Sherbert v. Verner* " which it did by explicitly articulating a strict scrutiny standard.[36] When the constitutionality of RFRA came before the Court, the Court had little difficulty in finding that Congress had exceeded its powers under the Fourteenth Amendment's enforcement clause, easily concluding that RFRA was not congruent and proportional to the Court's interpretation of the First Amendment's Free Exercise Clause as applicable to the states through the liberty clause of the Fourteenth Amendment.[37] This meant that although RFRA remained applicable to federal laws, state laws would be measured by the less rigorous *Smith* standard.

Shifting to its powers under the Commerce and Spending Clauses, Congress again sought to subject state laws to higher scrutiny but the scope was much narrower in the Religious Land Use and Institutionalized Persons Act (RLUIPA).[38] As the name implies, the statute affords greater protections for religious groups against land use regulations such as zoning and for persons who are incarcerated or otherwise institutionalized. Under RLUIPA, a prison rule that imposes a substantial burden on the religious exercise of a prisoner is invalid unless it is "in furtherance of a compelling governmental interest" and "is the least restrictive means of furthering that compelling governmental interest."[39] Yet the question of the constitutionality of RLUIPA itself soon surfaced. The Sixth Circuit, disagreeing with most of the other courts that had considered the constitutionality of RLUIPA, held the statute unconstitutional, beginning its analysis by quoting Justice Stevens's argument that "governmental preference for religion, as opposed to irreligion, is forbidden by the First Amendment."[40] The Sixth Circuit found that RLUIPA would have the effect of "encouraging prisoners to become religious in order to enjoy greater rights." The Supreme Court unanimously reversed the Sixth Circuit in *Cutter v. Wilkinson*.[41] Justice Ginsburg, writing for the Court, found the Sixth Circuit's reasoning too broad. She noted that it would invalidate the statute Congress passed in reaction to *Goldman v. Weinberger* that changed the law to allow members of the military to wear "conservative" religious apparel while in uniform.[42] Although the Court added that should "inmate requests for religious accommodations become excessive, impose unjustified burdens on other institutionalized persons, or jeopardize the effective functioning of an institution, the facility would be free to resist the imposition" and raise the constitutionality of RLUIPA as an as-applied challenge.

Given this complex history, it is not surprising that adjudications of prison religious accommodation claims suffer from doctrinal blurring and a level of incoherence.[43] Nevertheless, RLUIPA's elevation of the standard to strict scrutiny should be more favorable to an inmate's challenge. Philip Henderson, a Native American inmate in the California state prison system, claimed that the California Department of Corrections three-inch hair-length limit for men infringed upon the free exercise of his Native American religious beliefs in violation of the First Amendment; a panel of the Ninth Circuit concluded "the regulation at issue is reasonably related to legitimate penological interests."[44] The panel in *Henderson v. Terhune* explicitly stated that it expressed no opinion regarding whether or not the regulation would survive RLUIPA's higher standard. A few years later, the Ninth Circuit opinion in *Warsoldier v. Woodford* noted this explicit reservation and held in favor of another Native American inmate challenging the California three-inch hair-length regulation.[45] There is not only a hierarchy between claims but also between levels of legal representation necessary to navigate – and litigate – this hierarchy effectively. In *Warsoldier*, ACLU and private attorneys represented the inmate from the initial filing of the complaint through the appeals to the Ninth Circuit; in *Henderson*, the plaintiff represented himself pro se in all proceedings. Because most of the challenges by inmates are pro se, the better practice of courts would be to construe any religious claim as sounding in RLUIPA rather than under the First Amendment, but this is not always the case.[46]

In prisoner challenges to hair-length restrictions based on religious exercise claims, prison security is unwaveringly raised as a compelling governmental interest intended to satisfy the strict scrutiny standard of RLUIPA. The security interests generally include the possibility of prisoners hiding contraband in their hair with the related interest regarding the necessity of searching the prisoner's head, as well as the ease of prisoner identification while incarcerated, the risk that a prisoner will escape and evade recapture by cutting his hair thus making identification more difficult, and the institution's interest in maintaining hygiene. Most courts consider these interests compelling, especially the prevention of contraband, but there is more disagreement as to whether a per se hair-length rule is the least restrictive means of accomplishing such purposes.

In *Warsoldier*, the Ninth Circuit refused to defer to the "conclusory statements" of the California Department of Corrections (CDC) that no other regulations would adequately serve the security purposes. Instead, the court stated, the CDC had to demonstrate that it "actually considered and rejected the efficacy of less restrictive measures before adopting the challenged practice." The court found it highly relevant that Warsoldier was confined in a minimum security facility.

Moreover, the court in *Warsoldier* credited two arguments that other courts have rejected. First, the Ninth Circuit panel found "analytically useful" the practices of other prison systems. It noted that the Federal Bureau of Prisons operates the largest system in the nation and does not impose any hair-length policies for prisoners. Additionally, the panel considered that Colorado expressly provided for a religious exemption to the grooming regulations. The court found it troubling that the CDC did not explain why other prison systems were able to meet their similar security interests without infringing on their inmates' right to freely exercise their religious beliefs with regard to hair length.

Second, and even more uniquely, the Ninth Circuit panel in *Warsoldier* found CDC's gender disparity in its hair-length regulations relevant to the "least restrictive means" inquiry. Warsoldier's challenge was to this California Code provision:

> A male inmate's hair shall not be longer than three inches and shall not extend over the eyebrows or below the top of the shirt collar while standing upright. Hair shall be cut around the ears, and sideburns shall be neatly trimmed, and shall not extend below the mid-point of the ear.

On the other hand, the California Code provision regulating women's hair was more flexible, even as it included a conservative caveat:

> A female inmate's hair may be any length but shall not extend over the eyebrows or below the bottom of the shirt collar while standing upright. If hair is long, it shall be worn up in a neat, plain style, which does not draw undue attention to the inmate.

Given that the compelling governmental interests applied "equally to male and female inmates," the court reasoned that this suggested "the hair length restriction is not the least restrictive means to achieve the same compelling interests."[47]

Contrary to the Ninth Circuit, the Eighth Circuit in *Fegans v. Norris* rejected substantially similar arguments. Michael Fegans, an inmate in Arkansas and a member of the Assemblies of Yahweh, argued that the newly enacted hair-length regulation for male inmates did not withstand the "least restrictive means" requirement of RLUIPA. The Eighth Circuit, however, was not convinced by Fegans's arguments that the Arkansas policy was more restrictive than other prison policies and was also gendered, mandating hair above the ears and no longer than the middle of the nape of the neck in the back for male prisoners and the allowance of shoulder-length hair for female prisoners. The court found it important that these arguments were contradicted by the testimony of prison officials, even if the officials' statements seemed to be bare declarations. For example, Norris, the director of the Arkansas Department of Corrections, testified that more liberal policies would be "less effective" in the Arkansas system since "he had seen one of these policies at work in the past" and "security wasn't nearly as good then as it is now." Similarly, Director Norris had something to say about gender differences: "Women are not generally as violent as men. They are not as escape prone as men. They are not as prone to give us problems with contraband as men." In neither case did Fegans contradict this testimony.[48] As the dissenting judge in *Fegans v. Norris* correctly argued, however, Fegans did not have to refute Norris's statements.[49] Under RLUIPA, the prison authorities have the burden and mere assertions should not meet that burden.

Fegans v. Norris illustrates the precarious relationship between RLUIPA and the religion clauses of the First Amendment. One problem seems to be that despite RLUIPA's mandate of the strict scrutiny standard, some courts effectively apply the lower standard of the Free Exercise Clause established in *Smith*, or even the lowest standard for prison policies requiring only a legitimate penologic purpose enunciated by the United States Supreme Court in *Turner v. Safley*.[50] Although the Eighth Circuit opinion in *Fegans* does not refer to neutral laws of general applicability, it does state that to accept the prisoner's arguments would be to "allow accommodation of religious observances to override other significant state interests." Another problem flows from the U.S. Supreme Court's opinion in *Cutter v. Wilkinson* upholding the constitutionality of RLUIPA.[51] The Eighth Circuit in *Fegans v. Norris* was not concerned with *Cutter*'s Establishment Clause doctrine, however, but with the dicta regarding deference to prison officials. The Court in *Cutter* stated courts should give "due deference to the experience and expertise of prison and jail administrators in establishing necessary regulations and procedures to maintain good order, security and discipline, consistent with consideration of costs and limited resources."[52] The court in *Fegans v. Norris* used such language to eviscerate the strict scrutiny standard of RLUIPA. In this way, RLUIPA becomes RLU – effectively applicable only to religious land use.

However, RLUIPA and Free Exercise claims are more highly placed in the hierarchy of rights than are claims based upon gender discrimination. As in the employment and school contexts, differing hair lengths for males and females are superficially accepted. The Eighth Circuit in *Fegans* devoted two sentences to Fegan's equal protection claim, essentially accepting Norris's testimony that women are less troublesome prisoners than men. In contrast, the district judge in *Ashann-Ra v. Commonwealth of Virginia* applied intermediate scrutiny to a Virginia policy that allowed longer hair lengths for female inmates.[53] The judge conceded that some of state's arguments in favor of the sex-specific policy "have the hollow ring of sexual stereotypes," including its argument that "a haircut of one inch in length would be considered an extreme hair style for a female inmate and that such haircuts might be used to symbolize involvement in a homosexual relationship with another inmate." Nevertheless, the judge upheld the policy, noting that the inmate did not dispute the prison official's "unsupported statement that female inmates are not as prone to be violent, to hide weapons in their hair, or to escape as male inmates."[54]

Ashann-Ra, who the judge stated described himself as African American with coarse, kinky hair that hung halfway to his shoulders and could be put into two ponytails, braids, or plaits, did not have a gender claim. But he might have better success if he raised a claim as a Rastafarian, or a member of the African Hebrew Israelites of Jerusalem, or a member of a Native American religion, or an adherent of any other religion that eschews cutting of hair. Again, a person's mere personal preference is not constitutionally noteworthy, even as this raises Justice Stewart's "double-barreled dilemma" and Justice Stevens's warning of preferring religion over irreligion.[55] Yet this hierarchy of rights raises the possibility that a prisoner such as Ashann-Ra could strategically convert in order to maintain his hairstyle. Anxieties over religious fraud percolate throughout the prisoner cases.

To meet the threshold requirement for a RLUIPA claim, as for a Free Exercise claim, the prisoner must have a sincere religious belief in the practice to be accommodated. RLUIPA itself defines "religious exercise" as including "any exercise of religion, whether or not compelled by, or central to, a system of religious belief," although it states that the prisoner's belief must be "sincere." Eliminating the compulsion and centrality requirements prevents the risk of an Establishment Clause violation by judicial inquiry into the tenets of any religion. This risk also shapes the sincerity inquiry, although more obliquely. Reversing a district judge who concluded that the Rastafarian claim by Indiana inmate Homer Reed was "insincere," Judge Posner wrote for the Seventh Circuit in *Reed v. Faulkner* that mere inconsistent observance cannot be determinative.[56] Reed, who objected to cutting his hair based upon his beliefs, was seen eating meat, a violation of another Rastafarian creed. Posner reasoned "the fact that a person does not adhere steadfastly to every tenet of his faith does not mark him as insincere." To conclude otherwise would be to place prisons in the position of promoting "strict orthodoxy" by "forfeiting the religious rights of any inmate observed backsliding, thus placing guards and fellow inmates in the role of religious police."[57]

Additionally, although sincerity should be sufficient, the impermissible centrality or compulsion inquiries may resurface. In another instance of a Judge Posner opinion reversing a district judge's conclusion that a prisoner had no religious claim, the Seventh Circuit's 2012 decision in *Grayson v. Schuler* centered on Omar Grayson's dreadlocks.[58] Illinois prison officials had forcibly sheared the dreadlocks of Grayson, a member of the African Hebrew Israelites of Jerusalem, based upon the prison chaplain's representation that members of the sect were "not required by their faith to wear dreadlocks." Again, the problem is that the prison officials, including the chaplain – and perhaps especially the chaplain – may not "determine which religious observances are permissible because orthodox." While Posner's relatively brief opinion does not mention the Establishment Clause, it is doubtless the underlying issue.

Also at issue in both *Grayson* and *Reed* are distinctions among religions. While the pertinence of the First Amendment's religion clauses to distinctions between religion and irreligion remains a divisive issue, the rationale of the religion clauses as forestalling internecine conflicts is generally thought settled. Yet both *Grayson* and *Reed* demonstrate the persistence of religious divisiveness. In the earlier case of *Reed*, the Indiana prison admitted that it did not enforce the hair-length regulation against Native Americans and the federal district judge seemed to be the very judge who had issued an oral order to that effect. However, both the prison and the judge did not extend this rationale to Homer Reed as a Rastafarian. Indeed, the prison officials and the judge seemed to distinguish Rastafarians on the basis that dreadlocks symbolized a belief in "black superiority." For Posner, this raised the specter of a denial of equal protection.[59]

In Omar Grayson's case, it was the Rastafarians who had become the privileged group entitled to an exemption for dreadlocks. In addition to proclaiming his knowledge of the tenets of the African Hebrew Israelites of Jerusalem regarding hair, the prison chaplain also opined that only Rastafarians could wear dreadlocks under the policy prohibiting hair that created a "security risk."[60] This distinction among sects is precisely the type of discrimination the religious clauses were intended to prevent.

Yet in all religious accommodation cases there is an implicit discrimination among sects: the members of the dominant "sect" need no accommodation at all given that their religious practices are standard. A prison policy prohibiting "radical," "bizarre," or "exotic hairstyles" requires a normative judgment to enforce the regulation. In *Walls v. Schriro*, a Hare Krishna practitioner in an Arizona prison challenged such a policy as it was applied against his sikha, a shaved head except for a lock of hair at the base of the skull.[61] The federal district judge found that the prison's security interest in uniformity of prisoners was undermined by prison policies of allowing a wide variety of hairstyles not based upon religious beliefs (short hair, long hair, braided hair) as well as baseball caps, religious headgear, and Native American headbands. The judge's opinion suggested that Walls should be able to maintain his hairstyle but did not imply that the prison's policy was facially unconstitutional.

Among sects that are not the dominant sect, there is nevertheless a hierarchy. Claims rooted in some religions seem less likely to be accommodated. In their empirical work considering the success rates of religious accommodation claims, law professors Gregory Sisk and Michael Heise conclude that Muslims fare more poorly than any other group, including in prison litigation.[62] By their account, when all other explanatory variables are kept constant, Muslims succeed before a federal judge at a rate of 15.5 percent in prisoner cases, while non-Muslims succeed at a rate of 44.8 percent in prisoner cases: a Muslim prisoner raising a religious claim has only about a third the chance for success as a non-Muslim prisoner.[63] While not all claims from Muslim prisoners revolve around hair and headgear, many do. Notably, Muslim prisoner claims seek accommodation for religious practices of wearing a skullcap (kufi or taqiyah) or eschewing shaving.

Yet while religious claims by Muslims may be empirically less likely to succeed, courts – and prison officials – display the same strategies to deny the accommodation. The doctrinal blurring and resultant incoherence arising from the relationship between RLUIPA, the Free Exercise Clause, and the prison setting may lead a court to default to the lowest possible standard. One particularly troubling example is *Braithwaite v. Hinkle*, in which the federal district judge discussed RLUIPA and free exercises cases that had found constitutional problems with the same policy of the South Carolina Department of Corrections, but then applied the lowest possible standard of evaluating the policy, requiring only a logical connection to a legitimate penological interest.[64] The judge then opined that the no-beards policy was a neutral law of general applicability, not a religion-based rule. Additionally, the judge chastised the Sunni Muslim inmate for failing to "allege that he has no alternative means of exercising his religious rights," even after he was directed to "elaborate on whether he could or could not practice his religion in ways other than growing a beard." The Fourth Circuit summarily affirmed.[65]

In a 2011 Fifth Circuit case applying RLUIPA, *DeMoss v. Crain*, the court noted that the Texas prison officials had first disputed whether DeMoss's religious practice required him to wear a beard.[66] Instead, the central issues became RLUIPA's compelling governmental interest standard and its accomplishment through the least restrictive means. This government burden seemed to shift to the inmate to suggest alternatives to the no-beard policy. The two alternatives the pro se inmate suggested – a religious exemption or allowing all inmates to grow a quarter-inch beard – were found burdensome to the prison. The court reasoned that allowing a religious exemption would impose a "significant administrative burden on prison chaplains, who already spend the vast majority of their time on administrative duties." Presumably, the chaplains would be determining religious sincerity, and not engaging in the impermissible determinations of whether a beard was central or required by the religion, or risking Establishment Clause violations by making pronouncements such as only Rastafarians are allowed to have dreadlocks. As to the quarter-inch beards, the court reasoned that this would require the prison to "purchase additional grooming equipment and hire more barbers." The administrative costs and burdens on the prison were compelling governmental interests sufficient to defeat the inmate's suggestions of other less restrictive means. This is as much of a burden shifting to the inmate as the Eighth Circuit accomplished in *Fegans v. Norris* by expecting the inmate to effectively contradict the prison official's statement that "women are not as violent as men."[67] However, in *DeMoss*, no judge dissented to make this point.

Only two years earlier, the Fifth Circuit did appoint counsel to represent a pro se inmate Willie Lee Garner, an adherent of Islam, to argue a RLUIPA claim based upon the Texas prison policy limiting beards and the wearing of the kufi head covering. While denying the Free Exercise claim, the Fifth Circuit in *Garner v. Morales* found that the RLUIPA claim was particularly complex and novel, meriting the appointment of an attorney.[68] On remand to the district judge with appointed counsel, the court rejected the challenges to the no-beard and limited kufi policy. The judge also distinguished the policies, implicitly finding that the limited kufi policy was less burdensome. The limited kufi policy allowed the wearing of the kufi in the cell and in the location where religious services were held. The Muslim inmate wanted to wear the kufi on the way to and from religious services, but the judge noted that unlike facial hair, the kufi was easily removed and easily a hiding place for contraband. The judge concluded that the prison's compelling interest in security was served in the least restrictive means possible by its rule requiring removal of the kufi while the inmate was in transit.[69]

A different district judge did not engage in RLUIPA's compelling interest and least restrictive means inquiry, finding that the limited-kufi prison rule did not substantially burden the inmate's religion. In *Brown v. CMC*, the judge concluded that the inmate's belief regarding wearing the kufi prayer cap "at all times" was not substantially burdened by making the inmate remove his cap for identification purposes at the prison pharmacy because he was "permitted to wear the kufi cap at all other times."[70] The judicial ability to determine that a sincere religious belief requiring the wearing of a garment "at all times" is not substantially burdened by a prison policy that transforms "all times" into "sometimes" demonstrates the inability to accept a religious practice that might be viewed as "exotic" as a sikha hairstyle. It also risks an Establishment Clause violation by implicitly determining the contours of religious orthodoxy. But as law professors Gregory Sisk and Michael Heise argued, the empirical data suggest that claims based on Islam are at a particular disadvantage in the judicial arena, perhaps due to unarticulated biases regarding Muslims, exacerbated by the so-called 9/11 effect, ascribing a propensity toward violence as a Muslim characteristic.[71]

For women, any ascribed violence is complicated by an identification of their clothes, including headscarves and especially veils, with a stereotype of female subservience and anti-democratic impulses. Yet these hierarchal concerns easily become subsumed in the privileging of other hierarchical relationships.

III. THE IMPORTANCE OF LOOKING AT WOMEN

Hijab, with a linguistic provenance of "to prevent from seeing,"[72] invokes Muslim bias but also poses an obvious problem in the prison context given the emphasis on inmate identification and incessant surveillance. It also poses challenges for other types of identification such as drivers' licenses. In courtrooms, the identification is more subjective, raising issues of "demeanor" as well as the specter of a criminal defendant's constitutional right of confrontation under the Sixth Amendment. In classroom, some teachers are subject to still-existing historical bans on "religious garb." Other employees are also subject to employer uniform or "look policies." In all of these cases, international developments, anti-Muslim bias, notions of sexuality and democracy, and constitutional religious freedom theories inflect the – often indeterminate – outcomes.

In prison settings, the hijab as a headscarf (giving it the usual sartorial rather than conceptual meaning) would seem not to raise issues of identification because the face is not covered. Moreover, assuming that all women are less likely to carry contraband or be violent, as prison officials have testified to explain differences in male and female prisons, there should be little worry. Nevertheless, prison bans on "headgear" obviously include headscarves. A Ninth Circuit panel in *Safouane v. Fleck* found against a woman prisoner claiming wrongful removal of her headscarf.[73] Decided in 2007, the opinion demonstrated an astonishing ignorance of Islamic tenets by citing one of the evidentiary weaknesses as a failure to "indicate how" the "only proffered alternative arrangement – having Sarah Safouane handled only by female prison guards – had any relevance to the hijab policy."[74] In another, perhaps better litigated, case decided by a Ninth Circuit panel a few years later, *Khatib v. County of Orange*, it was incontrovertible that forcing the woman to remove her headscarf in the jail "violated her religious beliefs by forcing her with head uncovered to confront strangers, including men to whom she was not related."[75] The central gravamen of this litigation was whether the jail to which Souhair Khatib had been removed – the courthouse holding facility – was covered by RLUIPA. Reversing the panel decision that it was not covered, the en banc Ninth Circuit held

RLUIPA "plainly covers" such a facility.[76] Concurring, Judge Gould contended that a "Muslim woman who must appear before strange men she doesn't know, with her hair and neck uncovered in a violation of her religious beliefs, may feel shame and distress," and that this is "precisely" the kind of harm RLUIPA should remedy. On this court's view, then, there was little question of the type of accommodation that should occur.

Similarly, in the prison visitation case of *Bint-Ishmawiyl v. Vaughn*, a federal judge in 1995 found the accommodation of providing a female correctional officer to be sufficient. Bint-Ishmawiyl wore a veil, the removal of which the judge assumed would burden her free exercise of religion, although that was "perhaps debatable." As for the compelling governmental interest, there was no doubt the prison had an interest in making sure visitors were "indeed the persons they profess to be," and of "greater importance, that the person leaving the prison after a visit is indeed the same person as the visitor who entered the prison." The judge found this reasonable, despite the fact that the woman had to schedule her visits at times when a female correctional officer was available, which she could "readily learn, by a telephone call."[77] Although the judge's decision applied the then-applicable RFRA, the result would be the same under RLUIPA.

State enactments seeking to protect religious freedom – sometimes known as "little RFRAs" – introduce another layer of statutory protection for religious claimants, but for a Muslim women seeking to appear veiled on her driver's license photo, the Florida RFRA statute offered no relief. Sultaana Freeman had originally been photographed for her driver's license wearing a niqab, a full face covering except for her eyes. Although this original photographing occurred with little apparent fanfare, months later, and after the intervening tragedy of 9/11, the Florida department of motor vehicles informed Freeman that her license would be canceled unless she presented herself for a photograph unveiled. In the controversial case of *Freeman v. Department of Highway Safety and Motor Vehicles*, the question of accommodation was intertwined with the lack of a "substantial burden" on Freeman's religious beliefs.[78] The courts essentially eviscerated the Florida state RFRA, passed just as the federal RFRA was, to (re)impose the burden of strict scrutiny after the Supreme Court's decision in *Smith*. At the end of the final appellate opinion in Freeman's litigation, *Smith*'s essence is restated: "as long as the laws are neutral and generally applicable to the citizenry, they must be obeyed."[79]

Also interwoven was the issue of the sincerity of Freeman's religious beliefs. The trial judge found Freeman's stated belief prohibiting graven images, including photographs, was inconsistent: she has been "willing to have her picture taken many times, albeit veiled, and eyes are facial characteristics of living beings." Additionally, although she testified that she excised faces from cereal boxes so her children did not see them, there was the matter of her husband, who testified that "they hold their beliefs as a family unit and yet he has not objected to being photographed for his own driver's licenses or throughout this televised trial."[80] Given the finding of insincerity, Florida courts could disregard cases that recognized the similar beliefs prohibiting graven images of Christian Pentecostals, and exempted them from the driver's license photograph requirement.[81]

Instead, the courts imputed a religious belief to her based upon other Muslim women, a belief that could be accommodated. According the trial judge, "the State apparently has a practice of accommodating Muslim women holding similar beliefs on veiling." This consisted of state agents escorting a woman to a private room, with only a female license examiner present. Then there would be a "momentary" lift-ing of the veil in order to complete the digitalized image or photo, done in "private circumstances," and she could "place the photo license in her pocket and never show it to anyone, except perhaps to law enforcement officers in specific situations." The Florida appellate court affirmed, finding that Freeman's religious "veiling practice" was merely inconvenienced and not substantially burdened under the Florida RFRA.[82] To reach this conclusion, the appellate court recited the findings of the two experts who testified at trial. The state's expert, predictably, testified that "Islamic law" accommodates exceptions to the practice of veiling because of neces-sity, including the necessity of identification. Interestingly, he is described as an "American-educated law professor who also holds a Ph.D. and master's degree in Islamic law." Freeman's expert, equally predictably, testified the doctrine of necessity would not apply to a woman removing her veil for a driver's license photograph. He is described as an Imam, a local religious leader, who has been a practicing Muslim for twenty-seven years. The courts easily, if implicitly, elevated the more legal expert over the other one, performing the type of declaration of religious dogma that risks an Establishment Clause violation. The issue of the sincerity of Freeman's religious belief regarding wearing her niqab is obscured by expert opinions regarding the orthodoxy of her belief.

In addition to divisions of opinion regarding the stringency of wearing the reli-gious niqab, there is divisiveness about whether wearing a veil is a religious practice at all. This dispute fomented another controversial case, *Muhammad v. Paruk*, that began in a small claims court in Michigan, was the subject of federal litigation, and resulted in a change of the state rules of evidence.[83] In 2006, Ginnah Muhammad, wearing her niqab, was set to testify regarding disputed charges by Enterprise Rent-A-Car, but Judge Paruk told her to remove her veil because he needed to see her face to observe her "demeanor and temperament." Muhammad asserted her Muslim religion and requested a female judge. Judge Paruk stated that there was not a female judge available. He also asserted that her veil, unlike a headscarf, was not a "religious thing," but a "custom thing," a perspective he had ascertained from other practicing Muslim women he knew.[84] She disagreed, refused to remove her "clothes," and Judge Paruk dismissed Muhammad's case against the car rental company. Meanwhile, the car company's suit went forward, again before Judge Paruk, who denied Muhammad's request that he recuse himself. He ultimately awarded the car rental company damages against Muhammad.

Muhammad sought to vindicate her right to wear religious attire in state court by going to the federal courts, but the federal district judge's opinion did not resolve the issue. Instead, even as he discussed the facts and legal standards regarding the controversy, Judge Feikens ultimately relied upon constitutional principles of federalism, including the Eleventh Amendment, to withhold exercising federal power in the interests of not increasing "friction" between the federal and state courts. Part of Judge Feikens's rationale was that he would have to determine whether Judge Paruk had a neutral and generally applicable policy of "requiring witnesses to keep their faces visible while giving testimony," an inquiry that "would undoubtedly increase" federal-state friction. Although Muhammad appealed to the Sixth Circuit, she dismissed the appeal before oral argument.[85]

Meanwhile, Muhammad's niqab attracted the attention of Michigan judicial officials, resulting in the adoption of a new subsection of the Michigan Rules of Evidence. Rule 611(b), entitled "Appearance of Parties and Witnesses," was added:

> The court shall exercise reasonable control over the appearance of parties and witnesses so as to (1) ensure that the demeanor of such persons may be observed and assessed by the fact-finder and (2) ensure the accurate identification of such persons.

The Michigan Supreme Court's Order adopting the amendment thus substantially adopts the approach of small claims' Judge Paruk.[86] Applied to future litigants wearing a niqab, the rule is susceptible to challenge as violating the Free Exercise Clause with reference to two different doctrinal strands of the general doctrine. First, there is an argument that Rule 611(b) is not a neutral law of general applicability, although it might appear so on its face. The Michigan Supreme Court's Order adopting the amended rule specifically states that it arose from Muhammad's case in small claims court, raising the specter that it is similar to *Church of the Lukumi Babalu Aye, Inc. v. City of Hialeah*, in which the Court found that a city ordinance aimed at prohibiting ritual animal sacrifice was targeted at adherents of Santeria.[87] As a targeted rather than neutral law, the appropriate standard was strict scrutiny, and the Hialeah ordinance was easily found to be unconstitutional. The evidence that the Michigan Supreme Court targeted the Muslim women's wearing of the niqab is less persuasive than Hialeah's extended concern regarding Santeria sacrifices. Importantly, the Hialeah ordinance had several provisions that served to exempt other killings of animals, including the practice of Jewish kosher slaughter, so that Santeria slaughter was obviously the central prohibition. The Michigan rule appears much less targeted and it arguably simply restates the rule of judicial discretion. Nevertheless, the Michigan Supreme Court justices explicitly discussed Muhammad's case and the opinions also extensively discussed the niqab, including conclusions that it is not required religious wear in front of judges. This religious interpretation, combined with Michigan's large Muslim population and the court's failure to amend the evidentiary rule in previous situations involving sunglasses, hats, or disguises, does raise the possibility of the application of strict scrutiny rather than the more deferential test accorded to neutral laws of general applicability.

Second, Michigan Evidence Rule 611(b) could give rise to the type of "hybrid" constitutional challenge that Justice Scalia's opinion in *Employment Div., Dept. of Human Resources of Oregon v. Smith* distinguished in its effort to articulate a new doctrinal rule without overruling any previous cases.[88] These hybrid constitutional claims invoking not only free exercise of religion but also an additional constitutional right – such as freedom of speech or the press, or the due process rights of parents to direct the upbringing of their children, or possibly free association – presumably still merit strict scrutiny. The application of Rule 611(b) could possibly raise a hybrid claim. In *Muhammad v. Paruk*, for example, Muhammad also argued that she was denied her constitutional right of access to the courts, generally derived from the due process clause of the Fourteenth Amendment (or, for federal courts, the due process clause of the Fifth Amendment). Additionally, a niqab-wearing Muslim woman might raise an Equal Protection Clause claim, especially if the judge followed Paruk's example and proclaimed the veil a "custom thing." In either of these situations, a court might apply strict scrutiny to a court order based on Rule 611(b) for a Muslim woman to remove her niqab in court.

The rationale of the Michigan Supreme Court Justices in adopting Rule 611(b), however, is based less on the constitutional interests embedded in the religion clauses, or other rights of the niqab-wearing woman, than on those expressed by the Sixth Amendment's Confrontation Clause.[89] Although Muhammad's appearance in small claims court regarding a rental car contract was unarguably civil, the trepidation is that she might have just as easily been a witness for the prosecution in a criminal case. The Sixth Amendment provides that in "all criminal prosecutions, the accused shall enjoy" various rights, including "to be confronted with the witnesses against him." A witness whose face is obscured raises confrontation issues.

Stressing that the Confrontation Clause required visible faces, Justice Scalia writing for the Court in *Coy v. Iowa* discussed the origins of the word "confront," stating that simply as a matter of Latin, it combines "con -" (from "contra" meaning "against" or "opposed") and the noun "frons" (forehead).[90] Scalia then provided an excerpt from Shakespeare's play, *Richard II*, in which the eponymous regent says, "Then call them to our presence-face to face, and frowning brow to brow, ourselves will hear the accuser and the accused freely speak."[91] While the origins of the

Confrontation Clause's inclusion in the Constitution are less than clear, Scalia concluded that "there is something deep in human nature" that mandates an interpretation of the Confrontation Clause as requiring "face-to-face confrontation between
accused and accuser." Thus, the Court's majority found the Confrontation Clause
was violated when two prosecution witnesses, thirteen-year-old girls, testified with
a screen between the witness and the defendant, blocking him from their sight but
allowing him to see them dimly and to hear them.[92]

The Court left "for another day" whether there were any exceptions to this face-to-
face requirement of the Sixth Amendment's Confrontation Clause, and within
two years this day arrived. In *Maryland v. Craig*, Justice Sandra Day O'Connor
announced for the Court that "face-to-face confrontation" was not the "sine qua non
of the confrontation right."[93] Again considering child witnesses testifying about sexual assault, the Court upheld the constitutionality of their closed-circuit television
testimony, acceptable under the state evidence rules after an individualized assessment. Scalia, dissenting, seemed to disavow the opening left by *Coy v. Iowa* and
maintained that the text of the Sixth Amendment's Confrontation Clause unquali-
fiedly guaranteed a face-to-face confrontation.

Whether the importance of seeing a woman's face unobscured by cloth rises to
a constitutional right of a criminal defendant remains unresolved in the United
States, as does the relationship between any Sixth Amendment Confrontation
Clause right of the defendant and any First Amendment Free Exercise Clause right
of the niqab-wearing woman. However, the Canadian Supreme Court has grappled
with this situation and applied similar provisions and principles of the Canadian
Constitution. In *N.S. v. Her Majesty the Queen*, decided by the Canadian Supreme
Court in December 2012, the majority reached a very similar resolution to the
Michigan Supreme Court's adoption of the state evidentiary rule: the trial judge
should be accorded deference in making this difficult decision.[94] The Supreme
Court of Canada provided some guidance to judges seeking to balance the religious
rights of the witness against the confrontation rights of the accused, instructing them
to first determine whether accommodation was possible, and if not, to ask whether
"the salutary effects of requiring the witness to remove the niqab outweigh the deleterious effects of doing so." The majority explained:

> Deleterious effects include the harm done by limiting the witness's sincerely held
> religious practice. The judge should consider the importance of the religious prac-
> tice to the witness, the degree of state interference with that practice, and the actual
> situation in the courtroom – such as the people present and any measures to limit
> facial exposure. The judge should also consider broader societal harms, such as dis-
> couraging niqab-wearing women from reporting offences and participating in the
> justice system. These deleterious effects must be weighed against the salutary effects
> of requiring the witness to remove the niqab. Salutary effects include preventing

harm to the fair trial interest of the accused and safeguarding the repute of the administration of justice. When assessing potential harm to the accused's fair trial interest, the judge should consider whether the witness's evidence is peripheral or central to the case, the extent to which effective cross-examination and credibility assessment of the witness are central to the case, and the nature of the proceedings. Where the liberty of the accused is at stake, the witness's evidence central and her credibility vital, the possibility of a wrongful conviction must weigh heavily in the balance. The judge must assess all these factors and determine whether the salutary effects of requiring the witness to remove the niqab outweigh the deleterious effects of doing so.[95]

The Supreme Court of Canada thus rejected articulating a clear rule. Two concurring justices favored a rule that would always disallow the niqab, based on a rationale that a trial is a "dynamic" event in which evidentiary conclusions can change. A dissenting justice advanced a rule protecting religious freedom in the form of the niqab, based on a rationale that demeanor is a complex assessment and also stressing that the case was a sexual assault prosecution in which the defendants were members of the same religion as the witness.

While the Canadian provisions and principles of democratic constitutionalism are similar, although not identical, to those of the United States, the experiences of less similar nations such as Turkey, France, Germany, and Egypt regulating the wearing of hijab, niqab, and burka are often the subject of comparative constitutional scholarship.[96] A common point of comparison is the extent to which the nation has a commitment to secularism. For example, the banning of hijab in French schools is often explained in light of the French legal principle of secularism, or laïcité. Yet French laïcité is more similar to than different from the United States principle of separation of church and state. In the text of the U.S. Constitution, this is expressed in both the religion clauses of the First Amendment (prohibiting Congress from infringing on the free exercise of religion or from establishing a religion), as well as in Article VI's "test clause" ("no religious test shall ever be required as a qualification to any office or public trust under the United States"). It is also arguably expressed by the lack of "God," "Christianity," or any similar theocratic words in the text of the Constitution, unlike, for example, the Declaration of Independence's invocation of a "Creator" as the font of rights and equality, at least for men.

However, the First Amendment's Free Exercise Clause is generally proffered as the guarantee that public schools could not prohibit hijab as in France, or that governments could not promulgate wider prohibitions on hijab in universities and government offices as in Turkey.[97] But this view is mistaken, as illustrated by the complicated history and contemporary doctrine regarding teacher anti-religious garb enactments.[98]

The prohibitions of teachers wearing "religious garb" are linked to long-standing conflicts between public and religious education, often focusing on Catholic schools. For example, in 1925, the U.S. Supreme Court in *Pierce v. Society of Sisters of the Holy Names of Jesus and Mary*, held unconstitutional Oregon's law exempting private, including parochial schools, from fulfilling the state's compulsory education mandate, resting its decision on the due process rights of parents to direct the upbringing of their children, rather than religious freedom.[99] Another Oregon statute enacted in that era prohibited any teacher in a public school from wearing religious garb.[100] Such prohibitions were aimed at preventing nuns from wearing their habits while teaching, even as they reflect the reality that public schools often hired nuns as teachers. The danger of nuns dressed as nuns in the public schools was expressed by New York's highest court in *O'Connor v. Hendrick* in 1906: "There can be little doubt that the effect of the costume worn by these Sisters of St. Joseph at all times in the presence of their pupils would be to inspire respect, if not sympathy, for the religious denomination to which they so manifestly belong."[101]

In neighboring Pennsylvania, the state's highest court in 1894 rejected an attempt to enjoin a school district from employing as teachers members of the Sisters of St. Joseph, or if employed, to be enjoined from wearing religious dress. The Pennsylvania Supreme Court's majority and dissenting opinions in *Hysong v. Sch. Dist. of Gallitzin Borough* illustrate the opposing perspectives, not only about the doctrinal issues but also about the meaning of the nun's habit.[102] For the majority, the nun's habit was just another mode of dress, albeit religious, and similar to the apparel of other teachers that might indicate religious beliefs. As the court phrased it, "Quakers or Friends, Omnish, Dunkards, and other sects, wear garments which at once disclose their membership in a religious sect," but no one has yet "thought of excluding them as teachers from the school room on the ground that the peculiarity of their dress would teach to pupils the distinctive doctrines of the sect to which they belonged." In contrast, the dissenting judge described the nuns of the Sisterhood of St. Joseph as women whose "striking and distinctive ecclesiastical robes," "strikingly unlike the dress of their sex," serves to "proclaim their church, their order, and their separation from the secular world," wherever they go, by "constantly asserting their membership in a particular church, and in a religious order within that church, and the subjection of their lives to the direction and control of its officers." The Pennsylvania legislature, accepting the majority's invitation to change the law although the court expressed doubts any enactment would solve the problem, promptly passed a statute prohibiting teachers wearing religious garb in public schools, and criminalizing school officials who allowed such a practice to occur.[103]

Perhaps it should not be surprising that almost a century after it was enacted, the Pennsylvania teacher anti-garb statute would be applied to a Muslim woman wearing hijab. Perhaps more surprising, however, is that the Equal Employment Opportunity Commission, with now-U.S. Supreme Court Justice Clarence Thomas as chair, and the Department of Justice under President Ronald Reagan litigated *United States v. Board of Education for the School District of Philadelphia*, reaching the Third Circuit in 1990.[104] While not generally known for their enthusiastic enforcement of many aspects of employment discrimination,[105] the Thomas EEOC and Reagan DOJ pursued a complaint by Alima Dolores Reardon, described as a "devout Muslim" with a religiously held conviction requiring the wearing of a headscarf. Reardon was a substitute teacher, denied assignments unless she changed her attire. School officials relied upon the state religious garb statute and refused to conciliate Reardon's complaint with the EEOC. When the DOJ filed its complaint in federal court, it named as defendants both the Board of Education of Philadelphia and the Commonwealth of Pennsylvania. The district judge held that the Pennsylvania religious garb statute conflicted with equal employment opportunity guarantees of Title VII and enjoined the garb law's enforcement. Reversing, the Third Circuit relied on the U.S. Supreme Court's summary dismissal "for want of a substantial federal question" in *Cooper v. Eugene School District*, in which the Oregon Supreme Court had upheld a substantially similar anti-garb statute in a case involving a Sikh teacher who wore white clothes and a white turban.[106] While recognizing that the Supreme Court's summary dismissal in *Cooper* was not necessarily precedential, the Third Circuit nevertheless upheld the Pennsylvania anti-garb statute and also held that the anti-garb statute constituted an "undue hardship" under Title VII that excused the Board of Education from accommodating Reardon's headscarf. The Third Circuit minimized the relevance of any anti-Catholic bias in the legislative intent of the century-old statute and found it pertinent that the statute treated all religious attire in a similar manner. Echoing earlier judges who accentuated the effect of nun's habits on impressionable children, the concurring judge stressed that seeing Reardon's headscarf might provoke curiosity on the part of students, who then could believe that the school was endorsing religion, which would then risk an Establishment Clause violation. The United States apparently did not petition the Court to review this adverse decision. By 2012, however, Oregon had repealed its anti-garb statute, Pennsylvania legislators had introduced legislation to repeal its statute, and among the fifty states only Nebraska seemed determined to maintain its anti-garb law – a statute that criminalizes the wearing of any religious "dress or garb" by a public school teacher.[107]

But while the Third Circuit's opinion regarding Reardon's headscarf may have settled the issue with regard to Pennsylvania public schoolteachers' claims under Title VII, the Third Circuit considered employer bans on Muslim women's head coverings again in 2009 and 2010 in the context of Title VII and constitutional claims.[108] In *Webb v. City of Philadelphia*, the Third Circuit rejected a Title VII claim by Kimberlie Webb, a Philadelphia police officer, seeking accommodation to wear her headscarf, which the court called a "a khimar or hijaab."[109] Philadelphia rejected any accommodation, relying upon the undue hardship provision of Title VII. The City primarily asserted not an interest in uniformity but in impartiality, or "more precisely, the perception of its impartiality by citizens of all races and religions whom the police are charged to serve and protect." The court accepted this, although it buttressed the City's argument with other cases stressing the paramilitary aspect of the police department. Affirming summary judgment in favor of the City, the Third Circuit declined to consider Webb's sex discrimination and constitutional claims for procedural reasons. In *Equal Employment Opportunity Commission v. GEO Group Inc.*, the Third Circuit rejected a Title VII claim brought by the EEOC on behalf of several Muslim women working for a private prison contractor, GEO.[110] Only one of the women was a uniformed guard, while one was a nurse and the other an intake specialist; all three women had worn headscarves until GEO instituted a "zero tolerance policy" with regard to its rule prohibiting headgear except baseball caps with the GEO logo. The court noted that the headscarves at issue, labeled as khimars, were never particularly described in the litigation. This lack led to various disagreements between the majority and dissenting judges, including whether an inmate could use the khimar to strangle the employee. Dissenting, Ninth Circuit Judge Wallace Tashima, sitting by designation, argued that this was not necessarily true, because the khimar need not be worn tied under the chin at the neck, but could also be worn as a bandanna would be worn, or there could be a smaller "underscarf" as one of the women was already wearing. The majority, however, affirmed the grant of summary judgment in favor of the employer, accepting the interest that allowing headscarves would "compromise the prison's interest in safety and security and/or would result in more than de minimis cost." The majority accorded the prison "officials" great deference, despite the fact that GEO was a private for-profit corporation contractor.

Cases such as *GEO*, *Webb*, and *Board of Education of Philadelphia* belie simplistic assumptions that the First Amendment's religious protections prevent prohibitions of women wearing the hijab or niqab. They also support the empirical findings that among religious claims, those based upon Islam are disadvantaged in the judiciary, while also illustrating the divisive nature of the First Amendment's religion clauses. The intertwining of Title VII in these concerns, even when there are government employers subject to the First Amendment as in *Webb* and *Board of Education*, is illustrative of the doctrinal blurring to the detriment of individual rights.

But such cases also demonstrate – yet again – the ability of employers' interests to trump. Employers and employees still stand in relation to each other as masters and servants, despite the relatively recent abandonment of this legal description. This hierarchical relationship pervades not only the wearing of clothes but also their production.

7

Dressing Economically

The production, maintenance, trade, and transportation of clothes have been central to the development of constitutional doctrine, deeply implicating issues of hierarchy, democracy, and to a lesser extent, sexuality. The entwinement of slavery and cotton, the laissez-faire *Lochner*-era struggles in sweatshops and textiles mills, and the contemporary reign of international free trade have challenged and changed the constitutional contours of labor responsible for our attire. Just as Tudor sumptuary laws sought to channel sartorial options to maximize economic profits, so too has U.S. constitutional doctrine reckoned with cotton, cloth, and clothes as imperative to capitalist success.

One need not subscribe to the theories of Law and Economics, or Marxism, or Charles Beard's controversial 1913 book *An Economic Interpretation of the Constitution of the United States* to accept the premise that the Constitution concerns itself with economic relations.[1] Additionally, one need not reject Justice Holmes's dissent in *Lochner v. New York*, averring that the "constitution is not intended to embody a particular economic theory, whether of paternalism and the organic relation of the citizen to the State or of *laissez faire*."[2] Instead, it is sufficient to recall the oft-cited failings of the Articles of Confederation that led to the Philadelphia Constitutional Convention: the lack of power to regulate commerce and to tax, including the power to lay and collect duties, imposts, and excises.[3] These broad powers were allocated to Congress in the Constitution of 1787, and states were specifically prohibited from imposing duties on imports and exports. The power of Congress to "regulate Commerce with foreign Nations, and among the several States, and with the Indian Tribes" has proven to be Congress's most expansive power, and the basis of many of its worker protection and anti-discrimination laws. Yet the commerce clause has also been narrowly interpreted to limit congressional power to regulate the conditions of labor. Moreover, the Constitution safeguarded slavery.

I. SLAVERY AND COTTON

As cotton replaced wool as the fabric of world trade, the United States became an exporter of the raw cotton that English mills turned into textiles that could be then tailored into garments. But cotton as a staple crop in the United States was inextricably linked to slavery. As Gene Dattel has compellingly demonstrated in his excellent book *Cotton and Race in the Making of America*, it is difficult to imagine one without the other.[4] Yet this linkage was not an inevitable one. Instead, the Constitution itself created the conditions that facilitated the connection.

The 1787 Constitution enshrined slavery, albeit without using the term "slavery," in a number of provisions. First, Article I, section 2, clause 3, established that taxation and representation would be apportioned by counting persons who were free or indentured for a term of years, excluding Indians who were not taxed, and adding "three fifths of all other Persons." The three-fifths clause for the counting of slaves was championed by the slave-holding states; excluding slaves would have resulted in exceedingly low populations and thus lowered representation for such states. New Jersey's Gouverneur Morris famously excoriated such a compromise during the Constitutional Convention: "Upon what principle is it that the slaves shall be computed in the representation? Are they men? Then make them Citizens & let them vote? Are they property? Why then is no other property included?"[5] However, James Madison, the presumptive author of *Federalist* No. 54, argued that the Constitution was correct to view "our slaves" as possessing "the mixed character of persons and of property." Madison argued that this was "in fact their true character," although it was not necessarily a natural one: "it is only under the pretext that the laws have transformed the negroes into subjects of property, that a place is disputed them in the computation of numbers; and it is admitted, that if the laws were to restore the rights which have been taken away, the negroes could no longer be refused an equal share of representation with the other inhabitants."[6]

A second provision enshrining slavery guaranteed the importation of slaves for twenty years. Article I, section 9, clause 1, provided that "The Migration or Importation of such Persons as any of the States now existing shall think proper to admit, shall not be prohibited by the Congress prior to the Year one thousand eight hundred and eight, but a tax or duty may be imposed on such Importation, not exceeding ten dollars for each Person." The year 1808 was buttressed by a third provision, Article V, regarding amendments to the Constitution, exempted Article I, section 9, clause 1 from the amendment process until then.[7] A fourth provision was contained in Article IV, best known for requiring states to give "full faith and credit" to the proceedings of other states and to grant "all privileges and immunities" to citizens of other states. Article IV also mandated the recognition of slave status by all states: "No Person held to Service or Labour in one State, under the Laws thereof, escaping into another, shall, in Consequence of any Law or Regulation therein, be discharged from such Service or Labour, But shall be delivered up on Claim of the Party to whom such Service or Labour may be due." Last, and perhaps most obliquely, the Article I, section 8 powers of Congress include "calling forth the Militia to execute the Laws of the Union, suppress Insurrections and repel Invasions," expressing the possibility of slave rebellions.

Nothing could be more hierarchal, or less democratic, than slavery – a relationship in which some persons are deemed the property of others. As such, its appearance in the U.S. Constitution merits some explanation. There are many rationales for the compromises that constitutionalized slavery. The oft-touted justification is that the Northern abhorrence of slavery yielded to Southern demands in the interests of national unity. Yet Northern anti-slavery sentiment only erratically met the level of abhorrence, tempered as it was by racism and its own economic interests. However, there was some rationalization that the "peculiar institution" of slavery would not continue to be economically viable, even in the South. Thus, it is arguable that anti-slavery factions were willing to compromise because they believed time was on their side. In retrospect, such an opinion seems hopelessly naïve. But it is explicable because the intertwined relationship between American slavery and commercial cotton had not yet occurred.[8]

While the cultivation of "vegetable wool" was certainly in existence in the colonies as in India and the Caribbean,[9] it was seemingly not mentioned at the Constitutional Convention.[10] Instead, to the extent that textiles were implicated in the institution of slavery, it was by reference to indigo, a plant grown and processed for its blue dye.[11] Indigo, grown in the Carolinas and Georgia along with rice, as well as tobacco grown in Virginia and Maryland, were the staple crops and exports of the Southern states and they depended on slave labor for their production. Notably, in support of a suggestion that commercial legislation be passed by a two-thirds rather than a simple majority, Charles Pinckney of South Carolina contended that the regions had vastly different economic concerns: New England had its fisheries and West India trade; New York its "free trade"; and the Middle States their wheat and flour, while the "staple" of Maryland and Virginia was tobacco and the "staples" of South Carolina and Georgia were rice and indigo.[12] Similarly, Oliver Ellsworth of Connecticut, later chief justice of the United States, argued in favor of retaining the prohibition of taxing exports by states noting that "there are indeed but a few articles that could be taxed at all; as Tobo. rice & indigo, and a tax on these alone would be partial & unjust."[13] And in Gouverneur Morris's excoriation of the three-fifths clause, he referred to the "wretched slaves which cover the rice swamps of South Carolina."[14] Even a few years later, in a congressional proceeding in 1792, Representative Hugh Williamson mentioned "the great staples of the Southern States – tobacco, rice and indigo"[15]

However, by 1800, cotton was on the way to becoming the "king" it would be proclaimed to be by the eve of the Civil War. Central to the economy, cotton was the nation's leading export by 1803, comprising 60 percent of all exports by 1860.[16] It was also inextricably intertwined with slavery. The ascendancy of cotton and slavery were supported by two other events – the invention of the cotton gin and territorial expansion – both of which also raise constitutional concerns not entirely resolved by the Thirteenth Amendment.

The Cotton Gin

There are two opposing sets of stories regarding the invention of the cotton gin. In both versions, Eli Whitney, a son of New England, was an erstwhile law student who traveled to the South. In the common and singular story, Whitney was a genius inspired by his observation of a cat clawing through a fence to invent the cotton gin (cotton engine) as a means of separating the seeds from the fiber. In the alternate versions, Whitney was not the sole inventor, or perhaps not even an inventor, and there certainly is not a cat. Instead, the cotton gin was constructed at the behest of a woman, Catherine Littlefield Green, who suggested that the "practical mechanic" Whitney execute her idea while he was a guest at her house near Savannah, Georgia, in the winter of 1792–93.[17] Or, the cotton gin was appropriated from a slave known only as "Sam," who had developed a device based on his father's idea.[18] Or, the device was an ancient one and being modified for Southern cotton's especially difficult seeds around the same time as Whitney was working toward his own invention, with others seeking patents.[19] In all versions of the story, however, Whitney filed for a patent in 1793, corresponding with Secretary of State Thomas Jefferson, and being granted the patent by George Washington in 1794. That the white male entrepreneur would be the one to apply and be granted the patent was in accord with the existing hierarchal arrangements.[20]

But the notion of patent implicates broader issues of hierarchy as well as democracy as entrenched in the Constitution. The Patent and Copyright Clause, Article I, section 8, clause 8, grants Congress the power to "promote the Progress of Science and useful Arts, by securing for limited Times to Authors and Inventors the exclusive Right to their respective Writings and Discoveries."[21] Scarcely debated at the Constitutional Convention it may have seemed uncontroversial and based on familiar English practice of the monarchy granting licenses for a "new invention and a new trade within the kingdom" as was upheld in the famous 1615 *Clothworkers of Ipswich* case.[22] Yet even in *Clothworkers of Ipswich*, the court distinguished monopolies, which would "take away free-trade, which is the birthright of every subject."[23] This potential overlap between a patent and a monopoly is a site of the constitutional conflicts between hierarchy and democracy. Writing centuries later in *Graham v.*

John Deere Co. of Kansas City, U.S. Supreme Court Justice Tom C. Clark noted that Thomas Jefferson "like other Americans, had an instinctive aversion to monopolies."[24] For Clark, this American distaste was rooted in the "monopoly on tea that sparked the Revolution." Certainly Jefferson "did not favor an equivalent form of monopoly under the new government" and wrote to Madison in July 1788 from France urging a Bill of Rights provision restricting monopoly.[25] Yet according to Justice Clark, Jefferson's views "ripened," with Jefferson expressing approval of monopolies for limited periods to encourage ingenuity.[26] Although Jefferson's thinking on monopolies and patents did not necessarily evolve in a particular direction and may not be particularly salient, as secretary of state under George Washington he became the "first administrator" of the patent system, including granting one to Eli Whitney.[27]

Whitney's patent, unlike the invention, was far from successful. Along with his partner, Phineas Miller (who would later marry Catherine Littlefield Green), Whitney's attempt to profit from his claimed monopoly was chimeric at best. The reasons for failure were various: their business plan focused on (over)charging growers to do the "gin" work for them; the invention was easy to reproduce; other inventors procured patents on variations; and the legislative and litigation attempts to enforce the patent claim were largely unsuccessful.[28] Indeed, his application to renew his patent in 1812 was denied.[29] However, in 1810, he did prevail in the federal court case of *Whitney v. Carter*, with an award of $1,500. Part of the defense of the infringement was that Whitney's invention was not sufficiently novel, despite the existence of the patent.[30] In addition to distinguishing an earlier decision adverse to Whitney, the federal judge in Georgia waxed eloquently on the utility of the invention:

> With regard to the utility of this discovery, the court would deem it a waste of time to dwell long on this topic. Is there a man who hears us who has not experienced its utility? The whole interior of the Southern states was languishing, and its inhabitants emigrating, for want of some objects to engage their attention, and employ their industry, when the invention of this machine at once opened views to them which set the whole country in active motion. From childhood to age, it has presented us a lucrative employment. Individuals who were depressed with poverty, and sunk in idleness, have suddenly risen to wealth and respectability. Our debts have been paid off, our capitals increased, and our lands have trebled in value. We cannot express the weight of obligation which the country owes to this invention; the extent of it cannot now be seen. Some faint presentiment may be formed from the reflection that cotton is rapidly supplanting wool, flax, silk, and even furs, in manufactures, and may one day profitably supply the want of specie in our East-India trade. Our sister states also participate in the benefits of this invention; for, besides affording the raw materials for their manufactories, the bulkiness and quality of the article afford a valuable employment for their shipping.[31]

The argument that a patent promoted general economic and social utility supported the grant of the monopoly, as Whitney's attorneys had been arguing.[32] But the contrary is also true. Arguably, if Whitney's patent had been more of a successful monopoly, and thus used less extensively and more expensively, its impact might not have been so profound.[33] Nevertheless, the "utility" of the invention was an important consideration counterbalancing the suspicion of monopolies implicit in the constitution.

Territories and Expansion

The utility of the cotton gin is eclipsed by the usefulness of territorial expansion, including the Louisiana Purchase of 1803. Like the cotton gin, the Louisiana Purchase had a profound effect on the interwoven relationship between cotton and slavery. Again, there were also serious constitutional concerns.

Indeed, the constitutionality of the Louisiana Treaty was itself doubtful.[34] Even if the Treaty had merely been a simple contract for the sale of land, the Constitution did not provide the Executive – or the federal government – with explicit power to execute such a "real estate deal." The Constitution did include a Treaty Clause in Article II, section 2, clause 2, empowering the president, with the advice and consent of the Senate, to make treaties, "provided two thirds of the Senators present concur," although this clause was criticized as too expansive by some delegates. However, even after ratification of the Constitution, whether the treaty power could be used to acquire territory was unclear. It was unclear to the president who used it to enter into the Louisiana Purchase: Thomas Jefferson. Jefferson had been a staunch advocate of strictly construing enumerated powers, lest the Constitution become nothing more than a "blank piece of paper," but the unanticipated offer from France of such a vast tract of land during negotiations for the Port of New Orleans was not easily renounced. The Louisiana Treaty was executed and the Senate quickly gave its "advice and consent." Jefferson explored the possibility of a constitutional amendment, including drafting language, but this option was never seriously pursued.[35]

The constitutional option of judicial review was also not seriously pursued. The Louisiana Treaty and the Supreme Court's landmark *Marbury v. Madison* were both decided in 1803; arguably the notion of the Court as ultimate arbiter of constitutional issues was not established, or at least not solidly so.[36] It is also arguable that the Louisiana Purchase was more important to constitutional law than *Marbury*.[37] Nevertheless, the Supreme Court did eventually use its *Marbury* power to declare that the federal government had the power to engage in land deals such as the Louisiana Purchase in *American Insurance Company v. 356 Bales of Cotton, David Canter Claimant*, decided in 1828.[38] The underlying facts provide a glimpse into the economics and perils of the cotton trade. There were 584 insured bales of cotton (and about 300 other bales of cotton) on the ship *Point a Petre* when it wrecked off the coast of the territory of Florida on its journey from New Orleans to Havre de Grace, France, where it would be transformed into cloth and then clothes. Only a portion of the raw cotton was salvaged from the shipwreck. At an auction in Key West ordered by a Florida territorial court, David Canter bought 356 bales of the cotton, and in turn sold some of them at an auction in Charleston, South Carolina. The insurance company sought to recoup Canter's cotton money, arguing that the Florida territorial court had no power to order a salvage sale.

In writing the opinion for the Supreme Court in 356 *Bales of Cotton*, Justice John Marshall used the occasion to address larger issues, much as he did in *Marbury v. Madison*. As legal scholar Judith Resnik observed about 356 *Bales of Cotton*, "Marshall's opinion reads as a treatise on why Congress had the power, without constitutional amendment, to acquire land for the nation," a topic that was the subject of contemporary debate not only regarding the purchase of Florida from Spain but the Louisiana Purchase from France.[39] The issue more precisely before the Court was whether Congress had the power to establish territorial courts that were not Article III courts. The opinion in 356 *Bales of Cotton*, often called *American Insurance Co. v. Canter*, is thought by scholars to be the Court's first major Article III opinion.[40] It has come to stand for the proposition that Congress has the power to establish non–Article III courts, including for example, bankruptcy courts, but as Judith Resnik has suggested, this is a retrospective interpretation prompted by the relatively recent rise of various adjudicative structures.[41] Seemingly, it is more properly understood in the context of congressional power over territories, in which Congress is both the national and territorial legislature. Marshall's conclusion rested in part on the language of Article IV, section 3, clause 2 – the "Territory Clause" – empowering Congress "to make all needful rules and regulations, respecting the territory, or other property belonging to the United States."[42]

The notion of territory had – and has – broad implications for democracy and hierarchy.[43] The territories were not uninhabited. Indeed, from the congressional perspective, this was part of the problem. Solutions included the "relocation" of Native Americans and the offers of land to white Americans. One of the concerns regarding the Louisiana Purchase from France was that even its white inhabitants were largely non-English.[44] Moreover, in cotton-growing regions, the population was primarily people being held in slavery.

While 356 *Bales of Cotton* may have settled the constitutional issue regarding federal power to make land purchases from a foreign nation, it did not resolve the even more contentious issue governed by Clause 1 of Article IV, section 3. This was the process by which territories became states. Clause 1 simply provided that "New States may be admitted by the Congress into this Union," with the remainder of the provision being concerned with new states being formed from preexisting states.[45] It did not address the issue so vital to the increasingly booming commerce in cotton: whether the cotton-growing states would be "free states" or "slave states." The Louisiana Treaty had the potential to upset the carefully crafted compromise enshrined in the Constitution's three-fifths clause before "cotton fever." If the cotton-growing slave-holding states became a majority in the House of Representatives, this would result in disproportionate power for the voters of those states: white men.

Yet the compromise was always in jeopardy and the territorial or state power to allow slavery had been long debatable. The first Congress had adopted the Northwest Ordinance governing the territory northwest of the Ohio River. The ordinance set out a process for eventual self-governance, with a benchmark based on the number of "free male inhabitants," but it did prohibit slavery and involuntary servitude in its well-known Article VI.[46] Originally passed by the Congress of Confederation under the Articles of Confederation and often called the Ordinance of 1787, the Northwest Ordinance became the model for subsequent congressional approval of territories. It was the model for the Southwest Ordinance, approved in 1790 and governing the territory south of the Ohio River, with one notable exception: a proviso that "no regulations made or to be made by Congress, shall tend to emancipate slaves."[47] This territory later entered the Union as the slave state of Tennessee with the Mississippi River port of Memphis becoming known as a "Child of Cotton."[48] Other territorial statutes and state enabling statutes would incorporate the Northwest Ordinance, with the prohibition against slavery inconsistently – and at times circuitously – exempted.[49] But the provisos permitting slavery were far from erratic. They not only coincided with the territories and new states in which slavery was increasingly a feature but also mapped onto the land suitable for cotton cultivation.[50]

Congress did make attempts to legislate solutions, including the Missouri Compromise Act of 1820, prohibiting slavery in the territories of the Louisiana Purchase north of 36° 30".[51] The Supreme Court would hold the act unconstitutional in the infamous *Dred Scott* decision, *Scott v. Sanford*, rendered in 1857.[52] Justice Taney's opinion is most notorious for holding that Dred Scott was not a citizen entitled to avail himself of the federal courts,[53] but on the merits, the Court held that Congress lacked power to enact the Missouri Compromise statute. In reaching this conclusion, Taney misconstrued the 356 *Bales of Cotton* case, *American Insurance Co. v. Canter*, declaring that there was "not the slightest conflict" between the holding of *Dred Scott* and 356 *Bales of Cotton*: "it is only by taking a single sentence out of the latter and separating it from the context, that even an appearance of conflict can be shown." For Taney, the power of Congress under the Constitution's Article IV to make laws for a territory remained an open question in Marshall's opinion in 356 *Bales of Cotton*. Both of the dissenting justices in *Dred Scott*, in separate opinions, argued that Marshall's opinion had conclusively established that Congress did have the power to regulate territories, and that this power was grounded in the Constitution. The dissenters seem to have the better argument, and the 356 *Bales of Cotton* case could have determined the outcome in *Dred Scott*.

Instead, the *Dred Scott* opinion intensified the political arguments over slavery and statehood. Almost exactly a year later, South Carolina Senator James Hammond would deliver his "cotton is king" speech on the floor of the U.S. Senate on the "Kansas Question" regarding the terms of admission to statehood.[54] Hammond was a well-respected Southerner, despite his youthful homosexuality and adult molestation of underage female relatives, with a reputation for racial moralism.[55] His speech has less to say about "Bleeding Kansas" – as it came to be known for the violent skirmishes between slave staters and free staters – and more to say about slavery, cotton, and the result of any possible war: "No, you dare not make war on cotton. No power on earth dares to make war upon it. Cotton *is* king." This notion, often called King Cotton Diplomacy, relied on cotton not only to finance the war effort but also to induce Great Britain to enter the conflict on the side of the Confederacy because of its economic need for raw cotton.[56] As it turned out, Great Britain remained neutral, and the Confederacy was defeated. In 1865, the Reconstruction Congress passed the Thirteenth Amendment abolishing slavery and involuntary servitude; it was quickly ratified by two-thirds of the states.

While there remain some disputes regarding whether the Thirteenth Amendment or other Reconstruction Amendments complied with the Constitution's Article V amendment process, the Thirteenth Amendment became effective.[57] It was a drastic constitutional alteration of the legality of slavery as well as of federal-state relations, inserting the first (and still only) constitutional guarantee that reaches private action, and including the first (but duplicated in subsequent amendments) section granting Congress the power to enforce the amendment. However, the Thirteenth Amendment did not accomplish land redistribution and it did not abolish cotton. And it may not have truly abolished slavery, despite its explicit language.

The Thirteenth Amendment

Section One of the Thirteenth Amendment, taking its language from the Northwest Ordinance's Article VI, provides "Neither slavery nor involuntary servitude, except as a punishment for crime whereof the party shall have been duly convicted, shall exist within the United States, or any place subject to their jurisdiction." The exception in the amendment's Punishment Clause is an important one. It was the centerpiece allowing continuation of the slave system for cultivating and picking the crop that was transformed into the clothes worn by most Americans, the crop that was integral to the post–Civil War economic recovery and continued to be the nation's largest export until 1937.

As "slaves of the state," prisoners in the cotton states continued the work of slavery, although now more likely to be termed "involuntary servitude."[58] One arrangement was the convict-lease agreement in which a planter would contract with the state for convicts to work a planation. The fee, $9 a month per prisoner in post–Civil War Mississippi, was paid entirely to the government. The system was especially brutal – described as "worse than slavery" – because the planters did not even have an eco-nomic incentive to treat the workers humanely: workers were easily and cheaply replaced.[59] Convict-lease systems became the focus of legal reforms, in part because of conflicts between the planter elite class and the farmers lower in the hierarchy.[60] But the eventual demise of contract-labor did not change the conditions of work for all inmates. Instead, some state prisons entered the cotton business themselves. For example, Louisiana's Angola prison was the former Angola plantation: "prisoners were housed in the old slave quarters and worked in the now state-owned cotton fields."[61] The Mississippi legislature appropriated $125,000 for the purchase of three plantation land parcels of almost 8,000 acres in 1894, and in 1900 appropriated more money for the purchase of Parchman Plantation, which would become the notori-ous Parchman Farm.[62] Contemporary cotton growing continues on state prison land as does the mandatory work requirement for prisoners. As one warden admitted, it is like "a big plantation in days gone by."[63] Courts tend to treat a prisoner's Thirteenth Amendment claim for mandatory and uncompensated work as constitutionally friv-olous under the Punishment Clause exception, although scholars have argued for a more nuanced consideration of the arguments.[64]

However, even a broad reading of the Thirteenth Amendment's Punishment Clause exception is not sufficient to answer constitutional questions about the processes by which persons become prisoners. After the Civil War, the former Confederate states legislated "Black Codes" targeted at former slaves and "poorly disguised substitutes for slavery."[65] States also legislated more seemingly neutral laws that were neverthe-less aimed at the "Negro crime" problem, such as redefining grand larceny as theft of a farm animal in so-called pig laws.[66] Most problematic however, and most obvi-ously connected to cotton, were the vagrancy laws that expanded criminalization, as the Alabama 1865 statute did, to "a stubborn or refractory servant" or a "laborer or servant who loiters away his time." The vagrancy laws could be casually enforced: local law enforcement reportedly would round up the "idlers and vagrants" and take them to the fields when cotton was ripening.[67] Additionally, Alabama's statute made clear that the emancipation of slave into servant (or even apprentice) was a partial transformation. Servants could not leave a master or mistress without permission. And should anyone "entice away any apprentice from his or her master or mis-tress," there would be a $500 fine.[68] Contracts of service were enforced by criminal sanction; a person who "refuses to comply with any contract for a term of service without just cause" was defined as a vagrant.[69] The U.S. Supreme Court invalidated a subsequent version of Alabama's peonage provision in 1911, declaring in *Bailey v. State of Alabama* that the statute was contrary to the Thirteenth Amendment. The Court stated that although it would not impute "any actual motive to oppress," the "natural operation" of the law "furnishes a convenient instrument for the coercion" which the Constitution forbids: "There is no more important concern than to safeguard the freedom of labor upon which alone can enduring prosperity be based."[70] Sixty years later, in *Papachristou v. City of Jacksonville* the Court invalidated a broad vagrancy ordinance that criminalized among others "habitual loafers" and nightwalkers. Considering due process requirements, the Court concluded that it not only failed to provide adequate notice to potential offenders but also served as an impermissible law enforcement net "making easy the roundup of so-called undesirables."[71]

The earlier Supreme Court was less sympathetic. Indeed, in two landmark cases it rejected arguments under the Thirteenth Amendment. In the *Civil Rights Cases*, the Court in 1883 found that the Thirteenth Amendment's enforcement section did not empower Congress to pass the Civil Rights Act prohibiting racial discrimination in public accommodations.[72] The Court reasoned that it would be "running the slavery argument into the ground to make it apply to every act of discrimination," for even before the abolition of slavery the "thousands of free colored people in this country" were not thought to be equal to "white citizens." Thirteen years later, in *Plessy v. Ferguson*, the Court upheld a Louisiana statute that mandated racial segregation in railroad passenger cars, by again delinking racial inequality and slavery, and further reasoning that segregation is not necessarily a "badge of inferiority," unless "the colored race chooses to put that construction upon it."[73]

Neither the *Civil Rights Cases* nor *Plessy* involved cotton labor, and both also involved equally unsuccessful Fourteenth Amendment claims. Nevertheless, the Court spurned the promise of the Thirteenth Amendment's explicit language regarding the abolition of slavery. Instead, the Court implicitly proclaimed the rightful place of former slaves and their descendants: in them old cotton fields back home.[74]

II. LAISSEZ-FAIRE, LAUNDRIES, AND CHILD LABOR

The United States Supreme Court's constitutional interpretations did not necessarily become more democratic or less hierarchal as the Industrial Revolution transformed the methods of converting raw cotton into clothing. The mechanization of spinning and carding led to the development of the English mill factory system that had been so dependent on Southern cotton. The mill factory changed working life for those lower in the hierarchies. Work became desperate and joyless in ways made familiar by Charles Dickens in the novel *Oliver Twist* and Friedrich Engels in

Condition of the Working Class in England, 1844.[75] Yet constitutional doctrine did not embrace democratic and anti-hierarchal goals when confronted with the rise of sewing machines, laundries, or the southern textile industry.

Sewing Machines and Shirtwaists

The sewing machine may seem modest, but it was one of the great mechanisms of the Industrial Revolution. It was lauded as "epoch-making" and as one of the "seven wonders" of American invention, not only ushering in an era of "cheap clothes" but liberating "human fingers from one of the most monotonous, wearisome, and slavish of all forms of labor."[76] Even more than the cotton gin, it was an incremental invention, with various improvements and resultant patents. The "Sewing Machine War" of the 1850s witnessed intensive patent infringement litigation as well as lawsuits for libel, justifying Thomas Jefferson's notion to include an anti-monopoly provision in the Bill of Rights. The conflict's resolution was itself a monopoly: the "Sewing Machine Combination" took its place among the other commercial trusts of the Gilded Age, including the oil and railroad monopolies. It was one of a number of "odious" monopolies that prompted Congress to pass the Sherman Anti-Trust Act of 1890. While the Supreme Court did not declare the Anti-Trust Act unconstitutional, it seriously curtailed it in *United States v. E. C. Knight* by holding that congressional power to regulate commerce did not extend to the power to regulate manufacturing, otherwise "comparatively little of business operations and affairs would be left for state control."[77] The constitutional conflicts regarding states' rights were not solved by the Civil War or the Reconstruction Amendments.

Even apart from federalism concerns, the effect of the Reconstruction Amendments on labor was not limited to chattel slavery. In the famous "cotton is king" speech, Senator Hammond of South Carolina had specifically compared factory workers to slaves. He argued that "operatives" – as those who operated the machines in mills were called – were "essentially slaves" but with an important difference: "our slaves are hired for life and well compensated; there is no starvation, no begging," while the operatives in the North were "hired by the day, not cared for, and scantily compensated." He argued that the operative who "lives by daily labor, and scarcely lives at that, and who has to put out his labor in the market, and take the best he can get for it," is being degraded by being treated as less than a slave.[78] To be sure, Hammond supported his argument with white supremacist rhetoric and obscured the centrality of the concept of chattel in American slavery. Moreover, a slave or person bound by involuntary servitude did not have the all-important legal option to quit.[79] Nevertheless, the notion of "wage slavery" had increasing resonance after the Civil War into the Progressive Era.

Efforts of Northern states to alleviate "wage slavery" by Progressive legislation regulating minimum wages, hours, or other working conditions were thwarted by the constitutional notion of freedom of contract. There were two ironies in this. First, the ability to assert a constitutional claim of freedom of contract against a state was a product of the Reconstruction Amendments, specifically, the substantive aspect of the Due Process Clause of the Fourteenth Amendment. Second, the concept of freedom of contract was itself an abolitionist concept: slaves should not be chattel bound to labor but free persons entitled to contract for the terms of their labor. The apex of the Supreme Court's rejection of the constitutionality of labor protections was *Lochner v. New York*, a case involving bakeries, decided in 1905. The Court held unconstitutional a state law passed in 1897 providing that no employee "shall be required or permitted to work in a biscuit, bread, or cake bakery or confectionery establishment more than sixty hours in any one week." For the Court, the state law was unreasonable: "the freedom of master and employee to contract with each other in relation to their employment, and in defining the same, cannot be prohibited or interfered with, without violating the Federal Constitution."[80]

Thus, when garment workers in New York City sweatshops sought to reduce their working week to fifty-two hours and raise their pay, advocating for legislation had constitutional disadvantages. Instead, workers unionized and ultimately called a strike. Known as the "Uprising of the 20,000," the 1909 strike occasioned police brutality, arrests, and consignment to workhouses. The strikers were predominantly female, many under age eighteen, and almost all of them immigrants. Several scions of Gilded Age wealth supported the strikers, financially and otherwise, as part of their advocacy for women's suffrage. The strike was a modified success. Approximately one in seven of the 500 garment shops settled with the workers for a raise, a fifty-two-hour working week, and closed-union shops. The business that led the resistance to settling with the workers was the Triangle Shirtwaist Factory, owned by the so-called shirtwaist kings.[81]

Shirtwaists – women's blouses worn over plain long skirts in a "Gibson Girl" look – were extraordinarily popular, fashionable, and viewed as both democratic and a symbol of women's increasing equality.[82] The system for manufacturing the blouses, as with other items of clothing, included tenement sweatshops in which workers were "sweated" by contractors, as well as loft factories in which long rows of sewing machines could be powered by a single motor.[83] There were eight such rows on the ninth floor of the Triangle Shirtwaist Factory building when a fire broke out on the floor below, igniting discarded material and quickly spreading through the three floors of the factory. A combination of safety hazards contributed to the high death toll: crowded shop floor, lack of fire drill training, fire trucks in New York City that could only reach the seventh floor, rickety fire escapes, inoperable elevators, and doors locked from the outside. One hundred forty-six people, mostly young women, died.[84] The Triangle Shirtwaist fire became emblematic not only because of the number of deaths, but because it was a very public event, with a number of women jumping from the flames to the street below during the fire, bodies lined up on the sidewalk for identification afterward, and newspaper reports of skeletons bent over sewing machines.[85] It prompted a large commemoration, an unsuccessful prosecution of the shirtwaist "kings," and a state investigative commission that spear-headed a number of legislative reforms aimed at safety including a fifty-four-hour working week for children, minors, and women.[86]

The maximum hours law was soon challenged as an unconstitutional infringe-ment on liberty of contract. New York's highest court had previously declared unconstitutional a 1903 law that not only set a sixty-hour maximum work week for women, but also prohibited women from working after 9:00 P.M. In its opinion in *People v. Williams*, it cited a single case as authority, *Lochner v. New York*, in which the New York court had been reversed.[87] The court in *Williams* reasoned that a woman could not be the "special object of the paternal power of the state" because "she is entitled to be placed upon an equality of rights with the man." Yet when the post–Triangle Shirtwaist Fire statute came before a Brooklyn judge, he was rather dismissive of *Lochner*, quoting Justice Holmes's dissenting arguments in *Lochner* that the Constitution does not embody a particular economic theory, including laissez-faire.[88] The Brooklyn judge offered a stark assessment invoking slavery: the "liberty to contract to sell their labor may be but another name for involuntary ser-vice created by existing industrial conditions." However, his opinion, affirmed on appeal, rested most securely on the gendering of liberty of contract that occurred in the U.S. Supreme Court's 1908 opinion in *Muller v. Oregon*.[89]

Equal Protection and Laundries

Curt Muller, an owner of a large commercial laundry, challenged the constitution-ality of his conviction for violating an Oregon labor law prohibiting women from working in laundries and factories for more than ten hours per day. Like the 1903 New York law passed the same year, the Oregon law was part of the Progressive reform movement intended to improve working conditions in a range of industries. Targeting laws at women workers was a strategy that some thought would eventually lead to improvement for all workers, and that most thought would assist women workers who were more vulnerable than men. Women comprised the bulk of the workforce in garment shops, cotton mills, and laundries, with little bargaining power, given their limited skill and seemingly unlimited supply.[90]

Arguing to uphold the Oregon statute, attorney and future Supreme Court Justice Louis Brandeis filed what would become known as a "Brandeis Brief," emphasizing social facts rather than legal arguments.[91] Working with Progressive labor activists Josephine Goldmark and Florence Kelley of the National Consumers' League, Brandeis's brief conceded the applicability of liberty of contract as pronounced in *Lochner*, but contended that the state possessed a rational basis to infringe on this liberty in the case of women. It stressed the reproductive capacity of women and their comparative weakness to men. At times, the supporting quotations in the brief seem fantastical: a woman is "badly constructed for the purpose of standing eight or ten hours on her feet" because the "knee joint of a woman is a sexual characteristic" with women having a smaller patella (kneecap) than men.[92] At other times, the statistics adduced do not seem to support a finding that women are substantially more frail: in embroidery manufacturing, 302 men were sick compared to 332 women; in bleaching and dyeing, 279 men compared to 316 women.[93]

A unanimous Court upheld the Oregon statute, rejecting Muller's argument that women were entitled to equality. Instead, the Supreme Court found that the differences between women and men – in physical strength, in disposition and habits of life, in maternal functions – justified a "difference in legislation." Thus, "without questioning in any respect the decision in *Lochner v. New York*," the Court declared that the Oregon statute was constitutional "so far as it respects the work of a female in a laundry."[94]

As the Court's limitation of *Lochner* demonstrates, *Muller* also involved a different type of equality argument, that between laundries and other types of work. It is an argument that the Court does not explore, concentrating instead on gender hierarchies. However, Curt Muller had argued that the Oregon statute's application to "any mechanical establishment, or factory, or laundry" was not valid because the type of work was not unlawful, immoral, or dangerous to public health. The Brandeis brief spent the last section of its 113 pages discussing laundry work. This included situating laundry work within the "radical change" of the Industrial Revolution affecting other clothing work: "for good or for evil the washerwoman is passing under the influences which have so profoundly modified the circumstances of her sister of the spinning-wheel and the sewing needle. When the first washing machine and ironing roller were applied to this occupation, alteration in the conditions became as much a foregone conclusion as it did in the case of the textile or the clothing manufactures, when the spinning frame, the power loom, or the sewing machine appeared." Brandeis followed this argument with one that stressed that laundries were even worse than textile or clothing manufacturing, a superfluous argument under the statute's inclusive terms, but pertinent to Muller's specific claim regarding laundries. The Brandeis brief contended that laundry work must be done standing and it is hot and damp; the gas-heated irons give off fumes and there is the danger of hands being caught in the rollers. It is "not the light and often pleasant occupation of sewing or folding." Additionally, laundry work posed special moral hazards. Irregular and long hours dissuaded workers from being "early-risers" and punctual. And then there was beer: "Imagine the amazement of the master of a mill or weaving factory if his employees were to stop in a body for a quarter of an hour twice a day between meals to drink beer! Yet in many laundries the beer is kept on the premises for the purpose."[95]

The questionable status of laundries and the power of states to constitutionally regulate them consistent with the Fourteenth Amendment had been before the Supreme Court several times before *Muller*. In the late 1800s, San Francisco had passed ordinances that were the type of "class legislation" singling out laundries that raised issues under the Equal Protection Clause and to which Curt Muller had averred. San Francisco's ordinances were also the type of "class legislation" that targeted a class of people, albeit not as explicitly as the Oregon statute had. Yet it was well understood that the San Francisco laundry ordinances addressed Chinese immigrants; the vast majority of laundry operators were Chinese and a substantial proportion of all Chinese persons in the city worked in laundries.[96] The relevance of this overlap proved a difficult issue under developing equal protection doctrine. In the 1884 case of *Barbier v. Connolly*, the Court upheld the San Francisco ordinance prohibiting the operation of laundries between 6 P.M. and 10 A.M.[97] The Court focused on the permissibility of class legislation directed at laundries, which although it might be "necessarily special" in character, was permissible under the Fourteenth Amendment if "within the sphere of its operation it affects alike all persons similarly situated." The next year, the Court considered *Soon Hing v. Crowley*, another challenge to the constitutionality of the San Francisco laundry ordinance by a person arrested under it.[98] This challenge, however, explicitly raised the issue of the "hostile motives" of the city supervisors in passing the ordinance. The Court deflected the allegation, stating that the general rule was the "courts cannot inquire into the motives of the legislators"; not only do legislators have diverse motives but there is also "the impossibility of penetrating into the hearts of men and ascertaining the truth." The opinion did, however, mention the exceptions to this general rule: "except as they may be disclosed on the face of the acts, or inferable from their operation, considered with reference to the condition of the country and existing legislation."[99]

It was the latter exception that formed the basis for the Court to find a San Francisco laundry ordinance unconstitutional the very next year. In *Yick Wo v. Hopkins*, the ordinance at issue allowed laundry buildings made of brick or stone, but disallowed other types of buildings, for example, those made of wood, without consent from the city board of supervisors.[100] The ordinance appeared to be "fair on its face," but the Court found fault with the manner in which it was applied. The board of supervisors had withheld consent from the challengers "and from 200 other" applicants, all of whom "happen to be Chinese," while it had granted permission to eighty others, all of whom were not Chinese.[101]

Taken together, the "Chinese laundry cases" – as the trinity of *Barbier, Soon Hing,* and *Yick Wo* are sometimes called – illustrate two vital principles of equal protection doctrine. Importantly, they established that "subjects of the Emperor of China" and thus all noncitizens were included by the term person in the Equal Protection Clause. They also demonstrated, *Yick Wo* in particular, that the unequal application of a law could violate equal protection, a principle that is still controversial.

However, they also illuminate the rise of local "class legislation" aimed at regulating working conditions and public safety in an increasingly industrialized world that prized clothing. San Francisco was not yet focused on protecting workers, but one of its expressed concerns in the cases was fire; the city already had a history of fires and the laundries heated water and irons with flames. While the Court summarily rejected the *Lochner*-type arguments made by the challengers in *Barbier,* after *Lochner* was decided the arguments asserting freedom of contract were likely to prevail whether the government's legitimate rationale was public safety or worker protection. The exception was *Muller's* protection of women workers, given their "difference," although this protection would not extend during the *Lochner* era to paying women workers a minimum wage.[102] As a general rule, state and local laws regulating laborers in laundries, garment factories, and textile mills, as well as in other industries, were susceptible to constitutional challenge on the basis of freedom of contract claims under the Due Process Clause of the Fourteenth Amendment.

The Southern Cotton Manufacturers and Child Labor

Legislative inclination to enact worker protections was not only stymied by constitutional concerns but also by political choices made in various states. Prohibitions against child labor were not popular in many states in the South where the burgeoning post–Civil War textile industry relied on child labor.[103] Progressive reformers sought national legislation and were eventually successful with the Keating-Owen Act in 1916.[104] The act, however, was short-lived. Even before it was passed, the Southern Cotton Manufacturers organization strategized constitutional challenges in concert with prominent corporate attorneys. Despite successes such as *Muller* and an active labor movement, the dominant forces were decidedly free market. Indeed, the American Bar Association was described as a "sort of juristic sewing circle for mutual education in the gospel of Laissez Faire."[105] But constitutional challenges were not only available on the basis of freedom of contract under the Due Process Clause. In *Hammer v. Dagenhart,* the theory of laissez-faire was retrofitted to a state sovereignty argument; the central challenge became congressional power to regulate child labor and the concomitant Tenth Amendment "reservation" of unenumerated power to the states.[106]

Dagenhart, decided by the Court in 1918, is a study in social change litigation by conservative interests. The Southern Cotton Manufacturers hired excellent attorneys, selected a sympathetic judge, and then located an appropriate plaintiff in that judge's North Carolina district.[107] The plaintiff was Roland Dagenhart, on behalf of his two children, one younger than fourteen who would be precluded from working under the Keating-Owen Act, and the other who was fifteen and would have his working hours reduced to eight hours a day under the Act. The litigation proceeded apace, with the judge rather quickly finding that Congress had exceeded its power under the Commerce Clause. In the Supreme Court, the brief on behalf of the Dagenharts revived sentiments familiar from Senator Hammond's "cotton is king" speech. The Dagenhart brief stressed that the United States is a "vast territory" with various laws, income, climates, and races. New York, for example, "has statutes that relate to the employment of children in sweatshops, but sweatshops are unknown in North Carolina." Moreover, in the warmer parts of the nation, although "poverty still stalks" the "weather conditions may make possible constant fresh air even in a factory." Although the Dagenhart children were white, as were most cotton mill workers, the brief pertinently included mentions of the population of a race other than Anglo-Saxon, whose members "mature earlier."[108]

The gravamen of the legal argument was that congressional power to regulate interstate commerce only extended to preventing the "evils" attendant in the commerce itself, such as the "evile" of a lottery ticket in the Court's five to four decision in *Champion v. Ames*.[109] By contrast, there was nothing inherently wrong with textiles made by child labor; a person buying such textiles would not even be able to tell whether a child had been involved in their production. Over a sharp dissent written by Justice Holmes for four justices, including Justice Brandeis who was now a member of the Court, the majority found it fundamental that the "goods shipped are of themselves harmless." Adopting the argument on behalf of the Dagenharts, the Court concluded that to uphold congressional authority to regulate child labor in textile mills would have dire consequences: "all freedom of commerce will be at an end, and the power of the states over local matters may be eliminated, and thus our system of government be practically destroyed."[110]

The predominance of laissez-faire judicial interpretations of legislation regulating textile mill, laundry, or garment factory workers, whether accomplished through constitutional privileging of freedom of contract or state sovereignty, would be eroded by the New Deal era, including the passage of the Fair Labor Standards Act (FLSA), upheld in *United States v. Darby*, reversing *Hammer v. Dagenhart*.[111] Yet FLSA's minimum wage, maximum hours, and child labor provisions did not extend coverage to agricultural workers, including cotton laborers. Moreover, the provisions only cover "employees," exempting workers who are deemed "independent contractors" or whose work is subcontracted, a common practice in contemporary garment factories.[112] Additionally, FLSA's mandatory maximum hours provisions are focused on compensation for hours exceeding the maximum rather than a per se prohibition of excessive hours, another common practice in the contemporary garment industry.[113] Refusing to work six days a week remains a justifiable cause for termination; receiving state unemployment benefits would be unlikely unless the employee raised a First Amendment free exercise of religion claim under the Court's 1963 decision in *Sherbert v. Verner*, a case arising in a South Carolina cotton mill.[114]

Yet even the scattered constitutional and statutory protections for workers in the attire industry are precarious given the realities of globalization.

III. FREE TRADE AND FAIR TRADE

By 2010, the vast majority of wearable items purchased by consumers in the United States were made elsewhere. The American Apparel and Footwear Association, a trade group, reported "the percentage of the U.S. market that is supplied by apparel imports, again reached record levels in 2008–97.0 percent."[115] That would mean of the approximately sixty-five items of attire and eight pairs of shoes purchased by (or purchased on behalf of) each person in the United States in 2008, not even one item was "made in the USA."[116] In the 1960s, the ratio of imports and exports was essentially reversed, with imported clothing being a relative rarity. Yet consumers in 2010 bought more items of apparel and shoes than in previous decades and spent less of their total income on attire. If there remained a "king" in the realm of attire, it was no longer cotton, or any particular shirtwaist manufacturer, but low price.[117]

Price, of course, is not a new consideration. Neither is the relationship of price – and profit – to labor costs. Moreover, global trade is similarly not merely contemporary. Similar justifications supported arguments for slavery, sweated work, and child labor. Similar constitutional issues also arise in current controversies surrounding the production of clothing, including questions about the treaty power and the implicit process of constitutional amendment; the status of territories and their inhabitants; the Thirteenth Amendment's prohibition of slavery and involuntary servitude; and the constitutionality of monopolies.

Trademarks, Tariffs, and the World Trade Organization

Monopolies attach not only to inventions but also to objects. Trademarks, especially for luxury goods, pervade clothing and other items of attire. Indeed, while arguably luxury goods are of higher quality than their usual counterparts, their most distinctive feature may be their trademark. The constitutional authority for Congress to enact trademark protection laws, including the Lanham Act,[118] is not grounded in the Copyright and Patent Clause, but in the Commerce Clause. Unlike copyright and patent, trademark is thus not constitutionally limited to a term certain, but may endure indefinitely, or at least as long as the trademark is in use. Thus, trademarks are the very sort of perpetual monopoly that would "take away free-trade," the "birth-right of every subject," and are inconsistent with the American "instinctive aversion to monopolies." Certainly they would be inconsistent with the monopoly restriction as part of the Bill of Rights urged by Thomas Jefferson.[119]

Jefferson's eventual approval of monopolies for patent and copyright on the grounds of encouraging ingenuity has little applicability to the trademark context. The underlying rationales of granting a monopoly to a tangible mark of a business are to protect the accumulated goodwill of the company and to prevent consumer confusion. Moreover, in the case of attire, this "mark" may be an aspect of the style itself. As scholar Ann Bartow has argued, not only do the boundaries between coun-terfeits and copies ("knock-offs") need clarification, but copies should be legally permissible in the interests of economic equality.[120] She has noted that it is not only "manufacturers of uber-expensive luxury goods" that assert "monopolies over aes-thetic features," discussing the athletic shoe company Adidas' suit against the dis-count shoe company Payless. Adidas, having registered three diagonal side stripes as a trademark on its footwear, successfully used trademark law to prevent Payless from selling competing shoes bearing two – or four – similarly situated stripes.[121] For Bartow, this is an unjust result: stripes are hardly a unique design feature on attire.

Red is similarly not unique, even when it is trademarked as part of an "uber-expensive luxury item" such as Christian Louboutin women's shoes. In the summer of 2012, U.S. Customs Officers reportedly seized shipments from China of more than 20,000 pairs – worth an estimated $18 million – of "counterfeit" Louboutin shoes with the "distinctive red sole."[122] Seemingly, these shoes would have been sold as "genuine" Louboutin shoes, albeit at a deep discount. Meanwhile, the Second Circuit was considering a trademark infringement suit by Christian Louboutin against a fellow French high-end fashion company, Yves Saint Laurent, based on an entirely red shoe that included red soles. The district judge in 2011 ruled in favor of Yves Saint Laurent, reasoning that "conferring legal recognition on Louboutin's claim raises the specter of fashion wars":

> If Louboutin owns Chinese Red for the outsole of high fashion women's shoes, another designer can just as well stake out a claim for exclusive use of another shade of red, or indeed even Louboutin's color, for the insole, while yet another could, like the world colonizers of eras past dividing conquered territories and markets, plant its flag on the entire heel for its Chinese Red. And who is to stop YSL, which declares it pioneered the monochrome shoe design, from trumping the whole footwear design industry by asserting rights to the single color shoe con-cept in all shades? And these imperial color wars in women's high fashion footwear would represent only the opening forays. What about hostile color grabs in the

markets for low-fashion shoes? Or for sports shoes? Or expanding beyond footwear, what about inner linings, collars, or buttons on coats, jackets, or dresses in both women's and men's apparel?[123]

The Second Circuit reversed the conclusion that a "single color can never serve as a trademark in the fashion industry," but nevertheless interpreted Louboutin's trademark to be limited to "uses in which the red outsole contrasts with the color of the remainder of the shoe."[124]

In addition to the battleground of monopolies on colors of uber-luxury shoes, the "fashion wars" are waged even more vociferously on the terrain of low-priced imports. One persistent explanation for the dominance of "cheap" imported footwear and apparel in the United States is the current "free trade" regulatory regime embodied by NAFTA (North American Free Trade Agreement) and WTO (World Trade Organization). An international free trade policy, like a laissez-faire ideology, is a political rather than constitutional judgment. The Constitution evinces an explicit interstate "free trade" policy: it specifically prohibits a tax or duty on articles "exported" from any state.[125] It does, however, empower Congress to lay and collect duties, imposts, and excises, while generally prohibiting states from doing so.[126] The constitutional text seems to contemplate that the national government would impose tariffs, but arguably the Constitution is agnostic on the merits of the free trade with other nations.

There have long been trade agreements involving apparel as well as constitutional challenges to such arrangements. In *Marshall Field & Co. v. Clark*, the U.S. Supreme Court in 1892 considered duties "on woolen dress goods, woolen wearing apparel, and silk embroideries, imported by Marshall Field & Co., on silk and cotton laces imported by Boyd, Sutton, & Co.; and on colored cotton cloths imported by Herman, Sternbach & Co."[127] The companies challenged the constitutionality of the statute under which the duties were accessed, the Tariff Act of October 1, 1890, on several grounds. The first focused on the processes in Article I, section 7, governing how a bill becomes a law. The merchants contended that a section of the bill was not in the version authenticated by the signatures of the presiding officers of the Senate and House of Representatives and signed by the president. In rejecting this claim, the Court established the enrolled bill doctrine, concluding that the judiciary should not delve beyond the signatures of members of co-equal branches of government.[128] The second ground focused more directly upon the powers that Congress could delegate to the president. The companies argued that the Tariff Act's authorization to the president to suspend certain provisions was an unconstitutional delegation of legislative and treaty powers. Again, the Court rejected this argument, noting that this sort of delegation was especially important in the "execution of statutes relating to trade and commerce with other nations" as a way to protect the interests of "our people" against "unfriendly" regulations by foreign governments. The third challenge related to congressional authority under the taxing power to provide "bounties" to certain sugar producers, but the Court declined to reach the merits of this argument, concluding that even should the companies prevail, it would not effect the constitutionality of the Tariff Act's provision requiring them to pay duties on their clothing imports. The Court's decision in *Marshall Field* illuminates the complexity of tariff statutes, even before 1900, and the Court's long-standing lack of sympathy to constitutional challenges to such regulatory schemes.

Constitutional challenges to NAFTA have been similarly unsuccessful, although they have not reached the Supreme Court. The Eleventh Circuit in *Made in the USA Foundation v. United States* declined to reach the merits of a contention that NAFTA did not comply with the constitutional requirements for enacting a treaty (two-thirds of the Senate) given that it was passed as a simple legislation (majorities of Senate and House of Representatives).[129] The court discussed Congress's plenary powers to regulate foreign commerce and the president's inherent authority under Article II to manage foreign affairs, but ultimately held that the question of whether NAFTA constituted a "treaty" requiring Senate ratification presented a nonjusticiable political question. Thus, although scholars have divided on the constitutionality of NAFTA, the judicial assertion of separation of powers principles has truncated the constitutional discussion.[130]

The issues raised by the WTO are even more complex, at least in part because the WTO is not a single trade agreement but an organization involved in multiple agreements and adjudications under those agreements. In operation since 1995 when it replaced the post–World War II General Agreements on Tariffs and Trade (GATT), the WTO's perspective is decidedly "free trade." While not a treaty, and the agreements under it largely executive pursuant to delegated congressional power, there is an argument that the WTO policies have supplanted constitutional standards, and indeed affected a constitutional change without resort to the formal amendment process in Article V.[131] Moreover, on this view the WTO has wrought not only constitutional changes but also substantial alterations in daily life, affecting even "the clothes we wear."[132] This change was under way, however, before the WTO. The Multi-Fiber Arrangement, entered into in 1974, had as its goal the "progressive liberalization of world trade in textile products," with a gradual decrease in quotas and a favoring of developing nations with low labor costs.[133]

Balance of trade concerns are not the only ones. It is not simply that apparel purchased in the United States is produced elsewhere, contributing to a loss of employment in the United States, but there are also concerns that the attire is produced under substandard working conditions. These poor working conditions, as well as market forces, combine to contribute to increasingly shoddy products. While the argument in 1918 was that there was nothing obvious about the fabric milled in

Hammer v. Dagenhart to betray the use of child labor, an increasingly frequent contemporary contention is that clothes now reveal their origins the first time they are laundered and the hem unravels.[134] However, a "Made in USA" label is not necessarily an indication of high quality or exemplary working conditions.

Made in USA?

Attire "Made in the USA" is not necessarily manufactured under optimal conditions. It may be produced in a domestic sweatshop, in prison, or "overseas." In each instance, international free trade policies have had an impact on American working conditions.

First, while domestic sweatshops did not end with the Triangle Shirtwaist Factory, the contemporary struggle for fair working conditions operates in the shadow of the ability of retailers to use overseas outsourcing.[135] The free movement of clothes and other commodities but not persons across national borders has not only led to garment factories relocating overseas but also to the phenomenon of trafficked workers for garment production within the United States. While the vast majority of trafficked persons in the United States work in the sex industry, the garment industry has a notable portion. A constitutional issue under the Thirteenth Amendment may arise if conditions are tantamount to slavery or involuntary servitude, especially if the workers have had their travel documents seized or are kept captive.[136] Such claims can be part of an overall democratic activism, using litigation and government lobbying, as well as union and public relations organizing, to attempt to provide workers a "fair wage." An extended anti-sweatshop effort centered in Los Angeles is a model in this regard, but even it had mixed success given the overseas option.[137]

Second, prisoners not only cultivate cotton, they turn it, and other fabrics, into apparel. In the federal prison system, Federal Prison Industries (FPI), doing business as UNICOR, touts prisons as "factories with fences." One of UNICOR's components is the Clothing and Textiles Group (CTG), described as providing "a wide range of products, the majority of which are procured from a distinct cadre of customers on a contractual basis," including "military clothing such as army combat uniforms, physical fitness apparel, shirts and cold weather gear," as well as "specialty bags (for helmets, tools and the U.S. Postal Service), body armor, gloves, household items (mattresses, towels, linens, custom drapes, bedspreads), as well as screen printing, embroidery services and textile repair services."[138] Government is not the only customer for prison manufactured attire. For example, in 2012, UNICOR partnered with the retailer Woolrich Inc. to "manufacture two items, a fleece sweatshirt and a down parka which are now made exclusively outside of the U.S." The stated motivation of Woolrich was to "make these items in the United States" and the potential economic benefit was "$8 million in annual sales with nearly $600 thousand in projected earnings."[139] Like the prisoners in the cotton fields, inmates working in prison garment factories are exempt from wage and hour statutes, and Thirteenth Amendment claims have been rejected.

Third and last, the United States is even more vast than the attorney for Dagenhart described in his 1918 brief. Saipan is the largest of the islands in the Commonwealth of the Northern Mariana Islands (CNMI), an unincorporated territory of the United States. Located north of Guam in the Pacific Ocean, the islands have been "possessed" by Spain, Germany, and Japan. Saipan, like Guam, was invaded by the United States during World War II. After being part of the Trust Territory of the Pacific Islands, administered by the United States and the United Nations, the Northern Mariana Islands negotiated a formal relationship with the United States. The Covenant – formerly known as the Covenant to Establish a Commonwealth of the Northern Mariana Islands in Political Union with the United States of America – entered into in 1976 and approved by Northern Mariana Islanders continues to govern the relationship between CNMI and the United States.[140] The Covenant was validated by a Joint Resolution of Congress and thus did not conform to the constitutional requirements for a treaty.[141]

The Covenant specifically exempted U.S. laws on immigration and minimum wage from applicability to CNMI.[142] Other than tourism, the central aspect of CNMI's economy is garment manufacturing. Two-thirds of CNMI's working population is comprised of noncitizen, foreign workers.[143] Clothes manufactured in CNMI bear the "Made in USA" label; they are not subject to quotas or tariffs, even as such existed before free trade policies. This confluence of factors led to working conditions in garment factories that were described as involuntary servitude in a complaint in federal court filed against Saipan garment manufacturers and major clothing retailers such as The Gap, J. Crew, Jones Apparel, The Limited, Wal-Mart, Tommy Hilfiger, Nordstrom, and Levi Strauss.[144]

The district court dismissed the Thirteenth Amendment claim, stating that the Supreme Court's pronouncements left an "open question" about whether the Thirteenth Amendment by its own terms "did anything more than abolish slavery."[145] The district judge then turned to the federal involuntary servitude statute passed under the Thirteenth Amendment's enforcement power. The judge found that the allegations were not sufficient to demonstrate "the use or threatened use of physical restraint, physical coercion or legal coercion to compel labor," although acknowledging that threats of deportation could rise to that level and allowing leave to amend. However, subsequently, the judge found that the amended allegations were insufficient, concluding that the plaintiffs retained some "choice, however painful." The judge found it relevant that some of the plaintiffs had worked for more than one factory on Saipan, and also that the severe financial consequences of employment termination or deportation remained within the realm of choice.[146]

The plaintiffs' peonage claims likewise did not ultimately survive. Originally, the district judge found that the allegations were sufficient because they included plaintiffs' fear of the threatened consequences if they are unable to pay their recruitment fee debt, which plaintiffs allege is essentially a debt owed to their employer, and which the district judge found sufficient to impose liability on the retailer defendants.[147] However, subsequently, the judge found that the allegations were insufficient to sustain a claim of peonage. The judge reversed his conclusion that a debt to the recruiter was tantamount to a debt to the employer. Further, he found that the employers' assessment of food and lodging was an expense rather than a debt. And third, he concluded that the "performance deposits" of more than $1,000 that the employees paid to their employers were not debts that must be worked off; the employees had a choice to quit and forfeit the money.[148] Regarding the statutory peonage claim, the judge found that the "state action" required under the act was not satisfied by recruitment agencies working with the Chinese government.[149]

However, although the judge dismissed the plaintiffs' constitutional and quasi-constitutional claims, the judge did allow the civil Racketeer Influenced and Corrupt Organizations Act (RICO) claims to proceed. Relatively soon thereafter, the Saipan manufacturers and the clothing retailers – with the exception of Levi Strauss – entered into a settlement with the court-certified class of garment workers. The settlement included a requirement that the retailers adhere to a specified code of conduct – "CNMI Monitoring Standards" – in all future contracts with CNMI garment suppliers and that the CNMI garment manufacturers submit to independent workplace and living quarters monitoring, as well as the establishment of a settlement fund of $20 million to finance the monitoring.[150] The code of conduct included the CNMI (but not U.S.) minimum wage with no work to be done "off the clock," safety precautions such as fire alarms, no employer retention of passports, and limitations on recruitment and housing fees assessed to workers.[151]

Congress also acted by extending federal immigration laws to CNMI effective in 2009, a change that CNMI resisted by filing an action in federal court arguing that the change violated the Covenant. The federal district judge found that CNMI had Article III standing – discounting an argument that the federal government had rather amazingly advanced – but rejected CNMI's claim; the new immigration regime became effective.[152] Reportedly, the immigration change had negative consequences for the garment industry; but the industry was already suffering from the WTO free trade abolition of quotas for clothing imported to the United States.[153]

No-Sweat Procurement Policies

A different governmental strategy abandons the government as regulator in favor of the government as market participant. Anti-sweatshop procurement laws by local governments attempt to influence working conditions wherever they may occur, but these may provoke constitutional issues if they conflict with federal free trade policies. For example, New York City's "Apparel and textile services procurement" local law, passed by the City Council over the veto of the mayor in 2001, prohibited the city from purchasing apparel or textiles except from a "responsible manufacturer."[154] The council's legislative findings stated, "after almost a century of progress in the struggle against sweatshops in the apparel and textile sectors, there has been a recent resurgence of such exploitative and abusive workplaces in New York, the United States, and around the world." The law thus changed the usual lowest bidder process to require contractors and subcontractors to "provide a safe, non-discriminatory work environment and compensate their employees with a non-poverty wage" and included reporting requirements to effectuate those goals.

The mayor challenged the Local Law, contending it violated the City's Charter, the state constitution, and the Constitution's Supremacy Clause, Article VI. The New York court decision in *Mayor of City of New York v. Council of City of New York* did not reach the federal constitutional challenges that the Local Law was preempted by federal labor and wage and hour laws, as well as by the exclusive federal power to formulate foreign policy.[155] Instead, the New York court applied state constitutional principles and found the city's local law preempted by state law governing procurement. The state law, passed after the New York City law – and specifically referencing that law as part of a trend – was more lenient.[156] The state law required the manufacturer to attest that the "apparel was manufactured in compliance with all applicable labor and occupational safety laws, including, but not limited to, child labor laws, wage and hour laws and workplace safety." Applying state preemption doctrine and statutory construction principles, the court held that under the statute, localities had two choices: they could have no apparel procurement law or they could adopt the state's apparel procurement statute. Under the court's decision, New York City could not adopt a different – and seemingly certainly not stricter – local law.[157]

Yet even the weaker state law could raise constitutional issues. Although the law did not specifically mention other nations or other states, these applications could have constitutional implications. A state law interfering with foreign commerce could be subject to preemption under the rationale that the federal government has exclusive power in this realm. The exclusive federal foreign policy rationale had recently been used by the U.S. Supreme Court to invalidate a Massachusetts law prohibiting the state from doing business with companies in Burma (Myanmar) and a California law requiring insurance companies disclose information regarding their work during the Holocaust.[158] Moreover, a state law interfering with the interstate commerce and discriminating against goods from other states might run afoul of the dormant commerce clause.[159] But the statute would most likely survive such challenges if courts agreed that the statute prohibited purchase of certain goods regardless of their places of origin (such as Burma) but based on the conditions of their production.[160]

The New York statute, however, did not provoke a constitutional challenge during its short existence. When passed in 2002, it had a sunset provision with an automatic repeal of certain of its sections, including those regarding procurement, in 2008.[161] New York statutes retain a special task force on the apparel industry, but there is no mandate regarding state procurement policies.[162] The policies that do remain in effect, however, give priority to apparel and other commodities "produced by the correctional industries program of the department of corrections and community supervision."[163]

Additionally, the New York law provides that the state and city universities have the authority to implement sweat-free policies in their purchase of apparel or sports equipment.[164] Passed in 2003 and still valid in 2012, the statute recognizes the student anti-sweatshop movement that has been so influential. Democratic activism by students addressed the $4 billion collegiate apparel industry, forming United Students against Sweatshops in 1997, then later a Workers Rights Consortium, aimed at disclosing factory locations, monitoring and improving worker conditions, and then a Designated Suppliers Program, attempting to provide a living wage and job stability to workers producing university logo apparel and goods.[165] The Designated Supplier Program has the potential to run afoul of the same anti-trust statute prompted by Gilded Age monopolies such as the Sewing Machine Combination, but the Department of Justice in late 2011 issued an opinion that there was no anti-trust violation.[166]

Yet the government's role as market participant is modest. It is as a regulator that local, state, and territorial governments, as well as the federal government, most pervasively control the conditions of labor and work. The Constitution's Thirteenth Amendment, with or without a private right of action, sets an exceedingly low bar for standardizing working conditions. Instead, governments, albeit erratically, use their constitutional powers to eradicate hierarchy and to promote democracy, as well as to ensure sexual freedom for female garment workers, in the production of attire. This is no less true now than it was in eras of the Industrial Revolution, slavery, the American Revolution, and even the Tudors.

That government might limit the consumption of apparel, even indirectly through tariffs or quotas, has become unimaginable. It is even more difficult to imagine the Constitution empowering Congress with a Sumptuary Clause. However, the constitution does empower and allow the regulation of our attire and appearance in a multitude of ways. When we are barely, sexily, professionally, disruptively, or religiously dressed; when we have a tattoo or a hairstyle or a new pair of shoes; when we wear a jacket, a mask, a skirt, or a uniform; when we are at work, at school, in court, in prison, or in public; or when we launder silk shirts, or purchase cotton shorts or apparel we believe was made in the United States, our sartorial choices are inextricably linked with the Constitution.

Notes

1. DRESSING HISTORICALLY

1. Magna Carta, Paragraph 35. Initially known as the Charter of Liberties, the 1215 Magna Carta was confirmed in 1217 with the clauses concerning the use of the royal forests separated, so that it became known as the Great Charter to distinguish it from the Charter of the Forest. The 1215 document's less famous precursor is the 1100 Charter of Liberties, executed when Henry I ascended the throne.
2. 11 Edward III, c. 1–5 (1337), Statutes of the Realm 1: 280–281.
3. 10 Edw. III, Stat. 3 (1336), Statutes of the Realm 1: 278–279.
4. 37 Edward III, A Statute Concerning Diet and Apparel (1363), Statutes of the Realm 1: 378–383.
5. Id. (Chapter 9, applicable to "People of Handicraft and Yeoman").
6. 3 Edward IV c. 5, Act for Regulating Apparel (1463), Statutes of the Realm 2: 399–402; 22 Edward IV c. 1 (1482), Statutes of the Realm 2: 468–470.
7. 8 Henry V c. 3 (1420), Statutes of the Realm 2: 170.
8. 1 Henry VIII c. 14, Act against wearing of costly Apparell (1510), Statutes of the Realm 3: 8–9.
9. 6 Henry VIII c. 1, Act of Apparel (1514), Statutes of the Realm 3: 121–122; 7 Henry VIII c. 6 Act of Apparel (1515), Statutes of the Realm 3: 179–182; 24 Henry VIII c. 13, Act for Reformation of Excess in Apparel (1533), Statutes of the Realm 3: 430–432.
10. Maria Hayward, *Rich Apparel: Clothing and the Law in Henry VIII's England* (Farnham, England: Ashgate, 2009), pp. 29–39.
11. 1&2 Phil. & Mary c. 2–6, An Act for the Reformation of Excess in Apparel (1553), Statutes of the Realm 4(1): 239. The 1553 Act was targeted at the lower classes; it prohibited the wearing of silk in hats, bonnets, nightcaps, girdles, hose, shoes, scabbards, or spur leathers, by any person who was not heir apparent of a knight, or entitled to twenty pounds per year in land rental fees, or possessed assets of two hundred pounds. The penalty was imprisonment of three months and a fine of ten pounds for every day of violation.
12. Alan Hunt, *Governance of the Consuming Passions: A History of Sumptuary Law* (New York: St. Martin's Press, 1996), p. 143.
13. 18 & 19 Car. II c. 4, An Act for Burying in Wool Only (1666), Statutes of the Realm 5: 885–886.

14. 13 Elizabeth I c. 19, Act for the making of Cappes (1571), Statutes of the Realm 4(1): 555.
15. 5 Elizabeth I c. 3, An Act for Relief of the Poor (1563), 4 Statutes of the Realm: 411–414; Steve Hindle, "Dependency, Shame and Belonging: Badging the Deserving Poor, c. 1550–1750," *Cultural and Social History* 1 (2004), 6–35.
16. 8 & 9 Will. III c. 30, cl. II, An Act for supplying some Defects in the Laws for the Relief of the Poor of this Kingdome (1697), 7 Statutes of the Realm 281–283.
17. 1 Edward VI, c. 3, An Act for the Punishment of Vagabonds and for the Relief of the Poor (1547), 4 Statutes of the Realm: 5–8.
18. 22 Henry VIII c. 12, An Act Concerning Punishment of Beggars and Vagabonds (1530), 3 Statutes of the Realm: 328–332.
19. 3 & 4 Edward VI, c. 16, An Act Changing the Punishment of Vagabonds and Other Idle Persons (1549), 4 Statutes of the Realm: 115–117.
20. Karl Marx extensively discusses this history in the chapter entitled "Bloody Legislation Against the Expropriated, from the End of the 15th Century. Forcing Down of Wages by Acts of Parliament," in Karl Marx, *Capital: A Critique of Political Economy*, Vol. 1, edited by Friedrich Engels; translated by Samuel Moore and Edward Aveling (Charles H. Kerr & Co., 1906) (1867). Other scholarly works include William T. Chambliss, "A Sociological Analysis of the Law of Vagrancy," *Social Problems* 12.1 (1964), 67–77; C. S. L. Davies, "Slavery and Protector Somerset: The Vagrancy Act of 1547," *Economic History Review* 19.3 (1966), 533–549
21. 1 Henry VIII (1510) ("Provided also that this acte be not prejudiciall nor hurtfull to eny Woman or to …").
22. 3 Edward IV c. 5, Act for Regulating Apparel (1463), Statutes of the Realm 2: 399–402. A shorter version of this prohibition was included in Edward IV c. 1 (1482), Statutes of the Realm 2: 468–470.
23. The Records of the Parliaments of Scotland to 1707, K. M. Brown et al., eds. (St Andrews, 2007–2011), 1458/3/14, available at http://www.rps.ac.uk/trans/1458/3/14.
24. Ibid., 1567/12/53, available at http://www.rps.ac.uk/trans/1567/12/53.
25. Hunt, *Governance of the Consuming Passions*, p. 242.
26. Proclamations as to the dress of common women within the City, 24 Edward III. A.D. 1351. Letter-Book F. fol. ccviii. (Norman French), available at http://www.british-history.ac.uk/report.aspx?compid=57692#s2; Hunt, *Governance of the Consuming Passions*, p. 243.
27. E. R. Adair, "The Statute of Proclamations," *English Historical Review* 32.125 (Jan., 1917), 34–46; M. L. Bush, "The Act of Proclamations: A Reinterpretation," *American Journal of Legal History* 27.1 (Jan., 1983), 33–53; G. R. Elton, "Henry VIII's Act of Proclamations," *English Historical Review* 75.295 (Apr., 1960), 208–222.
28. Proclamation 464, in *Tudor Royal Proclamations*, Vol. II, edited by Paul L. Hughes and James F. Larkin (New Haven: Yale University Press, 1969), pp. 136–138.
29. Proclamation 494, ibid., pp. 192–194.
30. Proclamations 493, 495, 496, ibid., pp. 187–192, 195–203.
31. Proclamation number 496, entitled a "Briefing," provides a basic outline of the governing statutes, including the governing statute of Henry VIII, although the previous proclamation had begun with the declaration that "The Statute made in the 24th year of Henry VIII for the reformation of the abuse of apparel remaining now in force containeth so many articles and clauses as the same cannot be conveniently abridged, but is to be considered by reading and perusing the whole act at large." Proclamation 495, ibid., p. 195. Yet Proclamation 493 introduced a new regulation necessary because of the "use of the

monstrous and outrageous greatness of hose, crept alate into the realm to the great slander thereof." The prohibition did not relate to the cost color or fabric, but to the number of yards and even the style: men are prohibited from wearing (and tailors from making) hose with more than one yard and a half, or one yard and three-quarters at the most, and the lining of the hose "not to lie loose or be bolstered, but to lie just unto their legs as in ancient time was accustomed." The Proclamation also prohibited certain men from wearing the "outrageous double ruffs which now of late have crept in," at either the neck or sleeves of their shirts. Proclamation 493, ibid., p. 189.

32. Proclamation 646, ibid., pp. 454–462.
33. Proclamation 786, in *Tudor Royal Proclamations*, Vol. III, edited by Paul L. Hughes and James F. Larkin (New Haven: Yale University Press, 1969), pp. 174–179.
34. Proclamation 787, ibid., pp. 179–181.
35. Hunt, *Governance of the Consuming Passions*, pp. 312–313; N. B. Harte, "State Control of Dress and Social Change in Pre-Industrial England," in *Trade, Government, and Economy in Pre-Industrial England: Essays presented to F.J. Fisher*, edited by D. C. Coleman and A. H. Henry (London: Weidenfeld & Nicholson, 1976), pp. 132–165, 148.
36. 1 Jac. I c. 25, An Act for Continuing and Reviving of Diverse Statutes, and for Repealing of Some Others (1603–1604), Statutes of the Realm 4(2): 1050–1052.
37. Hunt, *Governance of the Consuming Passions*, pp. 321–323; Harte, "State Control of Dress and Social Change," pp. 148–149.
38. Hindle, "Badging the Deserving Poor," p.18, citing East Sussex Record Office, Lewes, Shiffner Archives SHR/1556, unfol.
39. Hindle, "Badging the Deserving Poor."
40. Kim M. Phillips, "Masculinities and the Medieval Sumptuary Laws," *Gender & History* 19.1 (2007), 22–42, 28.
41. Ibid. at p. 29.
42. Ibid.
43. Hindle, "Badging the Deserving Poor," p. 29.
44. 39 Elizabeth I, c. 4, An Act for the Punishment of Rogues, Vagabonds, and Sturdy Poor (1597), 4 Statutes of the Realm: 899–902.
45. Id.
46. 11 Edward III, c. 1–5 (1337), Statutes of the Realm 1: 280–281.
47. 6 Henry VIII c. 1, Act of Apparel (1514), Statutes of the Realm 3: 121–122.
48. 7 Henry VIII c. 6 Act of Apparel (1515), Statutes of the Realm 3: 179–182.
49. 25 Edward I c. 11 (1297), in Statutes and Ordinances and Acts of Parliament of Ireland: King John to Henry V, 211, edited by Henry F. Berry.
50. A Statute in the Fortieth Year of Edward the Third, Enacted in a Parliament held in Kilkenny, AD 1367, 14–15, edited by James Hardiman.
51. Margaret Rose Jaster, "Breeding Dissoluteness and Disobedience: Clothing Laws as Tudor Colonist Discourse," *Critical Survey* 13.3 (2001), 61–77, 65.
52. 10 Henry VII c. 16 (1495), Statutes at Large Passed in the Parliaments Held in Ireland, vol. I, 52–53.
53. 28 Henry VIII c. 15 (1537), Statutes at Large Passed in the Parliaments Held in Ireland, vol. I, 121. The statute became effective in 1539.
54. Id.
55. 33 Henry VIII c. 1 (1542), Statutes at Large Passed in the Parliaments Held in Ireland, vol. I, 176.

56. Act of Proscription, 19 Geo. II, c. 39 (1746) in The statutes at large, from Magna Charta, to the end of the last Parliament, 1761 in eight volumes, edited by Owen Ruffhead (London: printed by Mark Baskett, and by the assigns of Robert Baskett; and by Henry Woodfall and William Strahan, 1768–70), Vol. 6: 704–710.
57. Id. Section 17.
58. Id. Earlier in the statute, being sent to America to serve as a soldier was included in the possible punishments for possessing arms. Id. at sections I & II.
59. The Charter of the Colony of the Massachusetts Bay in New England, 1628–1629, in Nathaniel B. Shurtleff, ed., Records of the governor and company of the Massachusetts bay in New England: Printed by order of the legislature (1853), Vol. I, pp. 3, 10.
60. 12 Geo. I, c. 34 (1725), An Act to Prevent Unlawful Combinations of Workmen Employed in the Woollen Manufactures, and For Better Payment of Their Wages, section II, discussed infra.
61. Nathaniel Hawthorne, *The Scarlet Letter* (Boston: Ticknor, Reed & Fields, 1850). Page references are to The Centenary edition of the works of Nathaniel Hawthorne, Vol. 1, *The Scarlet Letter*, edited by Fredson Bowers (Columbus: Ohio State University Press, 1962).
62. Charles Ryscamp, "The New England Sources of The Scarlet Letter," *American Literature* 31.3 (1959), 257–272.
63. Hawthorne, *The Scarlet Letter*, pp. 51–52.
64. Nathaniel B. Shurtleff, ed., Records of the governor and company of the Massachusetts Bay in New England: Printed by order of the legislature (1853), Vol. II, p. 218.
65. Nathaniel B. Shurtleff, ed., Records of the governor and company of the Massachusetts bay in New England: Printed by order of the legislature (1853), Vol. I, pp. 112, 172, 248.
66. Hawthorne, *The Scarlet Letter*, p. 53.
67. Hawthorne, *The Scarlet Letter*, p. 82.
68. The setting of the novel is generally dated as 1642–1649; Ryscamp, "New England Sources of Scarlet Letter," pp. 260–261.
69. Nathaniel B. Shurtleff, ed., Records of the governor and company of the Massachusetts bay in New England: Printed by order of the legislature (1853), Vol. I, p. 126.
70. While a rayle could also be a cloak, the context here indicates it is closer to a scarf or neckerchief. A Tudor statute of 1482 similarly prohibited wives of men who were servants or laborers from wearing any "Reile called a Kerchief" whose price was more than twenty-pence. Edward IV c. 1 (1482), Statutes of the Realm 2: 468–470.
71. Nathaniel B. Shurtleff, ed., Records of the governor and company of the Massachusetts bay in New England: Printed by order of the legislature (1853), Vol. I, p. 183.
72. Nathaniel B. Shurtleff, ed., Records of the governor and company of the Massachusetts bay in New England: Printed by order of the legislature (1853), Vol. II, p. 84.
73. Nathaniel B. Shurtleff, ed., Records of the governor and company of the Massachusetts bay in New England: Printed by order of the legislature (1853), Vol. III, p. 243.
74. Nathaniel B. Shurtleff, ed., Records of the governor and company of the Massachusetts bay in New England: Printed by order of the legislature (1853), Vol. III, pp. 243–244.
75. *Palko v. Connecticut*, 302 U.S. 319 (1937).
76. *Benton v. Maryland*, 395 U.S. 784 (1969).
77. Body of Liberties (1641), in William Whitmore, ed., *Colonial Laws of Massachusetts*, Vol. I (Boston: Rockwell and Churchill, 1889).
78. Records and Files of the Quarterly Courts of Essex County, Massachusetts, Vol. I, 1636–1656, p. 274.

79. Ibid., p. 303.
80. Ibid., p. 304.
81. Ibid.
82. H. R. McIlwaine, ed., *Journals of the House of Burgesses, 1619–1658/59*, (Richmond, VA: Colonial Press, 1905; E. Waddey Co., Vol. I, p. 10).
83. No. 57, An Act for the Better Ordering of Slaves, 1790, in David J. McCord, ed., The Statutes at Large of South Carolina: Edited, Under Authority of the Legislature (1840), Vol. VII, p. 343.
84. No. 586, An Act for the Better Ordering and Governing Negroes and Other Slaves, section XXXVI, (1735), in David J. McCord, ed., The Statutes at Large of South Carolina: Edited, Under Authority of the Legislature (1840), Vol. VII, pp. 385, 396; No. 670, An Act for the Bettering Ordering and Governing Negroes and Other Slaves in this Province, section XL, (1740), in David J. McCord, ed., The Statutes at Large of South Carolina: Edited, Under Authority of the Legislature (1840), Vol. VII, pp. 397, 412.
85. No. 670, section XXXVIII. The act provided that "any person or persons, on behalf of such slave or slaves" could make a complaint to a justice. The provision included not only clothing but also "covering" and food.
86. *Britain v. State*, 22 Tenn. 203 (1842).
87. No. 314, An Act for the Better Ordering and Governing of Negroes and Slaves, section XIX, (1712), in David J. McCord, ed., The Statutes at Large of South Carolina: Edited, Under Authority of the Legislature (1840), Vol. VII, pp. 353, 359–360.
88. Arthur Lyon Cross, "The English Criminal Law and Benefit of Clergy during the Eighteenth and Early Nineteenth Century," *American Historical Review* 22.3 (1917), 544–565. C. B. Firth, "Benefit of Clergy in the Time of Edward IV," *English Historical Review* 32.126 (1917), 175–191.
89. No. 322, An Act to Put in Force in the Province the Several Statutes of the Kingdom of England or South Britain, Therein Particularly Mentioned, (1712), in Thomas Cooper, ed., The Statutes at Large of South Carolina: Edited, Under Authority of the Legislature (1837), Vol. II, pp. 401–582.
90. An Act concerning Women convicted of small felonies, 21 Jac. I. c. 6 (1623), 4 Statutes of the Realm 1216. The act is reproduced as part of No. 322, An Act to Put in Force in the Province the Several Statutes of the Kingdom of England or South Britain, Therein Particularly Mentioned, (1712), in Thomas Cooper, ed., *The Statutes at Large of South Carolina: Edited, Under Authority of the Legislature (1837), Vol. II, p.* 512.
91. *Rex v. Mellichamp, South Carolina Gazette* (Charlestowne), May 1–8, 1736, at 1 col. 1. Accessed at accessiblearchives.org, and NYPL.
92. Philip Hamburger, *Law and Judicial Duty* (Cambridge, MA: Harvard University Press, 2008), pp. 266–268.
93. The slave code of the state of South Carolina, in 1834, criminalized slaves learning to read, including penalties for teaching by whites and "free persons of color." No. 2639, An Act to Amend the Laws in relation to Slaves and Free Persons of Color, section I, in David J. McCord, ed., The Statutes at Large of South Carolina: Edited, Under Authority of the Legislature (1840), Vol. VII, p. 468. Earlier acts had criminalized writing by slaves, for example, in the Act of 1740, which also included a dress code, the act prohibited persons from teaching slaves to write or employing them as scribes, No. 670, An Act for the Bettering Ordering and Governing Negroes and Other Slaves in this Province, section XLV, (1740), in David J. McCord, ed., The Statutes at Large of South Carolina: Edited, Under Authority of the Legislature (1840), Vol. VII, p. 413.

94. No. 476, An Act for the Better Ordering and Governing Negroes and Other Slaves, section X, (1722), in David J. McCord, ed., The Statutes at Large of South Carolina: Edited, Under Authority of the Legislature (1840), Vol. VII, pp. 371, 374. No. 586, An Act for the Better Ordering and Governing Negroes and Other Slaves, section XI, (1735), in David J. McCord, ed., The Statutes at Large of South Carolina: Edited, Under Authority of the Legislature (1840), Vol. VII, pp. 385, 388.

95. Alex Lichtenstein, "'That Disposition to Theft, With Which They Have Been Branded': Moral Economy, Slave Management, and the Law," *Journal of Social History* 21.3 (1998), 413–440.

96. Brought to the Jail in Charlestowne, *South Carolina Gazette* (Charlestowne), May 1–8, 1736 at 3 col. 2. Accessed at accessiblearchives.org, and NYPL.

97. Nathaniel B. Shurtleff, ed., Records of the governor and company of the Massachusetts bay in New England: Printed by order of the legislature (1853), Vol. II, p. 105.

98. Ibid. p. 252.

99. Nathaniel B. Shurtleff, ed., Records of the governor and company of the Massachusetts bay in New England: Printed by order of the legislature (1853), Vol.. III, p. 397.

100. T. H. Breen, *The Marketplace of Revolution: How Consumer Politics Shaped American Independence* (Oxford: Oxford University Press, 2004).

101. 12 Geo. I, c. 34 (1725), An Act to Prevent Unlawful Combinations of Workmen Employed in the Woollen Manufactures, and For Better Payment of Their Wages, section II.

102. Christopher Tomlins, *Freedom Bound: Law, Labor, and Civic Identity in Colonizing British America, 1580–1865* (Cambridge: Cambridge University Press, 2010), pp. 349–350.

103. Leonard W. Labaree, ed., Royal Instructions to British Colonial Governors, 1670–1776 (1935) Vol. I, p. 161.

104. An Act for increase of Shipping, and Encouragement of the Navigation of this Nation, in Acts and Ordinances of the Interregnum, 1642–1660 (1911), 559–562, available at http://www.british-history.ac.uk/report.aspx?compid=56457; An Act for the Encouraging and Increasing of Shipping and Navigation, 12 Charles II c. 18 (1660), 5 Statutes of the Realm 246–250. An Act for the Encouragement of Trade, 15 Charles II c. 7 (1663), 5 Statutes of the Realm: 449–452.

An Act for the Encouragement of the Greenland and Eastland Trades, and for better securing the Plantation Trade, 25 Charles II c. 7 (1673), 5 Statutes of the Realm: 792–793.

105. Breen, *Marketplace of Revolution*, p. 61.

106. Ibid., pp. 62–63.

107. Ibid., p. 86.

108. Ibid., p. 92, citing Mason to Washington, April 5, 1769, in *The Papers of George Mason: Volume I, 1749–1778*, edited by. Robert A. Rutland (Chapel Hill, NC: 1970), 100.

109. 5 George II. c. 22 (1732) in The statutes at large, from Magna Carta, to the end of the last Parliament, 1761 in eight volumes, edited by Owen Ruffhead (London: printed by Mark Baskett, and by the assigns of Robert Baskett; and by Henry Woodfall and William Strahan, 1768–70), Vol. 6:89–91.

110. Id. at Section VII.

111. Thomas Jefferson, *A Summary View of the Rights of British America: Set Forth in Some Resolutions Intended for the Inspection of the Present Delegates of the People of Virginia, Now in Convention / by a Native, and Member of the House of Burgesses* (1774), available

at Yale Law School, The Avalon Project, Documents in Law, History, and Diplomacy, http://avalon.law.yale.edu/18th_century/jeffsumm.asp.

112. 4 George III c. 15 (1764), in The statutes at large, from Magna Carta, to the twenty-fifth year of the reign of King George the Third, inclusive, edited by Owen Ruffhead and Charles Runnington (London: printed by Charles Eyre and Andrew Strahan, [1786]), Vol. 7: 457–465.

113. Id.

114. The Examination of Dr. Benjamin Franklin, in A *third volume of interesting tracts, on the subject of taxing the British colonies in America* (London: printed for J. Almon, opposite Burlington-House, in Piccadilly, 1767), available at Eighteenth Century Collection Online. Breen discusses Franklin's testimony, Breen, *Marketplace of Revolution*, pp. 195–200.

115. Journals of the Continental Congress, The Articles of Association, available at Yale Law School, The Avalon Project, Documents in Law, History, and Diplomacy, http://avalon.law.yale.edu/18th_century/contcong_10-20-74.asp.

116. Breen, *Marketplace of Revolution*, p. 14.

117. Ibid., p. 206.

118. Ibid., pp. 263–264.

119. Max Farrand, ed. The Records of The Federal Convention of 1787, 4 vols. (1937; rev. ed., 1966). Volume 2: 344 (August 20, 1787).

120. Ibid. at 606 (September 13, 1787).

121. Ibid. at 607.

122. Linzy Brekke, "The 'Scourge of Fashion': Political Economy and the Politics of Consumption in the Early Republic," *Early American Studies* 3.1 (2005), 111–139, 123.

123. Ibid., quoting Pennsylvania Gazette, April 15, 1789.

124. John Adams, "Thoughts on Government," in *The Works of John Adams, Second President of the United States: with a Life of the Author, Notes and Illustrations, by his Grandson Charles Francis Adams,* 10 Vol. (Boston: Little, Brown, 1856), Vol. 4, pp. 193–200, 199.

125. Jeff Broadwater, *George Mason: Forgotten Founder* (Chapel Hill: North Caorlina University Press, 2006), pp. 44–45.

126. United States Constitution, Article I, section 8 cl. 3.

2. DRESSING BARELY

1. Thomas Paine, *Common Sense; addressed to the inhabitants of America, on the following interesting subjects* (London: H.D. Symonds, 1792), p. 3. available at http://galenet.galegroup.com/servlet/ECCO # CW3308134578.

2. *Evans v. Stephens*, 407 F.3d 1272 (11th Cir. 2005) (en banc).

3. Id.

4. *Bell v. Wolfish*, 441 U.S. 520 (1979). The trigger for the search in *Bell v. Wolfish*, however, was a contact visit with a noninmate.

5. *Florence v. Board of Chosen Freeholders*, 132 S. Ct. 1510, 182 L.Ed.2d 566, 566 U.S. ___ (2012).

6. 132 S.Ct. at 1524 (Alito, J., concurring) (emphasis in original).

7. *Mary Beth G. v. City of Chicago*, 723 F.2d 1263 (7th Cir. 1983).

8. Liptak, Adam. "No Crime, but an Arrest and Two Strip-Searches," *New York Times*, March 7, 2011, available at http://www.nytimes.com/2011/03/08/us/o8bar.html?_r=1.

9. *Monroe v. Pape*, 365 U.S. 167 (1961). The case and its background facts are discussed in Myriam E. Gilles, "Police, Race and Crime in 1950s Chicago: *Monroe v. Pape* as Legal Noir," in *Civil Rights Stories*, edited by Myriam Gilles and Risa Goluboff (New York: Foundation Press, 2008), pp. 41–59.

10. Gilles, "Police, Race, and Crime." p. 46. "As the 1950s progressed, Chicago remained a city marred by deep and unresolved racial tensions that were most strongly symbolized by the relationship between its police officers and minority residents."

11. *Monell v. Department of Social Services of the City of New York*, 436 U.S. 658 (1978).

12. *Los Angeles County, Cal. v. Rettele*, 550 U.S. 609 (2007).

13. *Safford Unified School Dist. No. 1 v. Redding*, 557 U.S. 364 (2010).

14. Id. at 374–375, citing Brief for *National Association of Social Workers et al.* as Amici Curiae 6–14; Irwin Hyman and Donna C. Perone, "The Other Side of School Violence: Educator Policies and Practices that May Contribute to Student Misbehavior," *Journal of School Psychology* 36 (1998), 7, 13 (strip search can "result in serious emotional damage").

15. Id. citing *New Jersey v. T.L.O.*, 469 U.S. 325, 342 (2008).

16. Id. at 397n.6 (Thomas, J., dissenting).

17. *Kastritis v. City of Daytona Beach Shores*, 835 F. Supp. 2d 1200 (M.D. Fla. 2011).

18. Id. at 1217, citing Fla. Stat. section 901.211.

19. Gary Taylor, "Exotic Dancers Win $195,000 Judgment in Strip-Search Case," *Orlando Sentinel*, July 7, 2011 available at http://www.orlandosentinel.com/news/local/volusia/os-st rip-search-exotic-dangers-illega20110707,0,4490925.story.

20. *Malinski v. New York*, 324 U.S. 401 (1945).

21. Id. at 413.

22. Major General George R. Fay and Lieutenant General Anthony R. Jones, U.S. Department of the Army, AR 15–6 Investigation of the Abu Ghraib Detention Facility and 205th Military Intelligence Brigade, (2004) available at http://fl1.findlaw.com/news. findlaw.com/hdocs/docs/dod/fay82504rpt.pdf. [hereinafter Fay/Jones Report], p. 88. For a discussion of the various reports, see Keith Rohman, "Diagnosing and Analyzing Flawed Investigations, Abu Ghraib as a Case Study," *Penn State International Law Review* 28 (2009), 1–44.

23. Fay/Jones Report, p. 88.

24. Paine, *Common Sense*, p. 3.

25. UN Commission on Human Rights, "Report of the Special Rapporteur on Torture and Other Cruel, Inhuman or Degrading Treatment or Punishment," A/59/324, September 1, 2004, paragraph 17, available at http://www.statewatch.org/news/2004/nov/un-torture-doc1. pdf.

26. Fay/Jones Report, pp. 64, 66, 74, 89.

27. Fay/Jones Report, p. 91 (Incident # 38) [emphasis added].

28. Office of Inspector General, U.S. Department of Justice, A Review of the FBI's Involvement in and Observations of Detainee Interrogations in Guantanamo Bay, Afghanistan, and Iraq (2008), 199, available at http://www.justice.gov/oig/special/s0805/final.pdf.

29. *Wilson v. Seiter*, 501 U.S. 294 (1991); *Estelle v. Gamble*, 429 U.S. 97 (1976).

30. *Warren v. District of Columbia*, 353 F.3d 36 (D.C. Cir. 2004) (lie on cold floor naked); *Gates v. Collier*, 349 F Supp 881 (D.C. Miss.) (fans turned on naked wet prisoners).

31. *O'Leary v Iowa State Men's Reformatory*, 79 F3d 82 (8th Cir. 1996) (behavior modification program included gradual restoration of underwear for good behavior); *Walker v. State*, 68 P.3d 872 (Montana 2003) (denial of all personal items, including clothing, pursuant to behavior modification plan).

32. A Review of the FBI's Involvement in and Observations of Detainee Interrogations, p. 200 ("Another agent stated in his survey response that detainees told him that the guards took away a detainee's clothing in response to repeated suicide attempts.").

33. *Jetter v. Beard*, 183 Fed. Appx. 178 (3rd Cir. 2006).

34. David Coombs, "The Truth behind Quantico Brig's Decision to Strip PFC Manning," March 5, 2011, available at http://www.armycourtmartialdefense.info/2011/03/truth-beh ind-quantico-brigs-decision-to.html; Glenn Greenwald, "The Inhumane Conditions of Bradley Manning's Detention," Salon.com, December 15, 2010, available at http://www. salon.com/news/opinion/glenn_greenwald/2010/12/14/manning/index.html.

35. Steve Fishman, "Bradley Manning's Army of One," *New York Magazine*, July 3, 2011, available at http://nymag.com/news/features/bradley-manning-2011–7/.

36. Juan E. Mendez, "Special Rapporteur on Torture and Other Cruel, Inhuman or Degrading Treatment or Punishment," Statement: USA: Unmonitored access to detainees is essential to any credible enquiry into torture or cruel inhuman and degrading treatment, says UN torture expert, United Nations Office of the High Commissioner for Human Rights, available at http://www.ohchr.org/en/NewsEvents/Pages/DisplayNews. aspx?NewsID=11231&LangID=E.

37. David Coombs, "Mail Policy for PFC Bradley Manning," May 10, 2011, available at http:// www.armycourtmartialdefense.info/2011/05/mail-policy-for-pfc-bradley-manning.html.

38. *Genies v. State*, 10 A.3d 854 (Md. App. 2010).

39. *Minor v. State*, 501 S.E.2d 576 (Ga. App. 1998), citing Georgia Code §16–6–8(d).

40. *Le Roy v. Sidley* (1663) 1 Sid. 168, 82 Eng. Reprint, 1036.

41. *Collins v. State*, 288 S.E.2d 43 (Ga. App. 1981).

42. *Weideman v. State*, 890 N.E.2d 28, 31 (Ind. Ct. App. 2008).

43. *Van Houten v. State*, 46 N.J.L. 160 (1884).

44. *Duvallon v. District of Columbia*, 515 A. 2d 724 (D .C. Ct. App. 1986).

45. Id.

46. *State v. Castaneda*, 245 P.3d 550 (Nev. 2010).

47. Id.; Grayned v. City of Rockford, 408 U.S. 104, 108–109 (1972).

48. Id.

49. *State v. Kueny*, 215 N.W.2d 215 (Iowa 1974).

50. *State v. Bauer*, 337 N.W.2d 209 (Iowa 1983).

51. *People v. O'Gorman*, 274 N.Y. 284, 8 N.E.2d 862 (1937).

52. Id.

53. *Ross v. State*, 876 So. 2d 684 (Fla. Dist. Ct. App. 4th Dist. 2004).

54. *Smith v. Doe*, 538 U.S. 84 (2003).

55. *Connecticut Dept. of Public Safety v. Doe*, 538 U.S. 1 (2003).

56. *Kansas v. Hendricks* 521 U.S. 346 (1997).

57. Joseph J. Fischel, "Transcendent Homosexuals and Dangerous Sex Offenders: Sexual Harm and Freedom in the Judicial Imaginary," *Duke Journal of Gender Law & Policy* 17 (2010), 277–311; Robert Jacobson, "'Megan's Laws': Reinforcing Old Patterns of Anti-Gay Police Harassment," *Georgetown Law Journal* 87 (1999), 2431–2467.

58. Cal. Penal Code § 290 (Deering 1949). The law, its history and enforcement is discussed in Robert Jacobson, "Reinforcing Old Patterns," pp. 2441–2444.
59. John Douard, "Sex Offender as Scapegoat: The Monstrous Other Within," *New York Law School Review* 53 (2008/2009), 32–51.
60. Liptak, "No Crime, but an Arrest and Two Strip-Searches."
61. *McJunkins v. State*, 10 Ind. 140 (1858).
62. The song is "Queen of the Highway" on the album "Morrison Hotel," released February 1970.
63. Jan E. Morris, "The Miami Incident," at http://doors.com/miami/one.html.
64. Gary Fineout, "Jim Morrison Is Pardoned in Indecent Exposure Case," *New York Times*, December 9, 2010, available at http://artsbeat.blogs.nytimes.com/2010/12/09/jim-morrison-is-pardoned-in-indecent-exposure-case/ (includes copy of letter from Governor Charlie Crist).
65. Video of Jim Morrison interview in Miami August 12, 1970, available at Ruthann Robson, "Jim Morrison's Possibility of Parole," http://lawprofessors.typepad.com/conlaw/2010/11/jim-morrisons-possibility-of-pardon.html.
66. *Southeastern Promotions, Ltd. v. Conrad*, 420 U.S. 546 (1975).
67. *Erznoznik v. City of Jacksonville*, 422 U.S. 205 (1975).
68. *Miller v. California*, 413 U.S. 15 (1973).
69. *Regina v. Hicklin* (1868 L. R. 3 Q. B. 360).
70. 18 U.S.C. § 1464, originally passed in 1948, actually provides "Whoever utters any obscene, indecent, or profane language by means of radio communication shall be fined under this title or imprisoned not more than two years, or both."
71. The implementing regulation of the FCC, 47 C.F.R. § 73.3999, provides: "(a) No licensee of a radio or television broadcast station shall broadcast any material which is obscene. (b) No licensee of a radio or television broadcast station shall broadcast on any day between 6 a.m. and 10 p.m. any material which is indecent."
72. *CBS Corp. v. F.C.C.*, 535 F.3d 167 (3rd Cir. 2008).
73. *FCC v. Fox Television Stations*, __ U.S. ___, 132 S.Ct. 2307, 183 L.Ed.2d 234 (2012).
74. The Court granted certiorari in *FCC v. Fox Television Stations* on June 27, 2011, to consider the First Amendment arguments; the Second Circuit held that the "fleeting expletives" policy by the FCC violated the First Amendment, *Fox Television Stations v. FCC*, 613 F.3d 317 (2nd Cir. 2010). In 2009, the Court had considered the administrative law issues in *FCC v. Fox Television Stations, Inc.*, 129 S. Ct. 1800 (2009). It vacated and remanded the Third Circuit opinion regarding Janet Jackson's fleeting nudity for further consideration in light of the fleeting expletives opinion in *FCC v. Fox Television Stations, Inc.*, 556 U.S. 502 (2009) (Fox I).
75. For a discussion of the oral argument, the transcript, and images and links to the friezes, see Ruthann Robson, "*FCC v. Fox* Argument: On Naked Buttocks, Regulated Media, and the First Amendment," January 10, 2012, available at http://lawprofessors.typepad.com/conlaw/2012/01/fcc-v-fox-argument-on-naked-buttocks-regulated-media-and-the-first-amendment.html.
76. The challengers asked the Court to overrule *FCC v. Pacifica Foundation*, 438 U.S. 726 (1978), famously involving comedian George Carlin's "seven dirty words" monologue. Justice Ginsburg concurred specially to stated that Pacifica was "wrong" when it was decided and bears reconsideration given the passage of time, technological advances, and the agency's "untenable rulings." __ U.S. at ___ (2012).

77. *Reno v. American Civil Liberties Union*, 521 U.S. 844 (1997).
78. Child Online Protection Act, 47 U.S.C. § 231.
79. *American Civil Liberties Union v. Mukasey*, 534 F.3d 181 (3rd Cir. 2008), cert. denied, *Mukasey v. American Civil Liberties Union*, 129 S.Ct. 1032 (2009). COPA was before the United States Supreme Court in *Ashcroft v. Am. Civil Liberties Union*, 535 U.S. 564 (2002), and Ashcroft v. Am. Civil Liberties Union, 542 U.S. 656 (2004).
80. CIPA, Pub. L. No. 106–554, tit. XVII, 114 Stat. 2763A-335 (2000) (codified in scattered sections of 20 & 47 U.S.C.).
81. *United States v. American Library Association*, 539 U.S. 194 (2003).
82. 539 U.S. at 212.
83. *National Endowment for the Arts v. Finley*, 524 U.S. 569 (1998).
84. *National Endowment for the Arts*, 20 U.S.C. § 954(d)(1).
85. *Finley*, 524 U.S. at 589.
86. *Erie v. Pap's A. M.*, 529 U.S. 277, 289 (2000) (plurality opinion).
87. *Barnes v. Glen Theatre, Inc.*, 501 U. S. 560, 565–566 (1991) (plurality opinion).
88. *Young v. American Mini Theatres, Inc.*, 427 U.S. 50, 70 (1976).
89. *Renton v. Playtime Theatres, Inc.*, 475 U.S. 41, 60 n. 4 (1986) (Brennan, J. dissenting) (findings of city council including crime, prostitution, rape, incest, assaults, property values); *Erie v. Pap's A. M.*, 529 U.S. 277, 297 (2000) (plurality opinion) (findings of the city council that "certain lewd immoral activities" are "highly detrimental to the public health, safety and welfare, and lead to the debasement of both women and men, promote violence, public intoxication, prostitution and other serious criminal activity").
90. *Young v. American Mini Theatres, Inc.*, 427 U.S. at 71 n. 34.
91. *Erznoznik v. City of Jacksonville*, 422 U.S. 205 (1975), see supra note 63.
92. *Erie v. Pap's A. M.*, 529 U.S. at 318 (Stevens, J., dissenting).
93. Id. at 321–330 (Stevens, J., dissenting).
94. Id. at 316–317 (Souter, J., dissenting).
95. Daniel R. Aaronson, Gary S. Edinger, and James S. Benjamin, "The First Amendment in Chaos: How the Law of Secondary Effects Is Applied and Misapplied by the Circuit Courts," *University of Miami Law Review* (2009), 63: 741–759 ("The law of secondary effects is a mess" and "The present state of the law is both confused and intellectually dishonest; the federal circuits are split on issues both large and small, and the guidance offered to lower courts resembles instructions for operating a Ouija board."); John Fee, "The Pornographic Secondary Effects Doctrine," *Alabama Law Review* (2009), 60: 291–338 ("the formal secondary effects doctrine is misleading and even dangerous on its own terms. As applied to most forms of protected speech, the secondary effects doctrine is both descriptively incoherent and normatively empty."); Seana Valentine Shiffrin, "Speech, Death and Double Effect," *N.Y.U. Law Review* 78 (2003), 1135–1185, 1148 ("the puzzling doctrine of secondary effects").
96. *Erie v. Pap's A. M.*, 529 U.S. at 301.
97. *Erie v. Pap's A. M.*, 529 U.S. at 310 (Scalia, J., concurring).
98. *Erie v. Pap's A. M.*, 529 U.S. at 313 n. 2 (Souter, J., concurring in part and dissenting in part).
99. *Erie v. Pap's A. M.*, 529 U.S. 277 at 323 (Stevens, J., dissenting).
100. *Salem Inn, Inc. v. Frank*, 501 F.2d 18, 21 (2d Cir. 1974) aff'd in part, rev'd in part sub nom. *Doran v. Salem Inn, Inc.*, 422 U.S. 922 (1975).
101. *United States v. Carolene Prod. Co.*, 304 U.S. 144, 152–53 n.4 (1938).
102. *Frontiero v. Richardson*, 411 U.S. 677, 686–87 (1973) (plurality opinion).

103. Davina Cooper, "Theorising Nudist Equality: An Encounter between Political Fantasy and Public Appearance," *Antipode* 43.2 (2011), 326–357.
104. *Bruns v. Pomerleau*, 319 F. Supp. 58 (D. Md. 1970).
105. Id. at 69.
106. F. Dickberry, *The Storm of London: A Social Rhapsody* (London: John Long, 1904), available at http://www.archive.org/details/stormoflondonsocoodickuoft. The identity of Dickberry is given as a pseudonym for "F. Blaze De Bury, probably Fernande Blaze De Bury" in *Edwardian Fiction: An Oxford Companion*, Sandra Kemp, Charlotte Mitchell, and David Trotter (Oxford: Oxford University Press, 1997), p. 99. Moreover, "Dickberry" is subject to its own ambiguities; as the *New York Times* noted in 1905, "H Dicksberry is the name of the author stamped on the cover of the book; F. Dickberry is his name on the title page," available at http://query.nytimes.com/gst/abstract.html?res=F70C17F63F 5512738DDDAC0994DF405B858CF1D3.
107. Darby Lewes, "Middle-Class Edens: Women's Nineteenth-century Utopian Fiction and the Bourgeois Ideal," *Utopian Studies* 4:1 (1993), 14–25.
108. Dickberry, *Storm of London*, pp. 45, 60, 180, 118.
109. *City of Seattle v. Buchanan*, 90 Wash. 2d 584, 584 P.2d 918 (1978).
110. *Hang On, Inc. v. City of Arlington*, 65 F.3d 1248, 1257 (5th Cir. 1995).
111. *Williams v. City of Fort Worth*, 782 S.W.2d 290 (Tex.App. 1989).
112. *U.S. v. Biocic*, 928 F.2d 112 (4th Cir, 1991).
113. Id.
114. *Craft v. Hodel*, 683 F.Supp. 289 (D.Mass. 1988).
115. *People v. Santorelli*, 80 N.Y.2d 875, 600 N.E.2d 232 (1992)
116. *People v. Craft*, 134 Misc. 2d 121, 509 N.Y.S.2d 1005 (City Ct. 1986) rev'd, 149 Misc. 2d 223, 564 N.Y.S.2d 695 (Co. Ct. 1991) rev'd sub nom. *People v. Santorelli*, 80 N.Y.2d 875, 600 N.E.2d 232 (1992).
117. *People v. Santorelli*, 80 N.Y.2d 875, 879, 600 N.E.2d 232, 235 (1992) (Titone, J, concurring).
118. *McGuire v. State*, 489 So.2d 729 (Fla. 1986).
119. *DeWeese v. Town of Palm Beach*, 812 F.2d 1365 (1987).
120. Id. at 1367, 1368n.9, 1370.
121. Janine Benedet, "On Indecency: *R. v. Jacob*," *Canadian Criminal Law Review* 3 (1998), 17–59.
122. 1993 Fla. Sess. Law Serv. Ch. 93–4 amending Fla. Stat. 800.03. The Act also amends other laws and encourages breast-feeding
123. *Forster v. Smith*, F.Supp.2d, 2006 WL 1663722 (E.D.Wis.).
124. *State v. McCapes*, 912 P.2d 419 (Or. App. 1996).
125. *City of Columbus v. Zanders*, 25 Ohio Misc. 144, 145, 266 N.E.2d 602, 603 (Ohio Mun. 1970).

3. DRESSING SEXILY

1. *City of Columbus v. Zanders*, 25 Ohio Misc. 144, 145, 266 N.E.2d 602, 603 (Ohio Mun. 1970).
2. Id.
3. *City of Chicago v. Wilson*, 75 Ill.2d 525, 389 N.E.2d 522 (Ill. 1978).
4. Id.

5. *Doe v. McConn*, 489 F.Supp. 76 (S.D. Tex. 1980).
6. *Mayes v. Texas*, 416 U.S. 909 (1974).
7. *City of Columbus v. Rogers*, 41 Ohio St. 2d 161, 324 N.E.2d 563 (1975).
8. Id.
9. Subdivision 7 of section 887, Code of Criminal Procedure. This statute is further discussed in Chapter 5, "Dressing Disruptively."
10. *People v. Luechini*, 75 Misc. 614,136 N.Y.S. 319 (1912), County Court, Erie County. The actual incident may have occurred earlier, given that the appellate judge's opinion is dated February 1912.
11. Id.
12. *People v. Archibald*, 58 Misc.2d 862, 296 N.Y.S.2d 834 (Appellate Term 1968).
13. *Fenster v. Leary*, 20 N.Y.2d 309, 282 N.Y.S.2d 739, 229 N.E.2d 426 (1967).
14. Id.
15. *People v. Simmons*, 79 Misc.2d 249, 252–53, 357 N.Y.S.2d 362 (N.Y.City Crim.Ct. 1974).
16. Aeyal Gross, "Gender Outlaws Before the Law: The Courts of the Borderland," *Harvard Journal of Law & Gender* 32 (2009), 165–231, citing *State v. Wheatley*, No. 97–1–50056–6 (Wash. Superior Ct. May 13, 1997); *People v. Clark*, No. 1994CR003290 (Colo. Dist. Ct. Feb. 16, 1996).
17. *Mayes v. Texas*, 416 U.S. 909 (1974).
18. *Troxel v. Granville*, 530 U.S. 57 (2000).
19. *Meyer v. Nebraska*, 262 U.S. 390 (1923).
20. *Pierce v. Society of Sisters*, 268 U.S. 510 (1925).
21. *Smith v. Smith*, No. 05 JE 42, 2007 WL 901599 (Ohio App. Mar. 23, 2007) appeal denied, 873 N.E.2d 1315 (Ohio 2007) (unpublished table decision).
22. Id.
23. Sarah E. Valentine, "Traditional Advocacy for Nontraditional Youth: Rethinking Best Interests for the Queer Child," *Michigan State Law Review* (2008), 1053–1113; Noa Ben-Asher, "Paradoxes of Health and Equality: When a Boy Becomes a Girl," *Yale Journal of Law & Feminism* 16 (2004), 275–311.
24. DSM-IV, Task Force on *DSM-IV*, American Psychiatric Association, *Diagnostic and Statistical Manual of Mental Disorders*, pp. 532–538 (4th ed. 1994).
25. American Psychiatric Association, DSM-V Development: Gender Dysphoria in Children: Proposed Revision & Rationale, updated May 4, 2011, http://www.dsm5.org/ProposedRevision/Pages/proposedrevision.aspx?rid=192# (last visited 9/22/2011) (emphasis added).
26. *Doe v. Bell*, 754 N.Y.S.2d 846 (N.Y. Sup. 2003).
27. Id.
28. *Karr v. Schmidt*, 460 F.2d 609 (5th Cir. en banc 1972).
29. *Crews v. Cloncs*, 432 F.2d 1259 (7th Cir. 1970).
30. *Reed v. Reed*, 404 U.S. 71 (1971).
31. *Karr v. Schmidt*, 460 F.2d 609 (5th Cir. en banc 1972) (Wisdom, J., dissenting).
32. *Tinker v. Des Moines Indep. Cmty. Sch. Dist.*, 393 U.S. 503 (1969).
33. *Ferrell v. Dallas Independent School Dist.*, 392 F. 2d 697 (5th Cir. 1968), cert. denied, 393 U.S. 856 (Douglas, J., dissenting from denial of petition for writ of certiorari); *Breen v. Kahl*, 419 F. 2d 1034 (7th Cir. 1969), cert. denied, 398 U.S. 937 (1970); *Jackson v. Dorrier*, 424 F. 2d 213 (6th Cir. 1970), cert. denied, 400 U.S. 850 (Douglas, J. dissenting without opinion); *Olff v. East Side Union High School Dist.*, 445 F.2d 932 (9th Cir. 1971), cert. denied, 404 U.S. 1042 (1972) (Douglas, J., dissenting from denial of petition for writ of certiorari); *Karr v. Schmidt*,

460 F. 2d 609 (5th Cir. 1972), cert. denied, 409 U.S. 989 (Douglas, J., dissenting without opinion); *King v. Saddleback Jr. College Dist.*, 445 F.2d 932 (9th Cir. 1971), cert. denied, 404 U.S. 979 (1971) (Douglas, J., and White, J., dissenting without opinion); *Lansdale v. Tyler Junior College*, 470 F. 2d 659 (5th Cir. 1972), cert. denied, 411 U.S. 986 (1973) (Douglas, J. dissenting without opinion); *Freeman v. Flake*, 448 F.2d 258 (10th Cir. 1971), cert denied, 405 U.S. 1032 (1972) (Douglas, J., dissenting from denial of petition for writ of certiorari); *Holsapple v. Woods*, 500 F.2d 49 (7th Cir. 1974), cert. denied, 419 U.S. 901.

34. *Ferrell v Dallas Independent School Dist.*, 393 U.S. 856 (1968) (Douglas, J., dissenting from denial of petition for writ of certiorari).

35. *Olff v. East Side Union High School Dist.*, 404 U.S. 1042 (1972) (Douglas, J., dissenting from denial of petition for writ of certiorari).

36. Id.

37. *Bishop v. Colaw*, 450 F.2d 1069, 1076 (8th Cir. 1971).

38. *Bishop v. Colaw*, 450 F.2d 1069, 1077 (8th Cir. 1971) (Aldrich, J., concurring).

39. *Craig v. Boren*, 429 U.S. 190, 197 (1976).

40. *Harper v. Edgewood Bd. of Educ.*, 655 F.Supp. 1353 (S.D.Ohio 1987).

41. Id.

42. *McMillen v. Itawamba County School Dist.*, 702 F.Supp.2d 699 (N.D. Miss. 2010).

43. *Logan v. Gary Community School Corporation*, Case No. 2:07-CV-431-JVB, Opinion and Order (N.D. Ind. 2008), available at 2008 WL 4411518.

44. *Logan v. Gary Community School Corporation*, Case No. 2:07-CV-431-JVB, [Discovery] Opinion and Order (N.D. Ind. 2008), available at 2008 WL 5062802. The settlement is reflected in the Docket. It occurred after the court found that the school's "scant document production" in compliance with Logan's discovery requests violated the federal rules of civil procedure and demonstrated a "lack of good faith effort to locate and produce documents."

45. *Doe v. Yunits*, No. 001060A, 2000 WL 33162199 (Mass. Super. Ct. Oct. 11, 2000), aff'd, 2000 WL 33342399 (Mass. App. 2000).

46. *Tinker v. Des Moines Indep. Cmty. Sch. Dist.*, 393 U.S. 503 (1969).

47. *Doe v. Yunits*, No. 001060A, 2000 WL 33162199 (Mass. Super. Ct. Oct. 11, 2000), aff'd, 2000 WL 33342399 (Mass. App. 2000).

48. *Sturgis v. Copiah County School District*, No. 3:10-cv-450 TSL-FKB, First Amended Complaint (2010), available at http://www.aclu.org/lgbt-rights/sturgis-v-copiah-county-school-district.

49. *Sturgis v. Copiah County School District*, No. 3:10-cv-450 TSL-FKB, Order (September 15, 2011), available at http://www.aclu.org/lgbt-rights/sturgis-v-copiah-county-school-district.

50. *Loving v. Virginia*, 388 U.S. 1 (1967).

51. *Youngblood v. School Board of Hillsborough County, Florida*, No. 8:02-CV-1089-T-24-MAP (M.D. Fl. 2002); settlement discussed at National Center for Lesbian Rights Newsletter, 12 (Fall 2004).

52. Mary Whisner, "Gender-Specific Clothing Regulation: A Study in Patriarchy," *Harvard Women's Law Journal* 5 (1982), 73–119.

53. Federal Bureau of Prisons, Visiting Room Procedures: General Information, available at http://www.bop.gov/inmate_locator/procedures.jsp.

54. Id.

55. Dep. Dir. Dennis Straub, Memo: Visiting Standards, 4–5, Michigan Department of Corrections, written July 26, 2010, emailed Aug. 4, 2010, effective Aug. 23, 2010.

56. New York State Department of Correctional Services, *Handbook for the Families and Friends of New York State DOCS Inmates* (2007) p. 13, available at http://www.docs.state. ny.us/FamilyGuide/FamilyHandbook.pdf.

57. *Holdman v. Olim*, 59 Haw. 346, 581 P.2d 1164 (Haw. 1978)

58. *Castle Rock v. Gonzales*, 545 U.S. 748 (2005).

59. Inter-American Commission on Human Rights, Report No. 80/11, Case 12.626, Jessica Lenahan, July 21, 2011, available at http://www.cidh.oas.org/Comunicados/English/2011/92–11eng.htm. The American Declaration of The Rights and Duties of Man, usually called the American Declaration, is available at http://www.cidh.oas.org/Basicos/English/Basic2. American%20Declaration.htm.

60. Office of the Commissioner for Human Rights, United Nations Human Rights, "Violence against Women: UN Expert Urges Full Policy Review after Regional Body Finds the U.S. Responsible of Rights Violations," available at http://www.ohchr.org/en/NewsEvents/ Pages/DisplayNews.aspx?NewsID=11325&LangID=E

61. *Carmichele v. Minister of Safety and Security*, 2001 (4) SA 938 (CC) (S. Afr.).

62. Section 12(1)(c) of Bill of Rights of the Constitution of South Africa (1996).

63. Marius Pieterse, "The Right to Be Free from Public or Private Violence after Carmichele," *South African Law Journal* 119 (2002), 27–39.

64. Carmichele, para 45.

65. Carmichele, para 54, 65.

66. Sonia Lawrence, "What Not to Wear," The Institute for Feminist Studies at Osgoode Hall Law School, February 17, 2011, available at http://ifls.osgoode.yorku.ca/2011/02/what-not-to-wear/ (rounding up and linking to sources discussing the incident).

67. Jane E. Workman and Elizabeth W. Freeburg, "An Examination of Date Rape, Victim Dress, and Perceiver Variables Within the Context of Attribution Theory," *Sex Roles* 41 (1999), 261–277; Roslyn Heights et al., "The Influence of Victim's Attire on the Adolescent's Judgments of Date Rape," *Adolescence* 30.18 (1995), 319–324. Mark Whatley, "The Effect of Participant Sex, Victim Dress, and Traditional Attitudes on Causal Judgments for Marital Rape Victims," *Journal of Family Violence* 20.3 (2005), 191–200.

68. Privacy Protection for Rape Victims Act of 1978, P.L. 95–520 (92 Stat. 2046) codified as Federal Rules of Evidence, Rule 412.

69. Ga. Code Ann., § 24–2–3(a) (1992) ("In any prosecution [relating to rape] … evidence of past sexual behavior includes, but is not limited to, evidence of the complaining witness's marital history, mode of dress, general reputation for promiscuity, nonchastity, or sexual mores contrary to the community standards"); Ala. R. Evid. Rule 412 (a)(3), (c) & (d) (1996) ("evidence of the complaining witness's marital history, mode of dress, and general reputation for promiscuity, nonchastity, or sexual mores contrary to the community standards and opinion of character for those traits" may only be introduced by the defense at the trial if the court finds during an "in camera" hearing "that such past sexual behavior directly involved the participation of the accused").

70. As the U.S. Supreme Court phrased it in *Strickland v. Washington*, 466 U.S. 668, 684–685 (1984), "The Constitution guarantees a fair trial through the Due Process Clauses, but it defines the basic elements of a fair trial largely through the several provisions of the Sixth Amendment." In Strickland, the focus was on the Sixth Amendment right to the assistance of counsel, but this is applicable to other Sixth Amendment rights such as confrontation and compulsory process.

71. *Johnson v. Moore*, 472 F.Supp.2d 1344, 1364 (M.D.Fla. 2007).

72. Fla. Stat. § 794.022.
73. N.H. Rev. Stat. § 632-A:6(III-a).
74. Opinion of Justices (Certain Evidence in Sexual Assault Cases), 662 A.2d 294 (N.H. 1995).
75. *State v. Nowlin*, 818 A.2d 1237 (N.H. 2003).
76. Duncan Kennedy, "Sexual Abuse, Sexy Dressing and the Eroticization of Domination," *New England Law Review* 26 (1992), 1309–1393. The essay was later included in the book, Duncan Kennedy, *Sexy Dressing Etc* (Cambridge, MA: Harvard University Press 1993).
77. Theresa L. Lennon, Sharron J. Lennon, and Kim K. P. Johnson, "Is Clothing Probative of Attitude or Intent? Implications for Rape and Sexual Harassment Cases," *Law & Inequality* 11(1993), 391, 395 and 402.
78. Duncan Kennedy, "Sexual Abuse," p. 1344.

4. DRESSING PROFESSIONALLY

1. Interpreter Protocols, 735 Ky. Admin. Regs. 2:040.
2. Ethical Standards, Okla. Admin. Code 612:10–13–21. See also, Code of ethics; interpreter manner and behavior, 460 Indiana Administrative Code, 2–3–11.
3. The Equal Employment Opportunity Act, 42 USC §2000e-2.
4. The Equal Employment Opportunity Act of 1972, codified at 42 U.S.C. §2000e.
5. The Congressional Accountability Act of 1995, Pub. L. No. 104–1, 1995 U.S.C.C.A.N. (109 stat), 2 U.S.C.A. §§ 1301 to 1348.
6. EMPLL § 8:1, Merrick Rossein, *Employment Discrimination Law and Litigation* (Eagan, MN: West 2011).
7. *Price Waterhouse v. Hopkins*, 490 U.S. 228 (1989).
8. *Jespersen v. Harrah's Operating Company, Inc.* 444 F.3d 1104 (9th Cir. en banc 2006).
9. Id. at 1113. Thus the Ninth Circuit rejected the applicability of the "double bind" language of the Hopkins plurality: "An employer who objects to aggressiveness in women but whose positions require this trait places women in an intolerable and impermissible catch 22: out of a job if they behave aggressively and out of a job if they do not. Title VII lifts women out of this bind." *Hopkins*, 490 U.S. at 251.
10. Paulette M. Caldwell, "A Hair Piece: Perspectives on the Intersection of Race and Gender," *Duke Law Journal* (1991), 365–396; Angela Onwuachi-Willig, "Another Hair Piece: Exploring New Strands of Analysis under Title VII," *Georgetown Law Journal* 98 (2010), 1079–1130; D. Wendy Greene, "Title VII: What's Hair (and Other Race-Based Characteristics) Got to Do with It?" *University of Colorado Law Review* 79 (2008), 1355–1393, esp. 1390–1391.
11. *Rogers v. American Airlines*, 527 F. Supp. 229 (S.D.N.Y. 1981). For discussions of Rogers, see Michelle L. Turner, "The Braided Uproar: A Defense of My Sister's Hair and a Contemporary Indictment of *Rogers v. American Airlines*," *Cardozo Women's Law Journal* 7 (2001), 115–162; Paulette M. Caldwell, "Intersectional Bias and the Courts: The Story of *Rogers v. American Airlines*," in *Race Law Stories*, edited by Devon W. Carbado and Rachel F. Moran (New York: Foundation Press, 2008), pp. 571–600.
12. D. Wendy Greene, "Black Women Can't Have Blonde Hair … In The Workplace," *Journal of Gender Race & Justice* 14 (2011), 405–430.
13. *Santee v. Windsor Court Hotel L.P.*, No. 99–3891 (E.D.La. Oct. 26, 2000) available at 2000 WL 1610775.

14. *Bryant v. BEGIN Manage Program*, 281 F. Supp. 2d 561 (E.D.N.Y. 2003).

15. *Burchette v. Abercrombie & Fitch Stores, Inc.*, No. 08 Civ. 8786 (S.D.N.Y.May 10, 2010) (Decision and Order Granting Motion for Summary Judgment) available at 2010 WL 1948322. An earlier decision by the same judge granted a motion to dismiss as to certain claims and certain defendants, *Burchette v. Abercrombie & Fitch Stores, Inc.*, No. 08 Civ. 8786 (S.D.N.Y. Mar. 30, 2009) (Decision and Order) available at 2009 WL 856682. Burchette did not file a claim pursuant to Title VII and did not invoke EEOC administrative proceedings, but instead filed a claim under 42 USC §1981 prohibiting race discrimination, although the doctrine is substantially similar. The judge dismissed her claim under New York City Human Rights Law on procedural grounds.

16. Dianne Avery and Marion Crain, "Branded: Corporate Image, Sexual Stereotyping, and the New Face of Capitalism," *Duke Journal of Gender Law & Policy* 14.1 (2007), 13–123. The authors focus on Jespersen, but their insights are certainly applicable more generally.

17. Richard H. Fallon Jr., "Constitutional Precedent Viewed through the Lens of Hartian Positivist Jurisprudence," *North Carolina Law Review* 86 (2008), 1107–1163, 1157.

18. Paul Boudreaux, "Federalism and the Contrivances of Public Law," *St. John's Law Review* 77 (2003), 564.

19. *Civil Rights Cases*, 109 U.S. 3 (1883).

20. *Heart of Atlanta Motel Inc. v. United States*, 379 U.S. 241 (1964); *Katzenbach v. McClung*, 379 U.S. 294 (1964).

21. Ruthann Robson, Bork's "75 page" Memo to Goldwater on the 1964 Civil Rights Act's Unconstitutionality, http://lawprofessors.typepad.com/conlaw/2011/10/borks-75--page-memo-to-goldwater-on-the-1964-civil-rights-acts-unconstitutionality.html.

22. Robert Bork, "Civil Rights – A Challenge," *The New Republic*, August 31, 1963, reprinted in Roy M. Mersky and J. Myron Jacobstein, *The Supreme Court of the United States: Hearings and Reports on Successful and Unsuccessful Nominations*, Volume 14-F (Buffalo, NY: William S. Hein 1991), pp. 7401–7405.

23. *Vinson v. Taylor*, 760 F.2d 1330 (D.C. Cir. 1985).

24. *Meritor Sav. Bank, FSB v. Vinson*, 477 U.S. 57, 73 (1986).

25. Eugene Volokh, "Freedom of Speech and Appellate Review in Workplace Harassment Cases," *Northwestern University Law Review* 90 (1996), 1029–1030.

26. *Hishon v. King & Spauling*, 467 U.S. 69 (1984).

27. David Bernstein, *You Can't Say That: The Growing Threat to Civil Liberties from Antidiscrimination Laws* (Washington, D.C.: Cato Institute, 2003), p. 198. See also, Richard A. Epstein, *Forbidden Grounds: The Case against Employment Discrimination Laws* (Cambridge, MA: Harvard University Press, 1992) (while Epstein focuses on liberty of contract, he makes some implicit First Amendment arguments; see pp. 305–306).

28. *Wisconsin v. Mitchell*, 508 U.S. 476 (1993) (bias enhancement upheld as constitutional); *Paris Adult Theatre I v. Slaton*, 413 U.S. 49 (1973) (obscene films).

29. *Washington v. Davis*, 426 U.S. 229 (1976).

30. *Ricci v. DeStefano*, 129 S. Ct. 2658, 2681–83 (2009) (Scalia, J., concurring).

31. Richard Primus, "The Future of Disparate Impact," *Michigan Law Review* 108 (2010), 1342–1387.

32. *Chisholm v. Georgia*, 2 U.S. (2 Dall.) 419 (1793).

33. Robert Middlekauff, *The Glorious Cause: The American Revolution, 1763–1789* (New York: Oxford University Press, 1982, 2005), pp. 522–525; Lynn Montross, *Rag, Tag and Bobtail: The Story of the Continental Army, 1775–1783* (New York: Harper & Bros., 1952).

34. Stuart Reid and Marko Zlatich, *Soldiers of the Revolutionary War* (Oxford: Osprey, 2002), pp. 15, 46, 89; Montross, *Rag, Tag and Bobtail*, pp. 314–315.
35. Doyle Mathis, "*Chisholm v. Georgia*: Background and Settlement," *Journal of American History*, 54:1 (1967), 19–29, 21. The Supreme Court described the underlying action as one for "military goods sold to Georgia," in *Atascadero State Hosp. v. Scanlon*, 473 U.S. 234, 281 (1985). Peter Irons describes the goods as "cloth and uniforms"; Peter Irons, *A People's History of the Supreme Court* (New York: Viking/Penguin, 1999), p. 93. Akhil Reed Amar states the breach is of a "war-supplies contract." Akhil Reed Amar, *America's Constitution: A Biography* (New York: Random House, 2005), p. 332.
36. Mathis, "*Chisholm v. Georgia*: Background."
37. Of the four Justices who held that Georgia did not have a claim of state sovereignty, two (John Blair and James Wilson) were signers of the Constitution; Wilson's influence over the Constitution is considered second only to James Madison's. Justice William Cushing was a Massachusetts jurist who shepherded the ratification of the Constitution through that state's process. Chief Justice John Jay was a co-author of *The Federalist Papers*. The dissenting justice, John Iredell, was a North Carolina federalist who unsuccessfully advocated for that state to adopt the Constitution; he had also originally ruled in favor of Georgia while "riding in the Circuit." Clyde E. Jacobs, *The Eleventh Amendment and Sovereign Immunity* (Westport, CT: Greenwood Press, 1972); Randy E. Barnett, "The People or the State? *Chisholm v. Georgia* and Popular Sovereignty," *Virginia Law Review*, 93 (2007), 1729–1758; John V. Orth, "The Truth about Justice Iredell's Dissent in *Chisholm v. Georgia*," 73 North Carolina Law Review (1994), 255–269.
38. The Eleventh Amendment provides "The judicial power of the United States shall not be construed to extend to any suit in law or equity, commenced or prosecuted against one of the United States by citizens of another state, or by citizens or subjects of any foreign state." The Court in *Hans v. Louisiana*, 134 U.S. 1 (1890) held that a Louisiana citizen could not sue Louisiana in federal court. Interestingly, again the case occurred at a time of anxiety over state solvency, this time from reconstruction debts. The Court has continued to apply the Eleventh Amendment in this manner, despite contentious disagreements between the Justices as in *Kimel v. Florida Board of Regents*, 528 U.S. 62 (2000).
39. *Goldman v. Weinberger*, 475 U.S. 503 (1986). *Goldman v. Weinberger* is further discussed in Chapter 7.
40. Bill Barnhart and Gene Schlickman, *John Paul Stevens: An Independent Life* (DeKalb: Northern Illinois Press, 2010), pp. 46–51.
41. 475 U.S. at 512.
42. Dwight Sullivan, "The Congressional Response to *Goldman v. Weinberger*," *Military Law Review* 121 (1988), 125–152.
43. Barry Goldwater, Statement, 132 Cong. Rec. S10699 (August 7, 1986).
44. 10 USC §774.
45. *United States v. Virginia*, 518 U.S. 515 (1996). Justice Ginsburg, writing for the Court, noted that the Virginia Women's Institute for Leadership (VWIL) established by Virginia in order to comply with the mandates of equal protection was not a "military-style residence and VWIL students need not live together throughout the 4-year program, eat meals together, or wear uniforms during the school day." This was contrasted with VMI where "cadets live in spartan barracks where surveillance is constant and privacy nonexistent; they wear uniforms, eat together in the mess hall, and regularly participate in drills."
46. Laura Fairchild Brodie, *Breaking Out: VMI and the Coming of Women* (New York: Random House, 2000).

47. Ibid., p. 135.
48. Ibid., p. 133.
49. 18 USC §702. The full statute provides: "Whoever, in any place within the jurisdiction of the United States or in the Canal Zone, without authority, wears the uniform or a distinctive part thereof or anything similar to a distinctive part of the uniform of any of the armed forces of the United States, Public Health Service or any auxiliary of such, shall be fined under this title or imprisoned not more than six months, or both."
50. 10 USC §772.
51. *Schacht v. United States*, 398 U.S. 58 (1970).
52. *United States v. O'Brien*, 391 U.S. 367 (1968).
53. "Certainly theatrical productions need not always be performed in buildings or even on a defined area and as a conventional stage. Nor need they be performed by professional actors or be heavily financed or elaborately produced. Since time immemorial, outdoor theatrical performances, often performed by amateurs, have played an important part in the entertainment and the education of the people of the world. Here, the record shows without dispute the preparation and repeated presentation by amateur actors of a short play designed to create in the audience an understanding of and opposition to our participation in the Vietnam war." 398 U.S. at 61.
54. 398 U.S. at 63.
55. United States v. Alvarez, __ U.S. __, 132 S. Ct. 2537, 183 L.Ed.2d 574 (2012).
56. 18 U.S.C. § 704 (2012) provides:
    (a) In general. – Whoever knowingly wears, purchases, attempts to purchase, solicits for purchase, mails, ships, imports, exports, produces blank certificates of receipt for, manufactures, sells, attempts to sell, advertises for sale, trades, barters, or exchanges for anything of value any decoration or medal authorized by Congress for the armed forces of the United States, or any of the service medals or badges awarded to the members of such forces, or the ribbon, button, or rosette of any such badge, decoration or medal, or any colorable imitation thereof, except when authorized under regulations made pursuant to law, shall be fined under this title or imprisoned not more than six months, or both.
    (b) False claims about receipt of military decorations or medals. – Whoever falsely represents himself or herself, verbally or in writing, to have been awarded any decoration or medal authorized by Congress for the Armed Forces of the United States, any of the service medals or badges awarded to the members of such forces, the ribbon, button, or rosette of any such badge, decoration, or medal, or any colorable imitation of such item shall be fined under this title, imprisoned not more than six months, or both.
57. *United States v. Alvarez*, 132 S. Ct. 2537, 2550–51 (2012), Justice Kennedy, writing for a plurality of the Court.
58. *City of San Diego v. Roe*, 543 U.S. 77 (2004).
59. Id. The Supreme Court opinion provides the basic facts; Roe's brief to the U.S. Supreme Court states that the videos were geared toward a "gay, male audience" and the Ninth Circuit's opinion notes that Roe was "partially masked" in the videos. Additionally, the district judge stated that Roe never identified himself as a San Diego police officer and went to some lengths to conceal his identity. All the opinions attempt to explain how Roe's supervisor happened upon the videos. *Roe v. City of San Diego*, 356 F.3d 1108 (9th Cir. 2004); *Roe v. City of San Diego* (S.D.Cal. 2001) available at 2001 WL 35936313; Roe's Brief in Opposition, available at 2004 WL 1877785 (U.S.).

60. *Boy Scouts of America v. Dale*, 530 U.S. 640 (2000).
61. Id. at 696 (Stevens, J., dissenting).
62. *Kelley v. Johnson*, 425 U.S. 238 (1976). Subsequent to Kelly, the Court dismissed a writ of certiorari as improvidently granted in a case involving a firefighter's goatee, *Quinn v. Muscare*, 425 U.S. 560 (1976).
63. *Zalewska v. County of Sullivan*, 316 F.3d 314 (2nd Cir. 2003).
64. Noel Cox, "Tudor Sumptuary Laws and Academical Dress: An Act against Wearing of Costly Apparel 1509 and an Act for Reformation of Excess in Apparel 1533," *Transactions of the Burgon Society*, 6 (2006), 15–43.
65. [Unsigned], "An English Judge's Dress," *Canadian Law Review* 3 (1904), 321–332.
66. *Miller v. Sch. Dist. No. 167*, Cook County, Illinois, 495 F.2d 658, 662 (7th Cir. 1974)
67. *E. Hartford Ed. Ass'n v. Bd. of Ed. of Town of E. Hartford*, 405 F. Supp. 94 (D. Conn. 1975) rev'd, 562 F.2d 838 (2d Cir. 1977), rev'd 562 F.2d 832, 856 (rehearing en banc 1977). Similarly in *Blanchet v. Vermilion Parish Sch. Bd.*, 220 So. 2d 534 (La. Ct. App. 1969), writ denied, 222 So. 2d 68 (1969), the court rejected the teacher's challenge to a mandatory necktie policy.
68. *E. Hartford Ed. Ass'n v. Bd. of Ed. of Town of E. Hartford*, 562 F.2d at 861, 862.
69. *Ramsey v. Hopkins*, 320 F. Supp. 477, 480–1 (N.D. Ala. 1970).
70. *Braxton v. Bd. of Pub. Instruction of Duval County, Fla.*, 303 F. Supp. 958, 959 (M.D. Fla. 1969).
71. *Domico v. Rapides Parish School Board*, 675 F.2d 100 (5th Cir. 1982).
72. *Bear v. Fleming*, 741 F. Supp. 2d 972 (D.S.D. 2010). However, he does not attend the ceremony because of his grandfather's death, [Unsigned], "Graduation Dress Dispute in South Dakota Ends," available at ttp://indiancountrynews.net/index.php?option=com_content&task=view&id=9211&Itemid=33.
73. Pennsylvania Rules Governing Standards of Conduct of Magisterial District Judges (judicial robes); Michigan Court Rules, Rule 8.115 (black robe); Alaska Rules of Administration, Rule 21 (a suitable black judicial robe); California Rules of Court, Rule 10.505 (the judicial robe must be black, extend in front and back from the collar and shoulders to below the knees, have sleeves to the wrists). While most state court judges wear black robes, the judges of Maryland's highest court, the Court of Appeals, wear scarlet robes with white collars. Rudolf Lamy, "A Study of Scarlet: Red Robes and the Maryland Court of Appeals" (2006), available at http://www.lawlib.state.md.us/aboutus/history/judgesredrobe.html.
74. John deP Wright, "Wigs," Green Bag 2d 9 (2006) 395; S. James Clarkson, "The Judicial Robe," 1980 Yearbook (Washington, D.C. Supreme Court Historical Society 1980), pp. 143–149; Charles M. Yablon, "Judicial Drag: As Essay on Wigs, Robes, and Legal Change," Wisconsin Law Review (1995), 1129–1153; Rob McQueen, "Of Wigs and Gowns: A Short History of Legal and Judicial Dress in Australia," in Misplaced Traditions: British Lawyers, Colonial Peoples, Law in Context 16:1 (1998), 31–58.
75. Jerome Frank, "The Cult of the Robe," *Saturday Review of Literature* 28 (October 13, 1945), 41, reprinted in Jerome Frank, *Courts on Trial: Myth and Reality in American Justice* (Princeton: Princeton University Press, 1949).
76. Ibid.
77. James Zagel and Adam Winkler, "The Independence of Judges," *Mercer Law Review*, 46 (1995), 795–834; see 814–816.
78. Opinion JE02–004, Standing Committee on Judicial Ethics and Election Practices (Nevada 2002); Opinion JE03–004, Standing Committee on Judicial Ethics and Election

Practices (Nevada 2003); Opinion JE06–014, Standing Committee on Judicial Ethics and Election Practices (Nevada 2006); Opinion JE08–006, Standing Committee on Judicial Ethics and Election Practices (Nevada 2008).

79. *Republican Party of Minneosta v. White*, 536 U.S. 765 (2002).

80. *Jenevein v. Willing*, 493 F.3d (5th Cir. 2007).

81. *Pickering v. Bd. of Educ. of Township High Sch. Dist.*, 391 U.S. 563 (1968); *Garcetti v. Ceballos*, 547 U.S. 410 (2006).

82. *Jenevein v. Willing*, 493 F.3d (5th Cir. 2007). The partial nature of Judge Jenevein's victory is apparent from the Fifth Circuit's refusal to grant the judge attorney's fees as a prevailing party, stating "the relief Jenevein received from the partial expungement of the commission's censure was de minimis." *Jenevein v. Willing*, 605 F.3d 268 (5th Cir. 2010).

83. William Rehnquist, "The Cult of the Robe," *Judges Journal* 15 (1976), 74.

84. Henry J. Reske, "Showing His Stripes: Operetta Inspires Chief Justice to Alter his Robe," *American Bar Association Journal*, 81.3 (1995), 35.

85. Ruth Bader Ginsburg, "In Memoriam: William H. Rehnquist," *Harvard Law Review* 119 (1995), 6–10.

86. Press Notice, Revised guidance on court dress at the UK Supreme Court (November 21, 2011) available at http://www.supremecourt.gov.uk/news/press-releases-archive.html.

87. Asha Rangappa, "God Save the Wig," *Legal Affairs*, May–June 2002, at 10.

88. Charles M. Yablon, supra.

89. Lawrence W. Jordan, Jr., "Are Robes for Counsel the Only Dress for Courtroom Success?" *Advocate* 26 (Sept.1983), 17–18.

90. NYCLA Eth. Op. 688 (1991), available at 1991 WL 755944 (N.Y.Cty.Law.Assn.Comm. Prof.Eth.).

91. Bethanne Walz McNamara, "All Dressed Up with No Place to Go: Gender Bias in Oklahoma Federal Court Dress Codes," *Tulsa Law Journal* 30 (1994–1995), 395–420.

92. John C. Coughenour et al., "The Effects of Gender in the Federal Courts; The Final Report of the Ninth Circuit Gender Bias Task Force," *Southern California Law Review* 67 (1994), 852–854.

93. NYCLA Eth. Op. 688 (1991), available at 1991 WL 755944 (N.Y. Cty. Law Assn. Comm. Prof. Eth.).

94. Maureen Howard, "Beyond a Reasonable Doubt: One Size Does Not Fit All When It Comes to Courtroom Attire for Women," *Gonzaga Law Review* 45 (2009–2010), 209–224 (discussing conservative advice, but also arguing for room for personal choice and comfort); Wendy Patrick, "Well Suited to the Courtroom: Women in Legal Advocacy," *Practical Litigation* 21:5 (2010), 7–10 (assumes that the suit is skirted, stating it would be a problem if there was "a run in her nylons").

95. Jeffrey Ross's shorts, *Ross v. State*, are discussed in Chapter 2.

96. *In Matter of De Carlo*, 141 N.J. Super. 42, 357 A. 2d 273 (1976).

97. *Friedman v. District Court*, 611 P.2d 77 (Ak. 1980).

98. *State v. Cherryhomes*, 840 P.2d 1261 (NM Ct. App. 1992).

99. As the court stated in *Cherryhomes*: "Cherryhomes contends that the issue before this court is whether his choice of neckwear disrupted the decorum of the court. He contends that his dress caused no disruption, that the judge required him to comply with a unique and personal interpretation of the local rule, and that the judge's ruling infringed his First Amendment right of free expression. We disagree with Cherryhomes's characterization of the issue." 840 P.2d at 1263. In *Friedman*, the Alaska Supreme Court stated that Friedman

contends that "the imposition of a dress code violates his rights to personal liberty and privacy under the Alaska Constitution," and that "an attorney's style of dress, so long as it is not disruptive of judicial proceedings, is beyond the power of the courts to control." 611 P.2d at 78. In *DeCarlo*, the appellate court does not attribute the disruptive standard to the attorney, but to itself: "Styles change and the promulgation of limits in dress is beyond precise articulation. Appellant was attired at oral argument in the clothes she wore in the trial court on January 28. In our view, they were not of the kind that could be fairly labeled disruptive, distractive or depreciative of the solemnity of the judicial process so as to foreclose her courtroom appearance." 357 A. 2d at 275.

5. DRESSING DISRUPTIVELY

1. *Tinker v. Des Moines Independent Community School District*, 393 U.S. 503 (1969).
2. Kristi L. Bowman, "The Civil Rights Roots of Tinker's Disruption Tests," *American University Law Review* 58 (2009), 1129–1165.
3. *Burnside v. Byars*, 363 F.2d 744 (5th Cir. 1966); *Blackwell v. Issaquena County Bd. of Educ.*, 363 F.2d 749 (5th Cir. 1966).
4. Bowman, "Civil Rights Roots," p. 1147.
5. *Defoe ex rel. Defoe v. Spiva*, 625 F.3d 324, 327 (6th Cir. 2010) cert. denied, 132 S. Ct. 399, 181 L. Ed. 2d 255 (U.S. 2011); *A.M. ex rel. McAllum v. Cash*, 585 F.3d 214, 223 (5th Cir.2009); *B.W.A. v. Farmington R-7 Sch. Dist.*, 554 F.3d 734, 741 (8th Cir. 2009). Earlier cases reaching similar results include *West v. Derby Unified Sch. Dist. No. 260*, 206 F.3d 1358 (10th Cir.), cert. denied, 531 U.S. 825 (2000); *Melton v. Young*, 465 F.2d 1332, (6th Cir.1972), cert. denied, 411 U.S. 951 (1973).
6. *Cash*, 585 F.3d at 223.
7. *Defoe*, 625 F.3d at 327.
8. *Cash*, 585 F.3d at 219.
9. In considering the prospect of two different experts on the history and meaning of the Confederate flag, the court stated:

    The problem, of course, is that both of them are correct. And they are correct not only in describing the different emotions this symbol evokes, but also in connoting the depth of those emotions through their choice of words. Words like "symbol," "heritage," "racism," "power," "slavery," and "white supremacy" are highly emotionally charged and reveal that for many, perhaps most, this is not merely an intellectual discourse. Real feelings – strong feelings – are involved. It is not only constitutionally allowable for school officials to closely contour the range of expression children are permitted regarding such volatile issues, it is their duty to do so.

    Scott v. Sch. Bd. of Alachua County, 324 F.3d 1246, 1249 (11th Cir. 2003).
10. *Defoe*, 625 F.3d at 338 (Rogers, J., concurring).
11. *Morse v. Frederick*, 551 U.S. 393 (2007).
12. The case involved students Heidi Zamecnik and Alexander Nuxoll, both of whom were originally minors: *Zamecnik ex rel. Zamecnik v. Indian Prairie School Dist. No. 204 Bd. of Educ.*, 2007 WL 1141597 (N.D. Ill. 2007), rev'd sub nom. *Nuxoll ex rel. Nuxoll v. Indian Prairie School Dist. No. 204*, 523 F.3d 668 (7th Cir. 2008), remanded to sub nom. *Zamecnik v. Indian Prairie School Dist. No. 204 Bd. of Educ.*, 710 F.Supp.2d 711(N.D.Ill. 2010), aff'd sub nom. by *Zamecnik v. Indian Prairie School Dist. No. 204*, 636 F.3d 874 (7th Cir. 2011).

13. "Then there is the common observation that homosexual men and heterosexual women are better dressed than either heterosexual men or homosexual women. Since men are sexually more aroused by visual cues than women are, we expect both men who are sexually interested in men, and women who are sexually interested in men, to dress better than either men who are sexually interested in women or women who are sexually interested in women." Richard A. Posner, *Sex and Reason* (Cambridge, MA: Harvard University Press, 1992), p. 106. For further analysis, see Ruthann Robson, "Posner's Lesbians: Neither Sexy Nor Reasonable," in *Sappho Goes to Law School* (New York: Columbia University Press, 1998).
14. *Nabozny v. Podlesny*, 92 F.3d 446 (7th Cir.1996).
15. *Cash*, 585 F.3d at 218 (fewer than sixty students out of 2,300); B.W. A., 554 F.3d at 741 (fifteen–twenty students).
16. "Sponsored by GLSEN, the Gay, Lesbian and Straight Education Network, the National Day of Silence is a day of action in which students across the country take some form of a vow of silence to call attention to the silencing effect of anti-LGBT bullying and harassment in schools." GLSEN, *Day of Silence Organizing Manual*, p. 1, available at http://www.dayofsilence.org/content/getorganized.html.
17. *Zamecnik v. Indian Prairie Sch. Dist. No. 204*, 636 F.3d 874, 876 (7th Cir. 2011), citing *R.A.V. v. City of St. Paul*, 505 U.S. 377, 394 (1992); *Boos v. Barry*, 485 U.S. 312, 321(1988).
18. *Harper v. Poway Unified School District*, 445 F.3d 1166 (9th Cir. 2006), cert granted and judgment vacated, 549 U.S. 1262 (2007) (Breyer, J., dissenting).
19. Id.
20. *Bethel School District v. Fraser*, 478 U.S. 675 (1986).
21. *H. v. Easton Area School District*, 827 F.Supp.2d 392 (E.D. Pa. 2011). The Third Circuit review of the case was still pending in February 2013.
22. *Palmer ex rel. Palmer v. Waxahachie Indep. Sch. Dist.*, 579 F.3d 502 (5th Cir. 2009), cert denied, __ U.S. __, 130 S.Ct. 1055 (2010).
23. *Canady v. Bossier Parish School Board*, 240 F.3d 437 (5th Cir.2001).
24. William Jefferson Clinton, State of the Union Address, January 23, 1996, available at http://www.washingtonpost.com/wp-srv/politics/special/states/docs/sou96.htm.[http://www2.ed.gov/PressReleases/02–1996/whpr28.html].
25. Neil H. Cogan, editor, *The Complete Bills of Rights: The Drafts, Debates, Sources, and Origins* (Oxford: Oxford University Press, 1997), pp. 143–145.
26. Id.
27. Irving Brant, *The Bill of Rights: Its Origin and Meaning* (New York: Bobbs-Merrill, 1965), pp. 55–56.
28. *The Peoples Ancient and Just Liberties Asserted, In the Tryal of William Penn and William Mead at the Old Bailey, 22 Charles II 1670, written by themselves*, in William Penn, *The Political Writings of William Penn*, edited by Andrew R. Murphy (Indianapolis: Liberty Fund, 2002), pp. 3–21. It appears as "The Trial of William Penn and William Mead, at the Old Bailey, for Tumultuous Assembly: 22 Charles II. 1670," in T. B. Howell, *A Complete Collection of State Trials*, Vol. 6 (London: T.C. Hansard, 1816), pp. 951–998. For discussions, see John D. Inazu, "The Forgotten Freedom of Assembly," *Tulane Law Review* 84 (2010), 565, 575–577; John S. Wilson, *The Importance of a Hat* (Chicago: Chicago Literary Club, 1999/2001), available at http://www.chilit.org/PublishedPapers.htm; Andrew Murphy, "The Trial Transcript as Political Theory: Penn-Mead in Anglo-American Political Thought," draft, available at http://papers.ssrn.com/sol3/papers.cfm?abstract_id=1914723.

29. Krista J. Kesselring, "Gender, the Hat, and Quaker Universalism in the Wake of the English Revolution," *The Seventeenth Century* 26.2 (2011), 299–322. See also Maryland State Archives, Vol. 53, Preface 44, p. xliv "In Kent a rule of court was adopted at the September, 1658 sessions, doubtless as the result of a recent offence, 'That noe man presume excepte a member of the Court to Stand wth his hat on his head in the prsence of the Court … or use any unscivill Language' (Arch. Md. liv, 139). At the next session held in October, Henry Carline, a Quaker, was fined 30 pounds of tobacco for disobeying this order (Arch. Md. liv, 146)." Available at http://www.msa.md.gov/megafile/msa/speccol/sc2900/sc2908/000001/000053/html/am53p–44.html.

30. T.B. Howell, Vol. 6, *A Complete Collection of State Trials*, p. 956.

31. Ibid.

32. The Penn and Mead trial is well known for its aftermath regarding the right of jury nullification, in Bushell's Case, in T. B. Howell, *A Complete Collection of State Trials* 999 – 1026, Vol. 6 (London: T. C. Hansard, 1816); Simon Stern, "Between Local Knowledge and National Politics: Debating Rationales for Jury Nullification after Bushell's Case," *Yale Law Journal* 111 (2002), 1815–1859; Teresa L. Conaway, Carol L. Mutzaai, and Joann M. Ross, "Jury Nullification: A Selective, Annotated Bibliography," *Valparaiso University Law Review* 39 (2004), 393–443.

33. John D. Inazu, "The Forgotten Freedom of Assembly," *Tulane Law Review* 84 (2010), 565–612.

34. *West Virginia State Bd. of Educ. v. Barnette*, 319 U.S. 624, 633 n. 13 (1943). The footnote also includes a reference to William Tell: "The story of William Tell's sentence to shoot an apple off his son's head for refusal to salute a bailiff's hat is an ancient one."

35. *West Virginia State Bd. of Educ. v. Barnette*, 319 U.S. 624, 642 (1943). The Court reversed *Minersville School District v. Gobitis*, 310 U.S. 586 (1940), decided only three years earlier.

36. *Bank v. Katz*, 08CV1033NGGRER, 2009 WL 3077147 (E.D.N.Y. Sept. 24, 2009) aff'd, 424 F. App'x 67 (2d Cir. 2011). The original dress dispute occurred in state court with Todd Bank, an attorney, appearing as a pro se litigant, wearing jeans as well as the baseball cap.

37. The best description of the robe incident occurs in the contempt case on remand, In the Matter of David T. Dellinger, 370 F. Supp. 1304 (N.D. Ill. 1973), aff'd 502 F.2d 813 (7th Cir. 1974), cert. denied, 420 U.S. 990 (1975); Pnina Lahav, "The Chicago Conspiracy Trial: Character and Judicial Discretion," *University of Colorado Law Review* 71 (2000), 1327–1364; Pnina Lahav, "Theater in the Courtroom: The Chicago Conspiracy Trial," *Law & Literature* 16 (2004), 381–448.

38. 18 U.S.C. §§ 2102, 2109 (1968), Pub.L. 90–284, Title I, § 104(a), Apr. 11, 1968, 82 Stat. 76.

39. In the Matter of David T. Dellinger, 370 F. Supp. 1304, 1347–8 (N.D. Ill. 1973) (APPENDIX quoting transcript)

40. In the Matter of David Dellinger, 461 F.2d 389, 402–465 (7th Cir. 1972) (Appendix to opinion).

41. In the Matter of David T. Dellinger, 370 F. Supp. 1304 (N.D. Ill. 1973). The judge directed that no sentence be imposed.

42. The United States Supreme Court definitely upheld a defendant's Sixth Amendment right to represent himself several years later in *Faretta v. California*, 422 U.S. 806 (1975).

43. *United States v. Seale*, 461 F.2d 345, 379 (7th Cir. 1972).

44. As the Seventh Circuit explained, Seale was restrained, bound, and gagged on the afternoon of October 29, 1969; his restraints were removed on November 3. "On November 5, after six

weeks of trial, the court sua sponte declared a mistrial as to Seale, and his trial was severed from that of his co-defendants." *United States v. Seale*, 461 F.2d 345, 350 (7th Cir. 1972).

45. *Illinois v. Allen*, 397 U.S. 337 (1970).

46. See *Tinker v. Des Moines Independent Community School District*, 393 U.S. 503 (1969) and the discussions in the earlier part of this chapter.

47. *Illinois v. Allen*, 379 U.S. 337, 351 (1970) (Douglas, J., writing separately).

48. Justice Douglas did not use the word "democracy," but wrote of the "social compact":

> Problems of political indictments and of political judges raise profound questions going to the heart of the social compact. For that compact is two-sided: majorities undertake to press their grievances within limits of the Constitution and in accord with its procedures; minorities agree to abide by constitutional procedures in resisting those claims.

> *Illinois v. Allen*, 397 U.S. at 356 (1970) (Douglas, J., writing separately).

49. *Illinois v. Allen*, 397 U.S. 337 (1970); *Estelle v. Williams*, 425 U.S. 501 (1976); *Holbrook v. Flynn*, 475 U.S. 560 (1986); *Deck v. Missouri*, 544 U.S. 622 (2005); *Carey v. Musladin*, 549 U.S. 70 (2006).

50. The Sixth Amendment provides: "In all criminal prosecutions, the accused shall enjoy the right to a speedy and public trial, by an impartial jury of the State and district wherein the crime shall have been committed, which district shall have been previously ascertained by law, and to be informed of the nature and cause of the accusation; to be confronted with the witnesses against him; to have compulsory process for obtaining witnesses in his favor, and to have the Assistance of Counsel for his defence."

51. *Allen*, 397 U.S. at 344.

52. *Deck v. Missouri*, 544 U.S. 622 (2005).

53. Id. at 630–632.

54. *Holbrook v. Flynn*, 475 U.S. 560 (1986).

55. Id. at 569–572.

56. *Estelle v. Williams*, 425 U.S. 501 (1976).

57. Id. at 509–513, see esp. 510n.5. Justice Brennan, joined by Justice Thurgood Marshall, issued a stirring dissent arguing that "identifiable prison garb robs an accused" of the presumption of innocence and also "entails additional dangers to the accuracy and objectiveness of the fact-finding process," including the defendant's consideration of the right to testify in his own defense.

58. *Carey v. Musladin*, 549 U.S. 70 (2006).

59. The Antiterrorism and Effective Death Penalty Act, 28 U.S.C. § 2254, passed in 1996, provides that

> An application for a writ of habeas corpus on behalf of a person in custody pursuant to the judgment of a State court shall not be granted with respect to any claim that was adjudicated on the merits in State court proceedings unless the adjudication of the claim –
>
> (1) resulted in a decision that was contrary to, or involved an unreasonable application of, clearly established Federal law, as determined by the Supreme Court of the United States.

60. *Carey v. Musladin*, 549 U.S. at 81–83 (Souter, J., concurring).

61. *People v. Pennisi*, 563 N.Y.S.2d 612 (Sup. Ct. 1990). Other cases include *Norris v. Risley*, 918 F.2d 828 (9th Cir. 1990) (anti-rape buttons), *State v. Franklin*, 327 S.E.2d 449 (W. Va. 1985)(MAAD buttons);*Woods v. Dugger*, 923 F.2d 1454 (11th Cir. 1991) (spectators wearing prison guard uniforms in prosecution for murder of prison guard). The

scholarship includes Jona Goldsschmidt, "'Order in the Court!' Constitutional Issues in the Law of Courtroom Decorum," *Hamline Law Review* 31 (2008), 1–102; Scott Kitner, "The Need and Means to Restrict Spectators from Wearing Buttons at Criminal Trials," *Review of Litigation* 27 (2008), 733–768; Sierra Elizabeth, "The Newest Spectator Sport: Why Extending Victims' Rights to the Spectators' Gallery Erodes the Presumption of Innocence," *Duke Law Journal* 58 (2008), 275–309; Meghan E. Lind, "Hearts on Their Sleeves: Symbolic Displays of Emotion by Spectators in Criminal Trials," *Journal of Criminal Law & Criminology* 98 (2008), 1147–1170; Elizabeth Lyon, "A Picture Is Worth a Thousand Words: The Effect of Spectators' Display of Victim Photographs during a Criminal Jury Trial on a Criminal Defendant's Fair Trial Rights," *Hastings Constitutional Law Quarterly* 36 (2009), 517–544.

62. Indeed, subsequent developments proved Anton McCray's sister correct. Although McCray and others were convicted in 1990, their conviction were vacated a decade later based upon newly discovered evidence, including a confession by another person and supporting DNA and forensic evidence. See *People v. Wise*, 194 Misc.2d. 841, 752 N.Y.S. 387 (2002).

63. *Musladin*, 549 U.S. at 83 (Souter, J., concurring)

64. *Pennisi*, 563 N.Y.S. 2d at 614–615.

65. Supreme Court of the United States, "Visitors Guide to Oral Argument," available at http://www.supremecourt.gov/visiting/visitorsguidetooralargument.aspx.

66. 40 U.S.C. § 13k; 40 U.S.C. § 6135.

67. *United States v. Grace*, 461 U.S. 171 (1983).

68. Id. at 185 (Marshall, J. dissenting).

69. *Potts v. United States*, 919 A.2d 1127, 1130 (D.C.2007); *Kinane v. United States*, 12 A.3d 23 (D.C. 2011), cert. denied, 132 S. Ct. 574, 181 L. Ed. 2d 424 (U.S. 2011).

70. Ruthann Robson, "Occupy Jacket-wearer Arrested at Supreme Court Building," Constitutional Law Professors Blog, January 21, 2012, available at http://lawprofessors.type-pad.com/conlaw/2012/01/occupy-jacket-wearer-arrested-at-supreme-court-building.html).

71. *People v. Cohen*, 1 Cal. App. 3d 94, 81 Cal. Rptr. 503 (Ct. App. 1969) rev'd sub nom. *Cohen v. California*, 403 U.S. 15 (1971); Clay Calvert, "Revisiting the Right to Offend Forty Years after *Cohen v. California*: One Case's Legacy on First Amendment Jurisprudence, *First Amendment Law Review* 10 (2011), 1–56; William S. Cohen, "A Look Back at *Cohen v. California*," *UCLA Law Review* 34 (1987), 1595–1614.

72. *Cohen v. California*, 403 U.S. 15 (1971).

73. Id.

74. Id. at 27.

75. For general discussions of saggy pants, see Nuriel A. Heckler, "That's What the Shovel's For: Atlanta's Sagging Baggy Pants Bill in a Liberal Society," *Guild Practice* 64 (2007), 216–224; Angelica M. Sinopole, "'No Saggy Pants': A Review of the First Amendment Issues Presented by the State's Regulation of Fashion in Public Streets," *Penn State Law Review* 113 (2008), 329–380; William C. Vandivort, "The Constitutional Challenge to 'Saggy' Pants Laws," *Brooklyn Law Review* 75 (2009), 667–705; Onika K. Williams, "The Suppression of a Saggin' Expression: Exploring the 'Saggy Pants' Style within a First Amendment Context," *Indiana Law Journal* 85 (2010), 1169–1195.

76. *People v. Martinez*, 29 Misc. 3d 263; 905 N.Y.S.2d 847 (Crim. Ct. Bronx County 2010), citing *People v. O'Gorman*, 274 N.Y. 284, 8 N.E.2d 862 (1937), discussed in Chapter 2.

77. Id.
78. Chief David R. Dicks, Memo to All Sworn Personnel, Subject: Indecent Exposure Enforcement (June 26, 2008); ACLU of Michigan, Letter to Chief David Dicks, Re: Illegal Stops and Searches of Men Wearing Sagging Pants (July 14, 2008). Both documents are available at http://www.aclumich.org/issues/search-and-seizure/2008–07/1267.
79. Ibid.
80. Dublin, Georgia, Code of Ordinances, §14–9(a)(7) & 14–9(c), available at http://library.municode.com/index.aspx?clientId=10664.
81. Riviera Beach, Wearing of Pants Below the Waist in Public, Ordinance 3043 (July 16, 2008) (copy on file with author); Eliot Kleinberg, "Judge Releases Teen, Criticizes Riviera Beach's Saggy Pants Law," *Palm Beach Post*, September 16, 2008, at 1A; Susan Spencer-Wendel, "Let 'em Sag, Judge Says," *Palm Beach Post*, April 23, 2009, at 1A.
82. AL House Bill 16 – Regular Session 2012, available at http://e-lobbyist.com/gaits/research/363108.
83. Howard P. Walthall Sr., "A Doubtful Mind: Understanding Alabama's State Constitution," *Cumberland Law Review* 35 (2005), 74–80; "Still Afraid of 'Negro Domination?' Why County Home Rule Limitations in the Alabama Constitution of 1901 Are Unconstitutional," *Alabama Law Review* 57 (2005), 545–563.
84. Fla. Stat. Ann. § 1006.07(d)(1) (2011). The language was added by SB 228 2010 Legislative Session, and signed into law by Governor Rick Scott on June 2, 2011. The similar Arkansas provision is codified at Ark. Code Ann. § 6–18–503 (c)(1), again mandating school districts to include a student discipline policy.
85. See *Rogers v. American Airlines*, 527 F. Supp. 229 (S.D.N.Y. 1981), discussed in Chapter 4.
86. *Bivens v. Albuquerque Pub. Sch.*, 899 F. Supp. 556, 558 (D.N.M. 1995)
87. ACLU of Michigan, "Letter."
88. In the Matter of Eli L, 947 P.2d 162 (Ct. App. N. M. 1997). Over a strenuous dissent, the appellate court in Eli L. found that law enforcement did not have reasonable suspicion under *Terry v. Ohio*, 392 U.S. 1 (1968) based upon his saggy pants, a fashion fad associated with gang membership.
89. *People v. Bunn*, 2009 Cal. App. Unpub. LEXIS 7080 (Ct. App. Cal. 2009).
90. *People v. Hicks*, 2009 Cal. App. Unpub. LEXIS 9957 (Ct. App. Cal. 2009). The appellate court thus found that the trial judge's denial of the defendant's motion under *Batson v. Kentucky*, 476 U.S. 79 (1986), was not erroneous.
91. *People ex rel. Gallo v. Acuna*, 14 Cal. 4th 1090, 1130, 929 P.2d 596, 621 (1997) (Chin, J., concurring and dissenting).
92. K. Babe Howell, "Fear Itself: The Impact of Allegations of Gang Affiliation on Pre-Trial Detention," *St. Thomas Law Review* 23 (2011), 620–659.
93. *Villegas v. City of Gilroy*, 363 F. Supp. 2d 1207, 1218 (N.D. Cal. 2005) aff'd, 484 F.3d 1136 (9th Cir. 2007) and aff'd sub nom *Villegas v. Gilroy Garlic Festival Ass'n*, 541 F.3d 950 (9th Cir. en banc 2008). For an excellent discussion of the case, see Megan Stuart, "Saying, Wearing, Watching, and Doing: Equal First Amendment Protection for Coming Out, Having Sex, and Possessing Child Pornography," *Florida Coastal Law Review* 11 (2010), 341 385.
94. Joshua D. Wright, "The Constitutional Failure of Gang Databases," *Stanford Journal of Civil Rights & Civil Liberties* 2 (2005), 115–142.
95. Ibid.

96. Christopher McGinnis, Sarah Eisenhart, "Interrogation Is Not Ethnography: The Irrational Admission of Gang Cops as Experts in the Field of Sociology," *Hastings Race & Poverty Law Journal* 7 (2010), 111–159; Hon. Jack Nevin, "Conviction, Confrontation, and Crawford: Gang Expert Testimony as Testimonial Hearsay," *Seattle University Law Review* 34 (2011), 857–887.

97. *City of Chicago v. Morales*, 527 U.S. 41 (1999).

98. *People ex rel. Gallo v. Acuna*, 14 Cal. 4th 1090, 1130, 929 P.2d 596, 621 (1997).

99. *People v. Englebrecht*, 88 Cal. App. 4th 1236, 1266–67, 106 Cal. Rptr. 2d 738, 760 (2001).

100. Howell, "Fear Itself."

101. *People v. Mejia*, B213993, 2010 WL 3788833 (Cal. Ct. App. Sept. 30, 2010); *People v. Vargas*, F037732, 2002 WL 1764180 (Cal. Ct. App. July 31, 2002).

102. *People ex rel. Gallo v. Acuna*, 929 P.2d 596, 623 (1997) (Mosk, J., dissenting), citing Reiner (1992), "Gangs, Crime and Violence in Los Angeles: Findings and Proposals from the District Attorney's Office" (Washington, DC: US Department of Justice, 1992), p. 121; Howell, "Fear Itself," p. 653; Wright, "Failure of Gang Databases," p. 25.

103. The Report considered two gang databases: African Americans represented 54 percent of those listed in the Gang Pointer File (1,324) and 42 percent of those listed in GangNet (7,108 persons). University of St. Thomas School of Law in collaboration with St. Paul NAACP, "Evaluation of Gang Databases in Minnesota & Recommendations for Change," Minnesota Department of Public Safety, SF 2725 Workgroup (2009) p. 22, available at http://twincities.indymedia.org/files/GangsofStPaulReport.pdf.

104. Id. at 19, 29, 40. This Report is discussed in Howell, "Fear Itself."

105. Charles Lawrence III, "The Id, The Ego, and Equal Protection: Reckoning with Unconscious Racism," *Stanford Law Review* 39 (1987), 317–388; Barbara Flagg, "'Was Blind But Now I See': White Race Consciousness and the Requirement of Discriminatory Intent," *Michigan Law Review* 91 (1993), 953–1017.

106. *Washington v. Davis*, 426 U.S. 229 (1976). The case involved a challenge to a District of Columbia policy, thus the equal protection clause was applied to the federal government through the Fifth Amendment's due process clause. The Court did say that intent could be inferred from impact, if the discrimination was "very difficult to explain on nonracial grounds."

107. Id. at 248. In a footnote, the Court stated that "minimum wage and usury laws, as well as professional licensing requirements" might also "require major modifications." Id. at 248 n. 14.

108. Enforcement Act of 1870, ch. 114, 16 Stat. 140 (1870), section 6 provided:

> That if two or more persons shall band or conspire together, or go in disguise upon the public highway, or upon the premises of another, with intent to violate any provision of this act, or to injure, oppress, threaten, or intimidate any citizen, with intent to prevent or hinder his free exercise and enjoyment of any right or privilege granted or secured to him by the constitution or laws of the United States, or because of his having exercised the same, such persons shall be held guilty of felony, and, on conviction thereof, shall be fined or imprisoned, or both, at the discretion of the court, the fine not to exceed $5,000, and the imprisonment not to exceed ten years; and shall, moreover, be thereafter ineligible to, and disabled from holding, any office or place of honor, profit, or trust created by the constitution or laws of the United States.

109. *United States v. Cruikshank*, 92 U.S. 542, 544 (1875). The case did not involve masking.

110. *State v. Miller*, 260 Ga. 669, 674, 398 S.E.2d 547, 552 (1990).

111. Id.; Oskar E. Rey, "Antimask Laws: Exploring the Outer Bounds of Protected Speech under the First Amendment – *State v. Miller* 260 Ga. 669, 398 S.E.2d 547," *Washington Law Review* 66 (1991), 1139–1158.

112. *Church of Am. Knights of the Ku Klux Klan v. Kerik*, 356 F.3d 197, 201 (2d Cir. 2004).

113. The Black Act, 9 Geo. I c. 22 (1723); Pat Rogers, "The Waltham Blacks and the Black Act," *Historical Journal* 17.3 (1974), 465–486; L. Radzinowicz, "The Waltham Black Act: A Study of the Legislative Attitude towards Crime in the Eighteenth Century," *Cambridge Law Journal* 9.1 (1945), 56–81.

114. L. 1845, c. 3 (New York Legislature 68th Session); Silas Wright, New York Governor Annual Message (1845), reprinted in *State of New York Messages from the Governors*, edited by Charles Z. Lincoln (1909), Vol. 4, p. 87; Reeve Huston, *Land and Freedom: Rural Society, Popular Protest, and Party Politics in Antebellum New York* (Oxford: Oxford University Press, 2000), p. 47.

115. Rogers, "The Waltham Blacks."

116. L. 1829, c. 270 (New York Legislature 52nd Session).

117. [Proposed] New York State Code of Criminal Procedure of New York §973(7), defining as a vagrant a "person, who, having his face painted, discolored, covered or concealed, or being otherwise disguised, in a manner calculated to prevent his being identified, appears in a road or public highway, or in a field, lot, wood or inclosure." The 1850 draft Code of Criminal Procedure was approved by the Legislature, but not signed by the governor. See William H. Manz, *Gibson's New York Research Guide* 197 (Buffalo, NY: William Hein, 2004).

118. "Current Topics," *Albany Law Journal*, 13.17 (1876).

119. L. 1876, c. 1 (New York Legislature 99th Session).

120. L. 1888, c. 552 §9 (New York Legislature 111th Session).

121. 4 Consolidated Laws of the State of New York, Article 68 §710 (1909).

122. New York State Temporary Commission on Revision of the Penal Law and Criminal Code, Third Interim Report, pp 26–27, Leg. Doc. 14 (1964).

123. *People v. Luechini*, 75 Misc. 614, 614, 136 N.Y.S. 319 (Co. Ct. 1912); see Chapter 3.

124. *Schumann v. State of N.Y.*, 270 F. Supp. 730, 731 (S.D.N.Y. 1967)

125. *People v. Aboaf*, 187 Misc. 2d 173, 175, 721 N.Y.S.2d 725, 727 (Crim. Ct. 2001); N.Y. Penal Law § 240.35 (McKinney). The 1909 statute was retitled and moved in the 1965 revised Penal Code, L. 1965, c. 1030 (New York Legislature 188th Session).

126. Ruthann Robson, "Loitering While Masked: The Wall Street Protest Arrests," September 22, 2011, available at http://lawprofessors.typepad.com/conlaw/2011/09/loitering-while-masked-wall_street-protests.html.

127. Evan Darwin Winet, "Face-Veil Bans and Anti-Mask Laws: State Interests and the Right to Cover the Face," *Hastings International & Comparative Law Review* 35 (2012), 217–251; Stephen J. Simoni, "'Who Goes There?' – Proposing a Model Anti-Mask Act," *Fordham Law Review* 61(1992), 241–274; Jack Swertfeger Jr., "Municipal Anti-Mask and Anti-Cross Burning Ordinance: A Model," *Journal of Public Law* 1 (1952), 193–197.

128. La. Rev. Stat. Ann. § 14:313.

6. DRESSING RELIGIOUSLY

1. *Bar-Navon v. Brevard County Sch. Bd.*, 290 F. App'x 273 (11th Cir. 2008).

2. *Iacono v. Croom*, 5:10-CV-416-H, 2010 WL 3984601 (E.D.N.C. Oct. 8, 2010).

3. Id.

4. *Bar-Navon v. Brevard County Sch. Bd.*, 290 F. App'x 273, 275 (11th Cir. 2008).
5. *Stephenson v. Davenport Cmty. Sch. Dist.*, 110 F.3d 1303, 1307 (8th Cir. 1997).
6. *Chalifoux v. New Caney Indep. Sch. Dist.*, 976 F. Supp. 659, 665 (S.D. Tex. 1997).
7. *Sherbert v. Verner*, 374 U.S. 398 (1963).
8. *City of Boerne v. Flores*, 521 U.S. 507, 537 (1997) (Stevens, J., concurring).
9. *Goldman v. Weinberger*, 475 U.S. 503, 514 (1986) (Brennan, J., dissenting).
10. Id. at 514.
11. *Reynolds v. United States*, 98 U.S. 145 (1878).
12. Id. Ruthann Robson, "Assimilation, Marriage, and Lesbian Liberation," *Temple Law Review* 75 (2002), 767–777.
13. *Employment Div., Dept. of Human Res. of Oregon v. Smith*, 494 U.S. 872 (1990).
14. *Goldman v. Weinberger*, 475 U.S. 503, 512–13 (1986) (Stevens, J., concurring).
15. *Welsh v. United States*, 398 U.S. 333 (1970); *United States v. Seeger*, 380 U.S. 163 (1965).
16. *Alabama & Coushatta Tribes of Texas v. Trustees of Big Sandy Indep. Sch. Dist.*, 817 F. Supp. 1319, 1329 (E.D. Tex. 1993).
17. See Chapter 4 for discussion of constitutional issues regarding Title VII.
18. *Cloutier v. Costco Wholesale*, 311 F. Supp. 2d 190, 196 (D. Mass. 2004) aff'd. on other grounds sub nom. *Cloutier v. Costco Wholesale Corp.*, 390 F.3d 126 (1st Cir. 2004).
19. Id. at 199 n. 10.
20. 42 U.S.C. § 2000e-1.
21. *Corp. of Presiding Bishop of Church of Jesus Christ of Latter-day Saints v. Amos*, 483 U.S. 327, 330 (1987).
22. *Amos v. Corp. of Presiding Bishop of Church of Jesus Christ of Latter-Day Saints*, 594 F. Supp. 791, 796 (D. Utah 1984) (AMOS I).
23. Id.
24. *Amos v. Corp. of Presiding Bishop of Church of Jesus Christ of Latter-Day Saints*, 618 F. Supp. 1013, 1018 (D. Utah 1985) (AMOS II).
25. *Amos*, 438 U.S. at 338. The Court also rejected the argument that the exemption "offends equal protection principles by giving less protection to the employees of religious employers than to the employees of secular employers," by declaring that the exemption "is rationally related to the legitimate purpose of alleviating significant governmental interference with the ability of religious organizations to define and carry out their religious missions." Although Title VII's statutory exemption as amended is not limited to a religious missions, the Court seemed to implicitly conclude that running a gymnasium was a religious activity, assuming it was nonprofit.
26. *Kennedy v. St. Joseph's Ministries, Inc.*, 657 F.3d 189, 190 (4th Cir. 2011).
27. *Hall v. Baptist Mem'l Health Care Corp.*, 215 F.3d 618, 624 (6th Cir. 2000).
28. *Hosanna-Tabor Evangelical Lutheran Church & Sch. v. E.E.O.C.*, __ U.S. __, 131 S. Ct. 1783, 179 L. Ed. 2d 653 (2011).
29. *Davis v. State*, 329 S.W.3d 798, 805–06 (Tex. Crim. App. 2010), reh'g. denied (Jan. 12, 2011), cert. denied, __ U.S. __, 132 S. Ct. 128, 181 L. Ed. 2d 50 (U.S. 2011).
30. *Davis v. State*, 329 S.W.3d at 805–06, quoting *Dawson v. Delaware*, 530 U.S. 159, 165 (1992).
31. *Robles v. Quarterman*, CIV.A. C-07–261, 2009 WL 594629 (S.D. Tex. Mar. 6, 2009).
32. *Davis*, 329 S.W. 3d at 804.
33. United States Commission on Civil Rights, *Enforcing Religious Freedom in Prison* (September 2008) at p. 22.
34. *Employment Div., Dept. of Human Res. of Oregon v. Smith*, 494 U.S. 872 (1990).

35. 42 U.S.C. § 2000bb et. seq.
36. 42 U.S.C. § 2000bb; 42 U.S.C. § 2000bb-1 provided that "Government may substantially burden a person's exercise of religion only if it demonstrates that application of the burden to the person –
    (1) is in furtherance of a compelling governmental interest; and
    (2) is the least restrictive means of furthering that compelling governmental interest."
37. *City of Boerne v. Flores*, 521 U.S. 507 (1997).
38. 42 U.S.C. § 2000cc et seq.
39. 42 U.S.C. § 2000cc-1.
40. *Cutter v. Wilkinson*, 349 F.3d 257, 261 (6th Cir. 2003) rev'd, 544 U.S. 709, (2005) citing *Boerne*, 521 U.S. at 536–37 (1997) (Stevens, J., concurring).
41. *Cutter v. Wilkinson*, 544 U.S. 709 (2005).
42. 10 U.S.C. § 774; *Goldman v. Weinberger*, 475 U.S. 503 (1986).
43. Melissa R. Johnson, "Positive Vibration: An Examination of Incarcerated Rastafarian Free Exercise Claims," *New England Journal on Criminal & Civil Confinement* 34 (2008), 391–427; James D. Nelson, "Incarceration, Accommodation, and Strict Scrutiny," *Virginia Law Review* 95 (2009), 2053–2128.
    Taylor G. Stout, "The Costs of Religious Accommodation in Prisons," *Virginia Law Review* 96 (2010), 1201–1239.
44. *Henderson v. Terhune*, 379 F.3d 709, 711 (9th Cir. 2004).
45. *Warsoldier v. Woodford*, 418 F.3d 989 (9th Cir. 2005).
46. In *Alvarez v. Hill*, 518 F.3d 1152, 1157 (9th Cir. 2008), considering various religious claims, including the denial of a Native American headband, the Ninth Circuit distinguished *Henderson v. Terhune*, and considered the heightened pleading requirements the United States Supreme Court articulated in *Bell Atl. Corp. v. Twombly*, 550 U.S. 544 (2007), but allowed the RLUIPA claim. In insisting that pro se claims were to be liberally construed, the panel noted that the inmate's original pro se complaint was on a form supplied by the prison that instructed inmates to state briefly the "facts of your case" (emphasis in original). A broader statement is in *Grayson v. Schuler*, 666 F.3d 450, 451 (7th Cir. 2012) ("The plaintiff doesn't mention the Act [RLUIPA], but he is proceeding pro se and in such cases we interpret the free exercise claim to include the statutory claim").
47. *Warsoldier v. Woodford*, 418 F.3d 989, 995 (9th Cir. 2005) citing, 15 Cal.Code Reg. § 3062(e) (male) and 15 Cal.Code Reg. § 3062(f) (female).
48. *Fegans v. Norris*, 537 F.3d 897, 905 (8th Cir. 2008).
49. Id. at 911–912 (Melloy, J., concurring in part and dissenting in part). Melloy dissented on the RLUIPA claims.
50. *Turner v. Safley*, 482 U.S. 78 (1987).
51. *Cutter v. Wilkinson*, 544 U.S. 709 (2005).
52. *Fegans v. Norris*, 357 F.3d at 905–6 quoting Cutter, 544 U.S. at 723.
53. *Ashann-Ra v. Com. of Va.*, 112 F. Supp. 2d 559 (W.D. Va. 2000).
54. Id. at 571.
55. *City of Boerne v. Flores*, 521 U.S. 507, 537 (1997) (Stevens, J., concurring).
56. *Reed v. Faulkner*, 842 F.2d 960, 963 (7th Cir. 1988).
57. Id.
58. *Grayson v. Schuler*, 666 F.3d 450.
59. *Reed v. Faulkner*, 842 F.2d 960.
60. *Grayson v. Schuler*, 666 F.3d at 451.

61. *Walls v. Schriro*, CV05–2259-PHX-NVWJCG, available at 2008 WL 544822 (D. Ariz. Feb. 26, 2008).
62. Gregory Sisk and Michael Heise, "Muslims and Religious Liberty in the Era of 9/11: Empirical Evidence from the Federal Courts," *Iowa Law Review* 98 (2012) 231–289.
63. Id. at 276–277.
64. *Braithwaite v. Hinkle*, 752 F. Supp. 2d 692, 693 (E.D. Va. 2010) aff'd, 412 F. App'x 583 (4th Cir. 2011). The judge distinguishes *Smith v. Ozmint*, 578 F.3d 246, 254 (4th Cir. 2009), in part because it involved the implementation of the policy through forcible shaving.
65. *Braithwaite v. Hinkle*, 752 F. Supp. 2d at 696.
66. *DeMoss v. Crain*, 636 F.3d 145, 154 (5th Cir. 2011).
67. *Fegans v. Norris*, 537 F.3d 897, 905 (8th Cir. 2008)
68. *Garner v. Morales*, 07–41015, 2009 WL 577755 (5th Cir. Mar. 6, 2009).
69. *Garner v. Livingston*, CA-C-06–218, 2011 WL 2038581 (S.D. Tex. May 19, 2011).
70. *Brown v. CMC*, CV 08–4587-VAP SH, 2010 WL 2674499 (C.D. Cal. May 18, 2010) report and recommendation adopted, CV 08–4587-VAP SH, 2010 WL 2674502 (C.D. Cal. July 1, 2010).
71. Sisk and Heise, "Muslims and Religious Liberty."
72. Aliah Abdo, "The Legal Status of Hijab in the United States: A Look at the Sociopolitical Influences on the Legal Right to Wear the Muslim Headscarf," *Hastings Race & Poverty Law Journal* 5 (2008), 441.
73. *Safouane v. Fleck*, 226 F. App'x 753, 763–64 (9th Cir. 2007).
74. Id.
75. *Khatib v. County of Orange*, 603 F.3d 713, 715 (9th Cir. 2010) reh'g. en banc granted, 622 F.3d 1074 (9th Cir. 2010) and superseded on reh'g. en banc, 639 F.3d 898 (9th Cir. 2011) cert. denied, __ U.S. __, (2011).
76. *Khatib v. County of Orange*, 639 F.3d 898 (9th Cir. 2011) cert. denied, __ U.S. __, 132 S. Ct. 115 (2011).
77. *Bint-Ishmawiyl v. Vaughn*, CIV. A. 94–7544, available at 1995 WL 461949 (E.D. Pa. Aug. 1, 1995).
78. *Freeman v. Dep't. of Highway Safety & Motor Vehicles*, 924 So. 2d 48 (Fla. Dist. Ct. App. 2006). For discussions of Freeman, see Kathleen M. Moore, "Visible through the Veil: The Regulation of Islam in American Law," *Sociology of Religion* 68 (2007), 237–251; Peter W. Beauchamp, "Misinterpreted Justice: Problems with the Use of Islamic Legal Experts in U.S. Trial Courts," *New York Law School Law Review* 55 (2011), 1097–1119; Christopher C. Lund, "Religious Liberty after Gonzales: A Look at State RFRAs," *South Dakota Law Review* 55 (2010), 466–497; Robert A. Kahn, "The Headscarf as Threat: A Comparison of German and U.S. Legal Discourses," *Vanderbilt Journal of Transnational Law* 40 (2007), 417–444.
79. *Freeman*, 924 So. 2d at 57.
80. *Freeman v. State*, 2002-CA-2828, 2003 WL 21338619 (Fla. Cir. Ct. June 6, 2003) aff'd sub nom. *Freeman v. Dep't of Highway Safety & Motor Vehicles*, 924 So. 2d 48 (Fla. Dist. Ct. App. 2006).
81. *Quaring v. Peterson*, 728 F.2d 1121 (8th Cir.1984); *Bureau of Motor Vehicles v. Pentecostal House of Prayer, Inc.*, 380 N.E.2d 1225 (Ind.1978). For an extended discussion of these and subsequent cases, see Lauren N. Harris, "You Better Smile When You Say

'Cheese!': Whether the Photograph Requirement for Drivers' Licenses Violates the Free Exercise Clause of the First Amendment," *Mercer Law Review* 61 (2010), 611–641.

82. *Freeman*, 924 So. 2d at 55.
83. *Muhammad v. Paruk*, 553 F. Supp. 2d 893 (E.D. Mich. 2008). For comments, see Adam Schwartzbaum, "The Niqab in the Courtroom: Protecting Free Exercise of Religion in a Post-Smith World," *University of Pennsylvania Law Review* 159 (2011), 1533–1576; Aaron J. Williams, "The Veiled Truth: Can the Credibility of Testimony Given by a Niqab-Wearing Witness Be Judged without the Assistance of Facial Expressions?" *University of Detroit Mercy Law Review* 85 (2008), 273–290; Sean Clerget, "Timing Is of the Essence: Reviving the Neutral Law of General Applicability Standard and Applying It to Restrictions against Religious Face Coverings Worn While Testifying in Court," *George Mason Law Review* 18 (2011), 1013–1043; Bruce W. Crews, "Michigan Rule of Evidence 611(b) and the Niqab: A Violation of Free Exercise of Religion," *Thomas M. Cooley Law Review* 27 (2010), 611–645; Joseph W. Tucker, "No Hats in Court: Michigan's Justifications for Free Exercise Indifference," *University of Toledo Law Review* 41 (2010), 1039–1062; Brian M. Murray, "Confronting Religion: Veiled Muslim Witnesses and the Confrontation Clause," *Notre Dame Law Review* 85 (2010), 1727–1757; Steven R. Houchin, "Confronting the Shadow: Is Forcing a Muslim Witness to Unveil in a Criminal Trial a Constitutional Right, or an Unreasonable Intrusion?" *Pepperdine Law Review* 36 (2009), 823–877.
84. Schwartzbaum, "Niqab in the Courtroom," p. 1567n.17.
85. *Muhammad v. Paruk*, 553 F. Supp. 2d 893 (E.D. Mich. 2008).
86. Mich. Sup. Ct. Admin. File No. 2007–13, Amendment of Rule 611 of the Mich. Rules of Evidence (Aug. 25, 2009), available at http://www.courts.michigan.gov/supremecourt/resources/administrative/2007–13–08–25–09-order.pdf [Michigan Rule 611 Order].
87. *Church of the Lukumi Babalu Aye, Inc. v. City of Hialeah*, 508 U.S. 520 (1993).
88. *Employment Div., Dept. of Human Res. of Oregon v. Smith*, 494 U.S. 872 (1990).
89. Michigan Rule 611 Order.
90. *Coy v. Iowa*, 487 U.S. 1012, 1016 (1988).
91. Id. quoting *Richard II*, Act 1, sc. 1.
92. Id.
93. *Maryland v. Craig*, 497 U.S. 836, 847 (1990).
94. *R. v. N.S.*, [2012] S.C.C. 72 (Can.).
95. Id.
96. Valorie K. Vojdik, "Politics of the Headscarf in Turkey: Masculinities, Feminism, and the Construction of Collective Identities," *Harvard Journal of Law & Gender* 33 (2010), 661–685; Clark B. Lombardi and Nathan J. Brown, "Do Constitutions Requiring Adherence to Shari'a Threaten Human Rights? How Egypt's Constitutional Court Reconciles Islamic Law with the Liberal Rule of Law," *American University International Law Review* 21 (2006), 379–435; Nathan J. Brown and Clark B. Lombardi, "The Supreme Constitutional Court of Egypt on Islamic Law, Veiling and Civil Rights: An Annotated Translation of Supreme Constitutional Court of Egypt Case No. 8 of Judicial Year 17 (May 18, 1996)," *American University International Law Review* 21 (2006), 437–460 (discussing the 1996 Supreme Constitutional Court of Egypt's "veiling" case); Douglas Laycock, "Conference Introduction: American Religious Liberty, French Laïcité, and the Veil," *Journal of Catholic Legal Studies* 49 (2010), 21–54; Ioanna Tourkochoriti, "The Burka Ban: Divergent Approaches to Freedom of Religion in France and in the U.S.A.," *William & Mary Bill*

Rights Journal 20 (2012), 791–852; Luna Droubi, "The Constitutionality of the Niqab Ban in Egypt: A Symbol of Egypt's Struggle for a Legal Identity," *New York Law School Law Review* 56 (2012), 687–709; Robert A. Kahn, "The Headscarf as Threat: A Comparison of German and U.S. Legal Discourses," *Vanderbilt Journal of Transnational Law* 40 (2007), 417–444; Oriana Mazza, "The Right to Wear Headscarves and Other Religious Symbols in French, Turkish, and American Schools: How the Government Draws a Veil on Free Expression of Faith," *Journal of Catholic Legal Studies* 48 (2009), 303–343; R. Vance Eaton, "Thinly Veiled: Institutional Messages in the Language of Secularism in Public Schools in France and the United States," *South Carolina Journal of International Law & Business* 6 (2010), 299–333; Hera Hashmi, "Too Much to Bare? A Comparative Analysis of the Headscarf in France, Turkey, and the United States," *University of Maryland Law Journal Race, Religion, Gender & Class* 10 (2010), 409–445.

97. Laycock, "Religious Liberty"; Vojdik, "Headscarf in Turkey."
98. For discussions of the religious garb statutes, see Holly M. Bastian, "Religious Garb Statutes and Title VII: An Uneasy Coexistence," *Georgetown Law Journal* 80 (1991), 211–232; Caitlin S. Kerr, "Teachers' Religious Garb as an Instrument for Globalization in Education," *Indiana Journal of Global Legal Studies* 18 (2011), 539–561; Linda Grathwohl, "The North Dakota Anti-Garb Law: Constitutional Conflict and Religious Strife," *Great Plains Quarterly* 13 (1993), 187–202; Edmund Reutter, "Religious Dress: A Century of Litigation," *Education Law Reporter* 70 (1992), 747–761.
99. *Pierce v. Society of Sisters of the Holy Names of Jesus and Mary*, 268 U.S. 510 (1925). More recently, the Court in *Zelman v. Simmons-Harris*, 536 U.S. 639 (2002), upheld an Ohio school voucher program that allowed parents to pay religious school tuition with tax-payer granted funds against an Establishment Clause challenge, and in 2011 the Court in *Arizona Christian School Tuition Organization v. Winn,)__ U.S. __ denied standing to challengers of an Arizona statute awarding tax credits for tuition at religious schools.
100. *Cooper v. Eugene Sch. Dist. No. 4J*, 301 Or. 358, 373, 723 P.2d 298, 308 (1986) (noting that the 1923 predecessor to ORS 342.650 "dates from the period of anti-Catholic intolerance that also gave us the initiative measure against private schools struck down in *Pierce v. Society of Sisters*").
101. *O'Connor v. Hendrick*, 184 N.Y. 421, 428, 77 N.E. 612, 614 (1906).
102. *Hysong v. Sch. Dist. of Gallitzin Borough*, 164 Pa. 629, 30 A. 482 (1894).
103. 1895, June 27, P.L. 395, §§ 1, 2 (24 P.S. §§ 1129, 1130), codified as 24 Pa. Stat. § 11–1112.
104. *United States v. Bd. of Educ. for Sch. Dist. of Philadelphia*, 911 F.2d 882 (3d Cir. 1990).
105. For a discussion of the EEOC under Thomas and Reagan, see Neal Devins, "Reagan Redux: Civil Rights under Bush," *Notre Dame Law Review* 68 (1993), 955–1001. The Reardon case could be an example of the preference for individual claims rather than more systemic litigation that Devins discusses, although the Reardon litigation did challenge the Pennsylvania statute.
106. *Cooper v. Eugene Sch. Dist. No. 4J*, 301 Or. 358, 723 P.2d 298 (1986), appeal dismissed, 480 U.S. 942 (1987) (Brennan, Marshall, and O'Connor dissenting).
107. Oregon (O.R.S. § 342.650, repealed by Laws 2010, c. 105 [1st Sp. Sess.], § 3, eff. July 1, 2011); Pennsylvania (2011 Pennsylvania House Bill No. 1581, Pennsylvania One Hundred Ninety-Fifth General Assembly – 2011–2012; Nebraska (Neb. Rev. Stat. § 79–898 [2012]).
108. For discussions, see Sadia Aslam, "Hijab in the Workplace: Why Title VII Does Not Adequately Protect Employees from Discrimination on the Basis of Religious Dress

and Appearance," *University of Missouri-Kansas City Law Review* 80 (2011), 221–238; Nathan K. Bader, "Hats Off to Them: Muslim Women Stand against Workplace Religious Discrimination in Geo Group," *St. Louis University Law Journal* 56 (2011), 261–300; Sami Hasan, "Veiling Religion in the Force: The Validity of 'Religion-Neutral Appearance' as an Employer Interest," *UCLA Journal of Islamic & Near East Law* 9 (2010), 87–110; Richard J. Ramones, "Religious Discrimination or Legitimate Uniform Policy? A Critique and Analysis of the Third Circuit's Decision to Uphold a Private Prison's Ban on Employees Wearing Khimars: EEOC v. The GEO Group, Inc.," *Rutgers Journal of Law & Religion* 12 (2010), 184–201.

109. *Webb v. City of Philadelphia*, 562 F.3d 256 (3d Cir. 2009).
110. *E.E.O.C. v. GEO Group, Inc.*, 616 F.3d 265, 270 (3d Cir. 2010).

7. DRESSING ECONOMICALLY

1. See generally, Charles Beard, *An Economic Interpretation of the Constitution of the United States* (New York: Macmillan, 1913); Symposium, "The Constitution as an Economic Document: A Symposium Commemorating the Bicentennial of the United States Constitution," *George Washington Law Review*, 56 (1987) 1–186.
2. *Lochner v. New York*, 198 U.S. 45, 75 (1905) (Holmes, J., dissenting).
3. Article I, §8 c. 1; Article I, §8 cl. 3. As then-Chief Justice Burger explained, in the Foreword to the Symposium on the Constitution,

> Because commercial problems had provided much of the impetus for the Philadelphia Convention following the Annapolis Convention of 1786, the delegates addressed those difficulties in detail. To assure that there would be a national monetary system, Congress was given the sole power to issue currency. Congress was given the power to borrow and the power to tax – thereby providing a solid fiscal foundation for government finance. The Constitution also gave Congress the exclusive powers to impose duties on foreign trade and to enter treaties, while limiting Congress to imposing only uniform duties and only duties on imports. This assured that the new federal government could not impose interstate tariffs, and that it could respond with a consistent policy to international trade restrictions by other countries.

Warren E. Burger, "Foreword: The Constitution as an Economic Document: A Symposium Commemorating the Bicentennial of the United States Constitution," *George Washington Law Review* 56 (1987), 2.
4. Gene Dattel, *Cotton and Race in the Making of America: The Human Costs of Economic Power* (Chicago: Ivan R. Dee, 2009), pp. 5–23.
5. Max Farrand, editor, *The Records of the Federal Convention of 1787*, 4 vols. (1937 rev. ed, 1966), Vol. 2, p. 222 (August 8, 1787) (New Haven: Yale University Press).
6. The *Federalist* No. 54, at 304 (James Madison), edited by Clinton Rossiter, 1961 (dated Tuesday, February 12, 1788).
7. Article V included "no Amendment which may be made prior to the Year One thousand eight hundred and eight shall in any Manner affect the first and fourth Clauses in the Ninth Section of the first Article." Section 9's fourth clause provided "No Tax or Duty shall be laid on Articles exported from any State" and was widely seen as protecting the staple crops of Southern states.

8. For discussions, see Paul Finkelman, *Slavery and the Founders* (New York: M. E. Sharpe, 1996); George William Van Cleve, *A Slaveholders' Union: Slavery, Politics, and the Constitution in the Early American Republic* (Chicago: University of Chicago Press, 2010); Robert McColley, *Slavery and Jeffersonian Virginia* (Urbana: University of Illinois Press, 1964).

9. Joyce E. Chaplin, "Creating a Cotton South in Georgia and South Carolina, 1760–1815," *Journal of Southern History*, 57:2 (1991), 171–200. Chaplain argues that before the widespread commercialization of cotton, its significance as a domestic product should not be underestimated, and that rural whites and blacks (whether slave or free) would have been familiar with its growth as well as cleaning, spinning, and weaving it into cloth.

10. Several searches of Max Farrand, editor, *The Records of the Federal Convention of 1787*, 4 vols. (1937; rev. ed., New Haven: Yale University Press, 1966) do not reveal the word "cotton." An electronic version of Farrand's *Records* is available through the Library of Congress website, at http://memory.loc.gov/ammem/amlaw/lwfr.html.

11. Terry G. Sharrer, "The Indigo Bonanza in South Carolina, 1740–90," *Technology and Culture* 12:3 (1971), 447–455. In addition to a detailed account of indigo cultivation and production into dye, Sharrer argues that indigo "paved the way" for the commercialization of cotton.

12. Farrand, *The Records of the Federal Convention of 1787*, Vol. 2, p. 449 (August 29, 1787). Pinckney had earlier mentioned the rice and indigo of the Carolinas and Georgia; id., Vol. 1, p. 510 (July 2, 1787).

13. Farrand, *The Records of the Federal Convention of 1787*, Vol. 2, p. 360 (August 21, 1787).

14. Farrand, *The Records of the Federal Convention of 1787*, Vol. 2, p. 222 (August 8, 1787).

15. Farrand, *The Records of the Federal Convention of 1787*, Vol. 3, p. 365 (February 3, 1792) (Statement of Hugh Williamson in the House of Representatives).

16. See Dattel, *Cotton and Race*, pp. ix–xi.

17. Maltida Joslyn Gage, the feminist and suffragist, begins her 1870 pamphlet, "Woman as Inventor," with this story. Matilda Joslyn Gage, "Woman as Inventor" ([New York State?]: serial number 1870), available at pds.lib.harvard.edu/pds/view/2575141.

18. Keith Aoki, "Distributive and Syncretic Motives in Intellectual Property Law (with Special Reference to Coercion, Agency, and Development)," *U.C. Davis Law Review* 40 (2007), 745–747, citing Portia James, *The Real McCoy: African American Invention and Innovation 1619–1930* (1989).

19. Mark A. Lemley, "The Myth of the Sole Inventor," *Michigan Law Review* 110 (2012), 718–19, citing Angela Lakwete, *Inventing the Cotton Gin: Machine and Myth in Antebellum America* (Baltimore, MD: Johns Hopkins University Press, 2004), pp. 58–61.

20. Aoki, "Intellectual Property Law," pp. 722, 745–747. Aoki argues that the patent system amplified racial subordination, including that caused by chattel slavery, deepening and widening distributional inequalities and inequalities of access to the American entrepreneurial system. Id. at 747.

21. Article I, section 8, clause 8. For a history of the patent and copyright clause, see Edward Walterscheid, "'Within the Limits of the Constitutional Grant': Constitutional Limitations on the Patent Power," *Journal of Intellectual Property Law* 9 (2002), 291–357.

22. *The Clothworkers of Ipswich*, (1615) 78 Eng. Rep. 147 (K.B.). For a discussion of this history, see Adam Mossoff, "Rethinking the Development of Patents: An Intellectual History, 1550–1800," *Hastings Law Journal*, 52 (2001), 1255–1321.

23. *The Clothworkers of Ipswich* (1615) 78 Eng. Rep. 147 (K.B.).

24. *Graham v. John Deere Co. of Kansas City*, 383 U.S. 1, 7 (1966).
25. *Graham* 383 U.S. at 7–8, citing *The Writings of Thomas Jefferson*, edited by Paul Leicester Ford (New York: G. P. Putnam's Sons, 1892–99), 10 vols.; Vol. 5, p. 47.
26. *Graham*, 383 U.S. at 8.
27. The Court in *Graham* states,

> Thomas Jefferson, who as Secretary of State was a member of the group, was its moving spirit and might well be called the "first administrator of our patent system." See Federico, "Operation of the Patent Act of 1790," 18 *Journal of the Patent and Trademark Office Society*, 237, 238. He was not only an administrator of the patent system under the 1790 Act but was also the author of the 1793 Patent Act. In addition, Jefferson was himself an inventor of great note. His unpatented improvements on plows, to mention but one line of his inventions, won acclaim and recognition on both sides of the Atlantic. Because of his active interest and influence in the early development of the patent system, Jefferson's views on the general nature of the limited patent monopoly under the Constitution, as well as his conclusions as to conditions for patentability under the statutory scheme, are worthy of note.
>
> *Graham*, 383 U.S. at 7.

Scholars of patent history in the United States criticize the Court in *Graham* as well as the courts and scholars more generally for both elevating and misusing Jefferson's comments to support their own conclusions. See Adam Mossoff, "Who Cares What Thomas Jefferson Thought about Patents? Reevaluating the Patent 'Privilege' in Historical Context," *Cornell Law Review* 92 (2007), 953–1012; Edward C. Walterscheid, "The Use and Abuse of History: The Supreme Court's Interpretation of Thomas Jefferson's Influence on the Patent Law," *Idea* 39 (1999), 195–224; Edward C. Walterscheid, "Patents and the Jeffersonian Mythology," *John Marshall Law Review* 29 (1995), 269–314.

28. Jeanette Mirsky and Allen Nevins, *The World of Eli Whitney* (New York: Macmillan, 1952); Dattel, *Cotton and Race*, pp. 33–35; Stephen Yafa, *Big Cotton* (New York: Viking, 2005), 79–88.
29. A copy of Eli Whitney's 1812 patent application requesting renewal is in the National Archives; available at http://www.archives.gov/education/lessons/cotton-gin patent/images/patent-petition-1.gif.
30. *Whitney v. Carter*, 29 F. Cas. 1070, 1072 (C.C.D. Ga. 1810).
31. Id. at 1072.
32. This argument is evident in *Whitney v. Carter*. Steven Lubar argues that Whitney's attorneys had been making it earlier; "The Transformation of Antebellum Patent Law," *Technology and Culture* 32.4 (1991), 932–959.
33. Kimberly D. Krawiec, "Privatizing Outsider Trading," *Virginia Journal of International Law* 41 (2001), 702–703, citing Jack Hirshleifer, "The Private and Social Value of Information and the Reward to Inventive Activity," *American Economic Review* 61 (1971), 561, 571.
34. For an excellent analysis, see Robert Knowles, "The Balance of Forces and the Empire of Liberty: States' Rights and the Louisiana Purchase," *Iowa Law Review* 88 (2003), 343–418.
35. Id.
36. *Marbury v. Madison*, 5 U.S. (1 Cranch) 177 (1803). For a discussion of whether *Marbury* established the concept of judicial review, see Ruthann Robson, "Judicial Review and Sexual Freedom," *University of Hawaii Law Review* 30 (2007), 1–46, esp. 6–7.

37. Sanford Levinson, "Why I Do Not Teach Marbury (Except to Eastern Europeans) and Why You Shouldn't Either," *Wake Forest Law Review* 38 (2003), 553–578, 556 (arguing that "truly the most important constitutional event not only of 1803, but, indeed, of the entire period between constitutional ratification and the outbreak of war in 1861" was the Louisiana Purchase).

38. *Am. Ins. Co. v. 356 Bales of Cotton, David Canter, Claimant*, 26 U.S. 511 (U.S.S.C. 1828).

39. Judith Resnik, "The Mythic Meaning of Article III Courts," *University of Colorado Law Review* 56 (1985), 581–617, 590.

40. Ibid. at 589.

41. Id. at 590n.38.

42. Article IV, section 3, clause 2 provides: "The Congress shall have Power to dispose of and make all needful Rules and Regulations respecting the Territory or other Property belonging to the United States; and nothing in this Constitution shall be so construed as to Prejudice any Claims of the United States, or of any particular State."

43. Uilisone Falemanu Tua, "A Native's Call for Justice: The Call for the Establishment of a Federal District Court in American Samoa," *Asian-Pacific Law & Policy Journal* 11 (2010), 246–292; Gary Lawson, "Territorial Governments and the Limits of Formalism," *California Law Review* 78 (1990), 853–911.

44. Knowles, "Balance of Forces," pp. 401–402.

45. Article IV, section 3, clause 1 provides: "New States may be admitted by the Congress into this Union; but no new State shall be formed or erected within the Jurisdiction of any other State; nor any State be formed by the Junction of two or more States, or Parts of States, without the Consent of the Legislatures of the States concerned as well as of the Congress." For an excellent overview of the process by which territories became states, see Eric Biber, "The Price of Admission: Causes, Effects, and Patterns of Conditions Imposed on States Entering the Union," *American Journal of Legal History* 46 (2004), 119–208.

46. Ordinance of 1787: The Northwest Territorial Government, 1 Stat. 50 (1789). For a discussion, see Paul Finkelman, "Slavery and the Northwest Ordinance, a Study in Ambiguity," *Journal of the Early Republic* 6.4 (1986), 343–370.

47. Southwest Ordinance, Act of May 26, 1790, ch. 14, 1 Stat. 123.

48. Dattel, *Cotton and Race*, p. 46.

49. For example, the Mississippi Enabling Act § 4, ch. 23, 3 Stat. 349 (1817), mentioned the Northwest Ordinance and then the "articles of agreement between the United States and Georgia." This agreement, in which Georgia ceded the land to the United States, also references the Northwest Ordinance in Article I, 5, with the proviso "that article only excepted which forbids slavery." Articles of Agreement and Cession, U.S.-Ga., Apr. 24, 1802, reprinted in Governor George Poindexter, *The Revised Code of the Laws of Mississippi in Which Are Comprised All Such Acts of the General Assembly, of a Public Nature, as Were in Force at the End of the Year 1823* (Natchez: Francis Baker, 1824), available at http://books.google.com/books?id=Ah5GAQAAIAAJ&dq.

50. Dattel, *Cotton and Race*, p. 51.

51. Missouri Compromise Act, Act Cong. March 6, 1820, 3 Stat. 545.

52. *Dred Scott v. Sandford*, 60 U.S. (19 How.) 393 (1857).

53. In this, the justices considered the particulars of Dred Scott's situation, but the necessity for doing has its roots not only in the Constitution's enshrining of slavery, but in the pre-constitutional Northwest Ordinance. The Ordinance did prohibit slavery and involuntary servitude, with an immediate proviso: "Provided, always, That any person escaping

into the same, from whom labor or service is lawfully claimed in any one of the original States, such fugitive may be lawfully reclaimed and conveyed to the person claiming his or her labor or service as aforesaid." Moreover, the recognition of certain rights to the "inhabitants" of the territory in Article 2 of the Northwest Ordinance, was compromised not only by the fugitive slave language in the Northwest Ordinance itself, but whenever the terms of Northwest Ordinance were extended to other territories with the exception of the prohibition of slavery.

54. James Henry Hammond, "On the Admission of Kansas, under the Lecompton Constitution," U.S. Senate, 4 March 1858, Congressional Globe, 35th Congress, 1st Session, Appendix, 68–71.

55. Martin Bauml Duberman, "'Writhing Bedfellows' in Antebellum South Carolina: Historical Interpretation and the Politics of Evidence," in *Hidden from History: Reclaiming the Gay and Lesbian Past* (New York: New American Library/Penguin Books, 1989), pp. 153–168.

56. Frank Lawrence Owsley, *King Cotton Diplomacy: Foreign Relations of the Confederate States of America* (Chicago: University of Chicago Press, 1931); Dattel, *Cotton and Race*, pp. 161–208.

57. First Reconstruction Act, Ch. 153, 14 Stat. 428 (1867). For a discussion of the adoption and constitutional process of the Thirteenth Amendment as well as the other Reconstruction Amendments, see Akhil Reed Amar, *America's Constitution* (New York: Random House, 2005), pp. 359–380; John Harrison, "The Lawfulness of the Reconstruction Amendments," *University Chicago Law Review* 68 (2001), 375–461.

58. *Ruffin v. Commonwealth*, 62 Va. (21 Gratt) 790, 796 (1871). Convict-lease systems arose not only for cotton but also for other crops, the production of turpentine, mining, and building railroad tracks and roads.

59. David M. Oshinsky, "Convict Labor in the Post–Civil War South: Involuntary Servitude after the Thirteenth Amendment," in *The Promises of Liberty: The History and Contemporary Relevance of the Thirteenth Amendment* (New York: Columbia University Press, 2010), pp. 100–116, esp. 109–110.

60. Ibid. at 110.

61. Andrea C. Armstrong, "Slavery Revisited in Penal Plantation Labor," *Seattle University Law Review* 35 (2012), 835n. 237 (citing Mark T. Carleton, *Politics and Punishment: The History of the Louisiana State Penal System* (1971), p. 92).

62. A Brief History of the Mississippi Department of Corrections, available at http://www. mdoc.state.ms.us/Brief_History.htm. For an extended discussion, see David M. Oshinsky, *Worse Than Slavery: Parchman Farm and the Ordeal of Jim Crow* (New York: Free Press, 1996).

63. Armstrong, "Slavery Revisited," p. 874.

64. *Wendt v. Lynaugh*, 841 F.2d 619, 619 (5th Cir. 1988) (the prisoner's "basic complaint is that he was forced to work without pay while in prison in violation of the Thirteenth Amendment. We agree that his case obviously is frivolous, and we affirm"); Armstrong, "Slavery Revisited"; Raja Raghunath, "A Promise the Nation Cannot Keep: What Prevents the Application of the Thirteenth Amendment in Prison?" *William & Mary Bill of Rights Journal* 18 (2009), 395–442.

65. *Goodman v. Lukens Steel Co.*, 482 U.S. 656, 672–73 (1987) (Brennan, J., concurring and dissenting in part). Justice Brennan states that Congress correctly perceived the "Black Codes," enacted in Southern States after the Thirteenth Amendment as "in fact poorly disguised substitutes for slavery." He then describes them: "They defined racial status;

forbade blacks from pursuing certain occupations or professions (e.g. skilled artisans, merchants, physicians, preaching without a license); forbade owning firearms or other weapons; controlled the movement of blacks by systems of passes; required proof of residence; prohibited the congregation of groups of blacks; restricted blacks from residing in certain areas; and specified an etiquette of deference to whites, as, for example, by prohibiting blacks from directing insulting words at whites." Id. at 673, citing H. Hyman and W. Wiecek, *Equal Justice under Law* (New York: Harper Collins, 1982), p. 319.

66. For example, Section 2901 of the Mississippi Code provided that "Every person who shall be convicted of taking and carrying away, feloniously, the personal property of another, of the value of ten dollars or more, shall be guilty of grand larceny, and shall be imprisoned in the penitentiary for a term not exceeding five years; but it shall be grand larceny to take and carry away, feloniously, any of the kind of horned cattle, or swine, or sheep, or goats, of any value." Quoted in *Golden v. State*, 63 Miss. 466, 467 (1886).

67. William Cohen, "Negro Involuntary Servitude in the South, 1865–1940: A Preliminary Analysis," *Journal of Southern History* 42.1 (1976), 31–60, esp. 50.

68. No. 120, An Act to define the relative duties of master and apprentice (Alabama 1866).

69. Id.

70. *Bailey v. State of Alabama*, 219 U.S. 219 (1911).

71. *Papachristou v. City of Jacksonville*, 405 U.S. 156, 170 (1972).

72. *The Civil Rights Cases*, 109 U.S. 3 (1883).

73. *Plessy v. Ferguson*, 163 U.S. 537 (1896).

74. Gene Dattel, *Cotton and Race*, argues extensively and convincingly that Northerners never expected that Southern Blacks would leave the rural South after Emancipation. The song "Cotton Fields" was written by Huddie Ledbetter, also known as Lead Belly, circa 1940.

75. Charles Dickens, *Oliver Twist: The Parish Boy's Progress* (London: Robert Bentley, 1838) (Twist's early days as a child laborer were believed to be modeled not only on Dicken's own experiences but on *A Memoir* of Robert Blincoe, who worked in a cotton mill beginning at the age of seven); Friedrich Engels, *Condition of the Working Class in England* (originally published in German, 1844; English translation, 1877).

76. Adam Mossoff, "The Rise and Fall of the First American Patent Thicket: The Sewing Machine War of the 1850s," *Arizona Law Review* 53 (2011), 202.

77. *United States v. E. C. Knight Co.*, 156 U.S. 1, 16 (1895). As the Court's 8–1 opinion explained, "Doubtless the power to control the manufacture of a given thing involves, in a certain sense, the control of its disposition, but this is a secondary, and not the primary, sense; and, although the exercise of that power may result in bringing the operation of commerce into play, it does not control it, and affects it only incidentally and indirectly. Commerce succeeds to manufacture, and is not a part of it. The power to regulate commerce is the power to prescribe the rule by which commerce shall be governed, and is a power independent of the power to suppress monopoly." Id. at 12.

78. Hammond, "On the Admission of Kansas," p. 71.

79. See James Gray Pope, "The Thirteenth Amendment versus the Commerce Clause: Labor and the Shaping of American Constitutional Law, 1921–1957," *Columbia Law Review* 102 (2002), 1–122.

80. *Lochner v. New York*, 198 U.S. 45 (1905).

81. David Von Drehle, *Triangle: The Fire That Changed America* (New York: Grove Press, 2003), esp. 6–86; Leon Stein, *The Triangle Fire* (New York: J. B. Lippincott, 1962); Arthur

F. McEvoy, "The Triangle Shirtwaist Factory Fire of 1911: Social Change, Industrial Accidents, and the Evolution of Common-Sense Causality," *Law and Social Inquiry* 20 (1995), 621–651, esp. 631–632.
82. Von Drehle, *Triangle*, pp. 44–45.
83. Ibid., p. 47.
84. Ibid.; Stein, *The Triangle Fire*; McEvoy, "The Triangle Shirtwaist Factory Fire."
85. McEvoy, "The Triangle Shirtwaist Factory Fire," pp. 629, 644.
86. Von Drehle, *Triangle*, pp. 216–218; Stein, *The Triangle Fire*; McEvoy, "The Triangle Shirtwaist Factory Fire." Compare Eric G. Behrens, "The Triangle Shirtwaist Company Fire of 1911: A Lesson in Legislative Manipulation," *Texas Law Review* 62 (1983), 361–387; Marcia L. McCormick, "Consensus, Dissensus, and Enforcement: Legal Protection of Working Women from the Time of the Triangle Shirtwaist Factory Fire to Today," *N.Y.U. Journal of Legislation & Public Policy* 14 (2011), 645–695.
87. *People v. Williams*, 189 N.Y. 131, 137, 81 N.E. 778, 780 (1907) (citing *Lochner v. New York*, 198 U.S. 45 [1905]).
88. *People ex rel. Hoelderlin v. Kane*, 79 Misc. 140, 145, 139 N.Y.S. 350, 354 (Sup. Ct. 1913) aff'd sub nom. *People v. Hoelderlin*, 161 A.D. 956, 146 N.Y.S. 1105 (1914).
89. *Muller v. Oregon*, 208 U.S. 412 (1908).
90. Nancy Woloch, *Muller v. Oregon: A Brief History with Documents* (New York: St. Martin's Press, 1996), p. 5.
91. Excerpts of the Brief appear in Woloch, *Muller v. Oregon*. The entire brief is available at the Louis D. Brandeis Collection, http://www.law.louisville.edu/library/collections/brandeis/node/235.
92. Woloch, *Muller v. Oregon*, p. 111; Brief in *Muller v. Oregon*, pp. 19–20.
93. Woloch, *Muller v. Oregon*, p. 114; Brief in *Muller v. Oregon*, pp. 20–21.
94. *Muller v. Oregon*, 208 U.S. at 422.
95. Brief in *Muller v. Oregon*, pp. 104–112.
96. For discussions of the cases and their social history, see David E. Bernstein, "Lochner, Parity, and the Chinese Laundry Cases," *William & Mary Law Review* 41 (1999), 211–294; Joel Kosman, "Toward an Inclusionary Jurisprudence: A Reconceptualization of Zoning," *Catholic University Law Review* 43 (1993), 59–108, esp. 63–70; Thomas H. Burrell, "Justice Stephen Field's Expansion of the Fourteenth Amendment: From the Safeguards of Federalism to a State of Judicial Hegemony," *Gonzaga Law Review* 43 (2008), 77–168.
97. *Barbier v. Connolly*, 113 U.S. 27 (1884).
98. *Soon Hing v. Crowley*, 113 U.S. 703 (1885).
99. Id.
100. *Yick Wo v. Hopkins*, 118 U.S. 356 (1886).
101. Id.
102. *Adkins v. Children's Hospital*, 261 U.S. 525 (1923). The Court overruled *Adkins* in *West Coast Hotel Co. v. Parrish*, 300 U.S. 379 (1937).
103. Seymour Moskowitz, "Dickens Redux: How American Child Labor Law Became a Con Game," *Whittier Journal of Child & Family Advocacy* 10 (2010), 101.
104. Pub. L. No. 64–249, § 432, 39 Stat. 675 (1916).
105. Stephen B. Wood, *Constitutional Politics in the Progressive Era: Child Labor and the Law* (Chicago: University of Chicago Press, 1968), p. 84.
106. *Hammer v. Dagenhart*, 247 U.S. 251 (1918).

107. Wood, *Child Labor*, pp. 81–110. Wood focuses on David Clark, who founded the *Southern Textile Bulletin* in 1911, as well as organizing the Executive Committee of Southern Cotton Manufacturers. Clark spearheaded the litigation that most believed would not be successful and announced its strategies in the *Southern Textile Bulletin*. Ibid., pp. 42–45; 80–87. A similar account appears in Elizabeth H. Davidson, *Child Labor Legislation in the Southern Textile States* (Chapel Hill: University of North Carolina Press, 1939), pp. 249–271. Davidson also discusses the state laws and efforts at reform.

108. Brief for Appellees, *Hammer v. Dagenhart*, p. 11.

109. *Champion v. Ames*, 188 U.S. 321 (1903).

110. *Hammer*, 247 U.S. at 276. The Brief had stated:

> *The question in this case is (and we make this statement with the utmost respect) whether those who earnestly favor an absolutely nationalized control of every function and activity of life, and the complete elimination of the States as political entities, have hit upon a new and yet unused tool to accomplish completely their purpose.*

   Brief for Appellees, *Hammer v. Dagenhart*, at 14 (italics in original).
   For an argument that the harmless goods doctrine was intellectually sustainable and that *Hammer* was not "an attempt to return American to an imagined laissez faire past," see Logan Everett Sawyer III, "Creating *Hammer v. Dagenhart*, *William & Mary Bill of Rights Journal* (draft available at http://papers.ssrn.com/sol3/papers.cfm?abstract_id=2033351).

111. *United States v. Darby*, 312 U.S. 100 (1941). Darby involved a lumber company.

112. Shirley Lung, "Exploiting the Joint Employer Doctrine: Providing a Break for Sweatshop Garment Workers," *Loyola University Chicago Law Journal* 34 (2003), 291–358.

113. Shirley Lung, "Overwork and Overtime," *Indiana Law Review* 39 (2005), 51–85.

114. *Sherbert v. Verner*, 374 U.S. 398 (1963).

115. American Apparel and Footwear Association, *TRENDS: An Annual Statistical Analysis of the U.S. Apparel & Footwear Industries* (2008), p. 5. Available at https://www.wewear.org/industry-resources/publications-and-statistics/.

116. The number of 65 is an approximation, derived from the consumption rate of 19.5 billion in 2008; 20.1 in 2007 of items of apparel, and 2.4 billion in 2008; 2.2 billion in 2007, pairs of shoes, according to American Apparel and Footwear Association, Id. Divided by the U.S. population in 2008 of 300 million, that's approximately 66 items of clothing bought per person and 8 pairs of shoes.

117. Elizabeth L. Cline, *Over-Dressed: The Shockingly High Cost of Cheap Fashion* (New York: Portfolio/Penguin, 2012), pp. 41–42 (imports), 12 (less proportion of income), 36 ("price is king").

118. The Lanham (Trademark) Act, Pub.L. 79–489, 60 Stat. 427, enacted July 6, 1946, codified at 15 U.S.C. § 1051 et seq. [15 U.S.C. ch.22].

119. See *supra* notes 25–28 and accompanying text.

120. Ann Bartow, "Counterfeits, Copying, and Class," *Houston Law Review* 48 (2012), 707–749.

121. Ibid. at 734–735, citing, *Adidas-Am., Inc. v. Payless Shoesource, Inc.*, 546 F. Supp. 2d 1029, 1053–54 (D. Or. 2008).

122. David Zahniser, "Thousands of Phony Christian Louboutins Seized by Customs Agents," *Los Angeles Times*, August 16, 2012, available at http://latimesblogs.latimes.com/lanow/2012/08/counterfeit-christian-louboutin-shoes-seized.html.

123. *Christian Louboutin S.A. v. Yves Saint Laurent Am., Inc.*, 778 F. Supp. 2d 445, 457 (S.D.N.Y. 2011).
124. *Christian Louboutin S.A. v. Yves Saint Laurent Am., Inc*, ___ F.3d ___ (decision September 5, 2012).
125. Art. I, §9 cl. 5.
126. Article I, §8 c. 1 provides:

> The Congress shall have Power To lay and collect Taxes, Duties, Imposts and Excises, to pay the Debts and provide for the common Defence and general Welfare of the United States; but all Duties, Imposts and Excises shall be uniform throughout the United States;

> Article I, §10, cl. 3 provides:

> No State shall, without the Consent of the Congress, lay any Imposts or Duties on Imports or Exports, except what may be absolutely necessary for executing its inspection Laws: and the net Produce of all Duties and Imposts, laid by any State on Imports or Exports, shall be for the Use of the Treasury of the United States; and all such Laws shall be subject to the Revision and Control of the Congress.

127. *Marshall Field & Co. v. Clark*, 143 U.S. 649 (1892).
128. For an argument that the enrolled bill doctrine should be abandoned, see Ittai Bar-Siman-Tov, "Legislative Supremacy in the United States? Rethinking the 'Enrolled Bill' Doctrine," *Georgetown Law Journal* (2009), 323–390.
129. *Made in the USA Foundation. v. United States*, 242 F.3d 1300 (11th Cir. 2001), cert. denied sub nom. *United Steelworkers of America, AFL-CIO, CLC v. United States*, 534 U.S. 1039 (2001).
130. Bruce Ackerman and David Golove, "Is NAFTA Constitutional?" *Harvard Law Review* 108 (1995), 799–929; Laurence H. Tribe, "Taking Text and Structure Seriously: Reflections on Free-Form Method in Constitutional Interpretation," *Harvard Law Review* 108 (1995), 1221–1303, esp. 1223; James J. Varellas, "The Constitutional Political Economy of Free Trade: Reexamining NAFTA-Style Congressional-Executive Agreements," *Santa Clara Law Review* 49 (2009), 717–792.
131. Chantal Thomas, "Constitutional Change and International Government," *Hastings Law Journal* 52 (2000), 1–45.
132. Ibid., p. 2.
133. Arrangement Regarding International Trade in Textiles (Multifibre Arrangement), Dec. 20, 1973, 25 U.S.T. 1001 (entered into force on Jan. 1, 1974).
134. Cline, *Over-Dressed*, pp. 81–82, 89–91.
135. Scott L. Cummings, "Hemmed In: Legal Mobilization in the Los Angeles Anti-Sweatshop Movement," *Berkeley Journal of Employment & Labor Law* 30 (2009), 1–84.
136. Samantha C. Halem, "Slaves to Fashion: A Thirteenth Amendment Litigation Strategy to Abolish Sweatshops in the Garment Industry," *San Diego Law Review* 36 (1999), 397–453.
137. Cummings, "Hemmed In."
138. UNICOR, Factories with Fences, p. 36, available at www.unicor.gov/information/publications/showpub.cfm?pubid=57.
139. UNICOR Board Minutes from January 2012, p. 7, available at http://www.unicor.gov/information/publications/pdfs/corporate/BOD_MEETING_MINUTES%20January%202012%20Washington%20DC%20-edits%203-23.pdf.

140. Pub. L. No. 94–241, 90 Stat. 263 (1976). For a discussion of the legal history of CNMI, see *U.S. ex rel. Richards v. De Leon Guerrero*, 4 F.3d 749 (9th Cir. 1993); *Commonwealth of the N. Mariana Islands v. United States*, 670 F. Supp. 2d 65, 71 (D.D.C. 2009). For critical discussions of the Covenant, see Marie Rios-Martinez, "Congressional Colonialism in the Pacific: The Case of the Northern Mariana Islands and Its Covenant with the United States," *Scholar* 3 (2000), 41–69; Marybeth Herald, "The Northern Mariana Islands: A Change in Course under Its Covenant with the United States," *Oregon Law Review* 71 (1992), 127–204.

141. Joint Resolution of March 24, 1976, 72 Pub.L. No. 94–241, 90 Stat. 263, reprinted in 48 U.S.C. § 1681 note.

142. Covenant §503, Pub. L. No. 94–241, 90 Stat. 263 (1976).

143. See *Commonwealth of the N. Mariana Islands v. United States*, 670 F. Supp. 2d 65, 72 (D.D.C. 2009).

144. For discussions of the litigation, see Farrah-Marisa Chua Short, "An Experiment in Protecting Workers' Rights: The Garment Industry of the U.S. Commonwealth of the Northern Mariana Islands," *University of Pennsylvania Journal of Labor & Employment Law* 7 (2005), 971–89; Robert S. Florke, "Castaways on Gilligan's Island: The Plight of the Alien Worker in the Northern Mariana Islands," *Temple International and Comparative Law Journal* 13 (1999), 381–410; Erin Geiger Smith, "Case Study: *Doe I v. The Gap, Inc.*: Can a Sweatshop Suit Settlement Save Saipan?" *Review of Litigation* 23 (2004), 737–771; Deborah J. Karet, "Privatizing Law on the Commonwealth of the Northern Mariana Islands: Is Litigation the Best Channel for Reforming the Garment Industry?" *Buffalo Law Review* 48 (2000), 1047–1097; Rose Cruz Cuison, "The Construction of Labor Abuse in the Mariana Islands as Anti-American," *Asian Pacific American Law Journal* 6 (2000), 61–85.

145. In *City of Memphis v. Greene*, 451 U.S. 100, 125–26 (1981), the Court stated that in *Jones v. Alfred H. Mayer Co.*, 392 U.S. 409, 439 (1968), "the Court left open the question whether § 1 of the Amendment by its own terms did anything more than abolish slavery. It is also appropriate today to leave that question open because a review of the justification for the official action challenged in this case demonstrates that its disparate impact on black citizens could not, in any event, be fairly characterized as a badge or incident of slavery."

The judge thus concluded: "Accordingly, the court finds that a claim for involuntary servitude or peonage is not available to plaintiffs under the Thirteenth Amendment because of the absence of a clear directive from the Supreme Court, the absence of a governmental actor in the present case, and the presence of other adequate remedies, either under federal law or state law, that address plaintiffs' claim. Because the Anti-Peonage Act addresses plaintiffs' claim for peonage, as discussed below, it is not appropriate to imply an independent cause of action for peonage under the Thirteenth Amendment." *Doe I v. The Gap, Inc.*, CV-01–0031, 2001 WL 1842389 (D. N. Mar. I. Nov. 26, 2001)

146. *Doe I v. The Gap, Inc.*, CV-01–0031, 2002 WL 1000068 (D. N. Mar. I. May 10, 2002).

147. *Doe I v. The Gap, Inc.*, CV-01–0031, 2001 WL 1842389 (D. N. Mar. I. Nov. 26, 2001).

148. *Doe I v. The Gap, Inc.*, CV-01–0031, 2002 WL 1000068 (D. N. Mar. I. May 10, 2002).

149. Id.

150. *Doe I v. The Gap, Inc.*, CV-01–0031, 2002 WL 1000073 (D. N. Mar. I. May 10, 2002) discusses the first settlement agreement. As Erin Geiger Smith explains, there were two

agreements, with the latter settlement being retroactively incorporated into the first. Erin Geiger Smith, "Case Study: Does I v. The Gap, Inc.: Can a Sweatshop Suit Settlement Save Saipan?" *Review of Litigation* 23 (2004), 737–771.

151. Smith, "Case Study: Does I," p. 755.
152. *Commonwealth of the N. Mariana Islands v. United States*, 670 F. Supp. 2d 65, 91 (D.D.C. 2009). For a discussion, see Robert L. Adair, "Closing a Loophole in the Pacific: Applying the Immigration and Nationality Act to the Commonwealth of the Northern Mariana Islands," *Asian Pacific American Law Journal* 16 (2011), 74–99.
153. In 2011, CNMI's governor blamed its economic recession in part on "the U.S. government for acting in ways that have been 'unnecessarily detrimental to our economy and the welfare of U.S. citizens and others living in our remote islands' over the past decade, with respect to world trade rules, immigration, and minimum wage." See Haidee V. Eugenio, "State of Commonwealth in Severe Disarray," *Saipan Tribune*, Jan. 3, 2011, at http://www.saipantribune.com/newsstory.aspx?cat=1&newsID=105838.
154. Local Law 20 (2001), codified at New York City, N.Y., Code § 6–124.
155. *Mayor of City of New York v. Council of City of New York*, 6 Misc. 3d 533, 789 N.Y.S.2d 860 (Sup. Ct. 2004).
156. New York State Apparel Workers Fair Labor Conditions and Procurement Act, 2002 Sess. Law News Of N.Y. Ch. 350 (A. 11831–A) (McKinney's), codified as, N.Y. State Fin. Law § 162, subsection 4-a (McKinney).
157. While the state legislature referenced the New York City local law as part of its rationale, it also expressly preempted "inconsistent" provisions in local laws. The court implicitly found that the stricter "nonpoverty wage" provisions were inconsistent, but rested its decision on field preemption and the ability of localities to opt out of the state procurement law. The New York Court also found a violation of the New York City Charter, concluding that the matter required a voter referendum.
158. *Crosby v. Nat'l Foreign Trade Council*, 530 U.S. 363 (2000); *American Insurance Ass'n v. Garamendi*, 187 539 U.S. 396 (2003).
159. See *C&A Carbone, Inc. v. Town of Clarkstown, New York*, 511 U.S. 383 (1994). An exception to this rule is the market participant doctrine: when the state is acting as any other participant in the market, it may discriminate just as any other participant might do; see *Hughes v. Alexandria Scrap Corp.*, 426 U.S. 794 (1976). Additionally, the state would argue that its actions were not discriminatory based on the origin of the goods and had only an incidental effect on interstate commerce; see *Exxon Corp. v. Maryland*, 437 U.S. 117 (1978).
160. Adrian Barnes, "Do They Have to Buy from Burma? A Preemption Analysis of Local Anti-sweatshop Procurement Laws," *Columbia Law Review* 107 (2007), 426–456.
161. New York State Apparel Workers Fair Labor Conditions and Procurement Act, 2002 Sess. Law News Of N.Y. Ch. 350 (A. 11831–A) (McKinney's), codified as, N.Y. State Fin. Law § 162, subsection 12 provided:

> This act shall take effect on September 1, 2002 and shall respectively apply to bids issued after such date; provided, however, that effective immediately, the addition, amendment and/or repeal of any rule or regulation necessary for the implementation of this act on its effective date are authorized and directed to be made and completed on or before such effective date; provided, however, that sections four through eight of this act shall be deemed repealed on September 1, 2005.

162. Article 12-A. Special Task Force for the Apparel Industry, N.Y. Lab. Law § 342–349A (McKinney).

163. N.Y. State Fin. Law § 162 subsection 2(a) (McKinney).

164. N.Y. Lab. Law § 213-a (McKinney).

165. Allie Robbins, "The Future of the Student Anti-Sweatshop Movement: Providing Access to U.S. Courts for Garment Workers Worldwide" (forthcoming).

166. Ibid.

Bibliography

CASES

A.M. ex rel. McAllum v. Cash, 585 F.3d 214 (5th Cir. 2009).

Adkins v. Children's Hospital, 261 U.S. 525 (1923).

Alabama & Coushatta Tribes of Texas v. Trustees of Big Sandy Independent School District, 817 F. Supp. 1319 (E.D. Tex. 1993).

Alvarez v. Hill, 518 F.3d 1152 (9th Cir. 2008).

American Civil Liberties Union v. Mukasey, 534 F.3d 181 (3rd Cir. 2008).

American Insurance Ass'n v. Garamendi, 539 U.S. 396 (2003).

American Insurance Co. v. 356 Bales of Cotton, David Canter, Claimaint, 26 U.S. 511 (U.S.S.C. 1828).

Amos v. Corp. of Presiding Bishop of Church of Jesus Christ of Latter-Day Saints, 594 F. Supp. 791 (D. Utah 1984); *Amos v. Corp. of Presiding Bishop of Church of Jesus Christ of Latter-Day Saints*, 618 F. Supp. 1013 (D. Utah 1985) ("Amos II"); *rev'd sub nom; Corp of Presiding Bishop of Church of Jesus Christ of Latter-Day Saints v. Amos*, 483 U.S. 327 (1987).

Arizona Christian School Tuition Organization v. Winn, ___ U.S. ___131 S. Ct. 1436 (2011).

Ashann-Ra v. Commonwealth of Virginia, 112 F. Supp.2d 559 (W.D. Va. 2000).

Ashcroft v. American Civil Liberties Union (Ashcroft I), 535 U.S. 564 (2002); *Ashcroft v. American Civil Liberties Union (Ashcroft II)*, 542 U.S. 656 (2004).

Atascadero State Hosp. v. Scanlon, 473 U.S. 234 (1985).

B.W.A. v. Farmington R-7 School District, 554 F.3d 734 (8th Cir. 2009).

Bailey v. State of Alabama, 219 U.S. 219 (1911).

Bank v. Katz, 08CV1033NGGRER, 2009 WL 3077147 (E.D.N.Y. Sept. 24, 2009), *aff'd Bank v. Katz*, 424 F. App'x 67 (2d Cir. 2011).

Bar-Navon v. Brevard County School Board, 290 F. App'x 273 (11th Cir. 2008).

Barbier v. Connolly, 113 U.S. 27 (1884).

Barnes v. Glen Theatre, Inc., 501 U. S. 560 (1991).

Batson v. Kentucky, 476 U.S. 79 (1986).

Bear v. Fleming, 741 F.Supp.2d 972 (D.S.D. 2010).

Bell Atlantic Corp. v. Twombly, 550 U.S. 544 (2007).

Bell v. Wolfish, 441 U.S. 520 (1979).

Benton v. Maryland, 395 U.S. 784 (1969).

Bethel School District v. Fraser, 478 U.S. 675 (1986).
Bint-Ishmawiyl v. Vaughn, CIV. A. 94–7544, 1995 WL 461949 (E.D. Pa. Aug. 1, 1995).
Bishop v. Colaw, 450 F.2d 1069 (8th Cir. 1971).
Bivens v. Albuquerque Public School, 899 F. Supp. 556 (D.N.M. 1995).
Blackwell v. Issaquena County Board of Education, 363 F.2d 749 (5th Cir. 1966).
Blanchet v. Vermilion Parish School Board, 220 So. 2d 534 (La. Ct. App. 1969), *writ denied*, 222 So. 2d 68 (1969).
Boos v. Barry, 485 U.S. 312, 321(1988).
Boy Scouts of America v. Dale, 530 U.S. 640 (2000).
Braithwaite v. Hinkle, 412 F. App'x 583 (4th Cir. 2011), *aff'd*, 752 F. Supp. 2d 692 (E.D. Va. 2010).
Braxton v. Board of Public Instruction of Duval County, Fla., 303 F. Supp. 958 (M.D. Fla. 1969).
Breen v. Kahl, 419 F.2d 1034 (7th Cir. 1969).
Brown v. C.M.C., CV 08–4587-VAP SH, 2010 WL 2674502 (C.D. Cal. July 1, 2010), rev'd, CV 08–4587-VAP SH, 2010 WL 2674499 (C.D. Cal. May 18, 2010).
Bruns v. Pomerleau, 319 F. Supp. 58 (D. Md. 1970).
Bryant v. Begin Manage Program, 281 F.Supp. 2d 561 (E.D.N.Y. 2003).
Burchette v. Abercrombie & Fitch Stores, Inc., 08 CIV. 8786 RMBTHK, 2009 WL 856682 (S.D.N.Y. Mar. 30, 2009); 2010 WL 1948322 (S.D.N.Y. May 10, 2010).
Bureau of Motor Vehicles v. Pentecostal House of Prayer, Inc., 380 N.E.2d 1225 (Ind.1978).
Burnside v. Byars, 363 F.2d 744 (5th Cir. 1966).
C&A Carbone, Inc. v. Town of Clarkstown, N.Y., 511 U.S. 383 (1994).
Canady v. Bossier Parish School Board, 240 F.3d 437 (5th Cir 2001).
Carey v. Musladin, 549 U.S. 70 (2006).
Carmichele v Minister of Safety and Security, 2001 (4) SA 938 (CC) (S. Afr.).
Castle Rock v. Gonzales, 545 U.S. 748 (2005).
CBS Corp. v. F.C.C., 535 F.3d 167 (3rd Cir. 2008).
Chalifoux v. New Caney Independent School District, 976 F. Supp. 659 (S.D. Tex. 1997).
Champion v. Ames, 188 U.S. 321 (1903).
Chisholm v. Georgia, 2 U.S. 419 (1793).
Christian Louboutin S.A. v. Yves Saint Laurent Am., Inc., 778 F. Supp. 2d 445, 457 (S.D.N.Y. 2011).
Church of American Knights of the Ku Klux Klan v. Kerik, 356 F.3d 197 (2d Cir. 2004).
Church of the Lukumi Babalu Aye, Inc. v. City of Hialeah, 508 U.S. 520 (1993).
City of Boerne v. Flores, 521 U.S. 507 (1997).
City of Chicago v. Morales, 527 U.S. 41 (1999)
City of Chicago v. Wilson, 75 Ill.2d 525 (Ill. 1978).
City of Columbus v. Rogers, 41 Ohio St. 2d 161, 324 N.E.2d 563 (1975).
City of Columbus v. Zanders, 25 Ohio Misc. 144 (Ohio Mun. 1970).
City of Erie v. Pap's A.M., 529 U.S. 277 (2000).
City of Memphis v. Greene, 451 U.S. 100 (1981).
City of San Diego v. Roe, 543 U.S. 77 (2004), *reversing* 356 F.3d 1108 (9th Cir. 2004), *reversing*, 01CV1760K (CGA), 2001 WL 35936313 (S.D. Cal. Dec. 21, 2001).
City of Seattle v. Buchanan, 584 P.2d 918 (Wa. 1978).
Civil Rights Cases, 109 U.S. 3 (1883).
Clothworkers of Ipswich, (1615) 78 Eng. Rep. 147 (K.B.)(Eng).
Cloutier v. Costco Wholesale Corp., 311 F. Supp. 2d 190 (D. Mass. 2004), aff'd, 390 F.3d 126 (1st Cir. 2004).

Cohen v. California, 403 U.S. 15 (1971).

Collins v. State, 288 S.E.2d 43 (Ga. Ct. App. 1981).

Commonwealth of the N. Mariana Islands v. United States, 670 F. Supp.2d 65 (D.D.C. 2009).

Connecticut Dept. of Public Safety v. Doe, 538 U.S. 1 (2003).

Cooper v. Eugene School District No. 4J, 723 P.2d 298 (Or. 1986), *appeal dismissed*, 480 U.S. 942 (1987) (Brennan, Marshall, and O'Connor, dissenting).

Coy v. Iowa, 487 U.S. 1012 (1988).

Craft v. Hodel, 683 F.Supp. 289 (D.Mass. 1988).

Craig v. Boren, 429 U.S. 190 (1976).

Crews v. Cloncs, 432 F.2d 1259 (7th Cir. 1970).

Crosby v. National Foreign Trade Council, 530 U.S. 363 (2000).

Cutter v. Wilkinson, 544 U.S. 709 (2005), *reversing*, 349 F.3d 257 (6th Cir. 2003).

Davis v. State, 329 S.W.3d 798 (Tex. Crim. App. 2010), *cert. denied*, __ U.S. __, 132 S. Ct. 128, 181 L. Ed. 2d 50 (2011).

Dawson v. Delaware, 530 U.S. 159 (1992).

Deck v. Missouri, 544 U.S. 622 (2005).

Defoe ex rel. Defoe v. Spiva, 625 F.3d 324 (6th Cir. 2010), *cert. denied*, __ U.S. __, 132 S. Ct. 399, 181 L. Ed. 2d 255 (2011).

DeMoss v. Crain, 636 F.3d 145 (5th Cir. 2011).

DeWeese v. Palm Beach, 812 F.2d 1365 (11th Cir. 1987).

Doe ex rel. Doe v. Yunits, 001060A, 2000 WL 33162199 (Mass. Super. Ct. Oct. 11, 2000).

Doe v. Bell, 754 N.Y.S.2d 846 (N.Y. Sup. 2003).

Doe v. McConn, 489 F.Supp. 76 (S.D. Tex. 1980).

Does I v. Gap, Inc., CV-01–0031, 2002 WL 1000068 (D. N. Mar. I. May 10, 2002), CV-01–0031, 2001 WL 1842389 (D. N. Mar. I. Nov. 26, 2001).

Domico v. Rapides Parish School Board, 675 F.2d 100 (5th Cir. 1982).

Doran v. Salem Inn, Inc., 422 U.S. 922 (1975).

Duvallon v. District of Columbia, 515 A. 2d 724 (D .C. Ct. App. 1986).

E.E.O.C. v. GEO Group, Inc., 616 F.3d 265 (3d Cir. 2010).

East Hartford Education Ass'n v. Board of Education of Town of East Hartford, 405 F. Supp. 94 (D. Conn. 1975), *aff'd*, 562 F.2d 838 (2d Cir. 1977).

Employment Division, Department of Human Resources of Oregon v. Smith, 494 U.S. 872 (1990).

Erznoznik v. City of Jacksonville, 422 U.S. 205 (1975).

Estelle v. Gamble, 429 U.S. 97 (1976).

Estelle v. Williams, 425 U.S. 501 (1976).

Evans v. Stephens, 407 F.3d 1272 (11th Cir. 2005).

Exxon Corp. v. Maryland, 437 U.S. 117 (1978).

F.C.C. v. Fox Television Stations, Inc., (Fox II), __ U.S. ___, 132 S. Ct. 2307 (2012), reversing, Fox Television Stations, Inc. v. F.C.C., 613 F.3d 317 (2nd Cir. 2010).

F.C.C. v. Fox Television Stations, Inc., 556 U.S. 502 (2009).

F.C.C. v. Pacifica Foundation, 438 U.S. 726 (1978).

Faretta v. California, 422 U.S. 806 (1975).

Fegans v. Norris, 537 F.3d 897 (8th Cir. 2008).

Fenster v. Leary, 20 N.Y.2d 309 (1967).

Ferrell v. Dallas Independent School District, 392 F. 2d 697 (5th Cir. 1968), cert denied, 393 U.S. 856 (1968)(Douglas, J., dissenting).

Florence v. Board of Chosen Freeholders of County of Burlington, __ U.S. __, 132 S. Ct. 1510 (2012).

Forster v. Smith, 04 C 171, 2006 WL 1663722 (E.D.Wis. June 8, 2006).

Freeman v. Flake, 448 F.2d 258 (10th Cir. 1971), *cert denied,* 405 U. S. 1032 (1972) (Douglas, J., dissenting).

Freeman v. Department of Highway Safety & Motor Vehicles, 924 So. 2d 48 (Fla. Dist. Ct. App. 2006), *affirming, Freeman v. State,* 2002-CA-2828, 2003 WL 21338619 (Fla. Cir. Ct. June 6, 2003).

Friedman v. District Court, 611 P.2d 77 (Alaska 1980).

Frontiero v. Richardson, 411 U.S. 677 (1973).

Garcetti v. Ceballos, 547 U.S. 410 (2006).

Garner v. Livingston, CA-C-06-218, 2011 WL 2038581 (S.D. Tex. May 19, 2011).

Garner v. Morales, 07–41015, 2009 WL 577755 (5th Cir. Mar. 6, 2009).

Gates v. Collier, 349 F.Supp. 881 (D.C. Miss.).

Genies v. State, 10 A.3d 854 (Md. Ct. Spec. App. 2010).

Goldman v. Weinberger, 475 U.S. 503 (1986).

Goodman v. Lukens Steel Co., 482 U.S. 656 (1987).

Graham v. John Deere Co. of Kansas City, 383 U.S. 1 (1966).

Grayned v. City of Rockford, 408 U.S. 104 (1972).

Grayson v. Schuler, 666 F.3d 450 (7th Cir. 2012).

H. v. Easton Area School District, 827 F.Supp.2d 392 (E.D. Pa. 2011).

Hall v. Baptist Memorial Health Care Corp., 215 F.3d 618 (6th Cir. 2000).

Hammer v. Dagenhart, 247 U.S. 251 (1918).

Hang On, Inc. v. City of Arlington, 65 F.3d 1248 (5th Cir. 1995).

Hans v. Louisiana, 134 U.S. 1 (1890).

Harper v. Edgewood Board of Education, 655 F.Supp. 1353 (S.D.Ohio 1987).

Harper v. Poway Unified School District, 445 F.3d 1166 (9th Cir. 2006), cert granted and judgment vacated, 549 U.S. 1262 (2007) (Breyer, J., dissenting).

Heart of Atlanta Motel Inc. v. United States, 379 U.S. 241 (1964).

Henderson v. Terhune, 379 F.3d 709 (9th Cir. 2004).

Hishon v. King & Spauling, 467 U.S. 69 (1984).

Holbrook v. Flynn, 475 U.S. 560 (1986).

Holdman v. Olim, 581 P.2d 1164 (Haw. 1978).

Holsapple v. Woods, 500 F.2d 49 (7th Cir. 1974), cert. denied, 419 U.S. 901.

Hughes v. Alexandria Scrap Corp., 426 U.S. 794 (1976).

Hysong v. School District of Gallitzin Borough, 164 Pa. 629 (1894).

Iacono v. Croom, 5:10-CV-416-H, 2010 WL 3984601 (E.D.N.C. Oct. 8, 2010).

Illinois v. Allen, 397 U.S. 337 (1970).

In Matter of De Carlo, 141 N.J. Super. 42, 357 A. 2d 273 (1976).

In the Matter of David T. Dellinger, 370 F. Supp. 1304 (N.D. Ill. 1973), *aff'd* 502 F.2d 813 (7th Cir. 1974), *cert denied,* 420 U.S. 990 (1975).

Jackson v. Dorrier, 424 F.2d 213 (6th Cir. 1970), *cert. denied,* 400 U.S. 850 (Douglas, J. dissenting).

Jenevein v. Willing, 605 F.3d 268 (en banc 5th Cir. 2010) *affirming,* 493 F.3d 551 (5th Cir. 2007).

Jespersen v. Harrah's Operating Company, Inc., 444 F.3d 1104 (9th Cir. 2006).

Jetter v. Beard, 183 F.App'x 178 (3d Cir. 2006).

Johnson v. Moore, 472 F.Supp.2d 1344 (M.D.Fla. 2007).

Jones v. Alfred H. Mayer Co., 392 U.S. 409 (1968).

Kansas v. Hendricks, 521 U.S. 346 (1997).

Karr v. Schmidt, 460 F.2d 609 (5th Cir. 1972), *cert. denied*, 409 U.S. 989 (Douglas, J., dissenting).

Kastritis v. City of Daytona Beach Shores, 835 F. Supp. 2d 1200 (M.D. Fla. 2011).

Katzenbach v. McClung, 379 U.S. 294 (1964).

Kelley v. Johnson, 425 U.S. 238 (1976).

Kennedy v. St. Joseph's Ministries, Inc., 657 F.3d 189 (4th Cir. 2011).

Khatib v. County of Orange, 603 F.3d 713, 715 (9th Cir. 2010) *reh'g en banc granted*, 622 F.3d 1074 (9th Cir. 2010) and *superseded on reh'g en banc*, 639 F.3d 898 (9th Cir. 2011), *cert. denied*, __ U.S. ___, 132 S. Ct. 115, 181 L. Ed. 2d 40 (2011).

Kimel v. Florida Board of Regents, 528 U.S. 62 (2000).

Kinane v. United States, 12 A.3d 23 (D.C. 2011), *cert. denied*, ___ U.S. __, 132 S. Ct. 574, 181 L. Ed. 2d 424 (2011).

King v. Saddleback Jr. College District, 445 F.2d 932 (9th Cir. 1971), *cert. denied*, 404 U.S. 979 (1971) (Douglas, J., and White, J., dissenting).

Lansdale v. Tyler Junior College, 470 F.2d 659 (5th Cir. 1972), *cert. denied*, U.S. 986 (1973) (Douglas, J. dissenting).

Le Roy v. Sidley (1663) 1 Sid. 168, 82 Eng. Reprint, 1036.

Lochner v. New York, 198 U.S. 45 (1905).

Logan v. Gary Cmty School Corp., CIV.A.207-CV-431JVB, 2008 WL 4411518 (N.D. Ind. Sept. 25, 2008).

Los Angeles County, California. v. Rettele, 550 U.S. 609 (2007).

Loving v. Virginia, 388 U.S. 1 (1967).

Made in the USA Foundation v. United States, 242 F.3d 1300 (11th Cir. 2001).

Malinski v. New York, 324 U.S. 401 (1945).

Marbury v. Madison, 5 U.S. 137 (1803).

Marshall Field & Co. v. Clark, 143 U.S. 649 (1892).

Mary Beth G. v. City of Chicago, 723 F.2d 1263 (7th Cir. 1983).

Maryland v. Craig, 497 U.S. 836 (1990).

Mayes v. Texas, 416 U.S. 909 (1974).

Mayor of City of New York v. Council of City of New York, 6 Misc. 3d 533 (Sup. Ct. 2004).

McGuire v. State, 489 So.2d 729 (Fla. 1986).

McJunkins v. State, 10 Ind. 140 (1858).

McMillen v. Itawamba County School District, 702 F.Supp.2d 699 (N.D. Miss. 2010).

Melton v. Young, 465 F.2d 1332, (6th Cir.1972), *cert. denied*, 411 U.S. 951 (1973).

Meritor Savings Bank, FSB v. Vinson, 477 U.S. 57 (1986).

Meyer v. Nebraska, 262 U.S. 390 (1923).

Miller v. California, 413 U.S. 15 (1973).

Miller v. School District No. 167, Cook County, Illinois, 495 F.2d 658 (7th Cir. 1974).

Minersville School District v. Gobitis, 310 U.S. 586 (1940).

Minor v. State, 501 S.E.2d 576 (Ga. App. 1998).

Monell v. Department of Social Services of the City of New York, 436 U.S. 658 (1978).

Monroe v. Pape, 365 U.S. 167 (1961).

Morse v. Frederick, 551 U.S. 393 (2007).

Muhammad v. Paruk, 553 F. Supp. 2d 893 (E.D. Mich. 2008).

Mukasey v. American Civil Liberties Union, 555 U.S. 1137 (2009).

Muller v. Oregon, 208 U.S. 412 (1908).

Nabozny v. Podlesny, 92 F.3d 446 (7th Cir. 1996).

National Endowment for Arts v. Finley, 524 U.S. 569 (1998).

New Jersey v. T.L.O., 469 U.S. 325 (2008).

Norris v. Risley, 918 F.2d 828 (9th Cir. 1990).

O'Connor v. Hendrick, 184 N.Y. 421, 428 (1906).

O'Leary v. Iowa State Men's Reformatory, 79 F.3d 82 (8th Cir. 1996).

Olff v. East Side Union High School District, 445 F.2d 932 (9th Cir. 1971), *cert. denied*, 404 U.S. 1042 (1972) (Douglas, J., dissenting).

Opinion of Justices, 662 A.2d 294 (N.H. 1995).

Palko v. Connecticut, 302 U.S. 319 (1937).

Palmer ex rel. Palmer v. Waxahachie Independent School District, 579 F.3d 502 (5th Cir. 2009), *cert denied*, __ U.S. __, 130 S.Ct. 1055, 175 L.Ed.2d 883 (2010).

Papachristou v. City of Jacksonville, 405 U.S. 156 (1972).

Paris Adult Theatre I v. Slaton, 413 U.S. 49 (1973).

People ex rel. Gallo v. Acuna, 929 P.2d 596 (Cal. 1997).

People ex rel. Hoelderlin v. Kane, 79 Misc. 140 (N.Y. Sup. Ct. 1913).

People v. Aboaf, 187 Misc. 2d 173 (N.Y. Crim. Ct. 2001).

People v. Archibald, 58 Misc.2d 862 (N.Y. Sup. Ct. 1968).

People v. Bunn, 2009 Cal. App. Unpub. LEXIS 7080 (Ct. App. Cal. 2009).

People v. Clark, No. 1994CR003290 (Colo. District Ct. Feb. 16, 1996).

People v. Cohen, 1 Cal. App. 3d 94 (Ct. App. 1969).

People v. Craft, 149 Misc. 2d 223 (N.Y. Co. Ct. 1991), rev'd, 134 Misc. 2d 121 (City Ct. 1986).

People v. Englebrecht, 106 Cal. Rptr. 2d 738 (Cal. Ct. App. 2001).

People v. Hicks, 2009 Cal. App. Unpub. LEXIS 9957 (Ct. App. Cal. 2009).

People v. Hoelderlin, 161 A.D. 956 (2nd Dept. N.Y. 1914).

People v. Luechini, 75 Misc. 614 (N.Y. Co. Ct. 1912).

People v. Martinez, 29 Misc. 3d 263 (N.Y. Crim. Ct. 2010).

People v. Mejia, B213993, 2010 WL 3788833 (Cal. Ct. App. Sept. 30, 2010).

People v. O'Gorman, 274 N.Y. 284 (N.Y. 1937).

People v. Pennisi, 149 Misc. 2d 36 (N.Y. Sup. Ct. 1990).

People v. Santorelli, 80 N.Y.2d 875 (N.Y. 1992).

People v. Simmons, 79 Misc.2d 249, 357 N.Y.S.2d 362 (N.Y.City Crim.Ct. 1974).

People v. Vargas, F037732, 2002 WL 1764180 (Cal. Ct. App. July 31, 2002).

People v. Williams, 189 N.Y. 131 (N.Y. 1907).

Pickering v. Board of Education of Township High School District, 391 U.S. 563 (1968).

Pierce v. Society of Sisters of the Holy Names of Jesus and Mary, 268 U.S. 510 (1925).

Plessy v. Ferguson, 163 U.S. 537 (1896).

People v. Wise, 194 Misc.2d. 841, 752 N.Y.S. 387 (2002).

Potts v. United States, 919 A.2d 1127 (D.C. 2007).

Price Waterhouse v. Hopkins, 490 U.S. 228 (1989).

Quaring v. Peterson, 728 F.2d 1121 (8th Cir.1984).

Quinn v. Muscare, 425 U.S. 560 (1976).

R. v. N.S., [2012] S.C.C. 72 (Can.).

R.A.V. v. City of St. Paul, 505 U.S. 377 (1992).

Ramsey v. Hopkins, 320 F. Supp. 477 (N.D. Ala. 1970).

Reed v. Faulkner, 842 F.2d 960 (7th Cir. 1988).

Reed v. Reed, 404 U.S. 71 (1971).

Regina v. Hicklin (1868) L. R. 3 Q. B. 360 (Eng.).

Reno v. American Civil Liberties Union, 521 U.S. 844 (1997).

Renton v. Playtime Theatres, Inc., 475 U.S. 41 (1986).

Republican Party of Minnesota v. White, 536 U.S. 765 (2002).

Rex v. Mellichamp, The South Carolina Gazette (Charlestowne), May 1–8, 1736 at 1 col. 1.

Reynolds v. United States, 98 U.S. 145 (1878).

Ricci v. DeStefano, 557 U.S. 557 (2009).

Robles v. Quarterman, CIV.A. C-07-261, 2009 WL 594629 (S.D. Tex. Mar. 6, 2009).

Rogers v. American Airlines, 527 F. Supp. 229 (S.D.N.Y. 1981).

Ross v. State, 876 So. 2d 684 (Fla. Dist. Ct. App. 2004).

Ruffin v. Commonwealth, 62 Va. 790 (Va. 1871).

Safford Unified School District No. 1 v. Redding, 557 U.S. 364 (2009).

Safouane v. Fleck, 226 F. App'x 753 (9th Cir. 2007).

Salem Inn, Inc., v. Frank, 501 F.2d 18 (2d Cir. 1974).

Santee v. Windsor Court Hotel Ltd. Partnership., CIV.A.99–3891, 2000 WL 1610775 (E.D. La.
     Oct. 26, 2000).

Schacht v. United States, 398 U.S. 58 (1970).

Schumann v. State of New York, 270 F. Supp. 730 (S.D.N.Y. 1967).

Scott [Dred] v. Sandford, 60 U.S. 393 (1856).

Scott v. School Board of Alachua County, 324 F.3d 1246 (11th Cir. 2003).

Sherbert v. Verner, 374 U.S. 398 (1963).

Smith v. Doe, 538 U.S. 84 (2003).

Smith v. Smith, No. 05 JE 42, 2007 WL 901599 (Ohio App. Mar. 23, 2007).

Soon Hing v. Crowley, 113 U.S. 703 (1885).

Southeastern Promotions, Ltd. v. Conrad, 420 U.S. 546 (1975).

State v. Bauer, 337 N.W.2d 209 (Iowa 1983).

State v. Castaneda, 245 P.3d 550 (Nev. 2010).

State v. Cherryhomes, 840 P.2d 1261 (N.M. Ct. App. 1992).

State v. Eli L., 947 P.2d 162 (N.M. Ct. App. 1997).

State v. Franklin, 327 S.E.2d 449 (W. Va. 1985).

State v. Kueny, 215 N.W.2d 215 (Iowa 1974).

State v. McCapes, 912 P.2d 419 (Or. App. 1996).

State v. Miller, 398 S.E.2d 547 (Ga. 1990).

State v. Nowlin, 818 A.2d 1237 (N.H. 2003).

State v. Vogt, 873 N.E.2d 1315 (Ohio 2007).

State v. Wheatley, No. 97–1–50056–6 (Wash. Superior Ct. May 13, 1997).

Stephenson v. Davenport Community School District, 110 F.3d 1303 (8th Cir. 1997).

Strickland v. Washington, 466 U.S. 668 (1984).

Sturgis v. Copiah County School District, No. 3:10-cv-450 TSL-FKB, First Amended
     Complaint (2010), available at http://www.aclu.org/lgbt-rights/sturgis-v-copiah-county-
     school-district.

Terry v. Ohio, 392 U.S. 1 (1968).

Tinker v. Des Moines Independent Community School District, 393 U.S. 503 (1969).

Troxel v. Granville, 530 U.S. 57 (2000).

Turner v. Safley, 482 U.S. 78 (1987).

United States ex rel. Richards v. De Leon Guerrero, 4 F.3d 749 (9th Cir. 1993).
United States v. Alvarez, ___ U.S. ___, 132 S. Ct. 2537 (2012).
United States v. American Library Ass'n, Inc., 539 U.S. 194 (2003).
United States v. Biocic, 928 F.2d 112 (4th Cir. 1991).
United States v. Board of Education for School District of Philadelphia, 911 F.2d 882 (3d Cir. 1990).
United States v. Carolene Products Co., 304 U.S. 144 (1938).
United States v. Cruikshank, 92 U.S. 542 (1875).
United States v. Darby, 312 U.S. 100 (1941).
United States v. E. C. Knight Co., 156 U.S. 1 (1895).
United States v. Grace, 461 U.S. 171 (1983).
United States v. O'Brien, 391 U.S. 367 (1968).
United States v. Seale, 461 F.2d 345 (7th Cir. 1972).
United States v. Seeger, 380 U.S. 163 (1965).
United States v. Virginia, 518 U.S. 515 (1996).
United Steelworkers of America, AFL-CIO, 534 U.S. 1039 (2001).
Van Houten v. State, 46 N.J.L. 160 (1884).
Villegas v. City of Gilroy, 484 F.3d 1136 (9th Cir. 2007), affirming 363 F. Supp. 2d 1207 (N.D. Cal. 2005), *reversed sub nom* Villegas v. Gilroy Garlic Festival Ass'n, 541 F.3d 950 (9th Cir. en banc 2008).
Vinson v. Taylor, 760 F.2d 1330 (D.C. Cir. 1985).
Walker v. State, 68 P.3d 872 (Mont. 2003).
Walls v. Schriro, CV05–2259-PHX-NVWJCG, 2008 WL 544822 (D. Ariz. Feb. 26, 2008).
Warren v. District of Columbia, 353 F.3d 36 (D.C. Cir. 2004).
Warsoldier v. Woodford, 418 F.3d 989 (9th Cir. 2005).
Washington v. Davis, 426 U.S. 229 (1976).
Webb v. City of Philadelphia, 562 F.3d 256 (3d Cir. 2009).
Weideman v. State, 890 N.E.2d 28 (Ind. Ct. App. 2008).
Welsh v. United States, 398 U.S. 333 (1970).
Wendt v. Lynaugh, 841 F.2d 619 (5th Cir. 1988).
West Coast Hotel Co. v. Parrish, 300 U.S. 379 (1937).
West v. Derby Unified School District No. 260, 206 F.3d 1358 (10th Cir. 2000), cert. denied, 531 U.S. 825 (2000).
West Virginia State Board of Education v. Barnette, 319 U.S. 624 (1943).
Whitney v. Carter, 29 F. Cas. 1070 (C.C.D. Ga. 1810).
Williams v. City of Fort Worth, 782 S.W.2d 290 (Tex.App. 1989).
Wilson v. Seiter, 501 U.S. 294 (1991).
Wisconsin v. Mitchell, 508 U.S. 476 (1993).
Woods v. Dugger, 923 F.2d 1454 (11th Cir. 1991).
Young v. American Mini Theatres, Inc., 427 U.S. 50 (1976).
Youngblood v. School Board of Hillsborough County, Florida, No. 8:02-CV-1089-T-24-MAP (M.D. Fl. 2002).
Zalewska v. County of Sullivan, 316 F.3d 314 (2nd Cir. 2003).
Zamecnik ex rel. Zamecnik v. Indian Prairie School District No. 204 Board of Education, 07 C 1586, 2007 WL 1141597 (N.D. Ill. Apr. 17, 2007), reversed and remanded sub nom Nuxoll ex rel. Nuxoll v. Indian Prairie School District No. 204, 523 F.3d 668 (7th Cir. 2008), *on remand Zamecnik v. Indian Prairie School Dist. No. 204 Board of Education*,

710 F.Supp.2d 711 (2010), aff'd, *Zamecnik v. Indian Prairie School District No. 204 Board of Education*, 636 F.3d 874 (7th Cir. 2011).
Zelman v. Simmons-Harris, 536 U.S. 639 (2002).

BOOKS, ARTICLES, AND OTHER SOURCES

Aaronson, Daniel R., Gary S. Edinger, and James S. Benjamin, "The First Amendment in Chaos: How the Law of Secondary Effects Is Applied and Misapplied by the Circuit Courts," *University of Miami Law Review* 63 (2009), 741–759.
Abdo, Aliah, "The Legal Status of Hijab in the United States: A Look at the Sociopolitical Influences on the Legal Right to Wear the Muslim Headscarf," *Hastings Race & Poverty Law Journal* 5 (2008), 441–507.
Ackerman, Bruce, and David Golove, "Is NAFTA Constitutional?" *Harvard Law Review* 108 (1995), 799–929.
ACLU of Michigan, Letter to Chief David Dicks, Re: Illegal Stops and Searches of Men Wearing Sagging Pants (2008), available at http://www.aclumich.org/issues/search-and-seizure/2008–07/1267.
Adair, E. R., "The Statute of Proclamations," *English Historical Review*, 32.125 (1917), 34–46.
Adair, Robert L., "Closing a Loophole in the Pacific: Applying the Immigration and Nationality Act to the Commonwealth of the Northern Mariana Islands," *Asian Pacific American Law Journal* 16 (2011), 74–99.
Adams, John, "Thoughts on Government," in *The Works of John Adams, Second President of the United States: With a Life of the Author, Notes and Illustrations, by His Grandson Charles Francis Adams* (Boston: Little, Brown, 1856). 10 vols. Vol. 4.
Alexandre, Michele, "When Freedom Is Not Free: Investigating the First Amendment's Potential for Providing Protection against Sexual Profiling in the Public Workplace," *William & Mary Journal of Women & the Law* 15 (2009), 377–413.
Allison, J. W. F., *The English Historical Constitution: Continuity, Change, and European Effects* (Cambridge: Cambridge University Press, 2007).
Amar, Akhil Reed, *America's Constitution* (New York: Random House 2005).
American Apparel and Footwear Association, "TRENDS: An Annual Statistical Analysis of the U.S. Apparel & Footwear Industries" (2008), 5, available at https://www.wewear.org/industry-resources/publications-and-statistics/.
American Psychiatric Association, "DSM-V Development: Gender Dysphoria in Children: Proposed Revision & Rationale" (2011), available at http://www.dsm5.org/ProposedRevision/Pages/proposedrevision.aspx?rid=192# (last visited 9/22/2011).
Aoki, Keith, "Distributive and Syncretic Motives in Intellectual Property Law (with Special Reference to Coercion, Agency, and Development)," *U.C. Davis Law Review* 40 (2007), 717–801.
Arkles, Gabriel, "Correcting Race and Gender: Prison Regulation of Social Hierarchy through Dress," *New York University Law Review* 87 (2012), 859–949.
Armstrong, Andrea C., "Slavery Revisited in Penal Plantation Labor," *Seattle University Law Review* 35 (2012), 869–910.
Arrangement Regarding International Trade in Textiles (Multifibre Arrangement), Dec. 20, 1973, 25 U.S.T. 1001 (entered into force on Jan. 1, 1974).

Aslam, Sadia, "Hijab in the Workplace: Why Title VII Does Not Adequately Protect Employees from Discrimination on the Basis of Religious Dress and Appearance," *University of Missouri-Kansas City Law Review* 80 (2011), 221–238.

Avery, Dianne, and Marion Crain, "Branded: Corporate Image, Sexual Stereotyping, and the New Face of Capitalism," *Duke Journal of Gender Law & Policy*, 14.1 (2007), 13–123.

Bader, Nathan K., "Hats Off to Them: Muslim Women Stand against Workplace Religious Discrimination in Geo Group," *St. Louis University Law Journal* 56 (2011), 261–300.

Baldwin, Frances Elizabeth, *Sumptuary Legislation and Personal Regulation in England* (Baltimore: Johns Hopkins University Press, 1926).

Bar-Siman-Tov, Ittai, "Legislative Supremacy in the United States? Rethinking the 'Enrolled Bill' Doctrine," *Georgetown Law Journal* 97 (2009), 323–390.

Barbarosh, Alison M., "Undressing the First Amendment in Public Schools: Do Uniform Dress Codes Violate Students' First Amendment Rights?" *Loyola of Los Angeles Law Review* 28 (1995), 1415–1451.

Barnes, Adrian, "Do They Have to Buy from Burma? A Preemption Analysis of Local Anti-sweatshop Procurement Laws," *Columbia Law Review* 107 (2007), 426–456.

Barnett, Randy E., The People or the State? *Chisholm v. Georgia* and Popular Sovereignty, *Virginia Law Review* 93 (2007), 1729–1758.

Barnhart, Bill, and Gene Schlickman, *John Paul Stevens: An Independent Life* (DeKalb: Northern Illinois Press, 2010).

Bartow, Ann, "Counterfeits, Copying, and Class," *Houston Law Review* 48 (2012), 707–749.

Bastian, Holly M., "Religious Garb Statutes and Title VII: An Uneasy Coexistence," *Georgetown Law Journal* 80 (1991), 211–232.

Beard, Charles, *An Economic Interpretation of the Constitution of the United States* (New York : Macmillan, 1913).

Beauchamp, Peter W., "Misinterpreted Justice: Problems with the Use of Islamic Legal Experts in U.S. Trial Courts," *New York Law School Law Review* 55 (2011), 1097–1119.

Behrens, Eric G., "The Triangle Shirtwaist Company Fire of 1911: A Lesson in Legislative Manipulation," *Texas Law Review* 62 (1983), 361–387.

Ben-Asher, Noa, "Paradoxes of Health and Equality: When a Boy Becomes a Girl," *Yale Journal of Law & Feminism* 16 (2004), 275–311.

Benedet, Janine, "On Indecency: *R. v. Jacob*," *Canadian Criminal Law Review* 3 (1998), 17–59.

Bernstein, David E., "Lochner, Parity, and the Chinese Laundry Cases," *William & Mary Law Review* 41 (1999), 211–294.

Bernstein, David E., *You Can't Say That: The Growing Threat to Civil Liberties from Antidiscrimination Laws* (Washington, DC: Cato Institute, 2003).

Biber, Eric, "The Price of Admission: Causes, Effects, and Patterns of Conditions Imposed on States Entering the Union," *American Journal of Legal History* 46 (2004), 119–208.

Bork, Robert, "Civil Rights – A Challenge" (*The New Republic* 1963), reprinted in *The Supreme Court of the United States: Hearings and Reports on Successful and Unsuccessful Nominations*, Vol.14-F, edited by Roy M. Mersky and J. Myron Jacobstein (Buffalo, NY: 1991), pp. 7401–7405.

Boudreaux, Paul, "Federalism and the Contrivances of Public Law," *St. John's Law Review* 77 (2003), 523–602.

Bowman, Kristi L., "The Civil Rights Roots of Tinker's Disruption Tests," *American University Law Review* 58 (2009), 1129–1165.

Brant, Irving, *The Bill of Rights: Its Origin and Meaning* (New York: Bobbs-Merrill, 1965).

Breen, T. H., *The Marketplace of Revolution: How Consumer Politics Shaped American Independence* (Oxford: Oxford University Press, 2004).

Brekke, Linzy, "The 'Scourge of Fashion': Political Economy and the Politics of Consumption in the Early Republic," *Early American Studies* 3.1 (2005), 111–139.

"A Brief History of the Mississippi Department of Corrections," available at http://www.mdoc. state.ms.us/Brief_History.htm.

Broadwater, Jeff, *George Mason: Forgotten Founder* (Chapel Hill: North Carolina University Press, 2006).

Brodie, Laura Fairchild, *Breaking Out: VMI and the Coming of Women* (New York: Random House, 2000).

"Brought to the Jail in Charlestowne," *The South Carolina Gazette* (Charlestowne), May 1–8, 1736, p. 3, col. 2.

Brown, Kathleen, *Good Wives, Nasty Wenches, and Anxious Patriarchs: Gender, Race, and Power in Colonial Virginia* (Chapel Hill: University of North Carolina Press, 1996).

Brown, Nathan J., and Clark B. Lombardi, "The Supreme Constitutional Court of Egypt on Islamic Law, Veiling and Civil Rights: An Annotated Translation of Supreme Constitutional Court of Egypt Case No. 8 of Judicial Year 17 (May 18, 1996)," *American University International Law Review* 21 (2006), 437–460.

Burger, Warren E., "The Constitution as an Economic Document: A Symposium Commemorating the Bicentennial of the United States Constitution," *George Washington Law Review* 56 (1987).

Burke, N. Denise, "Restricting Gang Clothing in the Public Schools," *Education Law Reporter* 80 (1993), 513–525.

Burnett, Paul Andrew, "Fairness, Ethical, and Historical Reasons for Diversifying the Legal Profession with Longhairs, the Creatively Facial-Haired, the Tattooed, the Well-Pierced, and Other Rock and Roll Refugees," *University of Missouri-Kansas City Law Review* 71 (2002), 127–149.

Burrell, Thomas H., "Justice Stephen Field's Expansion of the Fourteenth Amendment: From the Safeguards of Federalism to a State of Judicial Hegemony," *Gonzaga Law Review* 43 (2008), 77–168.

Bush, M. L., "The Act of Proclamations: A Reinterpretation," *American Journal of Legal History*, 27.1 (1983), 33–53.

Caldwell, Paulette M., "A Hair Piece: Perspectives on the Intersection of Race and Gender," *Duke Law Journal* 365 (1991), 367–396.

"Intersectional Bias and the Courts: The Story of *Rogers v. American Airlines*," in *Race Law Stories* (Devon W. Carbado and Rachel F. Moran, ed., Foundation Press, 2008), pp. 571–600.

Calvert, Clay, "Revisiting the Right to Offend Forty Years after *Cohen v. California*: One Case's Legacy on First Amendment Jurisprudence," *First Amendment Law Review* 10 (2011), 1–56.

Campanella, Major L. M., "The Regulation of 'Body Art' in the Military: Piercing the Veil of Service Members' Constitutional Rights," *Military Law Review* 161 (1999), 56–114.

Carleton, Mark T., *Politics and Punishment: The History of the Louisiana State Penal System* (Baton Rouge: LSU Press, 1971).

Chambliss, William T., "A Sociological Analysis of the Law of Vagrancy," *Social Problems* 12.1 (1964), 67–77.

Chaplin, Joyce E., "Creating a Cotton South in Georgia and South Carolina, 1760–1815," *Journal of Southern History*, 57.2 (1991), 171–200.

Clarkson, S. James, "The Judicial Robe," *Supreme Court Historical Society Yearbook* 90 (1980), 143–149.

Clerget, Sean, "Timing Is of the Essence: Reviving the Neutral Law of General Applicability Standard and Applying It to Restrictions against Religious Face Coverings Worn While Testifying in Court," *George Mason Law Review* 18 (2011), 1013–1043.

Cline, Elizabeth L., *Over-Dressed: The Shockingly High Cost of Cheap Fashion* (New York: Portfolio/Penguin, 2012).

Clinton, William Jefferson, State of the Union Address (1996), available at http://www.washingtonpost.com/wp-srv/politics/special/states/docs/sou96.htm.

Cogan, Neil H., *The Complete Bills of Rights: The Drafts, Debates, Sources, and Origins* (Oxford: Oxford University Press, 1997).

Cohen, William S., "A Look Back at *Cohen v. California*," *UCLA Law Review* 34 (1987), 1595–1614.

Cohen, William, "Negro Involuntary Servitude in the South, 1865–1940: A Preliminary Analysis," *Journal of Southern History* 42.1 (1976), 31–60.

Conaway, Teresa L., Carol L. Mutzaai, and Joann M. Ross, "Jury Nullification: A Selective, Annotated Bibliography," *Valparaiso University Law Review* 39 (2004), 393–443.

Congressional Globe, 35th Cong., 1st Sess. 959–62 (March 4, 1858).

Coombs, David E., "The Truth behind Quantico Brig's Decision to Strip PFC Manning," March 5, 2011, available at http://www.armycourtmartialdefense.info/2011/03/truth-behind-quantico-brigs-decision-to.html.

Cooper, Davina, "Theorising Nudist Equality: An Encounter between Political Fantasy and Public Appearance," *Antipode* 43.2 (2011), 326–357.

Coughenour, John C. et al., "The Effects of Gender in the Federal Courts: The Final Report of the Ninth Circuit Gender Bias Task Force," *University of Southern California Law Review* 67 (1994), 745–1106.

Cox, Noel, "Tudor Sumptuary Laws and Academical Dress: An Act against Wearing of Costly Apparel 1509 and an Act for Reformation of Excess in Apparel 1533," *Transactions of the Burgon Society* 6 (2006), 15–43.

Crews, Bruce W., "Michigan Rule of Evidence 611(b) and the Niqab: A Violation of Free Exercise of Religion," *Thomas M. Cooley Law Review* 27 (2010), 611–645.

Cross, Arthur Lyon, "The English Criminal Law and Benefit of Clergy during the Eighteenth and Early Nineteenth Century," *American Historical Review*, 22.3 (1917), 544–565.

Cuison, Rose Cruz, "The Construction of Labor Abuse in the Mariana Islands as Anti-American," *Asian Pacific American Law Journal* 6 (2000), 61–85.

Cummings, Scott L., "Hemmed In: Legal Mobilization in the Los Angeles Anti-Sweatshop Movement," *Berkeley Journal of Employment & Labor Law* 30 (2009), 1–84.

"Current Topics," *Albany Law Journal*, 13.17 (1876).

Dattel, Gene, *Cotton and Race in the Making of America: The Human Costs of Economic Power* (Chicago: Ivan R., 2009).

Davidson, Elizabeth H., *Child Labor Legislation in the Southern Textile States*, (Chapel Hill: University of North Carolina Press, 1939).

Davies, C. S. L., "Slavery and Protector Somerset: The Vagrancy Act of 1547," *Economic History Review* 19.3 (1966), 533–549.

Day of Silence, "Day of Silence Organizing Manual" (2012), 21, available at http://www.day-ofsilence.org/content/getorganized.html.

Devins, Neal, "Reagan Redux: Civil Rights under Bush," *Notre Dame Law Review* 68 (1993), 955–1001.

Dickberry, F., *The Storm of London: A Social Rhapsody* (London: John Long, 1904), available at http://www.archive.org/details/stormoflondonsocoodickuoft.

Dickens, Charles, *Oliver Twist: The Parish Boy's Progress* (London: Robert Bentley, 1838).

Dicks, Chief David R., Memo to All Sworn Personnel, Subject: Indecent Exposure Enforcement (June 26, 2008), available at http://www.aclumich.org/issues/search-and-seizure/2008–07/1267.

Douard, John, "Sex Offender as Scapegoat: The Monstrous Other Within," *New York Law School Law Review* 53 (2008/2009), 32–51.

Drehle, David Von, *Triangle: The Fire That Changed America* (New York: Grove Press, 2003).

Droubi, Luna, "The Constitutionality of the Niqab Ban in Egypt: A Symbol of Egypt's Struggle for a Legal Identity," *New York Law School Law Review* 56 (2012), 687–709.

DSM-IV Task Force on DSM-IV, American Psychiatric Association, *Diagnostic and Statistical Manual of Mental Disorders*, 4th ed. (Washington, DC: American Psychiatric Association, 1994), 532–538.

Duberman, Martin Bauml, "'Writhing Bedfellows' in Antebellum South Carolina: Historical Interpretation and the Politics of Evidence," in *Hidden From History: Reclaiming the Gay and Lesbian Past* (New York: New American Library/Penguin Books, 1989), pp. 153–168.

"Early Maryland County Courts," *Maryland State Archives*, 53 (1658–1666), 44, available at http://www.msa.md.gov/megafile/msa/speccol/sc2900/sc2908/000001/000053/html/am53p – 44.html.

Eaton, R. Vance, "Thinly Veiled: Institutional Messages in the Language of Secularism in Public Schools in France and the United States," *South Carolina Journal of International Law & Business* 6 (2010), 299–333.

Elizabeth, Sierra, "The Newest Spectator Sport: Why Extending Victims' Rights to the Spectators' Gallery Erodes the Presumption of Innocence," *Duke Law Journal* 58 (2008), 275–309.

Elliott, E. N., editor. *Cotton Is King and the Pro-Slavery Arguments* (Augusta, GA: Prichard, Abbott & Loomis, 1860), available at www.gutenberg.org/files/28148/28148-h/28148-h.htm.

Elton, G. R., "Henry VIII's Act of Proclamations," *English Historical Review*, 75.295 (1960), 208–222.

Engels, Freidrich, *Condition of the Working Class in England*, 1844 (originally published in German; English translation, 1877) (Stanford, CA: Stanford University Press, 1968).

"An English Judge's Dress," *Canadian Law Review* 3 (1904), 321–332.

Epstein, Richard A., *Forbidden Grounds: The Case against Employment Discrimination Laws* (Cambridge, MA: Harvard University Press, 1992).

Eugenio, Haidee V., "State of Commonwealth in Severe Disarray," *Saipan Tribune*, January 3, 2011, available at www.saipantribune.com/newsstory.aspx?cat=1&newsID=105838.

Fallon, Richard H. Jr., "Constitutional Precedent Viewed through the Lens of Hartian Positivist Jurisprudence," *North Carolina Law Review* 86 (2008), 1107–1163.

Farrand, Max, editor, *The Records of the Federal Convention of 1787*, 4 vols. (1937; rev. ed., 1966). (New Haven: Yale University Press, 1911).

Fay, Major General George R., and Lieutenant General Anthony R. Jones, "AR 15–6 Investigation of the Abu Ghraib Detention Facility and 205th Military Intelligence Brigade," *U.S. Department of the Army* (2004), 88–172, available at http://fl1.findlaw.com/news.findlaw.com/hdocs/docs/dod/fay82504rpt.pdf.

Federal Bureau of Prisons, "Visiting Room Procedures: General Information," available at http://www.bop.gov/inmate_locator/procedures.jsp.

Federico, Pasquale Joseph, "Operation of the Patent Act of 1790," *Journal of the Patent and Trademark Office Society* 18 (1936), 237–251.

Fee, John, "The Pornographic Secondary Effects Doctrine," *Alabama Law Review* 60 (2009), 291–338.

Fineout, Gary, "Jim Morrison Is Pardoned in Indecent Exposure Case," *New York Times*, December 9, 2010, available at http://artsbeat.blogs.nytimes.com/2010/12/09/jim-morrison-is-pardoned-in-indecent-exposure-case/.

Finkelman, Paul, "Slavery and the Northwest Ordinance, a Study in Ambiguity," *Journal of the Early Republic* 6.4 (1986), 343–370.
  Slavery and the Founders (New York: M.E. Sharpe, 1996).

Firth, C.B., "Benefit of Clergy in the Time of Edward IV," *English Historical Review*, 32.126 (1917), 175–191.

Fischel, Joseph J., "Transcendent Homosexuals and Dangerous Sex Offenders: Sexual Harm and Freedom in the Judicial Imaginary," *Duke Journal of Gender Law & Policy* 17 (2010), 277–311.

Fishman, Steve, "Bradley Manning's Army of One," *New York Magazine*, July 3, 2011, available at http://nymag.com/news/features/bradley-manning-2011-7/.

Flagg, Barbara, "'Was Blind But Now I See': White Race Consciousness and the Requirement of Discriminatory Intent," *Michigan Law Review* 91 (1993), 953–1017.

Florke, Robert S., "Castaways on Gilligan's Island: The Plight of the Alien Worker in the Northern Mariana Islands," *Temple International and Comparative Law Journal* 13 (1999), 381–410.

Fox, Michael W., "Piercings, Makeup, and Appearance: The Changing Face of Discrimination Law," *Texas Bar Journal* 69 (2006), 564–569.

Frank, Jerome, "The Cult of the Robe," *Saturday Review of Literature*, October 13, 1945, pp. 28–41. Reprinted in Jerome Frank, *Courts on Trial: Myth and Reality in American Justice* (Princeton: Princeton University Press, 1949), pp. 254–261.

Franklin, Benjamin, "The Examination of Dr. Benjamin Franklin," in *A Third Volume of Interesting Tracts, on the Subject of Taxing the British Colonies in America* (London: Printed for J. Almon, opposite Burlington-House, in Piccadilly, 1767), available at Eighteenth Century Collection Online.

Gage, Maltida Joslyn, "Woman as Inventor" [New York State?: s.n.], 1870, available at pds.lib.harvard.edu/pds/view/2575141.

Giles, Myriam E., "Police, Race and Crime in 1950s Chicago: *Monroe v. Pape* as Legal Noir," in *Civil Rights Stories*, edited by Myriam Gilles and Risa Goluboff (New York: Foundation Press, 2008), pp. 41–59.

Ginsburg, Ruth Bader, "In Memoriam: William H. Rehnquist," *Harvard Law Review* 119 (1995), 6–10.

Gohil, Neha Singh, and Dawinder S. Sidhu, "The Sikh Turban: Post-911 Challenges to this Article of Faith," *Rutgers Journal of Law & Religion* (2008), 54–57.

Goldschmidt, Jona, "'Order in the Court!' Constitutional Issues in the Law of Courtroom Decorum," *Hamline Law Review* 31 (2008), 1–102.

Goldwater, Barry, Statement, Congressional Record S. 132 (August 7, 1986).

"Graduation Dress Dispute in South Dakota Ends," available at http://indiancountrynews. net/index.php?option=com_content&task=view&id=9211&Itemid=33.

Grathwohl, Linda, "The North Dakota Anti-Garb Law: Constitutional Conflict and Religious Strife," *Great Plains Quarterly* 13 (1993), 187–202.

Greene, D. Wendy, "Black Women Can't Have Blonde Hair … In The Workplace," *Journal of Gender Race & Justice* 14 (2011), 405–430.

"Title VII: What's Hair (and Other Race-Based Characteristics) Got to Do with It?" *University of Colorado Law Review* 79 (2008), 1390–1391.

Greenwald, Glenn, "The Inhumane Conditions of Bradley Manning's Detention," Salon. com, December 15, 2010, available at http://www.salon.com/news/opinion/glenn_greenwald/2010/12/14/manning/index.html.

Gross, Aeyal, "Gender Outlaws before the Law: The Courts of the Borderland," *Harvard Journal of Law & Gender* 32 (2009), 165–231.

Halem, Samantha C., "Slaves to Fashion: A Thirteenth Amendment Litigation Strategy to Abolish Sweatshops in the Garment Industry," *San Diego Law Review* 36 (1999), 397–453.

Hamburger, Philip, *Law and Judicial Duty* (Cambridge, MA: Harvard University Press, 2008).

Hamilton, Alexander, James Madison, and John Jay, *The Federalist Papers*. A collection of essays written (1787–1788), 85, available at http://avalon.law.yale.edu/subject_menus/fed.asp.

Hammond, James Henry, "On the Admission of Kansas, Under the Lecompton Constitution," U.S. Senate, 4 March 1858, *Congressional Globe*, 35th Congress, 1st Session, Appendix, 68–71.

Harris, Lauren N., "You Better Smile When You Say 'Cheese!' Whether the Photograph Requirement for Drivers' Licenses Violates the Free Exercise Clause of the First Amendment," *Mercer Law Review* 61 (2010), 611–641.

Harrison, John, "The Lawfulness of the Reconstruction Amendments," *University of Chicago Law Review* 68 (2001), 375–461.

Harte, N. B., "State Control of Dress and Social Change in Pre-Industrial England," in *Trade, Government, and Economy in Pre-Industrial England: Essays Presented to F.J. Fisher*, edited by D. C. Coleman and A. H. Henry (London: Weidenfeld & Nicholson, 1976), pp. 132–165.

Hasan, Sami, "Veiling Religion in the Force: The Validity of "Religion-Neutral Appearance" as an Employer Interest," *UCLA Journal of Islamic & Near East Law* 9 (2010), 87–110.

Hashmi, Hera, "Too Much to Bare? A Comparative Analysis of the Headscarf in France, Turkey, and the United States," *University of Maryland Law Journal of Race, Religion, Gender & Class* 10 (2010), 409–445.

Haskins, George Lee, *Law and Authority in Early Massachusetts* (New York: Macmillan, 1960).

Hawthorne, Nathaniel, *The Scarlet Letter* (Boston: Ticknor, Reed & Fields, 1850).

Hayward, Maria, *Rich Apparel: Clothing and the Law in Henry VIII's England* (Farnham, England: Ashgate, 2009).

Heckler, Nuriel A., "That's What the Shovel's For: Atlanta's Sagging Baggy Pants Bill in a Liberal Society," *Guild Practice* 64 (2007), 216–224.

Heights, Roslyn, et al. "The Influence of Victim's Attire on the Adolescent's Judgments of Date Rape," *Adolescence* 30. 118 (1995), 319–324.

Herald, Marybeth, "The Northern Mariana Islands: A Change in Course under Its Covenant with the United States," *Oregon Law Review* 71 (1992), 127–204.

Hindle, Steve, "Dependency, Shame and Belonging: Badging the Deserving Poor, c. 1550–1750," *Cultural and Social History* 1 (2004), 6–35.

Hirshleifer, Jack, "The Private and Social Value of Information and the Reward to Inventive Activity," *American Economic Review* 61 (1971), 561–574.

Houchin, Steven R., "Confronting the Shadow: Is Forcing a Muslim Witness to Unveil in a Criminal Trial a Constitutional Right, or an Unreasonable Intrusion?" *Pepperdine Law Review* 36 (2009), 823–877.

Howard, Maureen, "Beyond a Reasonable Doubt: One Size Does Not Fit All When It Comes to Courtroom Attire for Women," *Gonzaga Law Review* 45 (2009–2010), 209–224.

Howell, K. Babe, "Fear Itself: The Impact of Allegations of Gang Affiliation on Pre-Trial Detention," *St. Thomas Law Review* 23 (2011), 620–659.

Hughes, Paul L., and James F. Larkin, *Tudor Royal Proclamations*, in 3 vols. (New Haven: Yale University Press, 1969).

Hunt, Alan, *Governance of the Consuming Passions: A History of Sumptuary Law* (New York: St. Martin's Press 1996).

Huston, Reeve, *Land and Freedom: Rural Society, Popular Protest, and Party Politics in Antebellum New York* (Oxford: Oxford University Press, 2000).

Hyman, H., and W. Wiecek, *Equal Justice under Law* (New York: Harper Collins, 1982).

Hyman, Irwin A., and Donna C. Perone, "The Other Side of School Violence: Educator Policies and Practices That May Contribute to Student Misbehavior," *Journal of School Psychology* 36 (1998), 7–13.

Inazu, John D., "The Forgotten Freedom of Assembly," *Tulane Law Review* 84 (2010), 565–612.

Irons, Peter, *A People's History of the Supreme Court* (New York: Viking/Penguin, 1999).

Jacobs, Clyde E., *The Eleventh Amendment and Sovereign Immunity* (Westport, CT: Greenwood Press, 1972).

Jacobson, Robert, "Megan's Laws: Reinforcing Old Patterns of Anti-Gay Police Harassment," *Georgetown Law Journal* 87 (1999), 2431–2467.

James, Portia, *The Real McCoy: African American Invention and Innovation 1619–1930* (Washington, DC: Smithsonian Institution Press, 1990).

Jaster, Margaret Rose, "Breeding Dissoluteness and Disobedience: Clothing Laws as Tudor Colonist Discourse," *Critical Survey* 13.3 (2001), 61–77.

Jefferson, Thomas, "A Summary View of the Rights of British America: Set Forth in Some Resolutions Intended for the Inspection of the Present Delegates of the People of Virginia, Now in Convention / by a Native, and Member of the House of Burgesses" (1774), available at Yale Law School, The Avalon Project, Documents in Law, History, and Diplomacy, http://avalon.law.yale.edu/18th_century/jeffsumm.asp.

Johnson, Melissa R., "Positive Vibration: An Examination of Incarcerated Rastafarian Free Exercise Claims," *New England Journal on Criminal & Civil Confinement* 34 (2008), 391–427.

Jordan Lawrence W. Jr., "Are Robes for Counsel the Only Dress for Courtroom Success?" *Advocate* 26 (September 1983), 17–18.

Kahn, Robert A., "The Headscarf as Threat: A Comparison of German and U.S. Legal Discourses," *Vanderbilt Journal of Transnational Law* 40 (2007), 417–444.

Karet, Deborah J., "Privatizing Law on the Commonwealth of the Northern Mariana Islands: Is Litigation the Best Channel for Reforming the Garment Industry?" *Buffalo Law Review* 48 (2000), 1047–1097.

Kemp, Sandra, et al., *Edwardian Fiction: An Oxford Companion* (Oxford: Oxford University Press, 2007).

Kennedy, Duncan, "Sexual Abuse, Sexy Dressing and the Eroticization of Domination," *New England Law Review* 26 (1992), 126–213.

Kerr, Caitlin S., "Teachers' Religious Garb as an Instrument for Globalization in Education," *Indiana Journal of Global Legal Studies* 18 (2011), 539–561.

Kesselring, Krista J., "Gender, the Hat, and Quaker Universalism in the Wake of the English Revolution," *The Seventeenth Century* 26.2 (2011), 299–322.

Kitner, Scott, "The Need and Means to Restrict Spectators from Wearing Buttons at Criminal Trials," *Review of Litigation* 27 (2008), 733–768.

Kleinberg, Eliot, "Judge Releases Teen, Criticizes Riviera Beach's Saggy Pants Law," *Palm Beach Post*, September 16, 2008, at 1A.

Knowles, Robert, "The Balance of Forces and the Empire of Liberty: States' Rights and the Louisiana Purchase," *Iowa Law Review* 88 (2003), 343–418.

Kosman, Joel, "Toward an Inclusionary Jurisprudence: A Reconceptualization of Zoning," *Catholic University Law Review* 43 (1993), 59–108.

Kramer, Ronald J., "Generation Y: Tattoos, Piercings, and Other Issues for the Private and Public Employer," *Urban Law* 38 (2006), 593–611.

Krawiec, Kimberly D., "Privatizing Outsider Trading," *Virginia Journal of International Law* 41 (2001), 693–715.

Labaree, Leonard W., editor, *Royal Instructions to British Colonial Governors, 1670–1776*, Vol. I (New York: Octagon Books, 1967 [© 1935]).

Lahav, Pnina, "The Chicago Conspiracy Trial: Character and Judicial Discretion," *University of Colorado Law Review* 71 (2000), 1327–1364.

"Theater in the Courtroom, the Chicago Conspiracy Trial," *Law & Literature* 16 (2004), 381–448.

Lakwete, Angela, *Inventing the Cotton Gin: Machine and Myth in Antebellum America* (Baltimore, MD: Johns Hopkins University Press, 2004).

Lamy, Rudolf, "A Study of Scarlet: Red Robes and the Maryland Court of Appeals" (2006), available at http://www.lawlib.state.md.us/aboutus/history/judgesredrobe.html.

LaVigne, Christopher M., "Bloods, Crips, and Christians: Fighting Gangs or Fighting the First Amendment?" *Baylor Law Review* 51 (1999), 389–417.

Lawrence, Charles, III, "The Id, the Ego, and Equal Protection: Reckoning with Unconscious Racism," *Stanford Law Review* 39 (1987), 317–388.

Lawrence, Sonia, "What Not to Wear," Institute for Feminist Studies at Osgoode Hall Law School, February 17, 2011, available at http://ifls.osgoode.yorku.ca/2011/02/what-not-to-wear.

Lawson, Gary, "Territorial Governments and the Limits of Formalism," *California Law Review* 78 (1990), 853–911.

Laycock, Douglas, "Conference Introduction: American Religious Liberty, French Laïcité, and the Veil," *Journal of Catholic Legal Studies* 49 (2010), 21–54.

Ledbetter, Huddie, a/k/a Lead Belly, "Cotton Fields" (1940).

Lemley, Mark A., "The Myth of the Sole Inventor," *Michigan Law Review* 110 (2012), 709–757.

Lenaham, Jessica, "Inter-American Commission on Human Rights," Report No. 80/11, Case 12.626, July 21, 2011, available at http://www.cidh.oas.org/Comunicados/English/2011/92–11eng.htm.

Lennon, Theresa L., et al., "Is Clothing Probative of Attitude or Intent? Implications for Rape and Sexual Harassment Cases," *Law & Inequality* 11 (1993), 391–402.

Levi, Jennifer L., "Misapplying Equality Theories: Dress Codes at Work," *Yale Journal of Law & Feminism* 19 (2008), 353–390.

Levinson, Sanford, "Why I Do Not Teach Marbury (Except to Eastern Europeans) and Why You Shouldn't Either," *Wake Forest Law Review* 38 (2003), 553–578.

Lewes, Darby, "Middle-Class Edens: Women's Nineteenth-century Utopian Fiction and the Bourgeois Ideal," *Utopian Studies*, 4.1 (1993), 14–25.

Lichtenstein, Alex, "'That Disposition to Theft, with Which They Have Been Branded': Moral Economy, Slave Management, and the Law," *Journal of Social History*, 21.3 (1998), 413–440.

Lind, Meghan E., "Hearts on Their Sleeves: Symbolic Displays of Emotion by Spectators in Criminal Trials," *Journal of Criminal Law & Criminology* 98 (2008), 1147–1170.

Liptak, Adam, "No Crime, but an Arrest and Two Strip-Searches," *New York Times*, March 7, 2011, available at http://www.nytimes.com/2011/03/08/us/08bar.html?_r=1.

Lombardi, Clark B., and Nathan J. Brown, "Do Constitutions Requiring Adherence to Shari'a Threaten Human Rights? How Egypt's Constitutional Court Reconciles Islamic Law with the Liberal Rule of Law," *American University International Law Review* 21 (2006), 379–435.

"London Unclothed," *New York Times*, 1905, available at http://query.nytimes.com/gst/abstract.html?res=F70C17F63F5512738DDDAC0994DF405B858CF1D3.

Lubar, Steven, "The Transformation of Antebellum Patent Law," *Technology and Culture*, 32.4 (1991), 932–959.

Lund, Christopher C., "Religious Liberty after Gonzales: A Look at State RFRAs," *South Dakota Law Review* 55 (2010), 466–497.

Lung, Shirley, "Exploiting the Joint Employer Doctrine: Providing a Break for Sweatshop Garment Workers," *Loyola University Chicago Law Journal* 34 (2003), 291–358.

"Overwork and Overtime," *Indiana Law Review* 39 (2005), 51–85.

Lyon, Elizabeth, "A Picture Is Worth a Thousand Words: The Effect of Spectators' Display of Victim Photographs during a Criminal Jury Trial on a Criminal Defendant's Fair Trial Rights," *Hastings Constitutional Law Quarterly* 36 (2009), 517–544.

Manz, William H., *Gibson's New York Research Guide* (Buffalo, NY: William Hein, 2004).

Marx, Karl, *Capital: A Critique of Political Economy, Vol. 1*, edited by Friedrich Engels, translated by Samuel Moore and Edward Aveling (Chicago: Charles H. Kerr, 1909) (1867).

Mathis, Doyle, "*Chisholm v. Georgia*: Background and Settlement," *Journal of American History* 54.1 (1967), 19–29.

Mazza, Oriana, "The Right to Wear Headscarves and Other Religious Symbols in French, Turkish, and American Schools: How the Government Draws a Veil on Free Expression of Faith," *Journal of Catholic Legal Studies* 48 (2009), 303–343.

McColley, Robert, *Slavery and Jeffersonian Virginia* (Urbana: University of Illinois Press, 1964).

McCormick, Marcia L., "Consensus, Dissensus, and Enforcement: Legal Protection of Working Women from the Time of the Triangle Shirtwaist Factory Fire to Today," *N.Y.U. Journal of Legislation & Public Policy* 14 (2011), 645–695.

McEvoy, Arthur F., "The Triangle Shirtwaist Factory Fire of 1911: Social Change, Industrial Accidents, and the Evolution of Common-Sense Causality," *Law and Social Inquiry* 20 (1995), 621–651.

McGinnis, Christopher, and Sarah Eisenhart, "Interrogation Is Not Ethnography: The Irrational Admission of Gang Cops as Experts in the Field of Sociology," *Hastings Race & Poverty Law Journal* 7 (2010), 111–159.

McIlwaine, H. R., editor, *Journals of the House of Burgesses, 1619–1658/59* (1905) (Richmond, VA: Colonial Press, E. Waddey Co.), Vol. I.

McNamara, Bethanne Walz, "All Dressed Up with No Place to Go: Gender Bias in Oklahoma Federal Court Dress Codes," *Tulsa Law Journal* 30 (1994), 395–422.

McQueen, Rob, "Of Wigs and Gowns: A Short History of Legal and Judicial Dress in Australia," *Law in Context* 16.1 (1998), 31–58.

Mendez, Juan E., "USA: Unmonitored access to detainees is essential to any credible enquiry into torture or cruel inhuman and degrading treatment, says UN torture expert," United Nations Office of the High Commissioner for Human Rights (July 12, 2011), available at http://www.ohchr.org/en/NewsEvents/Pages/DisplayNews. aspx?NewsID=11231&LangID=E.

Middlekauff, Robert, *The Glorious Cause: The American Revolution, 1763–1789* (New York: Oxford University Press, 1982, 2005).

Mirsky, Jeanette, and Allen Nevins, *The World of Eli Whitney* (New York: Macmillan, 1952).

Montross, Lynn, *Rag, Tag and Bobtail: The Story of the Continental Army, 1775–1783* (New York: Harper, 1952).

Moore, Kathleen M., "Visible through the Veil: The Regulation of Islam in American Law," *Sociology of Religion* 68 (2007), 237–251.

Morris, Jan E., "The Miami Incident," Doors, available at http://doors.com/miami/one.html.

Morrison, Jim, "Queen of the Highway" recorded by the Doors on "Morrison Hotel," Electra Records, (released February 1970).

Moskowitz, Seymour, "Dickens Redux: How American Child Labor Law Became A Con Game," *Whittier Journal of Child & Family Advocacy* 10 (2010), 89–153.

Mossoff, Adam, "The Rise and Fall of the First American Patent Thicket: The Sewing Machine War of the 1850s," *Arizona Law Review* 53 (2011), 165–211.

"Rethinking the Development of Patents: An Intellectual History, 1550–1800," *Hastings Law Journal*, 52 (2001), 1255–1321.

"Who Cares What Thomas Jefferson Thought about Patents? Reevaluating the Patent 'Privilege' in Historical Context," *Cornell Law Review* 92 (2007), 953–1012.

Murphy, Andrew, "The Trial Transcript as Political Theory: Penn-Mead in Anglo-American Political Thought," draft, available at http://papers.ssrn.com/sol3/papers. cfm?abstract_id=1914723.

Murray, Brian M., "Confronting Religion: Veiled Muslim Witnesses and the Confrontation Clause," *Notre Dame Law Review* 85 (2010), 1727–1757.

National Center for Lesbian Rights, Newsletter, 12 (Fall 2004).

Nelson, James D., "Incarceration, Accommodation, and Strict Scrutiny," *Virginia Law Review* 95 (2009), 2053–2128.

Nevin, Hon. Jack, "Conviction, Confrontation, and Crawford: Gang Expert Testimony as Testimonial Hearsay," *Seattle University Law Review* 34 (2011), 857–887.

New York State Department of Correctional Services, *Handbook for the Families and Friends of New York State DOCS Inmates* (2007), p. 13, available at http://www.docs.state.ny.us/FamilyGuide/FamilyHandbook.pdf.

New York State Temporary Commission on Revision of the Penal Law and Criminal Code, Third Interim Report Leg. Doc. 14 (1964), pp. 26–27.

New York State Temporary Commission on Revision of the Penal Law and Criminal Code, Third Interim Report, pp 26–27, Leg. Doc. 14 (1964).

Office of Inspector General, "A Review of the FBI's Involvement in and Observations of Detainee Interrogations in Guantanamo Bay, Afghanistan, and Iraq," U.S. Department of Justice (2008), available at www.justice.gov/oig/special/s0805/final.pdf.

Office of the Commissioner for Human Rights, "Violence against Women: UN Expert Urges Full Policy Review after Regional Body Finds the US Responsible of Rights Violations," United Nations Human Rights (2011), available at www.ohchr.org/en/NewsEvents/Pages/DisplayNews.aspx?NewsID=11325&LangID=E.

Onwuachi-Willig, Angela, "Another Hair Piece: Exploring New Strands of Analysis under Title VII," *Georgetown Law Journal* 98 (2010), 1080–1131.

Orth, John V., "The Truth about Justice Iredell's Dissent in *Chisholm v. Georgia*," *North Carolina Law Review* 73 (1994), 255–270.

Oshinsky, David M., "Convict Labor in the Post-Civil War South: Involuntary Servitude after the Thirteenth Amendment," in *The Promises of Liberty: The History and Contemporary Relevance of the Thirteenth Amendment* (New York: Columbia University Press, 2010), pp. 100–116.

Worse than Slavery: Parchman Farm and the Ordeal of Jim Crow (New York: Free Press, 1996).

Owsley, Frank Lawrence, *King Cotton Diplomacy: Foreign Relations of the Confederate States of America* (Chicago: University of Chicago Press, 1931).

Paine, Thomas, '*Common sense; addressed to the inhabitants of America, on the following interesting subjects*" (London: H.D. Symonds, 1792) 3, available at http://galenet.gale-group.com/servlet/ECCO # CW3308134578.

Parker, Will, "Still Afraid of "Negro Domination?" Why County Home Rule Limitations in the Alabama Constitution of 1901 Are Unconstitutional," *Alabama Law Review* 57 (2005), 545–563.

Patrick, Wendy, "Well Suited to the Courtroom: Women in Legal Advocacy," *Practical Litigation* 21.5 (2010), 7–10.

Peck, Alison, "Revisiting the Original 'Tea Party': The History of Regulating Food Consumption in America," *University of Missouri-Kansas City Law Review* 80 (2011), 1–43.

Penn, William, "The Peoples Ancient and Just Liberties Asserted, In the Tryal of William Penn and William Mead at the Old Bailey, 22 Charles II 1670, written by themselves," in William Penn, *The Political Writings of William Penn*, edited by Andrew R. Murphy (Indianapolis: Liberty Fund, 2002), pp. 3–21.

Phillips, Kim M., "Masculinities and the Medieval Sumptuary Laws," *Gender & History*, 19:1 (2007), 22–42.

Pieterse, Marius, "The Right to Be Free from Public or Private Violence after Carmichele," *South African Law Journal* 119 (2002), 27–39.

Ponte, Lucile M., and Jennifer L. Gillan, "Gender Performance over Job Performance: Body Art Work Rules and the Continuing Subordination of the Feminine," *Duke Journal of Gender Law & Policy* 14 (2007), 319–367.

Pope, James Gray, "The Thirteenth Amendment versus the Commerce Clause: Labor and the Shaping of American Constitutional Law, 1921–1957," *Columbia Law Review* 102 (2002), 1–122.

Posner, Richard, *Sex and Reason* (Cambridge, MA: Harvard University Press, 1992).

Primus, Richard, "The Future of Disparate Impact," *Michigan Law Review* 108 (2010), 1341–75.

Radzinowicz, L., "The Waltham Black Act: A Study of the Legislative Attitude towards Crime in the Eighteenth Century," *Cambridge Law Journal* 9.1 (1945), 56–81.

Raghunath, Raja, "A Promise the Nation Cannot Keep: What Prevents the Application of the Thirteenth Amendment in Prison?"*William & Mary Bill of Rights Journal* 18 (2009), 395–442.

Ramachandran, Gowri, "Freedom of Dress: State and Private Regulation of Clothing, Hairstyle, Jewelry, Makeup, Tattoos, and Piercing," *Maryland Law Review* 66 (2006), 11–93.

Ramones, Richard J., "Religious Discrimination or Legitimate Uniform Policy? A Critique and Analysis of the Third Circuit's Decision to Uphold a Private Prison's Ban on Employees Wearing Khimars: *EEOC v. The GEO Group, Inc.*," *Rutgers Journal of Law & Religion* 12 (2010), 184–201.

Rangappa, Asha, "God Save the Wig," *Legal Affairs* (May-June 2002), available at www.legalaffairs.org/issues/May-June-2002/scene_rangappa_mayjun2002.html.

Rehnquist, William, "The Cult of the Robe," *Judges Journal* 15 (1976), 74–98.

Reid, Stuart, and Marko Zlatich, *Soldiers of the Revolutionary War* (Oxford: Osprey Publishing, 2002).

Reiner, L., "Gangs, Crime and Violence in Los Angeles: Findings and Proposals from the District Attorney's Office" (Washington, DC: US Department of Justice, 1992).

Reske, Henry J., "Showing His Stripes: Operetta Inspires Chief Justice to Alter his Robe," *A.B.A. Journal* 81 (1995), 35.

Resnik, Judith, "The Mythic Meaning of Article III Courts," *University of Colorado Law Review* 56 (1985), 581–617.

Reutter, Edmund, "Religious Dress: A Century of Litigation," *Education Law Reporter* 70 (1992), 747–761.

Rey, Oskar E., "Antimask Laws: Exploring the Outer Bounds of Protected Speech under the First Amendment – *State v. Miller* 260 Ga. 669, 398 S.E.2d 547," *Washington Law Review* 66 (1991), 1139–1158.

Rhode, Deborah, *The Beauty Bias : The Injustice of Appearance in Life and Law* (Oxford: Oxford University Press, 2010).

Rios-Martinez, Marie, "Congressional Colonialism in the Pacific: The Case of the Northern Mariana Islands and Its Covenant with the United States," *Scholar* 3 (2000), 41–69.

Robbins, Allie, "The Future of the Student Anti-Sweatshop Movement: Providing Access to U.S. Courts for Garment Workers Worldwide" (on file with author).

Robson, Ruthann, "Assimilation, Marriage, and Lesbian Liberation," *Temple Law Review* 75 (2002), 767–820.

"Bork's '75 page' Memo to Goldwater on the 1964 Civil Rights Act's Unconstitutionality?" Constitutional Law Prof Blog (2011), available at Ruthann Robson, http://lawprofessors.

typepad.com/conlaw/2011/10/borks-75-page-memo-to-goldwater-on-the-1964-civil-rights-acts-unconstitutionality.html.

"*FCC v. Fox* Argument: On Naked Buttocks, Regulated Media, and the First Amendment," Constitutional Law Prof Blog (2012), available at http://lawprofessors.typepad.com/conlaw/2012/01/fcc-v-fox-argument-on-naked-buttocks-regulated-media-and-the-first-amendment.html.

"Jim Morrison's Possibility of Pardon," Constitutional Law Prof Blog, (2010), available at http://lawprofessors.typepad.com/conlaw/2010/11/jim-morrisons-possibility-of-pardon.html.

"Judicial Review and Sexual Freedom," *University of Hawaii Law Review* 30 (2007), 1–46.

"Loitering While Masked: The Wall Street Protest Arrests" (2011), available at http://lawprofessors.typepad.com/conlaw/2011/09/loitering-while-masked-wall_street-protests.html.

"Occupy Jacket-wearer Arrested at Supreme Court Building," Constitutional Law Professors Blog (2012), Available at http://lawprofessors.typepad.com/conlaw/2012/01/occupy-jacket-wearer-arrested-at-supreme-court-building.html.

"Posner's Lesbians: Neither Sexy Nor Reasonable," in *Sappho Goes to Law School* (New York: Columbia University Press, 1998).

Rogers, Pat, "The Waltham Blacks and the Black Act," *Historical Journal*, 17. 3 (1974), 465–486.

Rohmann, Keith, "Diagnosing and Analyzing Flawed Investigations, Abu Ghraib as a Case Study," *Penn State International Law Review* 28 (2009), 1–44.

Rossein, Merrick, *Employment Discrimination Law and Litigation* (Minneapolis, MN: West, 2011).

Russo, Charles J., and Tie Fatt Hee, "The Right of Students to Wear Religious Garb in Public Schools: A Comparative Analysis of the United States and Malaysia," *Education & Law Journal* 18 (2008), 1–14.

Ryscamp, Charles, "The New England Sources of *The Scarlet Letter*," *American Literature*, 31. 3 (1959), 257–272.

Sarke, Dena M., "Coed Naked Constitutional Law: The Benefits and Harms of Uniform Dress Requirements in American Public Schools," *Boston University Law Review* 78 (1998), 153–175.

Sawyer III, Logan Everett, "Creating *Hammer v. Dagenhart*," *William & Mary Bill of Rights Journal* (draft available at http://papers.ssrn.com/sol3/papers.cfm?abstract_id=2033351).

Schwartzbaum, Adam, "The Niqab in the Courtroom: Protecting Free Exercise of Religion in a Post-Smith World," *University of Pennsylvania Law Review* 159 (2011), 1533–1576.

Sharrer, G. Terry, "The Indigo Bonanza in South Carolina, 1740–90," *Technology and Culture*, 12.3 (1971), 447–455.

Shiffrin, Seana Valentine, "Speech, Death and Double Effect," *N.Y.U. Law Review* 78 (2003), 1135–1185.

Short, Farrah-Marisa Chua, "An Experiment in Protecting Workers' Rights: The Garment Industry of the U.S. Commonwealth of the Northern Mariana Islands," *University of Pennsylvania Journal of Labor & Employment Law* 7 (2005), 971–989.

Shurtleff, Nathaniel B., editor, *Records of the governor and company of the Massachusetts bay in New England: Printed by order of the legislature* (1853), Vol I–III (Boston: William White, 1853–54).

Simoni, Stephen J., "'Who Goes There?' – Proposing a Model Anti-Mask Act," *Fordham Law Review* 61(1992), 241–274.

Sinopole, Angelica M., "'No Saggy Pants': A Review of the First Amendment Issues Presented by the State's Regulation of Fashion in Public Streets," *Penn State Law Review* 113 (2008), 329–380.

Sisk, Gregory, and Michael Heise, "Muslims and Religious Liberty in the Era of 9/11: Empirical Evidence from the Federal Courts," *Iowa Law Review* 98 (2012), 231–289.

Smith, Erin Geiger, "Case Study: *Does I v. The Gap, Inc.*: Can a Sweatshop Suit Settlement Save Saipan?" *Review of Litigation* 23 (2004), 737–771.

Smith, Karen M., "Solving Worker Abuse Problems in the Northern Mariana Islands," *Boston College International & Comparative Law Review* 24 (2001), 381–407.

Spencer-Wendel, Susan, "'Let 'em Sag,' Judge Says," *Palm Beach Post*, April 23, 2009, p. 1A.

Stein, Leon, *The Triangle Fire* (New York: J. B. Lippincott, 1962).

Stern, Simon, "Between Local Knowledge and National Politics: Debating Rationales for Jury Nullification after Bushell's Case," *Yale Law Journal* 111 (2002), 1815–1859.

Stout, Taylor G., "The Costs of Religious Accommodation in Prisons," *Virginia Law Review* 96 (2010), 1201–1239.

Straub, Dennis, "Memo: Visiting Standards," Michigan Department of Corrections (July 26, 2010), pp. 4–5.

Stuart, Megan, "Saying, Wearing, Watching, and Doing: Equal First Amendment Protection for Coming Out, Having Sex, and Possessing Child Pornography," *Florida Coastal Law Review* 11 (2010), 341–385.

Sullivan, Dwight, "The Congressional Response to *Goldman v. Weinberger*," *Military Law Review* 121 (1988), 121–152.

Supreme Court of the United States, "Visitor's Guide to Oral Argument," available at http://www.supremecourt.gov/visiting/visitorsguidetooralargument.aspx.

Swertfeger, Jack Jr., "Municipal Anti-Mask and Anti-Cross Burning Ordinance: A Model," *Journal of Public Law* 1 (1952), 193–197.

Taubman, Elliot, "Headscarves, Skullcaps, and Crosses: Does Banning Religious Symbols in Public Schools Deny Human Rights?" *Rhode Island Bar Journal* 53(2005), 1–35.

Taylor, Gary, "Exotic Dancers Win $195,000 Judgment in Strip-Search Case," *Orlando Sentinel*, July 7, 2011, available at http://www.orlandosentinel.com/news/local/volusia/os-strip-search-exotic-dangers-illega20110707,0,4490925.story.

Thomas, Chantal, "Constitutional Change and International Government," *Hastings Law Journal* 52 (2000), 1–45.

Tomlins, Christopher, *Freedom Bound: Law, Labor, and Civic Identity in Colonizing British America, 1580–1865* (Cambridge: Cambridge University Press, 2010).

Tourkochoriti, Ioanna, "The Burka Ban: Divergent Approaches to Freedom of Religion in France and in the U.S.A.," *William & Mary Bill of Rights Journal* 20 (2012), 791–852.

The Trial of William Penn and William Mead, at the Old Bailey, for Tumultuous Assembly: 22 Charles II. 1670, in T. B. Howell, *A Complete Collection of State Trials*, Vol. 6 (London: T.C. Hansard, 1816), pp. 951–955.

Tribe, Laurence H., "Taking Text and Structure Seriously: Reflections on Free-Form Method in Constitutional Interpretation," *Harvard Law Review* 108 (1995), 1221–1303.

Tua, Uilisone Falemanu, "A Native's Call for Justice: The Call for the Establishment of a Federal District Court in American Samoa," *Asian-Pacific Law & Policy Journal* 11 (2010), 246–292.

Tucker, Joseph W., "No Hats in Court: Michigan's Justifications for Free Exercise Indifference," *University of Toledo Law Review* 41 (2010), 1039–1062.

Turner, Michelle L., "The Braided Uproar: A Defense of My Sister's Hair and a Contemporary Indictment of *Rogers v. American Airlines*," *Cardozo Women's Law Journal* 7 (2001), 115–162.

U.K. Supreme Court, Press Notice, "Revised Guidance on Court Dress at the UK Supreme Court," November 21, 2011, available at www.supremecourt.gov.uk/news/press-releases-archive.html.

UN Commission on Human Rights, "Report of the Special Rapporteur on Torture and Other Cruel, Inhuman or Degrading Treatment or Punishment," A/59/324, September 1, 2004, paragraph 17, available at http://www.statewatch.org/news/2004/nov/un-torture-doc1.pdf.

UNICOR Board Minutes, January 2012, p. 7, available at www.unicor.gov/information/publications/pdfs/corporate/BOD_MEETING_MINUTES%20January%202012%20Washington%20DC%20-edits%203-23.pdf.

UNICOR, "Factories with Fences," p. 36, available at www.unicor.gov/information/publications/showpub.cfm?pubid=57.

United States Commission on Civil Rights, "Enforcing Religious Freedom in Prison" (Washington, DC: United States Printing Office, 2008).

University of St. Thomas School of Law in collaboration with St. Paul NAACP, "Evaluation of Gang Databases in Minnesota & Recommendations for Change," Minnesota Department of Public Safety, SF 2725 Workgroup (2009), available at http://twincities.indymedia.org/files/GangsofStPaulReport.pdf.

Unsigned, Records and Files of the Quarterly Courts of Essex County, Massachusetts, Vol. I, 1636–1656.

Valentine, Sarah E., "Traditional Advocacy for Nontraditional Youth: Rethinking Best Interests for the Queer Child," *Michigan State Law Review* (2008), 1053–1113.

Van Cleve, George William, *A Slaveholders' Union: Slavery, Politics, and the Constitution in the Early American Republic* (Chicago: University of Chicago Press, 2010).

Vandivort, William C., "The Constitutional Challenge to 'Saggy' Pants Laws," *Brooklyn Law Review* 75 (2009), 667–705.

Varellas, James J., "The Constitutional Political Economy of Free Trade: Reexamining NAFTA-Style Congressional-Executive Agreements," *Santa Clara Law Review* 49 (2009), 717–792.

Vojdik, Valorie K., "Politics of the Headscarf in Turkey: Masculinities, Feminism, and the Construction of Collective Identities," *Harvard Journal of Law & Gender* 33 (2010), 661–685.

Volokh, Eugene, "Freedom of Speech and Appellate Review in Workplace Harassment Cases," *Northwestern University Law Review* 90 (1996), 1029–1030.

Walterscheid, Edward C., "Patents and the Jeffersonian Mythology," *John Marshall Law Review* 29 (1995), 269–314.

   "The Use and Abuse of History: The Supreme Court's Interpretation of Thomas Jefferson's Influence on the Patent Law," *Idea* 39 (1999), 195–224.

   "Within the Limits of the Constitutional Grant: Constitutional Limitations on the Patent Power," *Journal of Intellectual Property Law*, 9 (2002), 291–357.

Walthall, Howard P. Sr., "A Doubtful Mind: Understanding Alabama's State Constitution," *Cumberland Law Review* 35 (2005), 74–80.

Westerfield, Jennifer M., "Behind the Veil: An American Legal Perspective on the European Headscarf Debate," *American Journal of Comparative Law* 54 (2006), 637–678.

Whatley, Mark, "The Effect of Participant Sex, Victim Dress, and Traditional Attitudes on Causal Judgments for Marital Rape Victims," *Journal of Family Violence* 20.3 (2005), 191–200.

Whisner, Mary, "Gender-Specific Clothing Regulation: A Study in Patriarchy," *Harvard Women's Law Journal* 5 (1982), 73–119.

Whitney, Eli, Patent application requesting renewal, National Archives (1812), available at http://www.archives.gov/education/lessons/cotton-gin-patent/images/patent-petition-1.gif.

Williams, Aaron J., "The Veiled Truth: Can the Credibility of Testimony Given by a Niqab-Wearing Witness Be Judged without the Assistance of Facial Expressions?" *University of Detroit Mercy Law Review* 85 (2008), 273–290.

Williams, Onika K., "The Suppression of a Saggin' Expression: Exploring the 'Saggy Pants' Style within a First Amendment Context," *Indiana Law Journal* 85 (2010), 1169–1195.

Wilson, John S., "The Importance of a Hat," Paper CXVIII (Chicago: Chicago Literary Club, 1999/2001), available at http://www.chilit.org/PublishedPapers.htm.

Winet, Evan Darwin, "Face-Veil Bans and Anti-Mask Laws: State Interests and the Right to Cover the Face," *Hastings International & Comparative Law Review* 35 (2012), 217–251.

Woloch, Nancy, *Muller v. Oregon: A Brief History with Documents* (New York: St. Martin's Press, 1996), 5, available at http://www.law.louisville.edu/library/collections/brandeis/node/235.

Wood, Stephen B., *Constitutional Politics in the Progressive Era: Child Labor and the Law* (Chicago: University of Chicago Press, 1968).

Workman, Jane E., and Elizabeth W. Freeburg, "An Examination of Date Rape, Victim Dress, and Perceiver Variables within the Context of Attribution Theory," *Sex Roles* 41 (1999), 261–277.

Wright, John deP., "Wigs," *The Green Bag 2d* 9 (2006), 395–401.

Wright, Joshua D., "The Constitutional Failure of Gang Databases," *Stanford Journal of Civil Rights & Civil Liberties* 2 (2005), 115–142.

Wright, Silas, New York Governor Annual Message (1845), reprinted in *State of New York Messages from the Governors*, edited by Charles Z. Lincoln, Vol. 4, p. 87.

Yablon, Charles M., "Judicial Drag: An Essay on Wigs, Robes, and Legal Change," *Wisconsin Law Review* (1995), 1129–1153.

Yafa, Stephen, *Big Cotton* (New York: Viking, 2005).

Zagel, James, and Adam Winkler, "The Independence of Judges," *Mercer Law Review* 46 (1995), 795–834.

Zahniser, David, "Thousands of Phony Christian Louboutins Seized by Customs Agents," *Los Angeles Times*, August 16, 2012, available at http://latimesblogs.latimes.com/lanow/2012/08/counterfeit-christian-louboutin-shoes-seized.html.

Acknowledgments

This book started out as a very different project and I am grateful for the patience and indulgence of editor extraordinaire John Berger and the entire staff at Cambridge University Press.

I am indebted to the resources, collegiality, and dedication to social justice at my home institution, the City University of New York (CUNY) School of Law, where the largest portion of this book was researched and written. Dean Michelle Anderson has provided financial scholarship support, including funding students. The library staff has provided expert assistance, and I owe Douglas Cox for his enthusiasm for odd queries and Kathy Williams for her devotion to procuring books from far-flung libraries. At the CUNY Graduate Center, the assistance of librarian Polly Thistlethwaite provided important perspectives. I have been enriched by conversations, research, and suggestions from many in the CUNY School of Law community, including students in seminars such as First Amendment and Sexuality and Law. My colleagues and former colleagues Penelope Andrews, Janet Calvo, Shirley Lung, Andrea McArdle, and Jenny Rivera provided support at crucial junctures, and I benefited from the work of my colleagues K. Babe Howell and Merrick (Rick) Rossein. The opportunity to work with CUNY Law students as research assistants on various projects has always been a particular pleasure of working at CUNY and this book is no exception. I am especially thankful to CUNY law students and alums who made specific contributions, including proofreading: Lindsay Adams, Beena Ahmad, Joshua Carrin, Amitai Heller, Robert Hupf, Julie Pennington, Madeline Porta, Emile Primeaux, Sarika Saxena, and Kara Wallis.

During the writing of this book, I spent a year teaching at the West Virginia University College of Law as the John T. Copenhaver Chair. I am appreciative of Dean Joyce McConnell; of my students in Criminal Procedure, Comparative Constitutional Law, and Sexuality and Law; my research assistants Chad Webb and Rachel Livingood; and my colleagues Gregory Bowman, Atiba Ellis, Anne Marie Lofaso, and Alison Peck, especially for their insights about economics and trade.

For their enthusiasm for this project and valuable insights, I am grateful to David Rompf, Bruce Shenitz, and Scott Manning. I had the opportunity to present portions of this book at conferences such as American Association of Law Schools and the Law and Society Association and I greatly appreciate the comments of my colleagues.

In one iteration of this book, I intended to include personal stories of "dressing constitutionally," including my father's appearance in my high school principal's office defending my dress code violations, my mother's labor as a piecework seamstress and then as a member of the International Ladies' Garment Workers' Union, my child's mandated authentic apparel working at the Renaissance Festival (no zippers or Velcro allowed), my first post–law school employer, a federal judge, shaking my self-image by calling me a "modest dresser," and my lover's lovely tattoo that still shimmers decades later. Although I have omitted the long version of those recollections, they have deeply affected how I think about constitutionalism, hierarchy, democracy, and sexuality, as well as what I wear.

Index